39
38
37

R Grande

S. Feè

Yutas.   Mòqui   Zuñi

Òraibe.

Sierra delos Mimbres

Cuercomaches.   R. de S. Pedro Jaquesila

APA   Sierra de Mogollòn

Chemegues   R. de S. Bernabè

Yabipais cajuala

Martires   Jamajabas   Laguayepais   R. de la Asumpc.   R. de S. Francisco   Arrete de Mimbre

ta Maria   R. de la Asumpc.   CH   35

R. des.   R. de S. Francisco

Jalchedunes   Ybapais agua Apach   R. de S. Gila   S. Marcial   E   R   I   A   34

Yumas   R. de S. Pedro   Chiricagat

Pimas.

Cajuenches.   Cocomaricopas   33

Tuquiton   Sta. Cruz.   S. Bernardino   Janos.   32

PAPA   Sonotac   GUERIA.   Tubac   Cocospe   Cuquiarachi   Fronteras

Arroyo Salc.   Saric.   Calabas.   Terrenate

Jutobac.   Altar   Ati.   Tubutama   S. Ygn.   Dolor.   Bacuachi

Bisani   Pitiqui   Sta. Ana   Dolor.   Chinapa   NORA.

Caborca   Pimer ia Alta.   Tuape   Arispe   Cune   Guavabas   pasc

Opodepe   Bananchi   Opo   zura

Cieneguilla   Nacameri   Aconchi   S   O   30

Y. del Angostade   Babiacora   Bacadeguac   Basaracac

Canal de Ballenas   Y. del Tiburon   S. Mig.   Vres   31

S. Josè   Alamo   Batuco

Pitiqui   Nacori   Matape   29

Pimeria   S. Josè   Teopari   Natora

CA   GOLFO   Tecoripa   Aribechi

S. Marcial   Baja   Onapa   Taruqui

L   DE   Gumuripa   R. chico   28

I   Mobas   Yecora   Maicoba

F   CALIFORNIAS.   Buenavista   Prov. DE Ostimuri.   27

O   Pto. de Guaimas   Pueblos de Yaqui   Baroyeca

R   Botocosa

N   R. Yaqui   Tepague

I   A.   Conicari   26

Real delos Alamos

Once Upon A Desert

A BICENTENNIAL PROJECT

PATRICIA JERNIGAN KEELING
EDITOR

MOJAVE RIVER VALLEY MUSEUM ASSOCIATION
270 EAST VIRGINIA WAY, P.O. BOX 1282
BARSTOW, CALIFORNIA 92311

AMERICAN REVOLUTION BICENTENNIAL COMMISSION, BARSTOW,
CALIFORNIA OFFICIAL PUBLICATION

Published by the Mojave River Valley Museum association
P.O. Box 1282, Barstow, California 92312-1282

Cover Illustration "The Mojave Desert"

National American Revolution Bicentennial Administration - Project Number 76-37-028432

Library of Congress Catalog Card No. 76-50673

ISBN 0-918614-06-6 - ISBN 0-918614-07-4
    First Printing 1500 - 1976
    Second Printing 1000 - 1977
    Third Printing 2500 - 1994

PREFACE

Once Upon A Desert is by no means a complete history of the California deserts, but presents storied selections from a vast area of the Greater Mojave Desert.

Our articles are written by published and unpublished authors, who included their folklore, humor and interwoven family life with visions of tomorrow, forming a 200 year human interest account of people being people.

Like the painting of a desert landscape in various hues, these treasured tales give the coloring needed to bring the bicentennial legend to life. Our picture of the past shows the changes brought about through hardships, good times, sadness and laughter, high promise and some disappointment, life and death as lived on the Mojave Desert.

The purpose of the Mojave River Valley Museum is to preserve the heritage of the past for the future. The publication committee has collected and preserved hundreds of manuscripts, documents and photographs, and had the difficult task of selecting and editing these for publication. Unfortunately, all the material available for selection could not be used in this book.

A few stories which were based on personal experiences have not been researched for historical accuracy. Each author was responsible for the initial research needed to write his own manuscript. As time and resources permitted the editorial staff supplemented the author's investigations. The committee made every effort to include all sources for researched work in the bibliography.

For a rule of clarity we are using the spelling of Mohave for the Indian tribe and Fort and Mojave for all other references.

With the publication of this book valuable material has been preserved in print. We hope this accomplishment will stimulate further research and preservation of more of our heritage.

The Mojave River Valley Museum Association, solely supported by volunteer workers and donations, proudly presents *Once Upon A Desert.*

SAN BERNARDINO COUNTY

San Bernardino County is located in Southern California, bounded on the east by the Colorado River and the states of Nevada and Arizona, on the south by the counties of Orange and Riverside, on the west by Los Angeles and Kern Counties, and on the north by Inyo County. San Bernardino County is the largest county in the continental United States, containing 20,160 square miles, an area equivalent to the combined areas of the states of Massachusetts, Rhode Island, Connecticut, New Jersey, and Delaware. In distance the County measures about 275 miles from east to west and about 150 miles from north to south. Seventy-seven percent of the total area is publicly owned, including the San Bernardino National Forest, Death Valley National Monument, Joshua Tree National Monument, military reservations and the Bureau of Land Management lands.

There are four incorporated cities in the Greater Mojave Desert: Adelanto, Barstow, Needles, and Victorville. Current population in this desert region is estimated at 117,033, only 16.4 percent of the County's total. The desert region covers a major portion of San Bernardino County—almost 93 percent of the total land area. This awesome expanse of open space, which includes a significant portion of the "Greater Mojave Desert" does not fulfill the popular conception of a desert; instead, it is generally composed of a series of roughly parallel but disconnected mountain ranges rising several hundred feet above the surrounding areas. Between the ranges, alluvial slopes descend into valleys. The Mojave River cuts northerly and easterly for a distance of more than 100 miles, flowing intermittently above and underground from the San Bernardino Mountains into Soda Dry Lake near Baker. Producing a watershed of about 100,000 acre feet, this river is the principal water resource within the Greater Mojave Desert.

MOJAVE RIVER VALLEY MUSEUM ASSOCIATION

HISTORY

In 1963, several teachers and interested citizens from Hinkley, Lenwood, Barstow, Daggett and Yermo discussed the possibility of establishing a museum in the desert. The group selected temporary officers and directors. In 1964, interested persons held an election to establish the Mojave River Valley Chapter of the San Bernardino County Museum Association.

In 1974 the Chapter voted to dissolve affiliation with the San Bernardino County Museum Association and is now a non-profit private organization known as the Mojave River Valley Museum Association.

MOJAVE RIVER VALLEY MUSEUM ASSOCIATION
OFFICERS AND DIRECTORS 1976

OFFICERS

President	Robert I. Carlson
Vice President	Clifford Walker
Secretary	Emma Jean Petroff
Treasurer	Clara Beth Pinnell

DIRECTORS

R. Arden Dunton	William Mann
E. Henry James	E. W. "Al" Muncy
Robert Whitlock	

PAST PRESIDENTS

Albert Prince	1963-1965
Clifford Walker	1965-1968
Jane Chamberlin	1969
J. Paul Sweeney	1970
Clara Beth Pinnell	1971
Henry James	1972
Gordon Stricler	1973
William Mann	1974
Robert I. Carlson	1975

Once Upon A Desert

PUBLICATION COMMITTEE

Patricia (Jernigan) Keeling, Chairman
Celestia (Brown) Gilliam, Vice Chairman
Emma Jean (Barr) Petroff, Secretary

James Benton
Louella (Elliott) Bishoff
Thelma M. Carder
William Christiansen
Ray Conaway
K. Dean Elliott
Margaret (Kenney) Fouts

Helen (Cumins) Graves
Annice (Leak) Gibson
Louis Jackson
Caryl Krouser
Germaine (Ramounachou) Moon
Elizabeth (Nettles) Penton
Clara Beth (DePue) Pinnell

Kathy (Vialpando) Prescott
Mabel (Crouch) Purinton
La Rue Shaffer Slette
Clifford Walker
Leonard Waitman
Jack Westfall
June (Greane) Zeitelhack

Photography Laboratory
Fred Gibson, Director
Marvin Manness
Charles Monds
Harry Woodworth

Supervising Editor: Pat Keeling

Layout: Thelma Carder, Celestia Gilliam, Pat Keeling,
Germaine Moon, Jean Petroff

Editors: James Benton, Louella Bishoff, Thelma
Carder, Celestia Gilliam, Pat Keeling, Caryl Krouser,
Germaine Moon, Elizabeth Penton, Jean Petroff,
Mabel Purinton, Clifford Walker, Jack Westfall, June
Zeitelhack.

Publicity, Advertising and Financial: Celestia Gilliam,
Jean Petroff, Beth Pinnell

Bibliography: Louella Bishoff

Photographic Work: Fred Gibson, Marvin Manness,
Charles Monds, Harry Woodworth

Photographic and Art Layouts: Germaine Moon

Photographic Captions: Jean Petroff

High Desert Haiku: Louella Bishoff

Art Work: K. Dean Elliott, Germaine Moon, Kathy
Prescott

OTHER CONTRIBUTORS AND OFFICE WORK:

Typists: Louella Bishoff, Peggy Dunton, Jane Eddy, Annice Gibson, Pat Keeling, Margaret Westfall, Alice Mashburn, Jean Petroff, Candi Rosa, Betty Stanson, Maurine Walthall

Contract Typists: Taina Chutumil, Diana Dube, Ruth Jordon, Kerry Petroff, LaRue Slette, Ann Yednakovich

Graphics Arts Classes: J. F. Kennedy High School - Director Tom Percy

Photocopy Equipment: Barstow Stationers, Barstow College

CETA Assistants: Arlene Bryson, Mary Sprouls, Mildred Taylor

Maps: Sharon L. Hicks, City of Barstow, 1976 Back Flap

HISTORIC REVIEW AND ADVISORY MEMBERS

Gertrude (Hadley) Alf
Martha (Rollinson) Burnau
Leland A. Cochran
Ray Conaway
Phyllis (Burkart) Couch
Clarence "Bud" Crooks
Margaret (Kenney) Fouts
Helen (Cumins) Graves
Annice (Leak) Gibson
Fred Gibson
Arda Haenszel
Fred Harper
Ruby (Walthall) Smith Harper
Louis Jackson
Andrew Kitts
Eunice (Bush) Leak
Burton Leak
Caryl Krouser
Alice (Burnau) Mashburn
May (Henderson) Murray
E. J. Olsen
Laura (Honey) Olsen
B. A. Schilling
Gwiadys "Frankie" (Hughes) Simon
Mina (Conaway) Sutcliffe
Clifford Walker
Leonard Waitman

ACKNOWLEDGEMENT

There are no superlatives to express our sincere thanks to the devoted people listed above for their many hours of preparation of this book.

We thank the countless men and women who paused to share their time and memories with us.

To the members of the Mojave River Valley Museum, Barstow College, Barstow Women's Club, Barstow Chapter — American Association of University Women, Barstow Chamber of Commerce Staff, the City of Barstow, and Vernon and Jessica Tegland for their technical assistance in the project, — for their contributions and support — we thank you.

CONTENTS

Chapter I

Footpaths to Freeways

Saddle weary miles,
Lonely trails and travelers,
Horizons of hope.

FRANCISCO GARCÉS, A TRUE BICENTENNIAL HERO FOR THE SOUTHWEST

by Thelma M. Carder

History begins for the Mojave Desert in March 1776 when Francisco Garcés, a Spanish Franciscan priest, followed an old Indian trail along the Mojave River looking for a practical route from Arizona to northern California. With him were Mohave Indians Luis and Ventura and a former mission Indian Sebastián Taraval. Garcés' early death and the shortsightedness of Spanish authorities prevented recognition of his discoveries. But the journal of his exploratory trip is the first written account of travel in this area.

Garcés was a man well worth an honored place in America's bicentennial celebration. He was courageous, honest and considerate of his fellow human beings. He had a spirit of adventure equal to the best in the American tradition. Except that he could not swim and needed Indians to carry him across rivers, he was as self reliant as any individual in our history.

His diary leaves no doubt that he enjoyed exploring—that he always looked for what was *mas alla*, farther on. Before he walked through Barstow on his daring trek of 1776 he had already visited remote and unknown regions of the American Southwest. If Indian guides or companions refused to accompany him, Garcés went alone. Only reluctant obedience to authority and prudence when he lacked Indian help kept him from more discovery. He was seldom stopped by inhospitable terrain or the fear of Indian hostility. As historian Herbert Bolton wrote in 1917:

> Altogether, his pathfinding, accomplished without the aid of a single white man, covered more than a thousand miles of untrod trails, and furnished an example of physical endurance and human courage that has rarely been excelled.

Garcés' journal indicates that he was also a man of faith—faith in God and in human nature. The cynical reader will think him naive. He hoped that Indian tribes would follow his advice to stop fighting each other. He believed the Indians sincerely wanted Christian instruction. He assumed Spanish missions would benefit his Indian friends. He expected Spanish authorities to speedily and adequately support such missions. He even thought that if Spanish soldiers were accompanied by their wives they could protect the missions from Apache attack and leave Indian women alone. In the Yuma massacre of 1781 he died a martyr to such faith. With his death ended also his dreams. The Spanish would never build missions along the Gila and the Colorado Rivers or solve the problem of Apache raids. They would never use the travel routes he had discovered.

He also lost the prominent place in California and Southwestern history that he deserves. Recent concern for local history in Kern and San Bernardino Counties is changing that, but the change is not reflected in general texts. For example, a new book by Julian Nava and Bob Barger, *California: Five Centuries of Cultural Contrasts*, mentions only his death in 1781 and his usefulness to the Anza expedition. Older historians Herbert Bolton and Charles E. Chapman stress his contributions and accomplishments, while various writers have tried to precisely identify his routes through the desert. Elliot Coues, an army medical officer and naturalist, published a translation of Garcés' 1775-6 diary in 1900, including excerpts from journals of his own trips. In 1927 local writer Dix Van Dyke commented on Coues and suggested an alternative interpretation of the route Garcés followed. Recent works are John Galvin's new translation of the diary, 1972, and two short biographies: *Francisco Garcés: Pioneer Padre of the Tulares* by Ardis M. Walker, Visalia, 1974, and "Francisco Garcés Explorer of Southern California" by Raymund F. Wood, *Southern California Quarterly*, September 1969. Wood's article is scholarly and his excellent notes include comments important to the researcher interested in Garcés. Enough information exists to restore the missionary explorer of 1776 to his deserved place in history.

Born in the Villa de Morata del Conde, a town in the old Spanish kingdom of Aragon, Garcés was named after three saints—Francisco, Tomas, and Hermenegildo—and educated by his uncle Mozen Domingo Garcés, a curate. He began his religious study at age 15 and was ordained at 25. On student outings he often left his fellow classmates to talk to poor laborers. He so gained their confidence that one poor potter would confess to no priest other than Garcés.

He begged for missionary work in the Americas and was accepted for training at the *Colegio de la Santa Cruz* in Querétaro, Mexico, arriving there with a Spanish group in 1763. When northern missions were left without priests by the expulsion of the Jesuits in 1767, Garcés was one of fourteen Querétaran Franciscans sent from San Blas to Guaymas by sea and then overland. He began his work at the northernmost mission, San Xavier del Bac, near the present city of Tucson on June 30, 1768.

Although he did not spend much time at this post, he was seriously concerned about developing a process for religious conversion of the Indians and sought only their spiritual welfare. He befriended the Indians first and then introduced simple Christian concepts. The various sources give little information about the results of his missionary efforts.

In August 1768 he left with four Pima guides on the first of his exploratory ventures to establish friendly relationships with the Pimas and other tribes along the Gila River. On a second visit in 1770 he found the Pimas excited about having seen white people in the west, people Garcés inferred to be soldiers of the 1769 expeditions to Upper California. Garcés was also excited by this evidence that California could be reached from Arizona.

Meanwhile, his enthusiastic reports had gained him assurance from authorities in Mexico that they would support the establishment of more missions in Arizona. And the Indians of Arizona had begun to venerate him as their "old man," although he was still in his early thirties.

Accompanied by three Indian guides and taking one horse, he left on the most important of his early treks on August 8, 1771, intending to reach the Colorado River and follow up on the information he had gained from the Pimas. With the Gila River swollen by unusual rainfall, he did not recognize the Colorado at its junction east of Yuma. Traveling through the delta for several days, he lost his horse, found him again, crossed the river on rafts made by friendly Indians, and continued looking for the Colorado. Eventually, he decided to use the village of San Jacome near Cerro Prieto (Baja California) as a supply base for more exploration. In a three and a half day trek without water he sighted the San Jacinto mountains and San Felipe pass, his route for the Anza expedition to Mission San Gabriel three years later. He was very upset when Anza's men and horses in desperate need of water reached the obvious landmark Cerro Prieto and he could not find San Jacome again. He finally did encounter some former San Jacome inhabitants who told him they had abandoned the village for lack of water.

In October 1771 Garcés returned to his mission with information and accomplishments that would make him a key person in Spanish plans for the future. Particularly interested was Captain Juan Bautista de Anza, commander at nearby Tubac. Garcés had met Indians who had seen white men on the Pacific Coast, confirming accounts from the Pimas. He had befriended the Indian tribes controlling the Colorado, including the Yumas and their chief, Ollyquotquiebe, known by the Spanish name Salvador Palma. Garcés' report made possible Anza's long cherished ambition to head an overland expedition exploring feasible supply routes to Spain's precarious settlements in northern California.

These colonies were part of a larger Spanish design for defense against foreign encroachments—real and imagined—implemented in the 1760s and 70s. Though the land was potentially rich, the handful of early Spanish settlers in California could not provide for themselves. Food, animals, supplies and more settlers had to come either from Mexico or Spain. Tiny ships plying difficult waters between San Blas and San Diego or Monterey were never adequate to the task of transporting goods and settlers. An overland route was essential.

Monterey, founded by Gaspar de Portola in 1770, was suffering a "starving time" when Garcés returned to Arizona with news that the Pacific Ocean must be just over the mountains he had seen west of the Colorado. He was instrumental in gaining approval for Anza's first expedition from Viceroy Antonio Bucareli and the council in charge of appropriations in Mexico.

Garcés would serve as a guide for the first part of the trip. A second potential guide turned up in December 1773 just when Anza had gone back to Altar, Sonora, to replace animals and supplies lost in an Apache raid at Tubac. The newcomer was Sebastián Taraval, a Baja California mission Indian who had been taken to San Gabriel to help with Spanish mission efforts there. He had run away hoping to reach his old home. Accompanied by his wife and brother, he traveled up the San Jacinto Valley, crossed the mountains, came down Coyote Canyon, followed the Borrego Valley, and became lost crossing the desert to the Colorado. In a three-day stretch without water, his wife and brother had died of thirst. When he reached the Yuma villages, Chief Palma sent him to Altar to meet Anza.

Immediately employed as a guide for the first Anza expedition, Sebastián accompanied Father Garcés on most of his treks for the next four years. The Spanish nicknamed the new arrival *El Pelegrino*, the wanderer. But, he was no match for Garcés.

The trek of direct historical importance to the high desert began in connection with Anza's second expedition to bring colonists and supplies to California. This expedition left Tubac on October 23, 1775. Garcés and Tomas Eixarch, another priest, went along as far as the Yuma villages. They remained behind to explore the local area and determine the religious needs of Colorado River Indians.

In December Garcés, Sebastián, and two interpreters started south to the mouth of the Colorado River. On December 6 they overtook the Anza expedition and remained with it three days while Garcés negotiated for more interpreters to accompany him downstream. Father Pedro Font whose diary gives the most complete daily accounts of Anza's trip counseled Garcés "not to go alone . . . since just to see tribes he had already seen was no use. The purpose of his journey was to go with the interpreters to ascertain Indian wishes in the mater of catechism and Christianity." That night Father Font commented in his diary:

> Father Garcés is so well fitted to get along with the Indians and to go among them that he appears to be but an Indian himself. Like the Indians he is phlegmatic in everything. He sits with them in the circle, or at night around the fire, with his legs crossed, and there he will sit musing two or three hours or more, oblivious to everything else, talking with them with such serenity and deliberation. And although the foods of the Indians are as nasty and dirty as those outlandish people themselves, the father eats them with great gusto and says that they are good for the stomach and very fine. In short God has created him, as I see it, solely for the purpose of seeking out these unhappy, ignorant, and rustic people.

Garcés continued south, accompanied by Sebastián

and interpreters. Indians received him with affection, remembering him from his 1771 visit. They were proud of having followed his advice to remain at peace with their neighbors. Garcés recorded almost daily in his diary that he had counseled the Indians to give up war. To help the Indians understand "God and his mysteries," he displayed the canvas described in the introduction to his journal:

> Since I saw that in no way could I explain things better to the Indians than with pictures that they would understand at sight, I decided to take with me a canvas on one side of which was a painting of Mary Most Holy with the Divine Child in her arm, and on the other a painting of the damned man.

Variations in Indian languages made communication difficult, even with interpreters.

Eventually accompanied only by Sebastián, the missionary pushed south. On December 21 they "came to water that was of the sea . . . Its waves were high and it stretched northeast as well as south as far as one could see." To make sure, they went three miles farther down and Garcés had Sebastián get some water. "It was too salty to drink."

Returning to the Yuma villages January 3, 1776, Garcés talked to Apaches, Mohaves and representatives of other tribes, deciding first to visit the country of the Mohaves. He had long been hoping to find a shorter inland route to the northern Spanish settlements. He had been most disappointed when Anza's first expedition went north from San Gabriel without him and Anza ordered him to lead a party of soldiers back to the Colorado. Visiting the Mohaves might make such exploration possible.

Accompanied by a Mohave chief, one interpreter and Sebastián, Garcés reached a point across the river from the main Mohave rancherias on February 28. Many people came across the river to see him:

> I showed them the painting of the Virgin, which pleased them very much; of the Damned Man they said that he was very bad. I was the first Spaniard to enter their land, at which they rejoiced greatly on account of their desire to know us. They had heard said that we were brave, and they showed extraordinary pleasure at being friends of so valiant a people.

The next day Garcés talked with Mohave chiefs and

> . . . laid before them my desires to visit the Fathers living near the sea; they agreed and offered to accompany me, for they had heard of them and knew the way. As I was now short of supplies, I decided to leave at once and told them that on my return we should see each other at leisure. I left some of my baggage.

This baggage may have included his painted canvas. His journal does not mention the canvas again.

With Sebastián and three Mohave Indians for company, Garcés left the Colorado River on March 4 to begin the trek which would take him across the desert, along the Mojave River, through what today is Barstow and on to San Gabriel.

It is difficult to determine the exact route the small group followed from the Colorado River to the Mojave River, using only the Garcés journal as a reference. Several persons have tried to retrace his steps and locate his camping places. His first translator Elliot Coues compared his own trip across the Mojave in 1865 with the Garcés route:

> We shall be able to trace his very steps on this journey, as I once followed his route very closely, and have my own itinerary before me, October 30—November 14, 1865, from Mojave to San Gabriel. Besides myself the party consisted of John N. Goodwin, governor of Arizona; Lieutenant Charles A. Curtis, Fifth U.S. Infantry; two servants, one of them my Mexican boy Jose, whose full name I never knew, and the other Curtis' striker; and two teamsters, one of the four-mule ambulance in which we rode, the other of the six-mule wagon for our baggage and rations. The route in brief, was west to Soda Lake, then up the Mojave river, through the Cajon pass to San Bernardino valley, and thence to San Gabriel mission near Los Angeles. The clearest map of the road that I know of is one on a scale of 16 miles to the inch published by the Wheeler survey of 1875, being a topographical sketch of the route followed by a party under Lieutenant Eric Bergland, corps of Engineers, U.S. Army. This road does not agree well with the present railroad line, but in those earlier years it was the only road from Mojave westward. (Coues means Fort Mohave)

Coues, who gained knowledge of the Mojave desert while stationed at Ft. Whipple near Prescott, Arizona, often admits that his interpretation may not be accurate. Dix Van Dyke was much more acquainted with the area and tried personally to cover every inch of the Garcés route. Arda Haenszel and Dennis Casebier are currently collaborating on a new interpretation of the trek with evidence from archeological research. Neither of the recent biographers, Ardis Walker nor Raymund Wood, adds to the older accounts of this portion of the Garcés trip in his text, but Wood includes extensive comment in his notes.

Let Garcés and his interpreters tell it in their own words:

> *Father Garcés' Journal, 1776* (Translation by John Galvin, 1972). *Mar. 4, 56th day*—I set out to the southwest, accompanied by three Jamajab (Mohave) Indians and Sebastián. After two and a half leagues I arrived at some waterholes which I named the Pozos de San Casimiro. There was some pasturage.

> *Elliot Coues, 1900* (with notes from Coues' trip in 1865)—When I ferried across the river from Fort Mohave, October 30, 1865, I went three miles to some water called Beaver Lake; whence it was 22 miles to Piute Springs, the usual first camp out from the fort. The road was fair, though mostly up and down hill, and either sandy or rocky. But it appears that Garcés did not go exactly this way.

He started west from the river below Fort Mohave and took an Indian trail that runs approximately parallel with, but a few miles south of, the main wagon road I was on, joining the latter farther on.

Dix Van Dyke, 1927—The Colorado River, at the point where Garcés left it, on March 1, 1776, has an elevation of 450 feet. From that point, Garcés mounted gradually to a region with an elevation of three thousand feet, through which he passed during the two days following. He evidently followed the Piute Wash (a large gulch which, after leaving the river, runs southwest and then northwest), until he reached a suitable place to leave it and turn west. His camp, on March 4, was probably in this wash. At the present time there is water in it at Klinefelter, on the Santa Fe Railway. This point would be southwest of the point where he left the river, and leaving there on March 5, he would have had to follow the wash in a northwesterly direction for a time.

Garcés, Mar. 5, 57th day—Setting out northwest, I went eight leagues west by a quarter west-southwest through flat and grass-covered country and halted where there were holes with excellent water, but it was not very plentiful; Sebastián said that watering might be possible in two shifts.

Mar. 6, 58th day—I went five leagues west and three west-southwest through flat and grassy country and came to a mountain range (the Providence) with small pines; I called it the Sierra de Santa Coleta. The watering-place has little yield and is high up. Pasturage is ample and of good quality. Here I met four Indians who had come from Santa Clara to traffic in shell beads. They were carrying no food supply, nor even bows for hunting. Noticing my astonishment at this, where there is nothing to eat, they said, "We Jamajabs can withstand hunger and thirst for as long as four days," giving me to understand that they were hardy men.

Mar. 7, 59th day—In the afternoon I crossed the mountain range by a good pass and entered a small valley with sandy knolls at its sides; I called it the Cañada de Santo Tomás. Having travelled four leagues west-northwest (although I would have done better to follow the valley, as it had the firmest ground), I halted. At my stopping place there was herbage but no water.

Coues—No entry for Mar. 5 in our copy, by continued scribal omission, which I supply in brackets:
When I traveled the main road on Oct. 31, 1865 from Piute Springs it was 20 miles to Rock Springs, where I found no water and went two miles further to water at what were called Government holes in those days; total, 22 miles. Now Garcés is coming along his trail but little south of my road, and nearly parallel therewith. His eight leagues to-day, nearly west, takes him to the Sierra de Santa Coleta, in which range he finds a scanty aguage. This watering-place is Cedar Springs, in the Providence mountains of modern geography. Observe the name "Cedar" Springs, and the statement that the sierra "has

pines, though small ones.

Van Dyke—On the night of the 5th, he probably stopped north of Goffs, about where Vontrigger Spring now is, reaching Providence Mountain the next night. There is no mistaking his description of this mountain, for there is no other like it.

March 7, he tells of passing through a good gap, and at the outlet finding a "canyada" with sand hills on either side. This gap is a pass in the Providence Mountain, and the sand hills are the northeast edge of the "Devil's Playground." The canyada is merely a sandy wash that meanders through the sand hills and carries storm waters from the Providence Mountain towards Soda Lake. I traversed the same canyada, in an automobile, for the reason that, like Garcés, we found the footing there firmer than it was on the sands. These places are easily visible from the town of Kelso.

Casebier in *Camp Rock Springs* states that Garcés' "good gap" on March 7 was south of Cedar Canyon, probably Foshay Pass. Raymund Wood also argues that Foshay Pass fits Garcés description much better than does Cedar Canyon. No sand dunes lie west of Cedar Canyon, Wood notes, and instead that canyon would have led the priest out to Soda Dry Lake, a landmark he would surely have noted. He would also be too far north of the Mojave River sink and Afton Canyon.

Garcés—Mar. 8, 60th day—Six leagues to the west-southwest I came to some waterholes with an abundant supply; I named them after San Juan de Dios. Pasturage was sufficient. Here begins the territory of the Beñemé nation.

Van Dyke—March 8, Garcés evidently continued along the present route of the Union Pacific Railroad, and followed the sandy wash except in places where he could take short cuts across its curves. To the south of him was a range of rocky mountains, and to the north was a large area of sand dunes. He was picking the best route between. That night he camped at the edge of Soda Lake. The Beñeme nation he describes must have been Piutes.

Garcés—Mar. 9, 61st day—I went on five leagues and came to a pass in the mountains; I gave it the name Pinta because of the veins of various colors that are in it. I found a stream-bed with rather brackish water (the Mojave River) and named it the Arroyo de los Mártires. There was good pasturage.

Coues—"Mar. 9 is the memorable day on which Garcés discovers the Mojave river, never before seen by a white man. He has reached the sink of the river, modern Soda lake, and names it Arroyo de los Martires—a term appearing as "R. de los Martires" on Font's map of 1777, but "R. de los Martinez" by misprint on the reduced copy in Bancroft, and Rio de los Martires having originally been Kino's name of the Colorado in 1699. Hence arose some confusion; but there is not the slightest doubt of Garcés discovery and present position. Mojave river has no outlet, but sinks in the sand at Soda lake or marsh, a place which varies much in appearance at different seasons or conditions of water supply. The sink has an extent of about 20 miles from north to south, but is narrow in the opposite direction, and the main road takes directly across the middle of it from east to west when the water is low. When crossed it was nearly dry except in some reedy patches, and most of the surface was whitened with alkaline efflorescence; the water was bad, as Garcés says; the grass was poor, there was no wood and myriads of mosquitos tormented us, though water had frozen half an inch thick on our buckets on the night of Oct. 31. On the west side of the sink a road goes northward; the road to follow is the left-hand one, which runs about west-southwest and strikes the river a few miles higher up, as the river comes into the extreme south end of the sink. This is Garcés course for tomorrow. "arroyo arriba con rumbo al Oestsudoeste."

Van Dyke—March 9, he arrived at the Caves Canyon, through which the Mojave River flows. This canyon has walls several hundred feet high which are streaked with different colors. Except in flood times, all of the water flowing in this canyon rises from the ground a short distance above the upper end, and is heavily impregnated with alkali. This is the saltish water Garcés describes.

Coues has endeavored to show that thus far Garcés followed the course afterwards taken by American travelers, but he is in error. The latter route was more roundabout, and passed to the north of Providence Mountain. It was better for travelers with livestock and wagons, for it traversed country that was devoid of drift sand and that had watering places at intervals of a day's journey. It possessed no advantages for bare-footed Indians, who could easily out-travel horses. Until about 1870, or later, the desert Indians used horses only for eating, and never rode them. Indians carried but little baggage, and considered horses an encumbrance.

Caves Canyon today is called Afton Canyon, well worth a side trip from the freeway. The visitor should take his camera and plan to spend some time viewing this spectacular canyon which is inadequately described above by both Garcés and Van Dyke. Although he loved to travel, Garcés was probably too tired every night to wax eloquent about the natural world he was viewing. One would hardly know he was crossing a desert.

Garcés—Mar. 10, 62nd day—I continued six leagues west-southwest and stopped in the same stream-bed, where there are cottonwoods, pools of water, and much herbage.

Coues—The distance given should set Garcés in the vicinity of a place on the river called the Caves—a usual first stopping place in going up the river from Soda Lake.

Garcés—Mar. 11, 63rd day—Going on another league in the same direction, I came to some poor rancherías; they had nothing to eat but the roots of rushes. The inhabitants numbered about twenty-five. I gave them of what little I had, and they gave me of their roots, which my Jamajab companions swallowed with repugnance. The Indians showed disappointment at not being able to go hunting to get me food, but it was rainy and very cold and they were stark naked.

Here are found wild grapes, much pasturage, and mesquites including the screwbean. This nation is the same as that of San Gabriel, Santa Clara, and San José. They have some baskets like those of the (Santa Barbara) Channel (Indians), blankets of otter and rabbit, and some very unusual nets which they make from the wild hemp that grows here. The men are effeminate, and the women rather dirty like those of the mountains; but they are all very peaceable and not at all troublesome. They listened attentively to what I told them of God.

Van Dyke—March 10, he followed the course of the river, and camped four miles downstream from what became Camp Cady.

March 11, he camped at the site of Camp Cady. This is a stretch of timber about six miles long.

Coues—Hence it appears that about this time Garcés passes what was once a notable point on the Mojave river—the site of Camp Cady. This military post was occupied when I came by, Nov. 4, 1865, 16 miles from my camp at the Caves already mentioned. I find the following in my journal of that day: "Half a day's pull through heavy sandy and gravelly washes brought us to this God-forsaken Botany Bay of a place, the meanest I ever saw yet for a military station, where four officers and a handful of men manage to exist in some unexplained way in mud and brush hovels. The officers were Capt. West, Lieut. Forster, Lieut. Davidson, and Dr. Lauber—glad enough to see us—or anybody else."

Garcés—Mar. 12, 64th day—Having gone two leagues in the same direction, I stopped at a deserted ranchería on the same watercourse. The rain and cold continued; also our hunger, because there was not so much as rush roots; and as the inhabited rancherías were a long distance away I decided to have a horse killed to relieve our necessity. Not even the blood was wasted, and rationing was necessary until we got to other rancherías. The cold was so severe that one of the Jamajab Indians accompanying me started back. To one of the two who stayed on I gave a blanket to keep him warm, and to the other a woolen shirt. With the slaughtering of the horse there was much to eat, and they did not want to leave for three days.

Van Dyke—March 12, he camped at another river basin that was later called Forks of the Road.

Garcés—Mar. 15, 65th day—I moved on two leagues west-southwest and one and a half leagues northwest and halted on the same watercourse. Pasturage is plentiful.

Van Dyke—March 15, he camped between Daggett and Barstow.

Garcés—Mar. 16, 66th day—I went two leagues west-northwest, left the watercourse, and turned southwest. There I came to it again and followed it, going southward until I had completed four leagues. The herbage is good, and there are large cottonwoods, and cranes and crows like those of San Gabriel.

Coues—We have recovered Garcés' mileage, and we have him safe enough on the river. From what he says of his southwest course, and his anxiety at finding himself going so far below lat. 35º, I should suppose him to be somewhere between Grapevine and Cottonwood. From Camp Cady to Grapevine (Jacobi's) is about 25 miles: at 11 miles of this distance is a point called Forks of the Road, where a road to Salt Lake City branches. Most of the way is along the left bank, north side of the river; then comes a stretch off the river, which is regained at a place called Fish Pond: whence it is four miles further to Grapevine. The railroad now crosses the river in this vicinity, between stations Fish Pond and Waterman. I was last there in Dec., 1891.

Van Dyke—March 16, he cut across country to the east of Barstow to avoid a bend in the river, and camped about where Helendale now is. The government survey maps of 1856 show that, at that date, there was an extensive swamp opposite Helendale, into which the river flowed, and there was no river channel passing through it. Since then, floods have scoured a wide channel, and the old swamp is only a memory.

During the next four days, he wandered up the river, and on March 20, he took an observation either at the Victor Narrows or at the Lower Narrows between Victorville and Oro Grande.

Garcés—Mar. 17—I was there for the whole day because on crossing the stream the mule got stuck and everything got wet. I sent a Jamajab and Sebastián to look for inhabited rancherías. This place is at 34º 37'. There came to it five Jamajab Indians who had just returned from trading at San Gabriel, well pleased at their treatment by the Fathers, who had given them maize. These Indians imitated the bleating of the (mission's) calves.

Mar. 18, 67th day—Sebastián returned praising the hospitality he had received. I mounted and rode five leagues southwest up this watercourse to a ranchería of forty souls, of the same Beñemé nation. Because I had come below 35º (of latitude) I urged the Indians to take me toward the west, but they refused, saying they knew no other route. Here I was treated to hares, rabbits, and plenty of acorn gruel, with which we relieved our hunger.

Mar. 19, 68th day—I went one league south-southwest and reached the dwelling of the captain of these rancherías. He gave me a string of white seashells that was about two yards long. His wife sprinkled me with acorns and threw the basket, which is a sign of marked attention. Then she brought out some seashells and sprinkled me with them as if she were tossing flowers. Then his second wife came and expressed her sentiments

with the same attentions. I responded in the best way I could, astonished that among such rustic people there should be so expressive a show of feeling as their pouring out the shells that are their greatest treasure.

Mar. 20, 69th day—I travelled two and a half leagues east and southeast following the watercourse and came to a pass through which the stream flows; the position was 34º 18'. I continued in the afternoon and having gone five leagues south and southwest I arrived at a ranchería of perhaps seventy souls where the inhabitants received me with high spirits, some howling like wolves and others orating at the top of their voices. There were two captains. They and all the other men gave me seashells and the women made the same display of feeling as those at the ranchería last visited, tossing acorns even to the mules.

Coues—"Garcés continues up river, as he says he does; the words "est" "sursueste" and "sueste" are unmistakable in the handwriting before me. The road which I followed in 1865 crosses from left to right bank of the river a few miles above the Grapevine place said, continues past Cottonwood to Point of Rocks, 22 miles from Grapevine, on a southwest course; at Point of Rocks it turns due south to what was called Lane's, or the Upper crossing, and there leaves the river entirely to strike straight south by west for Cajon pass in the montains, reached in 19 miles from Lane's. This is the way I went, as my itinerary shows: "Nov. 9. To Martin's ranch, 29 miles South from Lane's crossing; more than half the distance in open country, and then we entered the Cajon pass in the mountains, where there is a tollgate. The pass is a narrow, deep, and tortuous cañon, the roughest I have ever traversed on wheels: there was 10 miles of this from the tollgate to Martin's ranch." Now Garcés has been sent through Cajon pass, with a query, as by Bancroft, but I do not think he went that way. Taking his courses on their face, he continued up the Mojave river, with considerable easting as said, passed Huntington's on the river, and then through Bear or Holcomb valley rounded up to the mountains directly north of the San Bernardino valley, and crossed them by the well-known trail into this valley.

Garcés—Mar. 21, 70th day—Striking out to the southwest from the stream and travelling two leagues, I crossed a ravine and some low hills, coming to a ranchería of five huts, and kept on south through a valley with many trees, pasturage, and water. In it there are many cottonwoods, alders, oaks, very tall conifers, and sightly junipers. A league further on I came to another ranchería of about eighty souls, which I called San Benito. I was joyfully received and treated to a shower of acorns.

Coues—"This cañada is the pass through which Garcés crossed the mountains, between the San Gabriel and the San Bernardino ranges, from Holcomb's valley into the beautiful one which became the site of the present city of San

Bernardino. He is tracing the Mojave river up to its very source, near which is the rancheria he calls San Benito.

Van Dyke—March 21, he left the river above Victorville, and cutting across a spur of the Hesperia Mesa, reached the Little Mojave River about where Las Flores Ranch now is.

Garcés—Mar. 22, 71st day—After three leagues I crossed the (San Bernardino) mountain range south-southwest. The trees mentioned yesterday reach to its top, whence the Ocean is in view, the Santa Anna River, and the San José Valley. On the downslope of the range there are few trees. At its foot I found a rancheria where they received me very gladly. I continued west-southwest and west, and having gone three leagues along the slope of the range I stopped in the Arroyo de los Alisos.

Coues—"Into the San Bernardino valley, which is Garcés Valle de San Joseph, on the upper reaches of his Rio de Santa Anna, which is the present name of this river, commonly in the form Santa Ana. This rises in the San Bernardino Mts., runs through the valley just said, and takes a mean S.W. course to the sea at Newport, under Point Lasuen. Garcés is about to fall upon the trail of the main expedition, and the names he uses for the river and valley are easily identified.

Garcés—Mar. 23, 72nd day—I travelled half a league west-southwest and a league south, at the urging of some Indians whom I met and who made me go to their rancheria, where we ate. After going another league west-southwest, I struck the path of the expedition. I followed it rapidly, going eight leagues northwest and west-northwest, well into the night, when I halted.

Mar. 24, 73rd day—Two leagues to the west-northwest brought me to San Gabriel Mission, where I was most kindly received by the Fathers. It made me very happy to see the improvement in this mission, both spiritual and temporal, since my former visit.

In San Gabriel Garcés hoped to get supplies and help to go north. He had already been disappointed, as he noted in his journal March 18, when the Indian trail turned south, but, it was now his misfortune to run into one of those second-rate administrators with whom mankind is often plagued. He would not be able to continue his trip very far. In fact it is apparent from his own account below that Fernando Xavier de Rivera y Moncada, military governor of Upper California, took a dim view of the entire project. He was particularly unhappy with Garcés for bringing Mohave Indians with him to San Gabriel:

My principal object on leaving the Jamajabs' country was to go straight to San Luis (Obispo) Mission, or further north, to make communication easier between the Sonora and Moqui provinces and Monterey (which is what His Excellency the Viceroy seeks); but not having succeeded in doing so because my Indian companions had refused to go with me, I decided to go from San Gabriel up to San Luis over the

Camino Real and then, striking eastward, to examine what reed marshes there are to the east of San Luis; and, continuing in the same direction, to return to the Jamajabs' country. For this journey I asked the corporal at San Gabriel for an escort and supplies, but he refused me. I appealed to Commander Rivera, who at the time was in San Diego, and he also, in writing, flatly refused my request. A few days after I received his reply, he arrived in San Gabriel and I set forth to him that matters were not impracticable as he had written, since many of the expedition's animals were there and that the Fathers, on his order, would give me supplies; also, since he was on his way to Monterey, I could go in his company past the (Santa Barbara) Channel, the most dangerous region, after which we would go our respective ways. Seeing how sensible, legitimate, and easy my proposal was, he took as an excuse not that it was beyond doing but that he had no order from His Excellency and therefore could not supply me anything. Finally, he let me have one of the expedition's horses.

I was persuaded by all this that the Commander had taken it very ill that I had come into these parts, the more since in his response to my letter he had said it did not in the least suit him that the Indians of the Colorado should come through to the establishments at Monterey. A little before my arrival, there had been at San Gabriel for their traffic in shells a few Jamajabs (those I have already said I met). When news of them reached the Commander, he wrote to the corporal at this mission to seize these Indians and take them toward their land a long way from here—an order that was not carried out because it arrived after they had left.

I don't doubt that the Commander must have had solid reasons for his decision, and have formed upon them his judgement that communications and dealings between the nations of the Colorado River and those of the coast would be harmful; but, begging his pardon, I shall say it is so far from being harmful that I rather consider it necessary if we are to carry forward with confidence the project of opening communications between those establishments and these provinces (Sonora and its neighbours).

In every nation, even advanced ones, it is common policy to deny passage to those who are going to favour one's enemies; but since communication between the Colorado River and the coast is a necessity, how are the Spaniards to go through if the nations of the one area are at odds with those of the other? The King our Sovereign orders that all Indians, even those unbaptized, be admitted into the presidios with displays of good-will. How, then, without thwarting His Majesty's intentions, can orders be given to seize them? The law of nations permits trade between one people and another. What reason, then, can there be to stop the harmless and long-established commerce of the river people with those of the sea, consisting as it does in some white shell-beads? If we preach to the heathen a law of peace and charity, how can we think of sowing discord?

Some of the nations nearest those establishments are justly provoked with the Spanish soldiers because of the abuses they have suffered, especially from deserters. Therefore, if the distant nations become exasperated, and the Indians make common cause, those establishments will not last, nor shall we be able to found others, and thus the wishes of our Catholic King will be set at nought. Because of all this I cannot give assent to the Commander's opinion; rather, it seems to me that it would have been more profitable, as well as correct, if he had ordered that the Indians be treated kindly, so that word of the Spaniards' good conduct should reach their land and spread among the heathen nations.

The Indians I have mentioned were returning contentedly, as I can personally testify, because the priests, the soldiers, and the mission's Indian converts had treated them well. It would have been otherwise if they had told of being seized; besides speaking ill of us to their own nation they would have complained to the Yumas, through whose territory Lieutenant-Colonel Juan Bautista de Anza was to return, and perhaps he would not have had the same good reception as on his outward journey. I have already related that the sudden calm at San Diego was occasioned when the Quemeyás who came with the news found that all the river Indians were now friends with the Spaniards, and at the same time met with the courtesy and kindliness of the Commander of the expedition. This is my view.

Garcés remains as diplomatic as possible in his criticism here of Governor Rivera. This is part of his official report to authorities in Mexico. He correctly points out, however, that the Indians had regular trade routes and means of communication. The word of Spanish behavior in one part of California reached Indians in other areas. He is also identifying some of the contradictions in Spanish policy which had already led to trouble in San Diego and would later cause the Yuma massacre and his own death. He does not state directly that Rivera may well have feared contact between the still free Mohave Indians and Indians at San Gabriel required to live in mission settlements.

The missionary explorer had come too far to let recalcitrant officialdom prevent his continued search for a northern route between Monterey and Arizona:

With regard to my supplies, the charity of my brothers did what Commander Rivera did not do. They also favoured my companions with presents. So I continued toward my goal, but not by the route past the (Santa Barbara) Channel since the Fathers impressed upon me that it was very risky. I stayed at San Gabriel Mission until April 9.

On April 9, still accompanied by Sebastián and the two Mohave Indians Luis and Ventura, Garcés traveled north avoiding the established route infested by rebellious Indians against whom he had no protection. His steps cannot be traced exactly, but Wood says he traveled to the east of the present-day Tejon Pass into the San Joaquin Valley. Successful with the first Indian communities he encountered, Garcés resolved to push on, but in the neighborhood of present-day Greenfield:

. . . they received me with great pleasure and fed me generously. They urged me not to go on; even Sebastián and the Jamajabs refused to accompany me. Seeing how reluctant they were, I stayed there until the 30th of April, although in that time I went out twice to have a look at the surrounding country. They were well aware of my desire to go on, but said that the people next them were not related to them and were very bad Noches. However, seeing me unhappy, an old man of that same Noche nation who had taken a wife in this ranchería offered to go with me.

83rd day—Telling Sebastián and the Jamajabs to wait for me there the four or five days that I should be away, I set out eastward with the old man.

His "four or five" days stretched into ten days as Garcés accompanied by various local Indians, explored the eastern San Joaquin Valley as far north as the White River. He discovered the Kern River where it comes out of the mountains, following it down to a place he could cross with the help of Indians who were good swimmers. Near the White River he met an Indian who was obviously a runaway from the Monterey missions. He knew that he was not far from San Luis Obispo. That same day, May 3, he decided to turn back in spite of being so near his goal. He feared that if he did not Sebastián and the Mohave Indians would desert him. Also, from the White River he could see the unbroken range of high mountains to the north. Ardis Walker infers that Garcés would have explored the Kern River as possibly the best route across the mountains had his Indian guides been willing to go along.

By May 8 on his return journey, he was beginning to worry about the safety of the three Indian companions he had left behind:

I went six more leagues as far as the territory of the Cuabajais. They were very festive because of my coming; there was a dance that night and the next day. But I was all the time worried at not finding any of my companions here. The next day Luis the Jamajab came with two animals and a message from the captain of San Pasqual asking me to go at once to the captain's ranchería; but as the message also said that Sebastián had gone looking for me along the San Felipe River (Kern) I decided to await him where I was. In the afternoon he arrived safe and sound.

His return to the village where he had left Sebastián and the Mohaves proved to him and to present historians that the Spaniards were discovering Indian trade routes long established:

I went to the ranchería of San Pasqual, where I found two Jamajabs who had recently arrived (of those who had journeyed with me there remained only Luis and Ventura); they were evidence to me of the regular trade between these nations and those by the sea. The people of the ranchería supplied us with rabbits, ground chia, and some little loaves made with other seeds. Everything was offered with much rejoicing, and I did not half make return with what I gave them. They asked me when I should come back another time. I spoke again with the captain, counselling him not to make war on the Indians of Santa Clara, where he had killed another captain. I tried to persuade them that the Spaniards are good people, but he did not acquiesce in this opinion, giving me to understand that those who passed through stole baskets and other valuables.

On May 11 Garcés with Sebastián and new Mohave guides "succeeded in returning" to the Colorado River "by a different route" unknown to the Indians who were used to traveling over Tejon Pass. For once the Spanish explorer was leading the Indians.

Crossing the Tehachapis and the Mojave Desert he was back at the future site of Helendale by May 19:

Garcés—May 18, 96th day—Travelling two and a half leagues in the same direction over an immense plain that clearly was in former times a lake-bed, I found another hole with a little water in it.

May 19, 97th day—Four and a half leagues further in the same direction I came to the Río de los Mártires (the Mojave River) near the place where an observation had read 34° 37'.

Van Dyke—On his return journey, he evidently descended from the Tehachapi Mountains and crossed the desert on some route between the present towns of Mojave and Helendale. There are two or three places there where water is near the surface, and the Indians probably had holes scooped out. There is now a cattle watering place midway, called Flowing Wells.

Sixty-eight years after Garcés, Frémont descended from the Tehachapi Mountains, following probably in Garcés footsteps. He recoiled, however, in fear of the desert, and instead of taking the direct route to Mojave River, as did Garcés, he followed around the southern edge, keeping close to the mountains; and somewhere near Cajon Pass he fell into the Spanish trail, following it northward to the river below Victorville.

Garcés—May 20, 21, 22—I returned the same way as far as the Pozos de San Juan de Dios.

May 23—Turning aside and going two leagues east-northeast, I halted at a sandy place where there was a Chemevet ranchería.

Van Dyke—May 23. There is a sandy plain stretching eastward from Soda Lake and north from the westerly route of Garcés. On the edge of Soda Lake and about four or five miles from the route Garces followed, there are some water holes with good water, known locally as Cow Holes. The Chemebet Rancheria he describes must have been within reach of this water, for there is no other near. The inhabitants were Chemehuevi Indians, who, within the memory of white men, have always lived on the Colorado

River. There are now very few of pure Indian blood left, although there are many of mixed Indian and white.

Garcés—May 24—I delayed here because some of the Jamajabs who had come to trade in shells were ill.

May 25, 98th day—I traveled four and a half leagues east-southeast to pass the region of sands and the Sierra de Santa Coleta (Providence Mountains).

Van Dyke—May 25—Garcés was retracing his steps of March 7.

Garcés—May 26, 99th day—Three leagues east-northeast and I halted at a watering-place with scant supply; I called it the Pozo de San Felipe Neri.

Van Dyke—May 26. He was now traveling northward along the east side of the Providence and New York Mountains. This is an elevated country, with plains four thousand feet high and peaks rising from five hundred to about two thousand feet higher. It has a rainfall of about eight inches, much of it falling in summer. It is the best watered section of the Mojave Desert. The plains abound in various kinds of grasses, brush, and yuccas. The heights have cedars and junipers, and in times past abounded in quail, rabbits, and wild sheep.

Garcés—May 27, 100th day—I went on five leagues east and northeast. The mountains have some trees and there is much pasturage.

May 28, 101st day—After one and a half leagues northeast I arrived at a good watering place which I called the Aguaje de la Trinidad, where there is a Chemevet ranchería. In the afternoon I went on a league and a half southeast and stopped at another ranchería. In the mountains there are large natural basins of water.

May 29, 102nd day—Two leagues to the east I found a waterhole with abundant supply. Seven more leagues, to the southeast, and I came to the Pozos de San Casimiro.

Van Dyke—The watering places here are too numerous to be identified in Garcés diary, but there is a wide plain rimmed part way round with hills, and he evidently followed a circuitous route, first paralleling the east side of the mountains until he reached approximately the southern Nevada boundary line. Thence, on the afternoon of May 28, he turned southeast to the hills now known as the Castle Mountains, about where the mining camp of Hart was later established. Thence he followed along the western slope of the Piute Mountains; and passing around their southern end, he evidently arrived, on May 29, at Piute Springs. It does not seem possible for him to have failed to visit Piute Springs. It is the only place where there is a flowing stream. Whipple described it, in 1855, as an Indian ranchería where crops were raised by irrigation. There is still a small stream of water flowing from these springs, but cloudbursts have washed away all of the arable land, leaving only a boulder-strewn wash. From Piute Springs, he could easily have reached the next camping place on May 29.

When he reached the Mohave villages on the Colorado on May 30 Garcés still wanted to do more exploring, to extend the trail he had already discovered to the Moqui (Hopi) communities in Arizona and from there by Escalante's route to Santa Fe. He ignored a letter from Anza urging him to return to the Yumas. The Anza party would long since have gone back to Tubac. A quarrel between the Mohaves and Hualapais gave him a chance to journey on to Oraibi with Indian guides.

Garcés—May 30, 103rd day—Travelling two leagues east-southeast, I again entered the country of the Jamajabs. Their joy at seeing me there once more would be hard to describe. They had sent word to the Tejua Yavipais, the Jaguallapais, the Chemevets, and the Jalcheduns, so that upon my arrival and in my presence they could talk together unhurriedly and celebrate peace. Even though they knew I had just received a letter from the Commander (Anza) urging me to return to the Yumas, they wanted me to stay a week. From the running about, the yelling, and the general hubbub of this meeting, and from the great heat, I feared I should fall ill. A general peace was concluded among the nations I have named, to their great pleasure and mine. I spoke at length with the Jaguallapais about the distance to Moqui and New Mexico and they supplied me information about the whole area. I wanted to go there, but the letter I had received obliged me to turn south to the territory of the Yumas.

On the following day (May 31) I took my leave, having given presents to all, especially to the Jaguallapais. As they started for home, some of the Jamajabs who were relatives of the men killed by them in past wars began to shout that they would kill them. The Indians in authority opposed this on account of the newly made peace and on my account too. They brought the Jaguallapais before me, terrified and suspicious (as I was too, for I did not trust the Jamajabs). On the spur of the moment I made up my mind to accompany them, and I told them not to be fearful, for I was going with them. No one opposed my resolve, though it is common enough that serious troubles attend such surprise moves. A Jaguallapai at once went forward with two Jamajabs to advise his nation that I was coming over to that land. Sebastián, who was the sole member of my company, refused to follow me though I begged him hard to do so, and thinking that I might never again see the Jamajab nation I told him to go down with the Jalcheduns to their lands.

Sebastián—El Pelegrino— had had enough wandering. Wood says he had developed a heart ailment. The Mohaves had their own work to tend to. But, Garcés was ready for more discovery. In the incredible journey to follow, this insatiable explorer twice visited the Havasupai Indians in their canyon village which every spring is the Mecca for hordes of modern wanderers. And at Oraibi he met a reception even more chilling than his welcome to San Gabriel.

Guided by Hualapai Indians who used him for safe passage through Mohave territories, Garcés crossed the Colorado on June 5 and in ten days reached Peach Springs. Descending into the "hideous abyss" of Cataract Canyon he spent five days among the Havasupai Indians who treated him very well, feeding him "deermeat and beef, maize, beans, greens and mescal." Guided by the Havasus he left the friendly canyon on June 25 and continued south and east traveling in the opposite direction a route taken 236 years earlier by one of Coronado's men, becoming the first white man to reach the Grand Canyon from the west. His description is short but he was impressed enough to name the Grand Canyon *Puerto de Bucareli* after the viceroy who had supported the Anza expeditions and Garcés' exploration.

Crossing the Little Colorado River on June 28 Garcés reached the hilltop town of Oraibi, "the first settlement of the Moqui," on July 2, the day that the Second Continental Congress in Philadelphia decided to formally declare independence from the British empire. The Hopis provided him with no hospitality whatsoever. He had to sleep in a secluded spot on the street and for food be satisfied with the little gruel he could heat on a corncob fire. His colleague Fray Francisco Velez de Escalante from New Mexico had had no better luck the year before.

Garcés wanted to push on to the Zuñi territory, but his Havasupai guides would go no farther and he feared the possibility of having to return through hostile Hopi country alone. Besides, he had already proved that a feasible route from New Mexico to California existed. He had traveled it to the Hopi settlements and Escalante and others had connected Oraibi and New Mexico. The trip was possible even in the heat of summer. He wrote a letter to inform the governor at Santa Fe and sent it off with Zuñi Indians who had befriended him. He dated his letter July 4, 1776.

On the way back to the Mohave villages he again visited the Havasupai and this time left their canyon by an easier route.

When he got back to the Colorado on July 25:

Garcés—As soon as they saw me, these people ran to embrace me, jumping with joy and telling me they had mourned me as dead because it had been reported to them that the Hopis had killed me. Moreover, they had advised the Cuercomaches that if I should return they (the Cuercomaches) should come with me. The Jamajabs also told me that Sebastián was bad, that he had given away the shells and other things I had left; that one of the mules had drowned and another had died. They never stopped talking and touching me.

He never mentions Sebastián again.

On his way back to San Xavier del Bac he was

received warmly by the Yumas and the Pimas and reached his home mission on September 17, 1776. He had traveled over 2000 miles, most of the time with only Indians for company. He had visited thousands of Indians who found him to be one Spaniard they could trust. Their great regard for him is evident in his own modest words in the excerpts included here from his journal.

Unfortunately for Garcés, and for the Indians who trusted him, Spanish interests in the Southwest were again in inept hands. Teodoro de Croix was made commandant-general of the frontier provinces in August 1776 with authority independent of Viceroy Bucareli. Bucareli died in August 1779. Croix neglected the Yuma Indian mission project, long recommended by Garcés and his colleagues, and instead set his mind on a grandiose scheme to conquer the Apaches.

The Yuma Indians never received the lavish gifts the Spanish had promised. Chief Palma lost credibility with his followers. When missionaries finally came to build missions, Croix sent rapacious Spanish colonists instead of well-supplied settlers as Garcés had recommended. He sent soldiers but not their wives, as Garcés had suggested. He allowed Fathers Garcés and Diaz and two other priests only the most meager supplies and no gifts at all for the Indians. And while the missions were built, the Spanish took the Yuma's best farm lands and let Spanish cattle graze in Yuma cornfields.

Then Garcés' old opponent Rivera came, leading colonists to Los Angeles. Rivera sent his colonists ahead and remained behind to fatten his cattle in the Yuma's ripening mesquite fields, depriving the Indians of their mesquite beans, a main source of food.

Garcés vociferously protested these appropriations of Indian land, but no one heeded his protests. Although his entreaties made the enraged leaders spare women and children, Garcés, his fellow missionaries Barreneche, Diaz and Moreno, and over fifty other Spaniards, including Rivera, were slaughtered in the Yuma massacre of July 17 to 19, 1781.

Garcés had not been idle in the years between 1776 and 1781, though he evidently was permitted no more exploring. He completed his journal and reports to Spain and recommended the routes he had followed, noting that these routes lacked sufficient water for large parties. He suggested alternative possibilities still to be explored. He also urged the establishment of missions on the Colorado and Gila Rivers, observing that they could be supplied most easily by small boats coming up the Gulf of California at favorable seasons to the mission door. Another means of supply would be by pack train from San Diego.

Garcés himself had paved the way for these missions, establishing a lasting friendship between himself and the Indians, gaining their veneration and respect. Friendship was an important first step in the process of conversion. Unfortunately, before his dreams could be carried out, both Garcés and the Indians ran afoul of the other side of the Spanish frontier advance—the governor, settler, soldier side.

With the Yuma missions gone, the Spanish abandoned Anza's route to California and for a time discredited Anza himself. They never solved the problem of the Apaches. And they failed to build up an adequate bulwark against Anglo-American expansion in the next century. During his wanderings in the San Joaquin Valley in 1776 Garcés evidently came closer than any other Spaniard to the gold hidden away in the California Sierra Nevada. God had saved the gold in California for American Protestants, as Goodykoontz puts it in a quote from the Home Mission Society literature of the 1850's:

> Why, Sir, did God preserve this whole country more than a century after its discovery, for the English race, turning the foot of the Spaniard to the sunny regions of the tropics? . . . Why did God keep this great country from the English until they had renounced the supremacy of the Roman Pontiff? And why did he keep it from the Protestants until they had purified the reformed faith from its still remaining Romish tendencies? . . . In fine, why were the immense treasures of California hidden from all the world, even from the keen-scented Spaniard, until she was annexed to this Republic? And tell me, if any one can, why it was that the title deed of transference had no sooner passed into our hands, than she gave up her mighty secret, and unlocked her golden gates? Is it possible not to see the hand of God in all this?

Spanish failures do not detract from Garcés, the man, or his achievements. His faith in his fellow human beings, his ability to relate to people of a different culture, and his zeal for exploration make him an historic figure with whom modern idealistic Americans can identify. He was a true martyr for the Church and a gentle hero of the most worthy kind for the high desert's bicentennial celebration.

LISITA PICO WILLIAMSON
by Louella Bishoff

Citizens of the Barstow area have had a part of California history living among them for 45 years in the person of 98 year old Lisita Pico Williamson.

Lisita's birthplace, the home of her parents Zenobio Alonzo and Mary Baxter Pico, was a two story house across the street from San Luis Obispo Mission.

Zenobio was the tax assessor for that area. Lisíta's memory of her childhood includes a happy family life with her parents and two brothers. They enjoyed performing in family musical entertainments and had many picnics together. Lisita is an accomplished pianist. She remembers going by horse and buggy to

Pismo Beach for picnics and across the street with her friends to play in the Old Mission buildings and grounds. With lace mantillas, then in vogue, and holy water from the church font, they held mock weddings at the old mission's altar.

Lisita's family later moved to Los Angeles so she could attend the University of Southern California. There she met her future husband, George R. Williamson. After a short courtship of only three months they were married. Following their wedding in Los Angeles they returned to George's boyhood home, Nashville, Tennessee, and there, in 1906, their son Ophelan was born. He was better known in Barstow as Bud.

George served overseas in World War I as a Captain in the Army Quartermaster Corps. He later moved his family to Jacksonville, Florida and Atlanta, Georgia, where Bud went to military school.

Lisita and George returned to Los Angeles where he worked at a Cadillac agency. On May 27, 1931, while their son was attending a university in Tucson, Arizona, they moved to Barstow for George's health. He first worked here as a bookkeeper in the old Barstow Garage.

When the "Victory Homes" housing project was built between Buena Vista and Mt. View in the early 1940's George acted as the manager. At that time Lisita helped her husband in his office. George Williamson died in 1955.

In 1936 Lisita became President of the Barstow Women's Club. She also served as president of the American Legion Auxiliary for two terms. Lisita loved beautiful clothes and big hats. One clue to her outstanding character is her devotion to the church. She was president of the St. Joseph's Altar Society five years, and for 23 years acted as a catechism teacher at the old St. Joseph Church when it was still on North Second Street.

Before she moved to Rimrock Convalescent Home Lisita lived in a house originally built by the Santa Fe Railroad. This house used to be in the 300 block on the south side of East Williams Street.

Lisita's son, Bud, was working in Raton, New Mexico, when doctors told him to move to a lower altitude. He decided to return to Sacramento where he had worked earlier. It was during a visit with his parents in Barstow that Bud decided to stay and make his permanent home here. He was working at the Marine Base in 1958 when he died.

Lisita's great-grandmother, Isabel Cota Pico, died in 1869 leaving over a hundred descendants. As a member of California's "first family" Lisita rightfully speaks of her Castilian heritage, of which she is very proud.

Historical Notes on the Pico Family of California:

Lisita's great grandfather, *Jose Dolores Pico,* who came to California as a soldier in 1790 founded the northern branch of the Pico family. He had 13 children, among them Lisita's grandfather, *Jose de Jesus Pico,* who was born in 1807.

Don Jose fought in several different campaigns, such as the Solis revolts in 1828, was prominent in Alvarado's revolution in 1836 and took part in the movement against Micheltorena in 1844. In 1846, ranking as a captain of the "defensores" and being "juez de pax" at San Luis Obispo, he was paroled with other officers but broke his parole and supported Flores in the Natividad campaign. In December he was arrested by U.S. Army Colonel John C. Frémont and condemned to death. However, through the emotional appeal of his wife and children who were supported by several hundred women at the San Luis Obispo Mission, he was pardoned by Frémont and became his most devoted friend.

In January 1847, Frémont, aided by Don Jose, entered into negotiations with General Andres Pico of the Californios, bringing about the treaty of Cahuenga which ended the war in California and paved the way for its entrance into the Union.

Don Jose, cousin of Andres and *Pio Pico* last Mexican Governor of California, was the grantee of Piedra Blanca, San Luis Obispo, and San Simeon Ranch; he was administrator of other ranchos as well. In 1878, the year Lisita was born, he dictated his recollections to early California historian H.H. Bancroft.

INDIAN - WHITE MAN RELATIONS

by Clifford Walker

In the westward movement of the United States a pattern of Indian-White man relations occurs over and over. The first white man contact with Indians was usually friendly—exchanging gifts, experiencing fellowships common to men. Then another group of trappers, traders, or settlers involved the Indians in a conflict of some type, quite often a fight. Next came some type of ambush or retribution on the part of the Indians against the third group of white men, usually innocent people not connected with the previous incident. If a fourth contact occurred, it was punitive, often disastrous to the Indians. At least, travelers were warned to enter the tribal area with extreme caution.

In 1826, Jedediah Smith's trappers spent two weeks with the Mohave Indians along the Colorado River north of Needles. The trappers rested, traded horses, and bought melons, squash, wheat, beans and corn from the agricultural Mohave. The Indians befriended Smith for the duration of the visit, helping him across the Colorado River, guiding him to Mission San Gabriel.

Then came another visit of trappers to the Mohave nation.

"OPENING THE MOJAVE RIVER TRAIL"

Excerpt—Trappers' First Fight With the Mohave

by Clifford Walker

(Reprint from San Bernardino County Museum Association Quarterly, Summer 1971, Vol XVIII, No. 4, pp 12-17)

. . . A group of mountain men and trappers were braving the desert frontiers. Although the records are vague, this assemblage of beaver men was probably under the command of Ewing Young. Evidence points to a membership of some thirty-odd men, including James Ohio Pattie; "Peg-leg" Smith; one of William Sublette's brothers; William Wolfskill; Antoine Leroux; and Manuel Rubidoux, most of whose French trappers were massacred either by the "Papawars" (Papagos) or the combined Maricopa-Pima forces.

After unbelievable experiences in central and southern Arizona, these men were successfully trapping along the Colorado River. On March 6, 1827 they marched directly through the first "Mohawa" village, where the women and children ran away screaming. Pattie narrated the unfortunate chain of events that followed. The trappers camped three miles above the village. Presently a chief demanded a horse for payment for the beavers taken from the Colorado. When the demand was instantly refused, the Indian yelled and shot an arrow into a tree. The captain of the trappers, according to Pattie, quickly raised his rifle and struck the arrow with a rifle ball. The perturbed Mohave left for the night. The next morning the "dark and sulky looking savage" again demanded a horse. He was loudly refused a second time, and as he galloped off he threw a spear through one of the trapper's horses. The chief's vindictiveness lasted just a second or so as he was felled by four bullets. The trappers fortified themselves on a bluff of the Colorado River and waited out the day and night. The expected Mohave came the next morning, let fly a shower of arrows, gave a war whoop and charged. At 150 yards the 30 or so trappers released a deadly fire. The Mohaves retreated, leaving 16 dead. From March 9 to 12, the trappers headed north, fortifying themselves each night. Exhausted, and considering themselves out of the Mohave range, they relaxed their vigilance on the twelfth day and were attacked, losing two trappers, who were killed, and another two wounded. There were 16 arrows in Pattie's bed where his bed partner had been killed. The next morning while a few trappers sadly buried the dead and cared for the wounded, 18 of them mounted horses and went after the Indians. They surprised and killed a "great part" of the band that had attacked them. "We suspended those we had killed upon the trees, and left their bodies to dangle in terror to the rest, and as a proof how we retaliated aggression."

The trappers left this sordid sight and continued up the Colorado, losing three more men on an eastern stream flowing into the Colorado, and losing some more men in the Rockies. They trapped in the southern Rockies, and on August 1, 1827 they arrived in Santa Fe, New Mexico, where disaster awaited them. Their

year of suffering, their 2,000 mile or more trek, and all their labor was rewarded by having their 29 pack mules and the furs confiscated by the new Governor, Manuel Armijo. Their loss was approximately $15,000 to $20,000. The pretext the Governor used was that the foreign trappers did not have a proper trapping license . . .

. . . As Jedediah Smith and his men started to cross the Colorado on a raft six months later, the Mohave helped them until the men were divided. Suddenly the Indians fell upon the trappers, killing nine and carrying off two Indian women who accompanied them. Smith rallied the nine survivors on a sandbar from where they could see their dead comrades as well as hundreds of Indians who might close in at any time. He threw some of their sinkable possessions into the river, and spread much of their stores across the sand to delay the Indians, who would, no doubt, fight over the spoils. Luckily Smith saved 15 pounds of dried meat. The desperate men then rushed about one-half mile away before the Indians began to close in around them. Maurice S. Sullivan, in his book *The Travels of Jedediah Smith: A Documentary Outline, Including the Journal of the Great Pathfinder,* includes these quotes from Smith's diary:

> We were not molested and on arriving on the bank of the river we took our position in a cluster of small Cotton Wood trees, which were generally two or three inches in diameter and standing verry (sic) close.

They chopped some trees down to clear a place to stand, the fallen trees making a slight breastwork. Having only five rifles among the 10 of them,

> We fastened our butcher knives with cords to the end of the light poles so as to form a tolerable lance, and thus poorly prepared we waited the approach of our unmerciful enemies.

Smith directed that only three of their five guns fire at a time, and then only at sure shots. The Indians closed in under cover so as not to incur another debacle like the charge on Young's men. Smith ordered the best shot to fire the first salvo, and "two indians fell and another was wounded. Uppon (sic) this, the indians ran off like frightened sheep . . ."

The hunters fled at dusk and traveling all night, reached the first spring the next morning. Since they had no way to carry water they rested and hid out in the daytime and again traveled all night. Smith pointed out the direction to his men and went ahead with a fast walker to find water. They found water and ate some of the dried meat. That day Smith climbed a mountain and ascertained that they were only five miles off the Mohave Indian trail. But instead of following the trail they headed directly for Soda Lake over a very hot and rocky route. Smith's men suffered from thirst and had some relief by chewing slips of "Cabbage Pear."

About eight miles up the Inconstant (Mojave) River, Smith found two lodges of Pauch (Paiutes). With some of the cloth, knives and beads that the trappers had saved, they purchased two horses, some cane-grass candy and pots for carrying water. He purchased two more horses from the Vanyumes (probably Serrano or Garcés' Beñeme) near what is now Victorville.

The American trappers spread the word: Be cautious around the Mohave Tribes; don't trust them. Indeed diaries and journals after 1827 had numerous examples to this effect.

REPORT UPON THE COLORADO RIVER OF THE WEST
EXPLORED 1857 and 1858
Excerpt—THE MOHAVE INDIANS
by Lieutenant Joseph C. Ives
Edited by Louella Bishoff
Introduction by Jean Petroff

The westward expansion of this new country was facilitated by exploration and survey parties sent out by the Secretary of War.

One such expedition, ordered in the spring of 1857, was led by First Lieutenant J.C. Ives, Corps of Topographical Engineers, United States Army. He was ordered to explore the River Colorado West. A thorough survey and mapping of the area was to be done and he was to provide a hydrographic report as to the navigability of the river.

That portion of the journey which began December 1, 1857, at the mouth of the Colorado in the Gulf of Mexico, extended north as far as the Mohave Villages which were a distance of 425 miles.

The following excerpts are taken from his journal dated February 10, 1858, Camp 41, Mohave Villages.

" . . . The men, as a general rule, have noble figures, and the stature of some is gigantic. Having no clothing but a strip of cotton, their fine proportions are displayed to the greatest advantage. Most of them have intelligent countenances and an agreeable expression. The women, over the age of eighteen or twenty, are almost invariably short and stout, with fat, good-natured faces. Their only articles of dress is a short petticoat made of strips of bark, and sticking out about eight inches behind. Some of the younger girls are very pretty and have slender, graceful figures. The children wear only the apparel in which they were born, and have a precocious impish look . . ."

"The position of Mohave chief is one of honor and dignity, but carries little authority with it unless his views happen to coincide with those of a majority of the tribe . . ."

In 1854, Lieutenant Amiel W. Whipple, an earlier

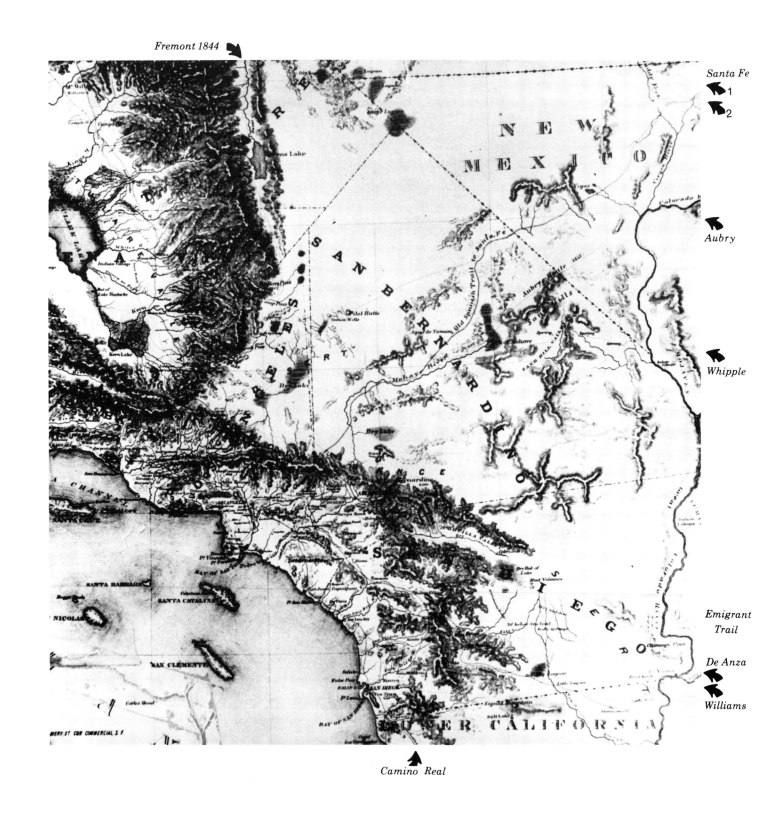

Fremont 1844

Santa Fe
1
2

Aubry

Whipple

Emigrant
Trail

De Anza

Williams

Camino Real

MAP 1857

railroad explorer, wrote the following opinion of Cairook and Ireteba, who acted as guides, " . . . They were noble specimens of their race, and rendered the party invaluable service . . ."

Upon meeting Ireteba, Lt. Ives states:

"I judged from his appearance that he was very poor, and gave him some blankets and other articles. When he and Cairook parted from Lieutenant Whipple they were loaded with enough presents to make them rich, according to an Indian's notions, for the rest of their lives . . ."

It was the custom of the Mohaves to burn the property of the deceased. After the body was placed on the funeral pyre, family and friends laid gifts on and near the body. They believed that the "spirits" of the gifts would be of use to the deceased in the "land of shadows." As Ives remarks, " . . . wealth is held by as uncertain a tenure as life."

" . . . Cairook is a noble looking man. He is nearly six feet tall and a half high, and has a magnificent figure and a fine open face. He seemed glad to see me, and laughed a great deal as he alluded to former adventures. He inquired particularly for Lieutenant Whipple, for whom he had conceived an exalted opinion. Many of his tribe remember, and have been recalling, incidents of that expedition. Among other things, they were inquisitive to learn something of the man who could carry his teeth in his hand; which brought to mind an amusing recollection of the astonishment with which they had seen a number of the party take out and replace one or two false teeth.

I now gave him some presents, which he forthwith distributed, as Jose had done, to his friends. The disposition of a few desirable articles that could not be divided occasioned him some perplexity. He made an earnest speech upon the subject, and at someone's suggestion it was decided to submit the matter to popular vote. A deafening clamor and hopeless confusion was the immediate result of this experiment in universal suffrage till Cairook, very sensible, threw the objects of strife into the midst of the crowd, to be scrambled for, which had the effect, after a fierce momentary tussle, of restoring peace.

There has been a great deal to interest us among the people of this valley, and I regret that we have had to pass so hurriedly and that we have been unable to learn more in regard to their habits and customs. Very few parties of whites have visited them, and none have remained longer than a few days. They are, therefore, in their native state, as they have existed for centuries. Of their religion or superstitions, I have not been able to learn anything. Government, they have so little of, that there cannot be much to learn. They are not at all communicative concerning their institutions. The marriage tie seems to be respected in more than an ordinary degree among Indians. I think that few, if any, have more than one wife.

Their minds are active and intelligent, but I have been surprised to find how little idea of the superiority of the whites they have derived from seeing the appliances of civilization that surround those whom they have met.

Fire-arms, and the Explorer's steam-whistle, are the only objects that appear to excite their envy. In most respects they think us their inferiors. I had a large crowd about me one day and exhibited several things that I supposed would interest them, among others a mariner's compass. They soon learned its use, and thought we must be very stupid to be obliged to have recourse to artificial aid in order to find our way. Some daguerreotypes were shown to them, but these they disliked, and were rather afraid of. I heard one or two muttering, in their own language, that they were 'very bad.' There being a few musicians and instruments in the party, the effect of harmony was tried, but they disapproved of the entertainment, as of everything else, and when the sounds died away, appointed two or three of their own musicians to show ours how the thing ought to be done. These artists performed a kind of chant, in a discordant, monotonous tone, and after making some of the most unearthly noises that I ever listened to, regarded us with an air of satisfied triumph. I tried, by showing them the boundaries upon a map, to make them comprehend the extent of our nation, as compared with their own, and to explain the relative numbers of the inhabitants. The statements were received simply as a piece of absurd gasconade, and had the same effect as the visits of some of the chiefs of the northwestern Indians to the Atlantic cities, which have resulted in destroying the influence of the unfortunate ambassadors, by stamping them forever, in the estimation of their own tribes, as egregious liars.

. . . For the sake of future parties that might visit the valley, I had determined not to encourage the expectation that they were to receive from the whites gratuities, but to exact always some equivalent in return for what should be given them. The others had rendered or agreed to render certain services, for which they had received payment, but of Sikahot (another chief) there was nothing to be asked. I told Cairook, and the other Indians, that if I met their friend (Sikahot) I could not give him anything, but that if he would bring flour I would pay him for it as I had paid them; that Indians never gave white men any presents, and ought not to expect any. This was an idea that had never occurred to them, and they could not help grinning at the fairness of the reasoning. All the crowd laughed when the remark was translated to them.

Gratitude seems to be an element foreign to their nature. The only emotion that benefits excite in their breasts is a desire to receive more. The Mohaves have been uncontaminated by the vices that the approach of civilization engenders among Indians, and are perhaps, rather superior to the generality of their race, but, as far as we can judge, they have with few exceptions, certain qualities common to the Indian character . . .

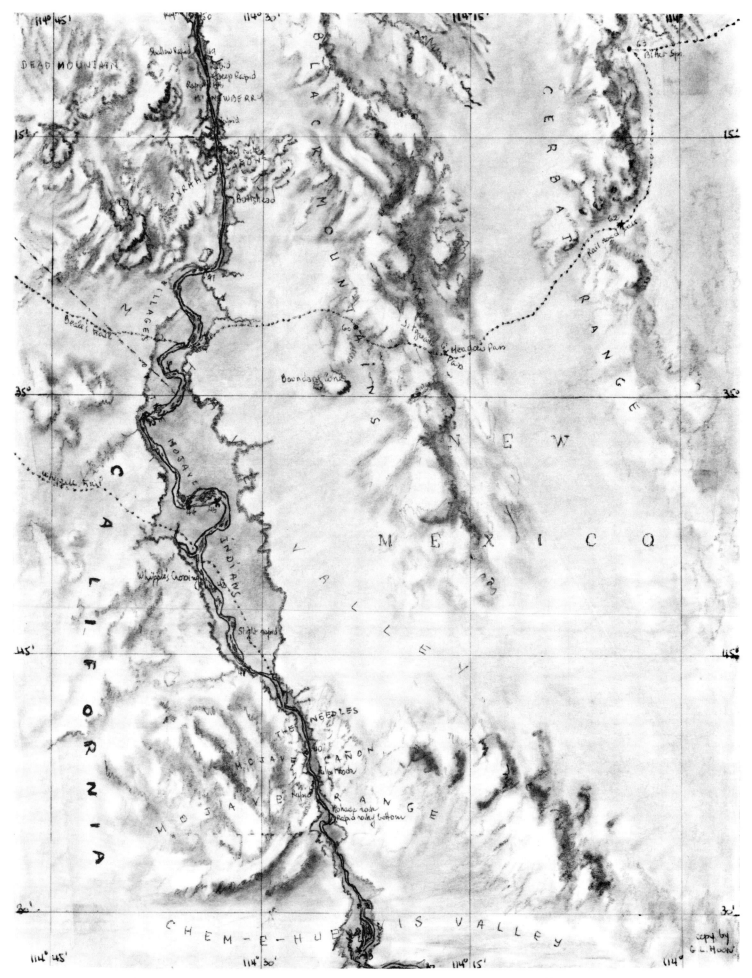

Rio Colorado Of The West - 1858   1st Lt. Joseph C. Ives   Top Eng. - Explorations and Surveys   War Department

They are beggars. Even Cairook is not exempt from this last frailty, though, to do him justice, the things he asks for are seldom for himself. Ireteba is the only one that I have never known to beg for anything.

We have had such agreeable intercourse with the Colorado Indians that it is pleasant to be able to notice one good quality in them, and that is the exactitude with which they fulfill an agreement. On several occasions this had been called to our attention, and I am disposed to give them all credit for so honorable a characteristic.

LIST OF EARLY SETTLERS ON TAX ROLLS OF SAN BERNARDINO COUNTY

1862, Parrish, H.E. — Land and improvements San Bernardino on Public Claim (Mojave) nine cows, five yoke oxen, 102 meat cattle, one stud, 40 stock horses, two wagon-harness and C. $1,672. Total Value $2,882.

1864, Dunlap

1864, Havens, John — Land improvements on Mohave River known as the Old Grocery.

1864, Lane, A.G. — Improvements on public land, on Mohave River known as "Lanes Station"

1864, Hemmenway, Doc

1864, Hymore Joseph

1864, Cline, Daniel — On Mohave River near Camp Cady.

1864, Allcorn, B. — Forks of road-large inventory. Went to San Bernardino.

ROUSSEAU DIARY

(Reprint: *Across the Desert to California: From Salt Lake City to San Bernardino in 1864* A Copy made from the original by George W. Beattie San Bernardino County Museum Association: Quarterly Vol. VI, No. 2 Winter 1958 pp 15-16)

Introduction by Jean Petroff

The pioneer woman had to be strong not only in body, but in mind, spirit and heart. One such woman was Mrs. Rousseau, the wife of Dr. J.A. Rousseau an early San Bernardino County Superintendent of Schools. Her diary of the 47 day journey from Salt Lake City, Utah, to San Bernardino, beginning November 1, 1864 and ending December 17, 1864, is an epic of great courage, untold physical expenditures, and an unshakeable faith in Almighty God. Excerpts are included below:

. . . Friday, December 9th. Got up quarter past four, a very pleasant morning. Got ready by sun up and started from camp . . . Went on to Bitter Springs . . . and stayed about three hours to cook our own dinner and cook bread enough to take us across the desert. Then got ready and went on, resting a good many times. The roads were dreadful bad, a great deal of heavy sand. One hill we had to go up, was 20 miles and sand all the way—very hard on the poor ponies. The men walked all the way, we still traveled on till three in the morning, then camped, tired enough. Met the old gentleman that keeps the ranch about 30 miles from Bitter Springs with some more grain for the horses, and a mule if we should need to put in with the ponies, one of the ponies appeared more tired than the rest and they put the mule in for a while.

Saturday, 10th. Got up about sun up, rather cool morning. Started from camp about half past seven, the roads bad but better than yesterday, being downhill most of the way. After a tedious travel arrived at the Mohave River at 3 p.m. The train having just got in the night before, they all came to see us and appeared glad we had got through.

Sunday, 11th. A pretty warm morning. Mr. Lindsay and his company left this morning for San Bernardino, Earps thinks of leaving in the morning. I hope we can leave in a day or two.

Monday, 12th. A warm but cloudy morning. The train left this morning for San Bernardino, leaving us here. We leave in the morning, we had to hire team to take us through, leave our horses there till we send our wagon back with a load for the gentleman that keeps the ranch. Then our horses, if they are able, will take the wagon back to San Bernardino. The Dr. is attending to a young man about to die, a son of Mr. Allcorn, he appears some better than he was, they seem real clever folks, the old gentleman is from Kentucky, his wife from South Carolina. They are secessionists, it is now a sunshiny day, quite warm, Libby is washing. I have been trying to cook a little.

Tuesday, 13th. A cool cloudy morning, raining some, has the appearance of raining considerably. We have to lay over another day for a span of mules to come in from San Bernardino to put in with the ponies. We expect they'll be here sometime today. We have been treated very kindly since we came here. It is now raining fast, there has been a good deal of rain lately in the settlements. The people seem to rejoice a good deal about it, it has been so dry for a year or two, some of the inhabitants have lost ten or 12 thousand head of stock from starvation.

Wednesday, 14th. Started from camp (on) the Mojave by sun up, cool and cloudy. It rained about all day yesterday. We got some freighters to let us have enough teams to take us through to San Bernardino. I hope we'll be there in a day or two. The roads were some better than they have been some times, although quite sandy. The rain did a great deal of good.

Thursday, 15th. A clear, frosty morning. Got up between 3 and 4 o'clock, want to start from camp early, there is a Prussian keeps the ranch, his home is Jacob, he lives most of the time alone. It is a lonesome looking place. I suppose we will get up with our train tonight. Heard the wolves last night. Got up with the train. Em and Eliza came over to see Libby. They had some singing. There is a very cold wind blowing. This is Nicholson's ranch. The old woman got drunk on whiskey. It is called Point of Rocks, a desolate looking place.

Friday, 16th. A cold, cloudy morning. Started from camp before daylight. The roads rough and hilly, went on to a ranch 14 miles from where we started in the morning. Ate our luncheon and fed the horses. Started on to the Cedars, where we camped. It was in the night when we got there. Very cold and cloudy. Very soon it commenced raining and turned into snowing. The wind blew very hard. It is a real stormy night . . .

THE OLD TRAIL
by G. Frank Mecham
(Reprint from the *Pioneer Cabin News*, San Bernardino
Society of California Pioneers, 1968)

The Emigrant Trail from Salt Lake came to the river a few miles east of Calico mountain . . . the Lower Crossing (later known as Hawley's Crossing.) Seven miles down the river, on the road to Arizona, was Camp Cady, military post established in 1860 for protection of the Trail from Indian attacks.

Coming up the river, the stations during the period from 1865 to 1872 were . . . the Fish Ponds (now location of Marine Corps Supply Center, Nebo), run by Lafayette Mecham; the Grape Vines (later Waterman, then Barstow), run by Jacoby; the Cottonwoods (possibly two miles above the present Hodge station), run by Bill Lightfoot; Point of Rocks (¾ mile below present station of Helendale), run by Saunders; Capt. A. J. Lane's, about 12 miles up the river from Point of Rocks; the Upper Crossing (above, the present Oro Grande). This station, on the south side of the river, was run by Doctor Andrews. From this point the road ran in a fairly straight line to the summit of Cajon.

When in 1867, Lafayette Mecham got a contract to supply 100 tons of hay to Camp Cady, he lined out a road from the Fish Ponds to the Little Meadow (later Victor Valley). He cut the hay in this valley and in the valley above the upper narrows . . . the Upper Meadow, where the grass grew tall and there were deer and antelope in great numbers.

Gus Yager, Alvy Downey and Mart Anderson hauled the hay, breaking through a road that was later used quite extensively. Sheldon Stoddard dug a well near the half-way point, thus improving conditions of travel. Twentyfive years later this road was used for hauling ore from the Silver King mine to the Oro Grande mill. This mill was run by water power. It was owned by a Mr. Sanger, who lived 'back East.' It was operated by Col. Markham, later Governor of California, and a Mr. Johnson.

Previous to the coming of the Americans from the East, there were no roads in this area. The Spaniards had no wagons, all their travel being by horseback, while supplies were transported by pack horses and mules. Their only wheeled vehicle was the crude carreta, used only around settlements.

The following letter appeared in the *San Bernardino Guardian* of August 16, 1868:

"My station is immediately on the river seven miles from the Upper Crossing. The land on the Mojave, at the point where I am is exceedingly fertile and comparatively free from alkali. It is of that peculiar character which retains moisture well, and consequently I am able to cultivate successfully without irrigation.

I irrigated the garden this season, but, planted at the proper time, it would not be necessary to do so. On the 160 acres of land which I have taken up as a homestead, there are 100 acres well adapted to farming purposes. My place is well timbered, and I have as good water as there is in the world.

I command grazing land sufficient for several thousand head of stock. You can judge the quality of grass when I tell you—my horses and cattle keep fat the year round. I am supplying Camp Cady with beef, and the soldiers swore it is the best they ever ate.

In conclusion, Messrs. Editors, allow me to give you an invitation to come and see me. I can feast you upon wild game and fish, as well as green corn and all sorts of vegetables, etc.

Yours,
A.J. (or G?) Lane."

DESERT HISTORY FROM OLD NEWSPAPERS

Yesterday there were seventeen bars of bullion brought in from the Ivanpah mines that will yield $17,000. Within the past three weeks, McFarlane has shipped in from these mines more than $45,000. worth of bullion.

Panamint shipped nearly $74,000. worth of bullion for the first half of this month. Pretty good for a played out camp. *San Bernardino Weekly Argus*, Vol. 3, No.

45, 11-1-1875.

Hartman's stage arrived from Resting Spring with five passengers on Saturday last. Mr. H. reports everything brisk and lively at Tecopa, and reports that the smelter will be started up in about a week.

A new voting precinct was also established at Resting Springs, to be known as Tecopa precinct. *Daily Morning Argus*, Vol. VI, No. 141, 7-5-1877.

The mill of the Ivanpah Mill and Mining Company is again stopped, owing to the breakage of some of the machinery. *Daily Morning Argus*, Vol. VII, No. 5, 7-21-1877.

Raspberry's stage leaves this morning for Ivanpah and Resting Springs. *Daily Morning Argus*, Vol. VII, No. 25, 8-15-1877.

(Advertisement) — Gem Saloon
Wm. Hawley, Propriet'r
Third Street

Best brands of Wines, Liquors, and Cigars, always on hand. *Daily Morning Argus*, Vol. VII, No. 31, 9-18-1877.

Fears are entertained for the safety of Hartman's stage. Two men came in on Tuesday night, and reported having passed Hartman 15 miles this side of Resting Springs, with three men and one woman on board; that his team was nearly given out, and he had about 20 miles more to travel before he reached water. The spring, 15 miles from the station, was dried up, which fact Hartman did not know. *Daily Morning Argus*, Vol. VII, No. 53, 9-13-1877.

A gentlemen from the Resting Springs Mining District says that the mines are looking better than ever, and there is every assurance of its being a permanent camp, with chances as good if not better than the Cerro Gordo mines in Inyo county. *Daily Morning Argus*, Vol. VI, No. 104, 5-23-1877—

The stage from Ivanpah, in charge of that Prince of Jehus, Mr. Raspberry, arrived in town yesterday afternoon. Mr. R. reports everything in a flourishing condition.

Several teams heavily laden with merchandise started out yesterday for Resting Springs and other points. Trade is improving.

Four bars of bullion, valued at $3,000. were brought in from the McFarlane mines yesterday, and will be shipped to San Francisco by the bank of San Bernardino today. *The Morning Argus*, Vol. VI, No. 106, 5-25-1877.

(Advertisement) Resting Springs Express and Stage
Line! From San Bernardino to Resting Springs

The undersigned has established a regular passenger and express line between San Bernardino and the Resting Springs Mining District. Will leave San Bernardino June 9th, and arrive back on June 22d, and leave again on the 24th inst. Passengers carried for $20. Freight 7 cents per pound.

H. Hartman, Prop.
Ed. Hall, Agent
(Ad carried in papers from 7-5-1877 to 4-3-1878)

EARLY DEVELOPMENT OF HINKLEY VALLEY

by Alta Langworthy — Barstow Women's Club 1938

As early as 1869, J.W. Robinson and his partner were exploring, searching for new cattle ranges, and decided that the then green pastures around Harper Lake would be an ideal place. There they made camp.

At that time there were but eight families in the entire Mojave desert—one at the Forks in the Road, where one road led to Utah, the other to Arizona.. There was one family each at Fish Ponds, Cottonwoods, and Helen; a single man six miles south of Helen; one family at old California Crossing—now Turner Ranch; one at Rancho Verde; and one at Las Flores Ranch. The government post at Camp Cady was the settlers' only protection from hostile Indians.

In 1872 C.S. Black established a cattle ranch on the site where Robinson had camped earlier. He built an adobe house which still stands. The cottonwood trees which surround it were set out by Robert Brooke in 1876. This place is still known as the Black Ranch. At this time the nearest source of supplies was San Bernardino, and the road was very difficult to travel.

In 1882, 13 years after Robinson came to this part of the country, the Southern Pacific built the railroad from Mojave to Daggett and this new territory was named Hinkley after an official of the railroad.

The development of Hinkley was very slow, and it was not until 1907 that settlers came, five men within two weeks of each other—O.S. Plotner, Evans, Vipond,

Cockrane and Howell. Evans completed the first house to be built besides the adobe. This house stood until 1915 when it was replaced by the Siemon bungalow. In 1908 the railroad built a small station house. The home of the agent was a boxcar. Evans installed the first pumping plant which had a five horsepower engine. He also was the first man to grow alfalfa in Hinkley. In 1913 he sold his ranch to Siemon.

Other settlers came to build their homes in this promising desert area—Sam Young, Petre, the Harlows, Gibbs, Harmons, Hills, and Hennings. Thomas Rafferty set up the first store in 1915.

The women of the community were anxious to do their part in the upbuilding of this new country. They felt the need of mutual understanding. On April 23, 1914, twelve ladies met in Mrs. Charles Rafferty's parlor, and the Women's Improvement Club of Hinkley was organized.

The development of this district has since been steady and progressive until it is famed far and wide for its fine alfalfa and efficient dairies.

Needles Nugget 2-7-41

Havasu Wildlife Refuge Established. Executive order by President Roosevelt has established the Havasu Lake National Wildlife Refuge, a measure of significance to residents of Needles . . .

MYSTERY OF BICYCLE LAKE
by Arda M. Haenszel

Approximately 35 miles northeast of Barstow, near Fort Irwin, is a playa called Bicycle Lake. The Mojave Desert abounds in unusual and colorful names, but the origin of this one is intriguing. Researching in reference books, and a letter to the United States Bureau of Geographic Names, revealed nothing about its origin. However, in conversation and correspondence with oldtimers of the desert area, some data was obtained about the background relating to the lake.

When Francis Marion (Borax) Smith took over borax operations from William T. Coleman in 1889, he shut down the Old Harmony Borax Works near Furnace Creek, which had hauled ore by 20-mule teams via Wingate pass to the shipping point at Mojave.

Activity was transferred to Borate, from which the ore was hauled down the picturesque Mule Canyon to Marion for roasting, then across the Mojave River to Daggett for shipment. Later, the mules were replaced by a small railroad.

Smith held the Amargosa Borax Works near Shoshone in reserve for later use. He had a road built from there to the Calico Mountains and thence to Daggett. This road went through Ibex Pass to Saratoga Spring, then via Denning and Cave Spring and Avawatz Pass, over Bicycle Lake to Garlic Spring and Langford Well, and over Coyote Lake to Borate and Daggett.

When the ore at Borate began to give out, Smith opened his Lila C. Mine, near Ryan, which was later called Old Ryan, on the east side of the Funeral Mountains. A road was connected with the earlier Shoshone road, and mule teams hauled this ore to Daggett. Expansion of business between 1889 and 1906 caused Smith to try tractor trains, unsuccessfully. The Tonopah and Tidewater Railroad was quickly built north from Ludlow to take over shipment.

Meanwhile, the borax road from Saratoga Spring to Daggett had begun to be used by the general public. Adrian Egbert, the desert samaritan who established emergency caches of water and supplies along the route for stranded travelers, operated a store at Cave Spring. For a time, the route became the principal southern entrance to the Death Valley area.

With this background, furnished by San Bernardino historian, L. Burr Belden, one can understand the story that was told to him by W. W. (Wash) Cahill, for 50 years an official of a borax company.

In the late 1880's or early 1890's some teamsters, with huge borax wagons, had pulled through Avawatz Pass and were rolling along onto our playa. Suddenly, they saw a most unexpected sight, part of a bicycle sticking up out of the solidified clay of the lake bed. It looked as if it had been mired after a rain on the dry lake. It was so deeply sunk into the sticky goo that the owner had, no doubt, given up and left it there.

Another interesting reminiscence was received in a letter from Charles B. McCoy of Barstow. Before the advent of Barstow, Daggett, boasting a population of over 5,000, was the main railroad supply and shipping point for mines. The local "blades" had an interesting pastime. It was for the amusement of young men, particularly on Sundays, to hold bicycle races on the smooth dry lake. To make it even more exciting, money was wagered on the competitors.

With these two related stories, one may have a clue connecting the sunken bicycle found by the teamsters to the name of . . . Bicycle Lake.

Perhaps we may never know who actually named the lake—the boys, or the teamsters, or someone else. But chances are these two incidents were somehow responsible for Bicycle Lake's unique name a decade or so before the turn of the century.

CALICO DAYS

A local newspaper, the 1885 Calico Print, furnishes some interesting facts about the life and activities of the times.

Transportation was of major concern and the ads state that the Calico Stage line was "restocked with relays of fine horses and a new light running, easy riding Concord Coach."

John M. Joy was a wholesale-retail dealer in "saddles, harnesses, whips, bridles, lap robes, lap dusters and horse clothing." The Calico Express Line made regular stops to Calico "every Monday and Thursday morning at seven o'clock."

VIA THE ANKLE EXPRESS
by Helen Graves

"Walking Weston" was his name, and he created quite a stir when he came through desert communities. Roy Walters, early day Hesperia resident whose family came to manage the famed brick three story hotel in 1905, recalls the health-minded traveler. Weston walked backward up the stairs, saying that the reverse ascent was of benefit to his legs.

Roy's two young sisters walked along the tracks with Weston toward Victorville and could hardly keep up with his fast pace.

It brought Weston into focus recently when the 1974 Old Farmer's Almanac included an item about Edward Payson Weston. He began an illustrious career as "The Father of Walking," leaving Boston February 22, 1861, and arriving the day of President Lincoln's inauguration in the nation's capital. The feat was motivated to settle an election bet. Amid other festivities Weston was given a hero's welcome.

During an unusual lifetime aboard "shanks mare" the walker gained note: Portland, Maine to Chicago, Illinois, 1326 miles in 26 days, repeating the journey when he was 70 years old and beating his previous time; in London, 1879, covering 550 miles in 141 hours, 44 minutes; 50 miles a day for 100 days in England, 1883, in support of the Church of England Temperance Society; and in 1910, age 72, walking from Los Angeles to New York in 77 days, a distance of 3483 miles, via the Mojave Desert.

Weston must have been pleased to learn that Hesperia was a Temperance Colony, one of several along the way.

EDITOR'S NOTE: Many early pioneers made derogatory statements about groups such as Indians, Chinese and Mexicans. Although prejudice shows in the writing and perhaps offends us today, the editors felt we should not cover up or omit this aspect of our past, negative as it is.

LIFE ON THE MOJAVE RIVER VALLEY

Excerpt—Freight Teams 1905
by Dix Van Dyke—Edited by G.L. Moon

Like many desert newcomers, Dix Van Dyke possessed visionary ideas of acquiring his first million in a hurry. Whenever he went to Daggett, he raced into town at full gallop, riding bareback. In front of Mike's Saloon, he usually hitched his mount.

Today, as he yanked his horse short, he noticed a small crowd on the sidewalk, and felt a subdued excitement in the air. "What's up?" he inquired. "Bert killed a man," replied Doc McFarlane. Incredulous, Dix looked about at Bert White plainly in distress amidst the group. He was only 17 years old and had never quarreled with anyone. He was good natured and never resentful and yet he admitted to deliberately shooting a man through the head with a rifle. Bert was still at liberty and it never occured to anyone to file a complaint with the Judge or consider that he might need restraint. Old Bob Johnson—Constable—and a companion had left with a team to get the body 35 miles away.

The Pacific Coast Borax Co. possessed many borax claims, some of them 150 miles north of here in the Funeral Mountains bordering Death Valley. To retain possession each year it was necessary to perform some sort of mining labor (called "assessment work") upon all claims.

On the floor of Death Valley at Furnace Creek, they raised alfalfa on a small irrigated ranch. Springs furnished the water, and Piute (Paiute) Indians did the work since few white men would stay during the midsummer months.

From Daggett to the Borax Company claims, a 12 mule freight team hauled the supplies. It was a ten day trip and few teamsters would drive even gentle mules without a swamper to assist in caring for the animals. Water, when available, was drawn from wells with a rope and bucket. After men and mules quenched their thirst barrels were filled for use the next day at dry camps. This was an arduous task always completed before retiring for the night.

Three days before the shooting, Shorty Smith's freight team, with Bert as swamper, departed from the Borax Camp on the north side of the Calicos. The supplies had arrived there by the branch railway which hauled ore to Daggett.

The first night's stop was a dry camp on the Alvord slope. The camping site was determined by the endurance of the team and any place was as good as another, so long as it was far enough to make possible the reaching of Garlock Well (Langford) the next afternoon.

Ahead were 12 miles, eight up the slope and four downgrade. The first four miles up-grade were so sandy that tracks made perhaps days before, were filled with sand. Such roads required "doubling up" and only one wagon would be hauled at a time, instead of using two wagons coupled together so that the first two wheels made a track for the rest to follow. The next four miles were slow going and the last four miles were easy traveling. The "doubling up" made it a 20 mile journey and 15 miles a day was deemed plenty for loaded teams.

At Garlock Well water was 60 feet below the surface and there was a rope, bucket and iron pulley wheel. Here the water barrels had to be filled as the next day's stop would be a dry camp high up on the Granite Ridge and as far as the mules could travel before becoming wearied. The grade was steeper, but the road better, therefore "doubling up" was not necessary, nor was there any choice of camp sites.

Far up the Alvord Slope, the freight team was overtaken by a livery team from Daggett, bringing a passenger, Bert Lee, who was the son of a Piute mother and an American father. In Daggett he had been engaged in the popular pastime of "blowing in" a stake for the past week. He now longed to reach his home in the desert, and learning of the freight team departure, he had hired the livery team and driver. The latter began its return journey and the freight team proceeded on its way.

The teamsters were glad to have Lee's company and

3   *Barstow in 1905. The yard, according to Walker, consisted of five long tracks with a capacity of 50 to 75 cars each, with a scale track for storage of "hold" passenger equipment. There were two main lines, known as Southern California and Mojave mains.*

aid during the long journey that lay ahead. He was an amiable young fellow, well liked and not to lessen his welcome, was well supplied with whiskey! Bert White was too young to care but Shorty Smith enjoyed soaking in it.

Shorty was an odd, quiet and reticent character, who never attracted attention when sober, but a few drinks of whiskey always stirred his imagination. Then he recounted wondrous tales of deeds of valor done in his youth. "He had been a famous Indian scout, serving under military commands and had often engaged in bloody frays with Indians." His imagination never failed until all the whiskey was gone or his listener's patience ended.

After a few drinks generously dispensed by Lee, Shorty's yarning began but it was not received with the derisive laughter of saloon loafers. Lee had lived all his life among Indians. His wits were addled by several days of drinking adulterated bar whiskey and he may have inherited some of the primitive passions of his mother's race. Anyhow, Smith's tales infuriated Lee, who drew his revolver and ordered Smith to get off the wagon so he could kill him on the ground. Only the most abject pleas induced Lee to refrain from doing so. However, he consented to spare Smith's life if he would immediately depart, on foot, toward Daggett. Smith hurried out of gun range and the team proceeded with Bert driving and Lee menacing him.

It was an appalling situation for even the bravest inured to danger. Bert was not accustomed to anything. He was just a fun loving boy marooned in a savage desert with an insane Indian. His mother was a poor widow who operated one of the dingy rooming houses. He was not old or strong enough to work in the mines and had been glad to get this job. Now he wondered whether he would ever see his mother again. He knew Smith would reach the Borax Camp the next day and then an armed posse would quickly be sent after them. Lee knew it too and boasted of the murderous deeds he would do when overtaken. If in insane fury he did not kill Bert, then the boy was liable to be slain in the battle that was impending. There was no escape for the terrified lad.

Late in the afternoon, the freight team arrived at Garlock Wells. The camp was on the edge of a large dry lake, in the bottom of a deep valley rimmed by barren hills. It was not a cheerful place at anytime.

Still menaced by Lee, Bert unhitched the team, tied the mules to the wagon and began removing their harnesses. Lee had left his rifle on the high seat of the freight wagon where he could observe and had retained his revolver. Going a short distance away, he squatted on his heels and momentarily forgetting Bert, gazed meditatively at the ground. Quickly springing up on the wagon wheel, Bert grasped the rifle and fired. It was a desperate gamble with death inspired by terror. The rifle contained only one shell and a miss would have doomed him. The bullet struck Lee in the top of the head.

After feeding and watering the mules, Bert mounted one of them and returned to the Borax Camp. On the way he overtook Smith. When Shorty heard the mule approaching, he thought it was Lee. Not taking any chance, he fled away from the road and hid.

The Coroner came, held a perfunctory inquest; the jury exonerated Bert and Lee was buried in the graveyard on the mountain slope above Daggett.

Far out in the desert, from the base of a small lava hill, a large stream gushes out and waters a natural meadow and groves of mesquites. Long ago the emigrants on the Old Spanish Trail tarried here to rest. It became known as Resting Springs.

Philander Lee, who had dwelt 40 years in the desert, had long made his home there with his Puite wife. Together they had raised a family in a well built house of stone and adobe. With the spring waters, he irrigated small fields and grew much of the family's food. From his meager means, he hired a young American woman (Molly Alf) to dwell with them and educate his sons and daughters. His many friends telegraphed the tragic news of Bert Lee's death to the railhead at Ivanpah from which a horseman was sent galloping over the desert to Resting Springs.

Only two days after the horseman's arrival a grief stricken old man drove a worn and jaded team into Daggett. "Kindly" friends had told him of the circumstances that attended his son's death, whereas he sent for Bert, and with tears streaming down his face, expressed forgiveness for his son's slaying. He assured Bert that neither he, nor any of his family would ever bear him ill will and that they would always be his friends. The pathos of it caused all present to weep.

LIFE ON THE MOJAVE RIVER VALLEY
Excerpt—Crackerjack 1906
by Dix Van Dyke—Edited by G.L. Moon

Sixty miles north of Daggett, on the barren slopes of the Avawatz Mountains, the town site of Crackerjack was surveyed. Flamboyant ads in Los Angeles papers offered "choice lots for sale" . . . "destined to be the richest camp of all," and "only a deep enough well was needed to insure plenty of water." Whereas, the town consisted of a few tents and water was sometimes hauled as far as seven miles.

The first successful auto-stage to operate on the desert was established. One touring car furnished transportation between Daggett and Crackerjack for $25. The traveler either paid the fare or made the two day journey by team and camp equipage. He stopped wherever night overtook him.

Miner's wages in the Nevada mining district were four dollars a day, and Chinese were barred from the new camps. At Crackerjack, only two gold mines were hiring, and they employed only a few men. One mine hired a Chinese cook; the workers did not object. On the contrary, they were glad to eat his grub which was better than that of his predecessor the "hobo cook." They wanted the Chinaman to stay! Not so; said some incipient millionaires who possessed mining claims in the locality. Stewing beans and "batching" tends to make men cranky! Furthermore, they could not afford to eat the Chinaman's cooking and the sight of him pained them.

An indignation meeting was held and it was decided that the dignity of the camp could only be maintained by enforcing the rules. It was resolved that the "Chinese must go!" Eight well-armed men descended upon the metropolis and announced their decision. They were land owners performing a public duty. (!) If there had been adobe houses, the cook's employers might have challenged the edict, but tents are poor defenses and the Chinaman was loaded on the out going stage. Mr. Florman, a loud talking gentleman who always wore a gun, defied the vigilantes and declared he would get himself a Chinese cook. He had none so they ignored his squawking.

The mining company tried to have the vigilantes prosecuted but the county authorities brought about a compromise and the Chinaman was allowed to return. So much ill feeling was engendered that the rival town of Avawatz City was founded two miles distant from Crackerjack.

Two of the vigilantes claimed ownership of Drinkwater Spring where the water was secured. There they ensconsed themselves and proclaimed that all comers must pay one dollar per barrel. A well armed and indignant gang from Crackerjack descended upon them and, after indulging in dire threats, filled their water barrels and left. So did the claimants, opposition being too strong for them.

A cold winter descended upon the desert. Five feet of snow fell at Crackerjack which was over 4000 feet high. The only fuel was branches of the creosote bush which, surely, were difficult to gather in the deep snow. The miners spent a miserable winter. Most of those who could not seek refuge in a mine tunnel descended to adjacent Death Valley or elsewhere.

A Frenchman had what he deemed a valuable cement claim near Crackerjack. Instead of doing assessment work, he filed a new location notice upon the same claim on the first day of each year. This was a common practice respected by local customs. Very rarely a contender tried to "jump the claim" by filing a prior notice.

The Frenchman, ill and fearful of losing his claim to some stranger, made the arduous trip by team and after his arrival died from exposure. Someone hired a team of mules and a light wagon from the Van Dyke ranch to fetch the body and take it home. The dead Frenchman was loaded in, the brake blocks removed from in front of the wheels to prevent snow from clogging them, and the 60 mile journey back to Daggett was made without an overnight stop. This procedure angered Dix. "No one cared for that Frenchman. He had no relatives. Why couldn't your bury him out there instead of nearly killing my mules hurrying in here to bury him?" he queried. This seemed to be a strange idea that never occurred to anyone.

That winter, the Nevada mining boom began its collapse but did not effect Daggett until the financial panic of 1907 swamped the whole country. Crackerjack was still full of lusty life. An eloquent talker persuaded George Mier to sell him $1,000 worth of merchandise on credit to start a store at the camp. Another enterprising gentleman procured enough liquor stock somewhere to start a saloon. Mr. Mier secured Van Dyke the job of hauling the stocks to Crackerjack. He was to receive $40 a ton for three ton loads.

During the flood stage of the Mojave River horses and wagons used the railroad bridge. There were few trains and, thus far, no objections from the railway company, which would have been futile anyway. Now, the river was low enough to ford and a few wagons had done so, thereby beating a track. With Funk's son, Buel, to assist in the crossing and two wagons drawn by six horses, Van Dyke started to ford when, in midstream, the leaders turned and could not be held by the lines. Handing a leather blacksnake whip to Buel, Van Dyke yelled: "Leap into the river, lash the leaders on their heads and straighten them out!" He did so effectively and the crossing was safely accomplished. If he had failed, the wagons, drawn from the beaten track, would have been mired in the quicksand.

Buel was a mile from home, shivering in clothes wet with icy water coming from mountain snows. Van Dyke broke open a case of bottled whiskey and poured some into Buel. "I intended to show them (Crackerjack's miners) that there was one teamster in this country who would not drink their rot gut," he grumbled, "but I don't want you to get sick, walking home in wet clothes."

The second night, camp was at Coyote Wells, a rather dismal place where the northern slope of the Calicos met the edge of a great dry lake four miles wide. The shallow well contained salty, brackish water. It was deemed an eerie place. Some 20 years before the Superintendent of the Calico Mine was progressing on horseback from Daggett to Calico carrying the miner's payroll. Enroute he encountered an ambitious footman who amazed the rider by flourishing a large revolver and depriving him of both horse and payroll. Such actions were unprecedented and it had not occurred to the Superintendent to avoid the man. The next day the Superintendent, accompanied by Johnny Ackerman and an Indian trailer, encountered the robber at Coyote Holes. Ackerman shot and killed him. Superstitious ones aver that the robber's ghost had been seen promenading about in the starlight. If alone, they would not camp there.

Van Dyke did not believe in ghosts, but he was alone, and the company of his revolver tucked beneath his pillow was cheering. He had retired late after filling his water barrels and caring for the team. He was restless and lay awake. Suddenly a weird moaning sound caused him to bounce to his knees and clutch his pistol. He was not scared but startled, and prepared for wailing banshees or anything else. It was only the siren horn of the approaching auto stage, and it was the first time he had heard one. The driver was alone, glad to chat and drink some whiskey.

The next night, camp was far up on the Alvord slope. Desert wagons had wide tires to roll atop the sand with a "tread" 62 inches apart. Autos had narrow tires with a "tread" 56 inches apart (wheel span 62" - 56"). Either one ruined a sandy road for the other. The auto preceded the freight team, having to break track up the sandy slope. For the team it was exhausting work though hauling one wagon at a time.

The team arrived at Garlock Well (Langford Well) in late afternoon. Dix was tired and thirsty. He had not known enough to carry a keg of drinking water from home and for two days had been drinking the salty water of Coyote Well. Even it had been exhausted before his arrival. Water! Here it was . . . sixty feet down. How sweet it tasted! After several buckets, up came a drowned owl, followed by a dead jack rabbit, and each had been immersed a long time! Mercy! For the next two days he must drink this!

Garlock Well was another dismal place where, not too long before, young Bert Lee had been killed. Dix was cheered by the company of three prospectors who camped overnight nearby. He treated them to whiskey and cigars and they assisted in filling the water barrels.

The road led up through rock strewn Black Canyon, over four miles of the flat dry bed of Bicycle Lake, and onward up the long slope of the Granite Ridge. It was hard ground and there was no more doubling up to do. On the lake, Dix left the trail wagon, piled most of its load on the other and proceeded. He had plenty of bottled beer and a canteen filled with strong boiled tea.

Neither was satisfactory. Both weather and beer were warm and the tea produced reminiscenses! The long slope of the Granite Ridge had a south exposure and was covered with grass and flowers. In mid-afternoon the team was grazed for two hours and the journey continued until late at night. Crackerjack City consisted of a few tents but the inhabitants gave a glad welcome. The saloon keeper, who had been impatiently waiting for his stock, dispensed hospitality. The only excitement was caused by a lizard who ran up a miner's pant leg. The victim emulated a quick change artist and yanked his pants off in a jiffy. He denied being frightened; said he was just curious. The next day Dix had to make the one and one quarter mile trip to Drinkwater Spring and back to secure water for the team.

Close beside the road, leading up the slope of the Avawatz Mountain, was a cairn of stones forming a monument for another gruesome tragedy. A few years before, Jack Anderson and Isaac Bateman had started on a prospecting trip. Near here Anderson, who had been on an extended drunk, became seized with delirium tremens. Leaping off the wagon, he fled over the desert seeking to escape from imaginary pursuers. Bateman went on a few miles to Cave Springs where he secured help and returned. They failed to find Anderson, and one of the party, Philander Lee, went to his home at Resting Springs, thirty miles farther out on the desert, and returned with Indian trackers. They found Anderson's body and said his tracks showed that he had been watching the first party seeking him and had eluded them. The body was unceremoniously placed in a shallow grave and stones heaped over it. It was no place for a coroner's inquest, nor could he have been induced to make the journey.

LIFE ON THE MOJAVE RIVER VALLEY
Excerpt—Automobiles 1909
by Dix Van Dyke

Automobiles were no longer a curiosity. Frank M. Byers was using one to deliver meat to Yermo. Dr. Linhardt had invested in one that looked like a buggy. It had high wooden wheels with narrow, solid rubber tires. It was nice appearing but failed to travel over the desert roads.

Joe Goodrich had been the master mechanic of the Pacific Coast Borax Company. He made a contraption to prospect with. On a wagon he mounted an air cooled engine, hitched it to a gear wheel fastened to the rear

wagon wheels and traveled at the rate of 10 miles an hour. It could traverse rough ground impossible for autos and was used for several years.

Autos were yet temperamental creatures and only good mechanics dared venture far from town. A transcontinental journey was still an endurance run made a few times a year and loudly ballyhooed by those who succeeded in reaching the Pacific Coast. But, in time automobiles were to revolutionize life on the desert.

A STORY LINKING SAN BERNARDINO AND INYO COUNTIES
by Celestia Gilliam

R.J. "Dad" Fairbanks was an old timer who observed first hand the growth of the desert in several directions.

Building of railroads brought Dad Fairbanks to the desert from his home in Utah in 1904. He used his team to do grading for the San Pedro, Los Angeles and Salt Lake Railroad between Salt Lake and Las Vegas. In Las

Vegas he heard of the plan to build a railroad between Las Vegas and Tonopah and also of the mining booms in Rhyolite, Beatty, Goldfield and Death Valley. Realizing that people would need services on their way and at the mining camps, he chose to set himself up in business in Ash Meadows because of the abundance of water there. Here he could pick up supplies at Johnny Siding on the Las Vegas and Tonopah with his team and haul them along with much needed water to the mining camps.

He sent for his wife Celestia and six sons and three daughters to join him and they set up three tents—one for eating, one for sleeping and one for a saloon. Here they fed travelers or gave overnight lodging for 50 cents. The girls helped their mother in cooking and making beds and the boys drove the team and also repaired wagons for travelers. Their main project was hauling water to the Copper Camp of Greenwater where they sold it for 75 cents a gallon. This was an endless job for they found it difficult to haul enough to sell and also satisfy the needs of the team.

Life was crude there and a drastic change for a family used to the green countryside and church-related activities in Utah. However, water and mesquite trees were abundant. The family had donkeys to ride and they were able to make friends with the local Paiute Indians who furnished them with vegetables. There was no school, but mother Fairbanks faithfully taught her children from readers she had brought, including the Book of Mormon.

They met many people who later became famous or infamous—Walter Scott (Death Valley Scotty), Shorty Harris and even Diamond Tooth Lil. They also saw their first car in Ash Meadows, a 1906 Thomas Flyer being driven by one of the owners of Greenwater Copper Company. In the thirties Standard Oil Company honored Dad Fairbanks, the oldest distributor in California. He sold gas, though not very much, out of thirty gallon drums.

His business venture in Ash Meadows was halted, however, when the Pacific Coast Borax Company completed the Tonopah and Tidewater Railroad from Ludlow to Beatty in 1907. It hauled borax out, but also brought supplies in from the South to Death Valley. From this time on, Death Valley Junction became the center of distribution. Fairbanks sold Ash Meadows and moved his family to Greenwater where he opened a saloon, but to this day Fairbanks Spring is a landmark on every map.

Greenwater Copper Camp was a mining promotion and lasted only three years, 1906-1909. Five thousand people were said to have rushed into camp in hopes of striking it rich, but by 1909 they were just as anxious to leave. Some of Fairbanks' sons returned to Utah. His older daughter, Betty, had married a mining man, Jack Lisle, in Ash Meadows. His wife, son Vern and two daughters were the only ones left at home. The Pacific Coast Borax Company asked him if he would like the job of moving any salvageable buildings from Greenwater to Shoshone and setting up a restaurant to serve passengers on the Tonopah & Tidewater Railroad. Once again the family packed up and moved to Shoshone where Fairbanks not only established an eating place, but also a small store building and "tourist cabins." It was while living here that his second daughter, Stella, married Charles Brown whom she had met in Greenwater. They got on the T and T in

Shoshone and went to Goldfield in 1910. Charles was a mining man and he followed his profession after their marriage by taking jobs at Lila C. Borax Mine, Dale, and Tonopah. In 1920, they returned to Shoshone with their three children to become partners with Dad Fairbanks in his business. They could see many possibilities since there was now a road south to Baker and north to Death Valley. They used their 1924 Studebaker-Eight to conduct tours of Death Valley for tourists arriving on the T and T and put up gas pumps to accomodate the few cars daring enough to drive through. Dad Fairbanks became the mentor of Death Valley and his knowledge of the desert saved many lives. He also helped map the new route for the paving of Highway 127 to Baker.

Urged by the Pacific Coast Borax Company, Charlie Brown ran for supervisor of Inyo County in 1924 and won. This gave representation to the desert which had formerly been neglected due to the high concentration of Inyo County population in Owens Valley. He fought fiercely for the improvement of roads into the Death Valley area. He attended monthly meetings at the County seat in Independence 185 miles away. However, because of the bad roads he would ride on the T and T, Shoshone to Ludlow where he would transfer to the Santa Fe to Mojave and then take the Aqueduct Railroad to Owens Valley.

At this same time, Art Doran of Barstow represented the desert area on the San Bernardino County Board of Supervisors and he and Charlie became good friends. The San Bernardino and Inyo County border line meets between Shoshone and Baker and the two men had a joint interest in paving Highway 127.

This was only the beginning of Charlie's political career as he in later years became a State Senator representing all of Inyo, Mono and Alpine Counties. He remained their representative in Sacramento until his death in 1963.

In 1926 Dad Fairbank's pioneer spirit of restlessness took hold once more. His youngest daughter, Vonola, had married Alex Modine and lived at China Ranch near Tecopa. Charlie and Stella had proved themselves capable of continuing their plans in Shoshone and besides Fairbanks had heard of a tremendous power line being built from Boulder Dam on the Colorado River all the way to Los Angeles. It would cross the Highway at Silver Lake, nine miles north of Baker. Also the main highway between Los Angeles and Las Vegas was being improved to say nothing of the fact that the T and T crossed that highway at Baker. In 1927 at the age of 70 he and mother Fairbanks, along with their son Dave and family, moved to Baker. Here they set up tents for living accommodations and opened the first service station called the "Big Blue." Shortly after, E.B. Failing and his wife Hazel moved from Midway between Barstow and Baker where they owned a small business to the opposite corner from Fairbanks in Baker. Though these original people are gone, the same two families operate these businesses today.

The move to Baker was with great foresight for it increasingly became a good business location and

4 Grandad's joy - Bernice Brown, L.D. Fairbanks, Celestia Brown, "Dad,"
Lionel Fairbanks, Charles Brown Jr., George Brown - Shoshone 1925

Fairbanks and Brown Clan

7 "Dad" Fairbanks - Baker 1930

5 Charles Brown's first store—Shoshone 1922
Building moved from Zabriskie Siding on
T & T R.R.

8 Stella and Senator Charles Brown - Bishop 1958

6 Death Valley Scotty and Celestia Brown - Shoshone 1928

9 Pauite Women at Brown's Store - Shoshone 1923

10 Main Street - Greenwater 1908

13 A Tall Drink - 300 gallons of bar whiskey for
    Fairbanks saloon - Greenwater 1908

11 Celestia and R.J. "Dad" Fairbanks - Baker 1930

Desert Enterprises

14 "Big Blue" - Dad Fairbank's first service station - Baker 1927

12 "Shorty Harris" well known prospector
    of Death Valley

15 Bulk Gas Plant fire at Baker Failings - 1935

remains so today. For some years the construction of the power line created a lot of activity and was an asset. Although the line went through Silver Lake, the center of activity at that time, a lot of action spilled over to Baker. Silver Lake had the Post Office which was not moved to Baker until 1933. If you were in Baker and wanted a ticket on the T and T, you had to go to Silver Lake for the main agent. All the drinking water was hauled for Baker on the T and T from Silver Lake. The activity in the area made possible a store and eating establishment. Some may remember "Ma" Palmer's wonderful dances in her tent-topped establishment, and the constable "Shorty" Williams who was pretty handy with a gun. People in the mining game from Silver Lake Talc, Riggs Mine and the Crackerjack added to the color.

With the completion of the power line job, activity at Silver Lake all but ceased and today there are only small reminders of the life that once existed there.

On the other hand, Baker began to grow. Highway 91 was paved to Las Vegas and also Highway 127 to Death Valley, which became a National Monument in 1933. Baker was a natural stop for tourists traveling in any direction, and still is. But for those who were there in 1927 life had been hard. The water was undrinkable because of the salt content and the service stations all had signs saying, "Do not drink this water." The heat was unbearable in the summer and there was no air conditioning in cars or houses. Many times residents would drive up the hill toward Las Vegas to Halloran Springs, Yucca Grove, Wheaton Springs or Mountain Pass in order to get one night's sleep out of the furnace blast. This was during the depression era and anyone at Baker during that time will tell you of the depressing migration of human beings on their way to California as depicted in the "Grapes of Wrath." Much to his credit, it is said that Dad Fairbanks never turned a hungry family away.

Others who helped pioneer Baker should be mentioned, "Death Valley" Jack Nickerson, Jack Hoveley, "Ma" Hardy, Bill Lawson and Betty Lisle. Others put their life's blood into small businesses along Highway 91. Elmo Proctor was one who had homesteaded at Crucero and moved his family to Cronese where he operated a service station long since eliminated by the freeway. Not to be forgotten are those people who lived off of Highway 91 in Nipton, Ivanpah, Cima and Kelso but traveled it, paved and unpaved, to obtain services in Baker.

Life, indeed, was hard then, but the people mentioned here also had their good times and became as close as families because of their common needs. On Saturday nights amazing numbers of people would appear for a dance at Ma Hardy's in Baker. They thought nothing of cranking up the Model T and driving miles over dirt roads for a get-together anywhere from Ludlow to Shoshone. They could get plenty of snake bite medicine at Whiskey Pete's at State Line (California-Nevada). Whiskey Pete is buried at State Line, on a little hill nearby. They had difficulty in digging a normal grave because of the hardness of the rock, but they drilled a hole straight down and Pete is buried standing up. You can still see the marker from the freeway.

During this era the road to Barstow was the dirt kind, but Barstow was the closest source of supplies. Dad Fairbanks bought all his lumber from H.C. Ryerson in Daggett, watermelons and vegetables from the Haimut-Skoebel ranch in Minneola and of course he knew Judge Dix Van Dyke, the Pendletons and Lubin J. Henderson. All these families sent condolences at his death in the early forties.

The history of our desert, as large as it is, strangely intertwines the lives of those who pioneered it. The Spanish Trail, one of our oldest routes, crosses both Inyo and San Bernardino Counties just as the Tonopah and Tidewater Railroad linked the two. As we pass through our beautiful desert on the freeways, in our airconditioned cars, we should reflect for a moment and pay tribute to those who went before in not quite so comfortable a manner.

YEARS AGO ON THE OLD MOJAVE, AS NARRATED BY "DOC" YATES

by A Student of Clifford Walker)

A roving group, consisting of a Coast and Geodetic Survey team and the Robinson Exploration Party arrived at Furnace Creek in Death Valley during the first part of August in 1926.

The survey team re-established some of the boundary lines of the Death Valley National Monument, while the exploration party, directed by Dr. John Robinson, a leading anthropologist of his day, gathered artifacts from old Indian camp grounds and burial sites. This was before the days of heavy tourism and a wealth of material was gathered by the party.

The Inn at Furnace Creek was a low squatty building, made of railroad ties from the old Tonopah and Tidewater narrow gauge railroad that once carried ore from Tonopah and Death Valley to San Pedro. At this time the railroad from Furnace Creek had been discontinued.

The trail from Furnace Creek to Las Vegas was strewn with large boulders and steep banked washes so that only burros and Model T Fords could travel over it. The party had to send their Dodge pickups around through Baker to Yermo to pick up supplies. The Union Pacific Depot at Yermo was brand new then, and the eating place did a flourishing business. Most of the travel across the desert at that time was on passenger trains.

A member of the Robinson party went to Las Vegas and witnessed an unusual gambling episode at the

Golden Nugget. A cattle rancher put up a ninety thousand acre ranch against his losses on the turn of a card while a house full of spectators watched. The manager rolled his shirt sleeves up to his elbows and shuffled the cards. The rancher declined to cut the cards and drew the top card. It was the Jack of Spades and looked like a sure winner. The manager took the next top card. It was the Queen of Hearts. He offered the rancher a job as foreman on the ranch. The offer was declined.

Meals were served family style at Furnace Creek. One of the boarders was Lord Baker who owned mining interests in that area. Baker, California was named after him. He was a red faced, beefy Englishman who had two black porters fanning him from behind with two large fans to circulate the air and drive away the flies. Members of the expedition used to race each other for a seat next to Lord Baker in order to gain a fringe benefit from this luxury. He only paid his porters six cents per day, and one day they vanished. It was rumored that they were getting six dollars per day at a soda mine.

There was not much difference between Barstow, Yermo and Daggett at that time. Barstow was a little larger. The Goldstone Club, named in honor of workers at the Goldstone Mines, did a lively and sometimes exciting business in Barstow, albeit the Volstead Act was still in effect. Visitors to the club can see bullet holes in the bar, the results of differences of opinion.

Yates has been a resident of Barstow since 1926. He came here from Kansas. In his narration he mentions a remarkable man named Charlie Brown. According to Brown's daughter, Celeste Gilliam of Barstow:

Charlie Brown, later on to become state senator, ran away from home in Georgia at the age of seventeen and worked his way to California. In San Francisco he heard of the mining copper strike at Greenwater. He met and married Stella Fairbanks and ran a business at Shoshone, a settlement between Baker and Death Valley. He and his wife are both buried on a hill there. Several years ago, a new highway from that area to Las Vegas was named the Charles Brown Highway. His son, Charles Brown Jr. is now a prominent Baker businessman.

THE EARLY ROADS
by Pat Keeling

In 1922, Bill Smart went from Needles to Klondike, west of Amboy, on the train, to buy a car. It was not necessarily the best method of travel in those days:

I bought a Ford Model "T" from a telegrapher, it was a late 1918-19 and did it ever go over the roads! The roads were all dirt at that time. Out of Klondike, the road was three ruts, two to drive in and one to turn out when and if you met another car. You seldom met another car at night.

I took a trip with the Kane family after the railroad strike in 1922. We left Needles at 8:30 at night to avoid the heat. It was slow driving and we had lots of tire repairs. We finally got into San Bernardino the next morning at 10:30. The old highway bridges had emergency water tanks (4-55 gallon barrels of water strapped to the bridge) for use in case of fire and for automobile radiators. The water wagon made the trip from Needles quite frequently to refill the tanks, as without water, travel by car was impossible.

WALT TERRY—CALIFORNIA HIGHWAY PATROLMAN
by Martha Burnau

During January 1937, the California Highway Patrol assigned a young recruit to Barstow as a resident officer for the Mojave Desert. The C.H.P. had hopes that he would stay in this "far-off" assignment for at least a couple of years. It turned out to last thirty years!

The C.H.P. issued Terry a uniform, motorcycle and a book with which to issue citations. Terry says "My beat was the California side of the Mojave Desert, Cajon Pass to Needles, East to Twentynine Palms, and over to the Kern County and Nevada State Line."

Because there was no C.H.P. office in Barstow, all emergency calls for Terry were taken at the Texaco Station at First and Main Street, or at Cunningham Drug Store directly across the street. A flashing red light was installed close to the street in front of the station. When an emergency call was received for the patrolman, the light was switched on, thus signaling Terry that he was needed. The motorcycle Terry had been issued was not equipped with a radio. When on patrol between Barstow and Needles there were few telephones available for him to use for contacting E.L. White, local druggist and mortician who also owned the ambulance service. He also had permission from the Santa Fe Railroad to use their dispatch telephones that were in booths along the tracks from five to ten miles apart. "This was fine" Terry says, "except that they weren't always working." There were also three private telephones for him to use, one at Daggett, Ludlow, and Amboy. In some cases emergencies were reported to the young patrolman by one of the "traveling Public."

One year Terry put 52,000 miles on one motorcycle while patroling the vast Mojave Desert. It wasn't until 1941 that squad cars came into existence.

Terry charged up and down the trailways twelve or more hours a day "he was on 24 hours call," nurturing a

16   Convertible 1917

Transportation

21   Delivery Rig 1907 - Mr. & Mrs. McCrary, Mrs. Wm. A. Gilham,
Nancy Gilham Gray, Wm. W. Gilham

17   Shopping at Dillingham's 1910

Foot

Power . . .

22   Riverbottom 1932

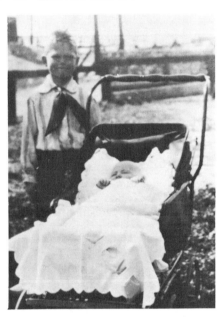

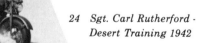

18   Bus Stop Failing's Midway Station 1925

23   Perambulator 1922 - Harry and
James Kelly

19   A Kiln for Trona

24   Sgt. Carl Rutherford -
Desert Training 1942

25   The Only Way To Go -
Death Valley R.R.

. . . To

Wings

20   Don Ramirez's Coche de Camino

26

large mustache, a growing love for the desert and consistently refusing any promotion which required him to transfer. He soon became a desert legend, celebrated in novels—and in one Hollywood film. The "Handle-barred-Officer" became Sergeant, one of the few men in the Highway Patrol to be promoted without being required to transfer his station. Sgt. Terry's promotion was an exception because his location was considered a "hardship" post.

Sgt. Terry retired from the C.H.P. after thirty years on March 31, 1965. Two minutes after midnight, Coroner Ed Doyle swore him in as the desert's resident deputy coroner. In this job Terry used a pickup truck for his runs. It had a shovel and broom mounted on each side of the cab. "Dig in with one, clean up with the other," he said. The truck became his trademark.

BARSTOW—TRUCKING CROSSROADS

by Elaine Marable
(Reprint from *Sun Telegram* 1974)

One of this city's slogans boasts that Barstow is the cross-roads of the high desert. That may soon change to "crossroads of trucking" if the big new Yellow Freight System Terminal is an indication of the future.

A little more than two years ago 40 drivers worked out of Yellow's relay station here—their number has now grown to over 225 and the base-of-operation is a modern terminal designed to handle 200 trailers.

This terminal, located on 35 acres on Lenwood Road just north of Interstate 15 and west of Barstow, is known as break-bulk terminal . . . A break-bulk terminal is the place where trucks from the East stop, and their cargo is diverted to Northern California cities or on into the Los Angeles metropolitan area. Conversely, eastbound trucks stop here, and cargo is sorted and put aboard trailers according to specific destinations.

From the time that freight leaves its point of origin, its movement is traced by computer so that its whereabouts and time of destination can be traced by the push of a button . . .

Line drivers working out of Barstow make runs to Los Angeles into one of five metropolitan terminals operated by the Yellow System; to San Diego, Fresno, Bakersfield, Stockton, San Jose, Oakland or to the farthest destination, Holbrook, Arizona. There, the drivers relay their cargo to drivers coming from the terminal at Albuquerque, New Mexico.

The newest of Yellow's 12 grouping stations opened in early February 1974. Along with the line drivers, the terminal has six dispatchers who schedule drivers' runs, a superintendent of drivers, Jack Jackson, eight mechanics, 46 dockmen, three communications clerks, a secretary and office manager. . .

The terminal has a 344-feet long dock equipped with 57 loading spaces. Freight is moved along a single-hook drag line in gondolas that automatically move onto trailers according to computerized pre-selection. Everything at the terminal is designed for expansion . . . An example is the above-normal high ceiling on the dock. This was constructed to accommodate a future overhead conveyor system.

All trucks arriving at the terminal get a safety inspection before they are refueled and sent to the docks for regrouping of cargo. The mechanics do minor repairs. Major work is sent to local truck mechanics. The terminal has room for a major overhaul repair shop, but this is part of the future . . . .

Chapter II

Working the Land

Rain on the desert —
Cloud-bursts, few and far between,
Healing hot dry lands.

A BRIEF HISTORY OF THE BLACK RANCH

by Beth Pinnell

Human occupation of the area known historically as the Black Ranch on the eastern shore of Harper Dry Lake, California, probably began at the same time as the shoreline of the Pleistocene Lake receded and left the ground dry. Evidence of Early Man has been found in the Coyote Gulch region northeast of the Black Ranch and it seems probable that man would also camp along the shores of the lake and gradually move inward as the water receded. Sites have been found all around the playa, but are concentrated in the sand dunes on the eastern side stretching all the way from the southeasternmost edge of the playa northward for several miles. Artifacts associated with the Pinto and Lake Mohave traditions have been found throughout this area, indicating an age of at least 10,000 years, while the Archaic material has been quite varied. Numerous grinding slabs and manos, pottery sherds, beads of bone, shell and pottery, stone and pottery pendants, steatite pipes, and a wide variety of projectile and other stone tools have been found. Glass trade beads found there indicate that the Indians occupied the area after contact with the white man, and probably until the 1850's when the influx of white travelers pushed them further back into the desert.

The primary or basic reason for this long period of human occupation in the area has been water—first the Pleistocene lake, and then springs. Until the last 15 years mesquite and cottonwood trees grew on the eastern side of the lake, indicating a shallow water table. The springs were recorded on the original survey map of Section 30 made in 1856. In 1919, David Thompson recorded data on three wells at the Black Ranch. L. C. Stucky was the owner of the wells according to Thompson. One well was hand dug, 15 feet deep with water standing at 11 feet, while the other two were flowing wells, six inches in diameter, depth unknown, but believed to be less than 200 feet. One of these wells was still flowing in the late 1950's, enough to provide water for wild life, but since then the water table throughout the Harper Lake basin has continued to drop so that artesian wells ceased flowing. The flowing wells were probably drilled by cattlemen to increase the yield of the original springs.

Just when these wells were drilled, or when white men first occupied the area is not known, but it may have been in the late 1860's when a number of ranches were established along the Mojave River. It is reasonably certain that the first white settlers at the Black Ranch were cattlemen, since the hard-pan soil produced grass and browse, but was unsuitable for agriculture.

William Wolfskill, who owned a ranch in what is now the Irvine area in Orange County, drove cattle to the Mojave to pasture in 1864. A severe drought had ruined most of the range throughout the state, and a slump in the cattle market, had caused Wolfskill's decision to send part of his cattle to the desert where he had previously noticed good pasture feed along the Mojave

River. Wolfskill's drovers made several excursions into the desert seeking other suitable range areas. It is quite likely that the cowboys rode over into the area of the Black Ranch, for it is less than 20 miles from where they were camped. The pasture at the Black Ranch could not have compared with the grass along the Mojave River, but the area must have been noted as a possible range because it did have water. Even though it was somewhat remote from the scattered settlements along the river and made men and cattle more vulnerable to Indian attack, the area was probably attractive enough so that cattle were brought in before 1870.

That the ranch was occupied by cattlemen in 1875 is certain. In that year an expedition headed by Lieutenant R. Birnie, Jr. traveled by way of Cajon Pass, Black's Ranch, and Pilot Knob to explore the country in the Owens Lake, Panamint, Death Valley, and Amargosa regions and he reported cattlemen living there then. There is also an entry in the San Bernardino County tax assessor's records for that year which lists a Charles R. Smith as claiming "Black's Ranch, Mohave Desert."

The tax assessor's records for the following year, 1876, list "Grant, James, Black's Ranch, claim and improvements, 80 acres known as Grant's Station." By this time the stage line between San Bernardino and the mining areas of the Panamints was established. The ranch was also serving as a stage stop.

James Grant is listed as the taxable owner for the next several years, and there are also entries indicating his claim to another location farther north of the Black Ranch, known as Grant's Well or Spring. A map of San Bernardino County, copyrighted in 1908, shows the Black Ranch in Section 30 and Grant's Spring about three miles north in Section 7. James Grant may have been a doctor—and businessman—who merely claimed the two locations, and employed others to run both the cattle business and stage station, for a directory of San Bernardino doctors for the years 1851-1881 lists a James Grant, M.D.

None of the names of the early owners of the Black Ranch so far uncovered reveal a Black for whom the place could have been named. An entry in Dix Van Dyke's journal reads as follows:

> Harper Lake, probably named after the nearest railway station which is named Harper before the homesteaders invasion about 1912, was called Black's lake. Black had a traveller station on the east end of the lake where the Panamint stage road passed. Ruins of his adobe house is beside cattle corrals and water troughs. Cal State Mine Bureau report for 1902 calls it Harper.

L.C. Stucky, a cattleman appears as owner on the tax assessor's records for 1912, and he apparently held possessory interest in the springs and area until he sold to Colon C. Campbell and E. Sandoz.

According to Sandoz's daughter-in-law, Ivy

Halstead Sandoz, her parents, the Albert Halsteads, and the Sandoz family were friends and neighbors in the Chino area prior to 1920 when both families moved to Hinkley where they secured adjoining properties. Sandoz, with his partner, Campbell, bought out Stucky's interest in the Black Ranch sometime in the 1920's, and Sandoz apparently lived there. The 1931 tax assessor's records show their having improvements worth $100, well and windmill at $500, and personal property at $2000. The personal property must have been cattle and horses, while the improvements may have included corrals and probably the old adobe stage station.

Sandoz's son, Henry, married Ivy Halstead in 1930, and when the elder Sandoz died in 1934, the couple moved to the Black Ranch to live with Henry's mother. In 1934 the records show that Henry Sandoz acquired patent to 40 acres which included the Black Ranch headquarters. He was the first person to actually acquire title to the ground.

Ivy Sandoz stated that she enjoyed living at the Black Ranch, and that she mopped the floor of the old cabin so much that the wood floor mildewed. She described the cabin, once the old stage station, as having two rooms with a porch added on. The adobe walls were 1½ feet thick, and on the outside walls various cattle brands had been carved into the adobe bricks. She could not remember whether the roof was of pole and sod construction or not, but mentioned that there were bullet holes in the door. Water from the flowing wells was piped directly into the house.

Sandoz owned 2,000 head of cattle at one time, and they ranged all over Harper Lake, up to Cuddleback Lake and the Granite Wells country, and even to Baker. They had three or four hired men working for them most of the time. They also owned a ranch near Barstow, located in the area along Soapmine Road, where they raised hay and pastured some of their stock.

During the late 1930's, there was a severe drought in Southern California, according to Mrs. Sandoz, and they sent most of their cattle to the San Bernardino mountains. Finally, in 1937, they sold out to Donato Ramirez. Ramirez continued to run cattle in the Harper Lake basin until the late 1940's when range conditions throughout the desert were too poor to make the venture worthwhile.

The mesquite groves have been dying out because of the gradual lowering of the water table within the entire Harper Lake and Hinkley Basins, and only a few of the cottonwood trees remain. The wells no longer flow, the corrals and fence posts continue to rot away or disappear as firewood.

Since then, there has been no one living there permanently. It is still used occasionally as a cow camp and in the early 1970's the wells were improved so that water was provided for small herds of cattle. Only a mound of earth remains of the adobe stage station, hardly distinguishable from the surrounding hard pan from which it was built by unknown hands over a century ago.

THE GREAT WATER CANAL

by Alice Salisbury and Dix Van Dyke—Edited by Margaret Fouts
(Reprint *Barstow Printer Review* January 5, 1950)

Here we have a story about a city half-way between Daggett and Newberry in a locale known today as Minneola. A dream city, fashioned entirely on paper, which flourished and collapsed three times before its final death. The historic struggle to get it off paper and established on land cost its optimistic creators and enthusiastic investors a half-million dollars before it passed into oblivion amid wrecked hopes and bewildering legal snarls.

Ever hear the term "Silver Valley" applied to Minneola region? It had nothing to do with silver or Calico. Silver was the name of optimist number one who organized and incorporated the Silver Valley Land and Water Company in 1889 and filed claim to 15,000 inches of Mojave River water to supply the great city to come. The filing record asked permission to use the water for agricultural, mining, manufacturing and culinary purposes.

The Silver Valley Land and Water Company acquired the land and water rights of Allan Marsh. In 1880 Marsh homesteaded 160 acres lying in the riverbottom area immediately below where the water sank underground. It was four miles upstream from Daggett. He filed appropriation notices for the Mojave River water in the south and north channels in 1880, and irrigated his lands for a year.

A dynamic real estate boom took shape and then blew sky-high in the depression of 1893. Ditch in trouble, debts neck-deep!

Next came the Southern California Improvement Company. The Mojave River water was to be diverted by a dam—100 feet on the bottom, 150 at the top and 10 feet deep. A submerged wooden flume-aqueduct canal 5 feet high, 4 feet wide, and 2100 feet long would carry 3000 feet of water to Daggett. The smaller canal from Daggett to Minneola was 6 miles long with a capacity of 7000 feet of water.

In spite of crude methods, scarce labor, an extravagant contractor and bankruptcy, that "Wind and Water" ditch (wind for much talk) actually was completed for 11 miles to the site of the Wonder City to be, Minneola, named after Mrs. Minnie Dieterle, wife of the secretary of the development company.

The Minneola Town Company now held the valley's future. The folders and posters issued by this group, whose members wore rose-colored glasses, are still a source of chuckles to old-timers who perused them.

Extravagant claims for the volume of water to be tapped from the elusive Mojave River was followed by the statement:

Near the Minneola water-power, first the town then the city will spring up. The city of Minneola will become one of the greatest manufacturing centers of Southern California, business center for one of the richest gold and silver producing sections of the Pacific Coast, with the greatest iron industry west of the Rocky Mountains, Minneola, Pittsburgh of the West!

A description of huge iron deposits in adjacent mountains and a recital of agricultural miracles followed.

The erection of a hotel, real estate office, school and some houses, launched the boom. To the optimistic and credulous, the project did look good! Dix Van Dyke, who supplied most of the foregoing wrote:

Before it lay the great level valley, behind it, a great range of desert mountains, extending east and west 100 miles. North, as far as one could see, the ranks of tinted mountains were endless. Plenty to stir the imagination and inspire belief in great achievement.

A dreary record followed. High hopes crushed to ruins; white city boundary stakes disappeared; inexperienced farmers ruined by blazing sun and hot winds; corrupt officials—bankrupt!

One more attempt was made. The Daggett Land Company incorporated in 1901, with Theodore Strong Van Dyke's sound knowledge and brilliant mind in control, brought ultimate success for the 320 adjacent acres that he farmed.

In 1896, local and national enterprise was at low ebb. With a three year drought preceding it, Calico silver mines closed, the Minneola electric plant and canal went bankrupt—the dream city became a slowly forgotten nightmare.

After that dream, Minneola made progress slowly. Deep-sunk wells and reservoirs, alfalfa fields, orchards, poultry, cattle and dude ranches appeared. Later, dozens of hard-working men such as Louis Skobel, Paul Haimut, Bill Smith, and others are viewing Minneola in Silver Valley without rose-colored glasses.

Minneola may yet get off paper and become an actual city.

"YES, VIRGINIA, THERE IS WATER ON THE MOJAVE"

by Beth Pinnell

To the millions of tourists who cross river bridges at Barstow that dry, sandy riverbottom sign "Mojave River" must seem quite a joke. Not enough water is in sight to wet a rattlesnake's whistle, let alone qualify for the name "river." But as any old timer can verify, the Mojave River is indeed worthy of the classification, and is one of the world's unique rivers in more ways than one. It runs backwards, upside down, crisscross, sometimes on top, usually underneath, all year in places, almost never in others, and its floods mark off the history of the desert as wars mark the history of the world.

The '38 flood stands out in capital letters in local history, while the '69 flood is still fresh in the minds of any who lived here during that spring. But who ever talks about the flood of 1921-22? According to official reports some 345,000 acre feet of water flowed past The Forks that year, while only 341,490 was measured there in 1968-69; and even less, about 219,000 acre feet was measured there in the '38 flood.

Reports of other major floods in the 1850's and 1860's, and a first hand report on the flood of 1883-84 are given in "Reminiscenses of Old Calico" by Herman F. Mellon. Mellon was 15 years old in 1882 when he and his father went to Calico to construct works for handling ore at the King Mine. He writes:

The winter of 1883-84 has taken its place in California history as the wettest one of which we have record. I can vouch for the fact that it was wet . . . In December the river rose some, but could still be forded; then the water receded until February. Though we had a great deal more rain and snow than usual on the desert, no one seemed to attach any importance to this fact. Early in February, after a couple of weeks of

beautiful, clear weather, the river suddenly began to rise. Word came to Daggett from Waterman (now Barstow) that the railroad bridge there was out and the river was still rising.

A Mr. Lott at Daggett attempted to ford the river with hay and barley for the teams at the mill just across the river on the north side, but the wagon was heavy and bogged down in midstream. He had much difficulty in freeing the team and getting them ashore, leaving the wagon almost hidden by the water. That left 24 mules at the mill with no feed, but the Oro Grande Company (at Elephant Mt.) had about a ton on hand, and they shared it with them. The next day the water had gone down, and Mellon rode across the river to Daggett after spikes which were needed in his carpentry work. While he was in Daggett the river rose again, and he almost drowned trying to ford back across. "I was thankful to be alive," he wrote, "with nothing worse to remind me of the incident than the loss of a piece of skin about the size of my hand just above my right knee, and a sore leg for a week."

The next day they were set to work building a boat for a ferry so that feed might be brought across the river for the mules. After the boat was built we had quite a time getting the rope system for guiding the boat across the river set up. First we shot a small line across the river, and, using it, pulled a one inch rope across. The large rope was stretched taut between two posts set deep in the ground on opposite banks. The nose of the boat was attached to a pulley running on this large rope. A small line parallel to the large one was also stretched across the river, and a man sitting in the stern of the boat held this line in such a manner as to keep the boat at an angle to the

1   *The Mighty Mojave, clockwise (from bottom) Coolwater Ranch, Daggett, U.S.M.C. Nebo, Barstow, Lead Mountain, West Yermo, Union Pacific Tracks, Yermo Annex, Repair Division, CALNEV gasoline storage, Elephant Mountain*

2 Old Town 1916 Flood

5 Willis Home on Crooks Street 1938

3 Prize winning photo of dramatic rescue during flood of March 1938. Damage reached $1,000,000.

6 Crooks Street looking west. Billy the Tailor Shop right foreground

7 East end Pierce Street - Stuchberry home a total loss - animals safe! G. Parks home on left

4 It Does Snow - Riverbottom December 1932 - Mrs. Stafford and Mr. Kelly

Nature's Fury

8 The only Survivor - Voisey cement block house near Ft. Irwin and Radio Rd.

river's current. The current did the rest, and did it right speedily. It was fun to see that boat shoot across. The first boat was a failure, however, as it was only 10 feet in length, so that when loaded with a bale of hay and the ferryman it shipped water, damaging the hay considerably and the temper of the ferryman more. The 16 foot boat we built a few days later worked to perfection . . .

Soon after building the larger boat a small French-Canadian put in an appearance one morning at our terminal of the ferry with a full camp outfit and two nice sharp axes. He wished to know who owned, "Le bon bateau," pointing to the little boat we had built first, laying bottom-up on the bank.

He told us that he had a contract to get mesquite wood out a couple of miles down the river, and he wished to obtain the boat to make the trip. He was told that the company owned the boat and to go up to the mill and see the boss about it, but that he was crazy to attempt the trip. He ignored this last information and went up to see the boss. Returning in a short time overjoyed to have been made a present of the boat, he proceeded to shape a paddle and then load his outfit and himself into the boat. He pushed the boat off heading at once for the middle of the river where the waves were two or three feet high and singing some Canadian boating song at the top of his voice. He was one happy Frenchy and left no doubt in our minds that he knew his business. We heard a few weeks later that he made the trip safely, was still all pepped up about the trip, and wished it could have lasted longer.

And so, the next time you travel the Yermo-Daggett Road and cross the Mojave River, squint your eyes a little to shut out the glare of that vast stretch of barren sand and visualize that time long ago when a French Canadian bravely dipped his paddle into the raging Mojave singing his song of triumph as he boated downstream with the flood.

Yes, the Mighty Mojave is indeed a river!

LIFE ON THE MOJAVE RIVER VALLEY
THE PIUTES OF 1904
by Dix Van Dyke — (Reprint Barstow Printer Review)

A few remnants of the once numerous Piute (Paiute) Indians roamed the desert in 1904. They no longer lived a savage life, having horses, wagons, guns, store clothes, and a hankering for white man's food. They were industrious, thrifty and occasionally worked at various jobs, not needing much to gratify their simple wants. The Newberry Mountains lay ten miles east of the Daggett ranch. Sheep thrived on the rugged heights and on each side of the mountains were springs where in hot weather they drank. Here the Indian hunters would patiently lie to wait for the sheep.

Where the point of the mountain extended into the valley there was a tract of damp land where grass, wild grapes and mesquite trees flourished. In summer it was a favored resort of a small band of Indians who eked out a meager living with mesquite beans and wild game. They brought to the Van Dyke ranch fine dressed sheep hides that, when cut in strips, wet and rolled in the hands and then dried, made the toughest and strongest of thongs.

The squaws had first scraped off all the hair and meat and smoked the hides. They then made them soft and pliable by rubbing and kneading the skins between their hands. The farmers bought a dozen for two dollars each and the Indian gladly assisted in harvesting the hay. The Indians' earnings were invested in food and merchandise with which they returned to their camp. Once a passing prospector gave one Indian too much wiskey. The Indian died! The next day the victim was buried and all his personal belongings were burned. The Indians believed this would insure their transportation to the same destination as the deceased. These were the last of the old hunting Indians. The next generation gravitated to the white settlements where they could slave and earn enough to possess automobiles and other new fangled contraptions their fathers had never dreamed of.

A FIELD TRIP TO THE VAN DYKE RANCH — 1962
by a student of "Frankie" Simon, Barstow High School teacher

Our first field trip was to the Van Dyke Ranch in Daggett, about eight miles east of Barstow. The ranch is owned and operated by Mr. and Mrs. Edward Strong Van Dyke.

The first thing we noticed were the trees— cottonwood, elm and pine. Mrs. Van Dyke then showed us a large bell set in a huge grinding stone. The date on the bell was 1906. It had the inscription "El Camino Real" which means The King's Highway. Mrs. Van Dyke told us that the grinding stone weighs approximately 2½ tons. It was made originally in Italy, and was found in a borax plant near Calico. It was part marble and part granite.

The bridge leading across the Van Dyke irrigation ditch was made by Mrs. Van Dyke. It consists of two old wagon wheels, approximately 200 pounds each, and rough hewn boards. It is self supporting.

On the large open screened-in porch we found an old fashioned coffee grinder, an old waffle iron, a wagon wheel brake, a rusty bommerang. All these articles were found together on the Van Dyke ranch.

As we went into the living room, Mrs. Van Dyke first showed us her collection of books written by John C. Van Dyke, Theodore S. Van Dyke, Woody Van Dyke and Paul Van Dyke. We also saw a listing of the family tree, a picture of Henry Van Dyke and a song which was

9   The Van Dyke Family

12   Daggett Ditch

10   Ed Millett and Ephraim Harris—Beekeeper 1912

13   Van Dyke Ranch 1935

Daggett Ranches

11   Ephraim Harris—well driller 1917

14   Bob Greer - Rancher 1916

dedicated to Henry Van Dyke.

In the kitchen, we met Mr. Van Dyke. We saw an old stove that burns gas as well as wood.

The antique-like dining room contained an old clock which Mrs. Van Dyke said did not run, a glass slipper which was a remembrance of her father, a silver service that was over 30 years old, and a picture of her grandmother's hut in the Hawaiian Islands.

We then began the tour of the surrounding grounds of the ranch. Outside the front door was an old wood-burning stove that had once been in the kitchen. Mrs. Van Dyke then showed us some fossils she had found. A well, 250 feet deep, had been drilled at the rear of the house. As we progressed, we saw an outhouse, the first Daggett jail, two adobe houses, a storeroom, a stable, a constable's house, a 100 year old wagon, a cactus with a lantern tree, stumps of petrified palm root and other stones.

At one time, eight families lived on the Van Dyke ranch, which stretched from Daggett to Camp Cady.

Mrs. Van Dyke is, indeed, a practical joker. She and Mr. Van Dyke both love children. Mrs. Van Dyke is 62 years old. She and Mr. Van Dyke have been married since 1915.

Editors Note 1976 (Edward S. Van Dyke was Theodore's nephew and had inherited the ranch after the death of Dix Van Dyke on October 10, 1952. Edward Van Dyke passed away on July 7, 1964, and Evelyn Van Dyke now resides in the Los Angeles area. The ranch has been sold to the Gordon Striclers, who have retained many of the outbuildings They remodeled the old homestead into a modern home.)

HINKLEY VALLEY
by Jessie McCormick

In 1869, early settlers searched the country around Hinkley Valley for new ranching areas. In 1872, Mr. Black established a ranch and in 1882 Southern Pacific built a railroad from Barstow to Mojave and gave Hinkley its name.

In 1908 others came, houses were built and wells dug. Since there were no well-drilling outfits, each person had to dig his own. A small railroad station was built with a house for the station agent. Mr. Evans installed a pumping plant with a five horse power engine. He grew the first crop of alfalfa, others started planting their fields.

Until 1915 supplies were shipped in from Los Angeles and San Bernardino. A small grocery store was built in the shade of two mesquite trees. It is still standing. The Post Office was moved into the same building from the corner of the railroad station where it had been located.

In 1914 the ladies of the area felt the need for recreation. One of them invited the others to her home and they organized the "Women's Improvement Club" with 13 charter members. One of the members, Grace Hill, lived in Hinkley. The club is still active as the Hinkley Women's Club.

In 1912 a small school house named Todd School was built. The building was used for meetings and potlucks. Most of the dinners were chicken, because that's what everyone raised.

The ladies decided that the school yard needed cleaning up, so they all met there one spring day with basket lunches. After working all day they enjoyed the picnic food. It reminded me of the poem,

There once was a smiling girl, from Niger,
Who rode back and forth on a tiger.
On the return ride, the girl was inside
And the smile was on the face of the tiger.

The farmers in the area planted buffalo berries, black locust, russian mulberry, cottonwood, tamarisk, cedar trees and lilac bushes. Also many wild grape vines grew.

On July 4 there was a big picnic as on other occasions. These projects were coordinated through the Women's Improvement Club. They also organized a small newspaper circular which everyone in the Valley enjoyed. Most of the projects were to raise money for the needy or to improve the community. If they raised seven or eight dollars it was a big amount.

When the Marine Base opened in Barstow, many of the farmers gave up their farms and went to work there. They had become discouraged on their farms because of the lack of water.

Many organizations were formed in Hinkley to help develop the community. These included the Chamber of Commerce, the Farm Bureau, and the Grange. A large Grange Hall was built and is still active today. In 1958, a large cement building was built to house a grocery store, library and Post Office. A big celebration was held for the dedication of the Post Office, called "Hinkley Valley Days," which has become an annual event. A fire hall was built for the fire equipment and meetings.

In 1921, the second Hinkley School was built of cement blocks. It had three large rooms, an auditorium with a stage, basement, kitchen, inside bathrooms, and dressing rooms. The curtains and equipment were furnished by the Women's Club. Later, Hinkley, Todd, and Harper Lake Schools unified. School busses were obtained for local use, and one to take children to Barstow High School. Eventually this school building was torn down and a new one built by the Unified District.

A Boy Scout Organization, sponsored by the Women's Club, had Russell Riley as its first Scoutmaster.

The Women's Club had exchange meetings with the Barstow Women's Club and Harper Lake Club. Speakers from The Barstow Women's Club were: Miss Abby Waterman, who presented a program on Red Cross work and Mrs. Stella White, who interested the ladies in making gowns for hospital inpatients.

As automobiles became popular, Hinkley needed a service station. The first one was built at Dixie corner.

15 Waterman Ranch

19 Hinkley Station 1908

Ranches and Communities

16 Shopping Center 1920

17 Ranching on the slash X -
Lee Berry, Cathy Westmoreland

20 Black Ranch - Adobe - Stagecoach stop

21 Goldstone remains

18 Farming at Harper Lake

22 Thelma and Hazel DePue

People bought gas there for 14 cents a gallon. Later a grocery store was added.

As the area of Hinkley grew, a paved highway was put through, streets laid out, a mail route established, and numbers put on the houses. For those who could not get delivery the Post Office had locked boxes. The school house was used as a church and Sunday School, but soon two new church buildings were erected.

The Pacific Gas and Electric Company built a huge pumping plant in Hinkley for conveying gas from Texas to Washington through pipelines. It provided employment for many men in the area, and helped to build the community.

Many people have settled here, staying throughout the years. Mr. and Mrs. Ernest Shephard came in the early 1930's, bought a large ranch, and planted alfalfa and many fruit trees. These dear people have been of great service to the community. They celebrated their 71st wedding anniversary in 1975 and still live on the same ranch.

From 1869, when only two families camped on the desert, a community named Hinkley sprang, now complete with farms, businesses and people.

HISTORIAN EXPLORES WILLIS WELLS
by Helen Graves

Before the summer heat comes again, visit Willis Wells. You will walk in the tracks of early Indians and see petroglyphs etched on the granite boulders. you can hunt for lost caves said to have pictographs on their walls.

In the stillness of a hiding place used later by horse thieves, you will feel the vibrations which once propelled Mildred Willis, for you will view remnants of a dream almost fulfilled.

In 1865 there was a rush to the Ord mountains where a golden magnet drew a population of at least 150 souls to one settlement. Can you find where the town of Marblehead is said to have been located? It was somewhere on the west side of the Ord Mountains, so the story goes. By 1869 claims had been consolidated into one or two large holdings. The several springs were also taken over by the mines and the Ords became closed to most people.

George and Mildred Willis lived in the best sections of various mining towns during the booms of Goldfield, Rhyolite, and Greenwater. Luck played out for the active mining promoter who brought his wife over into California. He was broke, but ready for a new start. Occupationally limited, George had been handicapped a few years before when he tried to wrest a knife from a drunken Mexican who had gone berserk. The blade had severed a tendon in George's right arm rendering it useless.

Ranching along the Mojave near Yermo in 1908, George took his pay in cattle, gradually building up a herd. Finding employers discouraged by floods, the couple felt ready to settle down on their own spread.

Aided by his geological knowledge, George in 1915 found a long narrow valley on the north side of the Ords, and at the base of a huge pile of jumbled rock found evidence of water seepage. It had been a watering place for roving Indians. Mildred was the physical "manpower" for the next 10 years. She dug a well 20 feet deep to water trapped in an underground basin.

The site was the best open range on the slopes of the Ord mountains, on the edge of a natural bowl that spreads from the base of the mountain.

At first the couple sought shelter in a habitable cave, one of several still to be found. Then they built a crude mud hut 10 feet square with two windows and a dirt floor. Canvas hung at the doorway.

Mildred's dream began to impel her. She had one of the greatest plans ever conceived in desert country. She had seen pictures of Scottish castles, and planned a magnificent house of stone. She loved gardens, flowers, orchards, and she visualized her landscaping.

Walls must be built to keep hungry cattle away from the gardens and house. The valley was strewn with pebbles, rocks and boulders. George could help drive the horses using a crude drag-on-winch that could load rocks, be hauled and unloaded when needed.

For 10 years Mildred cared for her husband as he became increasingly handicapped, and she cared for the herd. She drew water with a rope and a bucket hand-over-hand, standing for hours at the well which had planks laid across it. Visitors dropped by sometimes offering to help and tiring after four or five buckets-full. One account tells of an offer to provide a pump, but George refused under the impression that Mildred would not be content unless she had plenty to do.

Later, George located and built another well on the south side of the mountain, and had a small gasoline engine installed so that he could pump the water himself. A visitor was amazed to see Mildred approaching over the mountain with a pan of stew in her hand. The shack was 4 miles distant with extremely rough country in between.

Mildred planned earth-filled platforms bound by stone. First she would build a long wall across the opening of the basin in front of the cabin. It would be 350 feet long, and would run east and west starting with a huge pile of rock and reaching out to the long ridge that extended to the valley floor. Large rocks would make two parallel walls five feet apart and four and a half feet high. She would use small rocks to fill in between the two walls. After completion of the main wall, she would build a corral on the west side and a lateral wall westward to close the basin.

Mildred had been reared in a good family and was well educated. She was a slender, delicate woman, five feet three inches tall, and weighed about 125 pounds. The great wall of China, the pyramids and great temples were built by brawny men, some slaves under a lash. Mildred was lashed on by a labor of love and an incredible dream to build, single-handed and unaided a wall 660 feet long and 16 feet wide. At Willis Wells one may still see stonework measuring 10,560 cubic feet, containing 1,372,000 pounds of material, all placed by one pair of small hands. Some stones weighed more than the frail builder who lifted them. She used no mortar in constructing the wall of uniform four-foot thickness.

The rock work was done in Mildred's spare time. She came out of her self-imposed exile only twice in 10 years—once for dental work and once to sign a deed before a notary.

One day George became ill and the couple left to seek outside medical treatment for him. He died in San Diego.

After George's death, Mildred must have gone to San Francisco. After several years a miner received a letter from her inquiring about a mining claim. Her letter indicated that a city was the loneliest place in the world. Never interested in material riches, she had long known that money could not buy happiness for she had found contentment in shaping up her dream.

Her stone walls still endure, virtually untouched, but the rest of her paradise must endure only in written account and in the memory of the few who knew her.

Be sure to take along a camera when you visit Willis Wells, for you may have to prove that you have seen traces of a miracle, a story too strange to believe.

THE THURSBY FAMILY

by Celestia Gilliam
(From an interview with Gladys Thursby McGinnis)

In 1901 Richard Chilson homesteaded 80 acres of land on Soapmine Road, known then as the Fish Pond area. He was no stranger to the desert for, before this, he had discovered the Odessa Silver Mine near Calico. At Calico he had met his future wife, Mary Alice, a dancehall girl. After their marriage they lived in Victorville where he served as post-master. He had moved his wife and twin daughters, Alice and Adele, to the Fish Pond area and drilled a well on the homestead. It became the watering place for travelers, and also a boarding home for young ladies. One such young lady was Eunice Bush (now Mrs. Burton Leak), the teacher at Fish Pond School. The Chilson twins, and the children of their neighbors, the Comptons and the Mitchells, all attended this school and later rode horseback around Sugarloaf Mountain to attend high school in town. Occasional trips to San Bernardino by horse and buggy would take several days, but most of the shopping was done at Walter Alf's store in Yermo.

Many young men came courting at the Chilson Ranch, and eventually Alice's sister Adele married Ruby Griffith. His brother, Richard Arnold Griffith, was the serviceman for whom our local Legion Post is named. Edna Compton married Charles Mitchell and Alice Chilson went to work for Dr. Anderson in his office.

At about this time, Retson Frear Thursby arrived in Barstow at the age of nineteen and went to work for the Santa Fe. He was born in Stranraer, Scotland and spoke with a brogue. He was soon tagged with the nickname "Scotty." He met and married Alice Chilson and they became the parents of Lucille, Gladys, Roy and Leslie.

In 1922 Scotty left the railroad and became one of the first people to move to Main Street after going into the building business. He built the family home at what is now 236 East Main and also a tourist court with cabins to rent. Alice made handmade quilts for the beds and all the children helped to run the business. Scotty built the house of handmade adobe brick and straw, mixed in a wheelbarrow, not an easy task. The children would be enlisted to water down the brick for curing purposes.

Crooks and Pierce Streets had shade trees to rest under and watch the Mojave River run. The children were often sent with their father's lunch pails across an old wooden foot bridge over the river and the tracks. Before the 1938 flood, Gladys remembers going to the ball park on Crooks Avenue in the triangle between the Santa Fe tracks and Pierce Street. Everyone in town would turn out for a very happy time.

Scotty was also a musician, playing the piano, drums and saw, all by ear. He organized a band and played for dances and parties all over the desert. He passed away in 1946, Alice in 1948. Their daughter, Gladys, still resides on the original Chilson Ranch.

THE CROOKS FAMILY

by Celestia Gilliam
(From an interview with Clarence Crooks, Jr.)

Samuel Crooks brought his family to Barstow in 1902. His children were Clifford, Lynn, Jessie, Mollie and Clarence. They had formerly lived in Inglewood, California. They took up homestead property from the North Line of the Santa Fe behind the then Harvey House. The street, now known as Crooks Avenue, ran in front of the property. They lost the property during the depression, but Samuel retained land on what is now Irwin Road, called Burke's corner, and also ten acres where Radio Station KWTC now stands. Mexican laborers were hired to build an adobe wall around the area adjoining the Crooks' property on the North and

23 Samuel and Leona (Mitchell) Crooks 1911. Alfalfa Ranch north of Buzzard Rock later - Hawes Ranch

26 Holdup Waterman Road (Irwin) 1912 - Bandit Edna Mitchell, Charlie Mitchell, Leona Mitchell Crooks, "Dutch" and Lavella Crooks

24 Mr. and Mrs. Clarence Crooks 1918 - Clarence Jr., Mary Alice, Marie

The Crooks Family

27 The water boy 1918 - Bud, Marie, Mary Alice

25 Rooster protecting his harem

28 Three for the road

owned by the Gilhams. Walt Terry now lives there and some of the adobe wall still stands.

Samuel's son, Clarence, known as "Dutch," worked for the Santa Fe in "old Barstow." He met La Villa Mae Fisher, who had arrived in town from Bellefourche, North Dakota, after answering an ad for a housekeeper for Mrs. Lubin J. Henderson. Dutch and La Villa were married in 1913 and took up residence on the Burke's corner property. For Irwin Road, then known as Waterman Road, led to the famous Waterman Mine and was also a route to Death Valley. Clarence and La Villa had six children—Marie, Mary-Alice, Clarence Jr., Ann, Faye and Emma. They all attended Waterman School and were all taught in the first grade by Ruth Thomson. At first they walked the old wooden foot bridge over the tracks to school. Later they were picked up by a bus coming from Harper Lake.

Several families lived in the North area of old Barstow: the Marvins, Hawes, Redmans, Mitchells, Uptons, Jensens and the Clarks. Their children contracted all of the standard childhood diseases, carrying them to the others who lived between the tracks in town, and vice-versa. A good snow-pack in the San Bernardino Mountains could cause the Mojave River to flow with water as late as the first of July. The Santa Fe would hold a barbeque down at the Richard Harlan Ranch. Families could also attend dances at the Compton Dairy. Children would fall asleep in a chair. No babysitters in those days.

The Crooks family would make up a freezer of ice cream on hot summer nights and take it by horse and buggy to Coolgardie much to the delight of the miners who did not get into town except for supplies. La Villa also made her own butter and cottage cheese. She kept the excess butter in the Harvey House cooler with the understanding that the manager could make use of it on occasion.

Christmas was a big time for the Crooks and they remember a bachelor, Charlie McIlroy, who came for the festivities and a home-cooked meal. He always brought gifts for the children. Charlie was a grave-digger for White and Platt, receiving $5.00 for each job. (Charlie McIlroy had a gold mine out North which he worked and turned his gold into the Express Office to send to San Francisco.)

Ed Harris was the Santa Fe Special Officer or "bull," and also town constable. Lubin J. Henderson was the judge. The only crimes in those days were bootlegging or swimming nude in the pond west of "B" Hill. The passengers on the train could get a good view of those early day streakers and the town leaders did not approve.

At that time, 23 trains, express mail and passenger, stopped at Barstow in a 24 hour span. Pullman cars were air-cooled, but the economy unit or chair car had only fans to circulate the air. Clarence Jr. sold ice-cream cones to the passengers during the summer. He charged 10 cents, but people would have given more after stepping from the train onto the hot brick pavement. A counter thermometer was said to always register over 100 degrees.

Clarence Sr. passed away in 1952, La Villa in 1962. Clarence Jr. married June White, who was also born in Barstow. She still has her fathers' receipt from Dr. Anderson for the delivery. The cost of having a child was $35. Her father, Jules Verne White, worked for Gilham's Dry Goods in old Barstow at that time.

The Crooks family has had the same Post Office Box, #94, since 1906.

FIFTY YEARS AGO
by Clarence "Bud" Crooks

One day in 1925 Dad came home with the "talk" of the town. Some citizens were agitated, especially the town mortician. An Indian family beat him out of the $15 fee he usually received from the county for burial of the very poor.

Pat, the deceased, was the elder of his Indian family. The family worked and lived at the Waterman Ranch. Apparently, the old man clung to the old ways because when he died his family built a pyre of mesquite wood and cremated his remains. Then lovingly they gathered Pat's bones, ground them, and cast the dust to the winds. Thus, no $15 fee for the mortician.

Next time you bend to admire a desert flower, pause . . . Ashes of the lords of this land gave our desert earth this life.

THE MITCHELL FAMILY
by Celestia Gilliam
(From an interview with Charlie and Edna Mitchell)

Franklin and Cecilia Mitchell were married in 1892 and lived on a farm in Minnesota. They became disenchanted with the extreme cold and decided to sell the farm machinery and move to sunny California. After living in Los Angeles and Colton, they were fascinated by the thoughts of moving to the desert. In 1908 Franklin homesteaded available land in North Barstow, now on Highway 91. By this time the Mitchells were parents of four boys and three girls—Leona, Charlie, Howard, Joseph, John and twins, Mary and Martha.

They chose to build their house on the lower river bottom portion of their land, but after the flood of 1910 were forced to move to higher ground. It was during this flood that they tried to put Grandpa Mitchell, 90 years old, on the kitchen table to keep him above the flooded floor. When told what they were doing, Grandpa Mitchell said, "Hell, what's a little water? Put me down and I'll swim out." A testimony to the hardiness of our ancestors!

The Mitchell children grew. Times were hard. Charlie quit school in the sixth grade and went to work for Santa Fe in order to help the family. All the children helped on the ranch tending to the horses and cattle. Cecilia, their mother, had her own vegetable garden and milk cows. She also made sure that they attended Mass each Sunday and was later instrumental in the building of the Catholic Church then on Second Street.

The children went to Waterman Elementary School and each day walked over the foot bridge. It was not long before Charlie began carrying Edna Compton's books and also occasionally meeting her for roller skating at Fletcher's Opera House. Life was good, although the school at Waterman had its problems, caused by several "big mean boys" that women teachers could not handle. School was closed entirely at one point until a male teacher could be imported. With parental consent, he developed a technique of grabbing unruly boys by the ears and banging their heads against the wall. After a few exhibitions of this treatment things simmered down and school continued.

Petite Edna Compton, Charlie's love, lived with her family on a neighboring ranch. She was one of five children to graduate from the eighth grade at Waterman School in 1915, and attended the first high school established in Barstow the same year. The school, located where the El Rancho Motel is now, was in a private home rented from a woman by the name of Jesse Flint.

Charlie continued to court Edna and, in 1920, they were married in the home of Charlie's sister, Leona. Leona had wedded Lynn Crooks and they lived at what had formerly been Grapevine Station. The famous desert priest, Father Crowley, performed the ceremony. Charlie went to work at Black's Ranch near Hinkley, and later at the P K Ranch, where he and his bride made a home out of whatever was available, a tent or a shack. They were happy honeymoon years and Charlie loved to tease his gullible bride. On one occasion he told her to get all dressed up and he'd take her to the big city of Ballarat. He added that they would drive the Model T and park on the edge of town and take the streetcar in because of the traffic. One can well imagine her surprise when she actually arrived at her imagined metropolis!

By 1925 old Barstow was moving to Main Street and Charlie became involved in this process. He had owned and operated a garage on their original property in North Barstow and now decided to build a new one at what is now Seventh and Main. He bought the used brick from the Gilham's building which had been destroyed by fire in 1923 and used this in his new construction. He gave his old Buick (Moon) car to a Mexican laborer in return for cleaning the bricks. Through the years, he operated his garage, was a part-time rancher and also involved himself in the construction and rental businesses. He and Edna became the parents of three boys, Art, Bob and Pat.

The original Mitchell homestead has been kept through the years and two of the boys still reside on the property. Edna and Charlie have indeed played a part in the history and development of Barstow. They are happily retired at a delightful ranch nestled in the Charleston Mountains where Charlie, with a twinkle in his eye, is still not above teasing his bride of 55 years.

THE HILL FAMILY
by Melvin Hill as told to Thelma M. Carder

I was born on a homestead ranch in a railroad-tie house. Mother and Dad, along with my six older brothers, had homesteaded the 160 acres in 1908. Dad was then working at the Bagdad-Chase mill located on the west side of what is now "B" hill.

The family moved onto the property in the spring of 1908 with a team of mules and a tent, plus a lot of fortitude and ambition. Dad put down the first well here, and many others around the community, mostly by hand, with one-mule power.

Watermelon applesauce, made from watermelon rind, was the fruit preserves of the time.

The old orchard, planted in 1910, is set on the bias from the rest of the ranch because that was the easiest way to level the land for irrigation.

Sharing memories, my sister Mabel Hill Dyer said:

"About 1907, 'The Place,' the Hill home was located between the Mojave River and the railroad tracks in Barstow. My father still worked as an engineer at the Bagdad-Chase Mill, but he had moved his family to town to be nearer the school. When school started, I left my shoes at home. Mother protested but I assured her that most of the children went barefooted.

All went well with my liberated feet until the day of reckoning arrived. The school pictures were sent home. There was little Mabel, proud in starched pinafore and pigtails, and the only one in the front row without shoes.

One memorable summer we had a vacation. Mother, an older brother, and baby Melvin stayed back to look after the ranch. Father loaded the rest of his family into the farm wagon drawn by two big mules. The wagon was already piled high with food stuffs, cooking utensils, dishes, bedding, etc. I think it took two days to get to Big Bear Lake, our destination. Our camp was in a pine grove near the lake. Trees, water, grass, mountain air! What a blissful change from our desert sand and sage brush! We fished from a row boat, but I don't remember any fish dinners. We splashed in the lake but no one knew how to swim. One challenge was to throw a pine cone over the tall trees, I can't remember if we ever made it.

The camping must have been primitive, but I don't recall any complaints. The evening campfires were a special treat.

We arrived back home a week or so later, probably a very dirty and disheveled crew, but also very happy. We were of the elite. We had had a vacation!"

Then Mabel added the story about her cooking for the family while Mother was away. Mabel was 11 or 12 at the time she said. She baked some bread and forgot the salt. By serving very salty gravy and extra salty butter she managed to get the stuff eaten up, never even considering chucking it out and starting over. You just didn't throw any kind of food away.

My oldest sister Elizabeth was the first white child born in Holcomb Valley, near Big Bear.

In 1914 when I came along, mother was active in school work. In 1915, she and Abby Waterman of the Waterman mine were successful with a petition to establish a high school. Three of my older brothers and sisters graduated in the same class in 1919, with the other four following as we came along.

One of the first things I can remember is the old Model T that my oldest brother drove to peddle milk in Barstow.

I especially remember the great Fourth of July picnics in the Tappy Woods. There were trees along the river then. The people walked the half mile back and forth to our reservoir to swim because it was about the only place around to swim safely.

I attended Todd Grammar School, a little one-room schoolhouse (10' x 15') that the farmers would move on a hay wagon to wherever the most children lived. One acre of our property in the northwest corner of the old homestead is still deeded to the Todd School District for a place to put the school. A few years back, when we were enlarging the reservoir with two D8 cats and carryalls, both drivers and myself stopped to look at a four-foot square of soil uncovered that was a different

color. I had to think way back. It was the privy hole for the old school.

When I started walking to grammar school in 1920, its building was located one and a half miles away, where it stayed. A concrete building was built about 1924. I still have the old wooden one-room schoolhouse.

The parties, ice-cream socials they called them then, when the whole community would gather by wagon or buggy, were joyous occasions. Everybody knew everybody for 25 miles around, and they would all turn out.

My first memory of a church experience was riding with dad in the Model T to Harper Lake for Sunday School. A minister would drive from Long Beach for this group of six families.

Dad was active in the Farm Bureau as long as he was able to get around, and I can remember raising onions as a 4H project in 1925. I was a member, in 1928, when we named the local club "Hinkley Rollicking Ranchers."

Years later, many neighbors and myself were leaders of the club which is still active, and has won many awards over the years. For the County Fair we used the idea of growing plants in flats to have a green live exhibit booth with an operating sprinkler system. Jackie Simmons pumped the water.

The outstanding trip of my life was with 25 members from California to the 4H Club Congress in Chicago. I rate 4H Club members high anyway, and one in a thousand got to go on this trip.

Since I graduated from high school in the "hungry '30's" very few of us went away for more schooling. In the spring of 1957 when I was chairman of the High School Board, I began thinking about that. We asked the superintendent, Dr. Robert Hilburn, to investigate the possibilities of a junior college in this area.

The Hill family has been living in the Mojave River Valley, mining and ranching, for nearly 70 years. Chances are there will be Hills many years to come.

MARY BEAL—BOTANIST

by Margaret Fouts

Mary Beal of Daggett went on to become a nationally known botanist after leaving her life as a librarian and recovering her health in the dry Mojave Desert climate. Her cottage was built where she first pitched her tent on the Van Dyke Ranch in April, 1910.

During early days she travelled on horse back and by horse and buggy, familiarizing herself with every desert plant she could find. Her desert herbarium of 1000 botanical specimens, which she mounted and catalogued herself, was incorporated in the Jepson Herbarium at the University of California, Berkeley in 1951. Miss Beal worked with Dr. Willis Linn Jepson, author and world renowned botanist, from 1930 until his death several years later.

Miss Beal photographed thousands of desert flowers

and did beautiful oil paintings of others. Her pictures and articles are found in national magazines and used in high school and university science and botany classes. Noted visitors, professors and students consulted her on desert flowers and asked her guidance on field trips.

She spent much of the 15 years between 1937 and 1952 in the Providence Mountains botanizing and identifying plants bordering the stony trail to the Mitchell's Caverns, owned by Jack and Ida Mitchell.

In June 1952, honors were accorded to Miss Beal for her work in the field of botany, especially in the desert area. The Mary Beal Botanical Trail at Mitchell's Caverns was dedicated in her honor.

SPETH HOMESTEAD

by Shirley Wasco

Robert Speth was born to Anthony Speth and Sophia Matuska Speth on October 29, 1911. He moved to Hinkley from Los Angeles with his parents at the age of five, a long trip by train. His father had a severe case of rheumatism and was given only two years to live. Robert Speth had two younger brothers, Frank and George.

His father leased out the land in Hinkley from 1916-18, and came to stay in 1918. In 1919 electric power arrived—a big day for everyone.

The property consisted of 40 acres obtained under the Desert Homestead Act. They raised oats and alfalfa and in the early 20's put in a large orchard north of the house—the same place the small orchard is today. Only two pecan trees remain of the Speth's orchard.

The house, built in 1916, consisted of a kitchen, two bedrooms, bathroom and service porch. The kitchen and service porch faced east, but about 1925 they moved the house so that the kitchen faced south, adding a living room and dining room, which were divided by bookcases. At the same time the front porch was cemented and carpentry work done by Charles Brass. His wife was a teacher at the high school and Robert Speth was a student in her Math class at that time. The cellar was dug at that time also.

According to Speth, their indoor bathroom was the "first" in the Hinkley area—a real luxury. The windows in the living room all seem to have the original panes. The view is very distorted and rippled as streaks seem imbedded in the glass. The house is built of cedar siding and is holding up very well.

Speth said that the septic tank was put in as a demonstration for the whole area under the direction of the Farm Advisor in 1922 or 1923. It was an excellent set up. Had we known the extent of the system when we moved in, we could have saved several hundred dollars and much hard work.

Surrounded by trees, the house never needed cooling. Pictures taken throughout the time that the Speths lived there show that much vegetation could grow on the desert.

The Speths also raised turkeys. At that time there were few diseases of fowl and it was simple to raise them. When diseases hit, they discontinued their turkey line.

His mother heated her wash water outside in a copper bottomed tub and dumped it into a washing machine that worked as our modern day clothes dryers do in their tumbling action. Speth states that it was an effective way of washing as their clothes came out exceptionally clean.

They later worked 40 more acres across Somerset Road on the present Willie Walker residence. They had built a weir to force water through pipe lines to irrigate, but when they wanted to irrigate land across the road, they had to build the stone weir higher because the ground level was higher on the Walker place. Speth was a high school student when the weir was built.

About that time they built the reservoir at the end of the road, then purchased their own forms and cast the cement pipe that would go from the weir to the reservoir. It was a very neat and systematic operation. He and his brother also dug much of the ditch and helped make and lay the cement pipe on the ranch.

Speth and his brother rode a horse to school until they were too big for the horse, at which time their father got a carriage for the horse to pull. The first school was white with a big church-type steeple. In 1924 it burned down, so they met in a warehouse, and later a house. Still later, a brick school was built. It was eventually torn down and the present Hinkley School built.

Before electricity they had a food cooler, shaped like a pyramid with wool and burlap draped around it. Water was held in sacks at the top and allowed to drip down the sides. A large single cylinder distillate fueled engine was used on the farm for pumping irrigation water before electricity.

In 1937 Speth's father and 17 year old brother, George, were killed in a farming accident. The hay stacker they were moving touched electrical wires. The high school closed that day, in his brother's honor. His father's funeral was so well attended that people had to stand outside the church during the service. Later that same year his distraught mother passed away of a broken heart, and as if to add salt to open wounds, his faithful dog, Scotty, was shot, making it home in time to die before his master. Left completely alone, Speth sold the entire 80 acres in 1938 for $16,500.

On the lighter side, Mr. Speth told of the cider which he and his brother made in the cellar with the apples from their orchard. They made so much, however, that they could not possibly consume it all before it turned to vinegar. Not knowing what else to do when he sold out in 1938, he left thirty-five gallons of vinegar in the cellar.

Speth attended the University of Redlands from February 1929 to February 1933, majoring in economics. He joined the service, eventually meeting his wife, Rose Moran, in Pecos, Texas where she was a Lieutenant in the Army Nurse Corps. He was also a Lieutenant. They were married October 18, 1943. Her people came from the same area as my mother's—near Reading, Pennsylvania. They had two children, Robert John Jr., of San Bruno and Ellen Louise Gutierrez of Glendale.

Speth moved back to Hinkley after deciding that being a banker in Los Angeles behind four walls was not healthy. He owned the farm across the road west from the present Nelson Dairy, but sold out when the water level receded in the wells. They moved to the Daggett Ranch, part of Coolwater Ranch in Daggett, and then back to Barstow. He still works at the Daggett Ranch.

Speth told of the abundance of water and how he and Dix Van Dyke drove from house to house collecting money in 1924 or 1925 for an attorney to fight for their water against Pasadena—helping to save another Owens Valley catastrophe in the Barstow area.

The depth of water was about 19 feet during Speth's time. They used a windmill as well as a centrifugal pump. In the first seven years we were here the water level had not dropped, but when we replaced the pump in 1965 the level was 93 feet.

The house is the same as when Speth left but for the addition of a side porch and dinette area to the south of the kitchen, built in 1943.

The property had changed hands many times before we acquired it in 1965. It was run down to the point that we believed we would have to tear the house down and start from scratch. However, with a lot of energy, money and love we have come to cherish the house as it is. Seeing the pictures of the land during the Speth ownership and learning just a bit of the history of the land makes it that much more appreciated.

LEAK CROSSING

by Annice Leak Gibson

The place known as "Leak's Crossing" was where Highway 66, intersected the railroad tracks east of Barstow and continued on the north side of town. Both the railroad tracks and Highway 66 ran through the corner of the Leak's homestead. Thus their intersection was known as "Leak's Crossing." Many travelers used it to go over the railroad from East Main Street to Riverside Drive.

Charles Leak brought his wife, Grace, and their four sons, Burton, George, Donald, and Elmer to Barstow in 1914. Mrs. Leak suffered from asthma and hoped the dry desert climate would improve her health. They homesteaded 160 acres, the area where Henderson & Barnes Heating and Cooling, Desert Villa Trailer Park, Victorville-Barstow Truck Line, and Citizen's Savings & Loan Association are now located.

Leak built a home and planted fruit trees nearby, but the soil was too poor and a shortage of water made fruit growing impractical. In 1916 he worked for the railroad on the riptrack and in 1917 as a butcher for Frank Ryerse in Daggett.

In June 1917 Burton Leak married Eunice Bush who had been teaching at the Fish Pond School. They lived at Daggett on the Funk Ranch where Burton worked.

In 1918, desiring independence, Charles Leak purchased a farm and hogs from Mr. Howard directly across the river from the Leak homestead. The family moved to the farm. Charles planted a vegetable garden, alfalfa, and raised chickens. With a team and wagon he collected garbage from the restaurants in Barstow as well as from the Santa Fe Harvey House to feed his hogs. Thus, the road over the riverbed to their farm also became known as "Leak's Crossing."

The following year the hogs caught cholera. It was costly to vaccinate their entire herd. Some died and the others were left in a weakened condition. The chickens did not fare well for a lack of grit in their diet.

In 1920 the family moved back to the Leak homestead bringing their livestock with them. They tore down the farm house and with the lumber added a room onto the homestead house. They also built hog pens and both brooder and laying coops for their chickens. That same year a fifth son, Frank, was born. They continued to grow alfalfa and vegetables on the farm, and used both Leak's Crossings as they traveled back and forth between their farm and homestead.

When George Leak graduated from high school in 1922, he and his father went into partnership. In 1923, George went to the University of California, Davis, for a short course in "Poultry Husbandry." Following his return home, the Leaks raised white Leghorn chickens, selling both chickens and eggs. They had as many as 1,000 chickens at one time, which was a large number in those days. They also continued to raise hogs. They bought a one ton Model T Ford truck and had a special metal bin made for hauling garbage.

George bought a one room homestead cabin from Miss Mary .Etta Cook, a neighbor and local music teacher, and moved it to the Leak homestead for his sleeping quarters. With the help of Billy King, a local carpenter, he started building two additional rooms. Dutch Dorrance, a farmer from Newberry, built the fireplace.

In June 1924, George married Margaret King, the carpenter's daughter, before the house was completed. George tells the story of the night their friends shivareed them. The window panes were still missing and a bat flew into their bedroom. They had put the lights out when the "shivareers" arrived. The visitors thought the bride and groom were trying to make an escape, when they were really trying to get rid of the bat which was in their closet.

In 1926 George and his father dissolved their partnership and George found work in town. Charles Leak continued raising chickens and hogs on the homestead with the help of his remaining younger sons.

THE HENDERSON STORY—1976

by Grace Denney Hart

I, Fanella Grace Henderson Denney Hart, have lived on the desert most of my life. My father and mother, Mr. and Mrs. Newton "Newt" Henry Henderson came from Fillmore, Ventura County, to Newberry, California, in

32 *Prime rib on the hoof*

Ramirez Rancho

29 *Donato "Papa," Tommy Ramirez (back row) Carl Alton Hughes, Jr. (grandson), Andrew, Arthur, Mary Lou Ramirez - 1951*

30 *Corral, barn and slaughter house*

31 *Donato selects your next steaks*

33 *Felix, Catherine (Hughes), John, Donato, Margaret Ballejos (wife of Felix) Ramirez (back row) John Hughes, Robert Ramirez, Alton Carl Hughes, Jr., Anna Marie, Diana, Virginia Ramirez - 1952*

January 1921, with a family of ten children.

My father raised cattle on the river bottom north of Newberry. When we were lucky enough to have heavy rains in the San Bernardino mountains, the Mojave River would flow.

All of us children, except the eldest, Eliza and Newton, attended a one room school house on Newberry Road. The school had a well complete with a windmill. The wind blew enough to keep the water tank full. Toilets, outhouses or two-holers as they were then called, were outside, the girl's on one side of the yard, the boy's on the other. Today the school has a modern building.

After having raised cattle for a short time, my father worked and grew alfalfa on Dix Van Dyke's ranch. Later, we returned to Simi in Ventura County where my father was killed on December 3, 1928.

Most of the children were grown and some married when my mother remarried Charles B. McCoy. We moved back to Newberry where McCoy was a pumper for Santa Fe Railroad. After he retired, they lived in Barstow until their deaths.

My brother, Newton, worked a few years for Santa Fe, in Barstow, as a repairman at the rip track, until he was promoted wrecker engineer. In 1934 he decided to run for the office of Constable; he was elected and held the position for 23 years, 'till his death, October 27, 1957.

My husband, Clifton Denney, worked for Santa Fe as a wrecker engineer after Newton's departure. He remained with the company until his death, October 12, 1959. As a wrecker engineer, he had the honor of using Barstow's large wrecking crane to unload "the large eye" (I imagine, the lens of the 200 inches Palomar telescope), which was transported, by rail, to Pasadena. Later, it was taken to Mount Palomar and installed at the Observatory.

My mother-in-law, better known as Ma Denney, lived in Barstow for many years. She had a nursing home on the Old Hawes Ranch, which was destroyed by the 1938 Mojave River flood; she started another home on Arrowhead Avenue.

My father-in-law, Perry Denney, was a plumber (in Barstow), and quite active until retirement. Both have been deceased for many years.

My brothers and sisters have married, had children, and now have grand-children, some great grand-children. Six of us are still living and enjoying life to the fullest.

CAMP CADY IN THE 1930's
by Henry James

My mother, Mrs. Mintie N. James, and Mrs. Melville bought Camp Cady from E. Bryen Sinces in the fall of 1930. Cecil Wilhelm, brother of Walt and Kenneth, was the cowboy on the ranch; my brother Eugene, was our cowboy. The ranch proper had about 1200 acres within the outside fence, which was cut up into many pastures and two alfalfa fields. There were about 300 head of cattle that were ranged along the river, where ever there was food and water, from about the Mitchell ranch on the west, down through the ranch proper and on down to Soda Lake. Much of the river bottom was open grassy land. New Fort Cady was in the lower end of our best alfalfa field. At the upper end of the field, where the best alfalfa grew, maybe 400 yards from the Fort was an artesian well. The well pipe came up out of the ground several feet. At about waist height a regular garden faucet was screwed into the pipe and it ran a nice stream of water. Right beside it was a small pump house with a gasoline engine driven pump that pumped water up to the alfalfa field.

The house and barn area was just about like it is now. The big house is by the river and about 300 feet back is the little house. East of the little house is the big barn that Mr. Sinces called the racehorse barn, and out west of the little house was a small stock barn. We used the small barn the most. Between the two barns, and south of the little house, was a wooden fence. Along this fence ran what I believe was the old Government Road. Across the road from the small barn were several small buildings, one made out of logs. There was still a sign hanging on the front of this one that said, "Short Order Cafe." The Wilhelms said that it was the stage stop. We used the road as a ranch road.

My brother and his wife lived in the little house. It was a nice house but it's only convenience was running water. Kerosene lamps were used for lights, and a wood stove, using mesquite wood, was used for cooking and heat. Clothes were washed on a scrub board, and with a cyclone washer (up and down plunger). They traded at Ryerson's in Daggett where they could get credit and pay when cattle were sold. Barstow was too far so we traded at Daggett and Yermo. One day, while we were in Bell's store in Yermo, the fire bell rang. The west end house of a string of houses was burning, and the west wind was blowing hard. The fire equipment was two hose carts. They got the hoses going on the house but just didn't have enough water to put it out. Then the second house caught on fire. They tried to put it out but again just didn't have enough water. When the third house was threatened they turned their hoses on it and saved it.

Quite often we needed an extra man, so when we did we hired Drew Tankersley, who lived about three miles south of us on a homestead. He was our man Friday. He helped us in many ways. He knew cattle and ranching, so he helped us manage the stock, break horses and do everything that has to be done on a cattle ranch. When my brother lost his wife in the winter 1932, and was in an emotional turmoil, Drew and his wife and little girl moved into the little house and managed the ranch for us. During this time when we were at the ranch we lived in the big house. On one of our trips to the ranch Drew came over one evening and said; "It's snowing outside." We went out to see, and sure enough it was. In the morning everything was covered with about 3 inches of snow. I believe it was the first snow that I saw here on the desert. We had several pigs on the ranch that ran loose and foraged for their food. One of them, a large boar, wandered up to the Mitchell ranch and gored one of their horses. When Drew was told about it he got his 30-30 rifle out, hunted up the boar and killed it. He said that with his little girl playing in the yard he didn't want to take a chance. My mother told him she was glad he did, because she didn't want to take a chance either.

When the mortgage was almost due we knew we couldn't make the payment. So we put the ranch up for sale. We sold it to the current owner, Mr. Smith. We moved our things back to Fillmore, where we were living when we bought the ranch.

LEE BERRY
by Louella Bishoff

Was he the Mojave Desert's "Cattle Baron" as some people have proclaimed, or just a fool as others said when he began ranching in the desert?

Some who know Lee Berry consider him a shrewd business man who took opportunities as they presented themselves and made the most of them. Berry, himself, has said "a man's success in business depends on a large amount of luck, plus a lot of help from God Almighty . . . We just ain't smart enough to do all the things we do sometimes."

Berry was born in Oklahoma on April 15, 1901. However, he lived most of his early life on ranches in New Mexico and Arizona, where his family had moved in 1904. It was while he was in Amarillo, Texas that he learned another trade, barbering and ladies' hair styling.

In 1932 a friend from Texas, the late George Patton, convinced Berry to come to California and set up a barber shop. He went into partnership with Ada Hill, who had opened the first beauty shop in Barstow. Their business was located on the alley behind Lubin J. Henderson's clothing store (then on the northeast corner of First and Main.)

After about six months in Barstow, Berry decided to move to Red Mountain where he opened a barbering and hair stylist shop at the corner of "The Owl" an establishment which was, in the words of Berry, "as good as any fancy place you could find in San Francisco at the time." It was run by a Greek named Harry Moss, who furnished it with fabulous decor, excellent entertainment, gourmet food, and the best "cribs" for miles around! The orchestra used top-rate musicians. Moss employed a bevy of beautiful young girls from all over the United States.

Berry's barbering clientele were mostly miners from the surrounding area. One of Berry's customers was the famous "Death Valley Scotty," builder of Scotty's Castle. Berry was also the women's hair stylist. In addition to an occasional marcelle-wave, the girls often had their hair color-tinted to please their clients.

The working hours at the shop were from four in the afternoon to midnight. Although business was good in Red Mountain, Berry decided to move back to Barstow where he could have better working hours. He opened a barber shop next door to Brooks Tabor's Pool Hall and the Melrose Hotel, which were in the middle of the 100 block on East Main street.

In 1938 Berry married Mary Weaver from Victorville. She was working at the Barstow WPA office, which was located in the basement of Dillingham's Market, at the northwest corner of Second and Main. She was a true help-mate when Berry went into cattle ranching. While he commuted between his ranch, which was east of Helendale at the time, and the barber shop in Barstow (a 50-mile round trip over rough roads), she used to hand-pump a trough of water for their herd, which began with about 30 head.

They lived in a tent at that time. As the cattle business was expanding, Berry began to spend less and less time at the barber shop and, in 1947, he sold it.

As the cattle business was growing, Berry also leased other acreage at such places as the Martin Ranch (Circle C) near the Mojave River. The ranch's business expanded further when Berry went into partnership with the late Jim Cox and Howard Foster of Imperial Valley. Cox was an old friend from New Mexico.

In 1948 Berry acquired the land now known as the Slash X, where they eventually ran around 3,000 head of cattle. The partnership was dissolved in 1951. Berry subsequently began to raise quarter horses, and now trains dogs. He has since sold some of his ranch properties.

One of the most famous horses he ever owned was the well known "Joker B" who was the sire of several generations of prize Appaloosas. Joker was born at a quarter horse ranch in Colorado in 1941. He was almost destroyed as a foal because the first owner didn't want his stock to be known to contain the Appaloosa coloring. But Joker was rescued and subsequently bought by Tommy Young who boarded him on acreage near Las Vegas, Nevada, where Berry bought him in 1946 for $1,500.

The Appaloosa breed was not thought of as a preferred strain at the time, but Berry recognized the great quarter horse conformation of Joker, different than most inbred Appaloosas, and knew he would make an excellent stud. He then added the "B" to Joker's name.

At first Joker B's stud fee of $50 was thought to be too high and there were few takers. Meanwhile Berry had bred his own mares and a few others in the area. He then sold Joker B to a Long Beach man who eventually sold him to Carl Miles, an oilman from Texas for

$10,000. Miles spent a million dollars advertising Joker B, and later sold him to a syndicate in Texas for $26,800 when he was about 25 years old. Joker B died of a heart attack soon after that!

Besides Berry's cattle ranching, horse breeding and dog training, he is especially noted for his Brahma bull, "Old Jim," which he broke and rode in many parades; he was a big hit. Old Jim was among the first Brahmas ever brought into California from Orange, Texas. Berry stated that only a few Brahmas are capable of being trained. He said "You have to look at them to tell if they have a disposition for it."

One of Berry's regular activities includes driving a team of burros hitched to a chuck wagon all the way to Death Valley each November for the annual celebrations held there. He takes his fiddle along and plays tunes around the camp fires.

Berry said that during the 1940's many of his acquaintances told him he shouldn't spend so much time at the ranch, that if he would just stay in town he could make a million. His reply:

"Well, I was buildin' up somethin', see? So, they didn't do it; what they did with their money is to get drunk, play poker, and they all died a bunch of damn paupers. Every damn one of them didn't have a nickle. I may die the same way, but I've had something in the meantime . . . "

BLACK FAMILIES IN THE BARSTOW AREA
by T. L. Merchant

Mr. and Mrs. Cook came from Oklahoma, arriving in the Barstow area June, 1940. Cook planned to find work in Bakersfield, but needed money, so he stopped here.

The Cook's first night in Barstow was spent where the Marine Base (Nebo) is now built. Cook saw nothing but sage brush and one light on the hill when they awakened in the morning. (He referred to the sloping hill that now includes East Barstow and the Montara area.) As the sun came up, they saw only one house on that side of the hill. They found out later that Elmer Leak had a hog ranch near there, located on Main Street below Yucca.

The first residence of the Cook family was a ranch near the Mojave River, west of the present Lenwood Road, where they raised pigs and cattle. The calves were watered by digging a hole in the pasture, because the water level was only four feet below the surface.

The Cooks lived near the river for 10 years and then moved to a ranch in Hinkley, where the family experienced several floods. During the 1943 flood, Cook remembers crossing the river by crawling on a cable from the washed-out bridge.

One of Cook's first jobs was picking peaches. He was offered a job mending ladders when the employer found more green peaches than ripe ones in the crating boxes. He then worked in a dairy, and was offered a job working in the alfalfa field at $1.50 per day. According to Cook, it was not good pay, but all you could get, and lucky at that.

In 1941 Cook helped clear the brush so Camp Irwin could be rebuilt. He later worked at Camp George near Victorville. His next job was in Oro Grande with Southern County Rock Co. Since then, he has remained at his present ranch where he cultivates alfalfa.

In the 1940's the Prelows, Sharps, and Mrs. McKinney were some of the other black families in the area. Prelow was a bricklayer in Los Angeles, and working part-time, built "practically all of the old brick buildings in Barstow." Sharp worked for the W.P.A. in the highway department.

The construction of Camp Irwin and the Marine Base attracted many new black families. As the area grew, they began to take their place along side the other citizens, working in the progress of the community.

Chapter III

Saddles to Satellites

Way stations and forts
Succor traveling horsemen,
Mankind in transit.

A SHORT HISTORY OF THE MOJAVE DESERT FORTS

by Leonard B. Waitman

Many years before white men entered the desert wastes of the Mojave, Indians traversed the region using trails their forefathers had established before them, stopping at natural springs or water-holes along the way. Desert Indians treated these trails with great respect, for only by careful use and conservation of spring water, surrounding grasses, and woodlands could man long survive while crossing the desert.

The topography of the area, in general, is typical of that existing throughout the Great Basin. The region is marked by broad level stretches of sand and gravel from which irregular barren ridges and hills rise abruptly. On the whole, the area receives scant rainfall. The sparse vegetation consists of cactus, yucca, and bunch grass. The water-holes were formed, in most cases, by seepage of water up through the low sandy terrain.

The Indians used these natural camp-sites by resting, feasting, and then moving on. The most common visitors were Piutes, Mohaves, Chemehuevis, and Amargosas. Petroglyphs and pictographs throughout the desert bear mute testimony of their visits.

The first white man to travel the Mojave wastelands between the Colorado River and the California settlements was the Franciscan, Fray Francisco Garcés, whose fourth entrada from Pimeria Alta to the Gila and Colorado rivers in 1775-76 resulted in an historically significant journey across the Mojave desert to San Gabriel Mission in Alta California. After spending time among the Indians on the lower Colorado and Gila Rivers, Garcés journeyed northward from the vicinity of present day Yuma to visit the "Yamajabs" (Mohaves).

California mission Indians also used the Mojave River route to flee from Alta California to the Colorado. Furthermore, Indian forays from the desert areas into the California frontier around the San Gabriel mission area were annoyingly frequent. In 1819, the California military commander, Gabriel Moraga, led an expedition into the Mojave River Corridor to track down the guilty parties. Little is known of the success of his mission.

In 1826, an American fur trapper, Jedediah Smith, led a small party across the Mojave, guided by two runaway San Gabriel Mission neophytes. This notable entrance into California originated from the Great Salt Lake area. Smith's party of 15 men left Great Salt Lake August 22, 1826, seeking new fur territory. They traveled down the Virgin River to the Colorado River and visited the Mohave Indians, whom Smith states, called themselves "Ammuchabas." After obtaining supplies and the guides, the party took 15 days to reach the California settlements. Smith followed approximately the same route followed by Garcés across the Mojave Desert, up the Mojave River, across the San Bernardino Mountains to Mission San Gabriel. In July, 1827, he left the fur trapper rendezvous on Bear Lake in northeastern Utah and returned to California in August of that year along the same general route he had followed the previous year. This time, however, because of a previous incident involving another fur trapping party, the Mohaves attacked Smith's party as it was crossing the Colorado River and killed ten of his eighteen men.

In 1829, another party of trappers from New Mexico led by Ewing Young and including Kit Carson, also crossed the Mojave basin to Mission San Gabriel and the California settlements.

Between 1829 and the 1840's travel along the Mojave River route from or to the old Spanish Trail and the Colorado River area increased with a complex interweaving of explorers, trail makers, packers, home-seekers, horse thieves, slave catchers, path makers, dispatch bearers, and Mormons. Prior to the gold rush

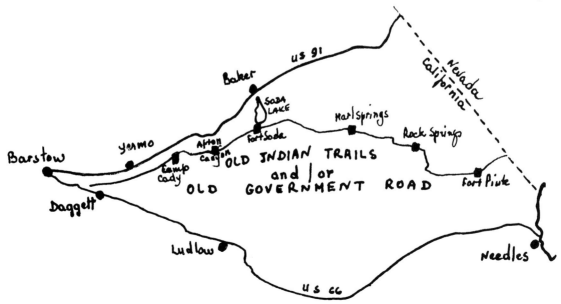

period, the Indians were often friendly and at times even helpful, but, when the gold rush of 1849 began, an avalanche of immigrants advanced across the trails and this endangered the life structure of the Indians in the desert. Therefore, increasingly they took up arms in order to stop the white man's inroads. Numerous contemporary newspaper records attest to the hostility of the desert Indians, and a cry for Army protection and forts along the trails of travel resounded among the citizenry.

By the late 1850's and early 60's the situation had grown desperate and the merchants of Los Angeles and Salt Lake, who had built up a lucrative trade, demanded protection for freight wagons and travelers using what later became the Old Government Road.

To carry out the task at hand the army established a series of forts and redoubts along the major trails of travel. These were strategically placed at the water holes along the trails.

The first bastion to be established as the western anchor was Camp Cady which was soon followed by Rock Springs, Marl Springs, and Soda Lake, later renamed Hancock Redoubt. Fort Mohave on the Colorado, the eastern anchor was built in 1858, serving until 1861 when it was abandoned. It was reoccupied at the outbreak of the Civil War.

Soldiers at these outposts provided escorts for the mails, protected the wagon trains, and aided the miners and ranchers in the desert. Each fort or redoubt was supplied via the nearest large bastion which in turn drew its supplies from either the Upper Colorado Army District, as in the case of Fort Mohave, or from Camp Drum, in Wilmington, as in the case of Camp Cady.

The army redoubts were conveniently placed approximately two days march apart so that horses could be changed for new relay teams. Even so, the toll in horse-flesh and mules was extremely high. A good horse seldom lasted over six months, if indeed that long. Escort duty was brutal to the animals and men alike.

ARMY DUTIES

Army duties at the forts consisted of patrolling the roads and clearing them of marauding Indians, escorting the freight wagons, accompanying the mails, and protecting the miners and ranchers in the area.

Escort duty acted as a welcome relief from post routine even though it was for the most part arduous, boring, and possibly dangerous. The escort usually consisted of three to five men. The men carried their own supplies, their guns—some spencer rifles, but often muzzle loaders—and bag of forage for each animal. Each man was given approximately fifteen rounds of ammunition all of which he turned in after his duty was completed. The horses were given the once over inspection by the officer or non-commissioned officer in charge. When the escort returned from its duty, the horses were inspected once again. Each man was held responsible for any damage to his mount.

Men and officers alike complained about the boredom of escort duty, the heat, and the poor mounts supplied by the army. Either they were too wild to handle or so poor that the rider often questioned the animal's ability to complete the ordered duty. Visiting the miners and the few stock ranchers proved equally hard since these men were often well off major roads and the journey was that much rougher on the animal and rider alike.

Duties in camp included routine menial tasks, such as cleaning out the blockhouses, the corral, or currying the horses.

Reveille was sounded at five in the morning at which time enlisted men and officers readied themselves for breakfast. The morning meal was served at 5:30 sharp. Early drill call was scheduled for six o'clock. Drill usually consisted of the use of firearms and the manual of arms. Although horse soldiers, the men were also expected to drill on foot as infantry.

Sick call was at 6:30 when those too sick for the daily routine reported to the dispensary. The men at the camp—despite their boring monotonous routine—were for the most part healthy. The most frequent disease in camp was dysentary, usually attributed to poor food or more often, poor sanitary habits.

Those who were well enough to carry on with the day's routine policed the area grounds, prepared the block-house for inspection, cut wood for the day's needs, and fed the horses and mules. In addition to these tasks, men were assigned to guard duty, mess duty, and other army camp duties.

Army posts located in the desert changed schedules but little until the beginning of summer. The summer desert heat was unbearable. All but those assigned specific chores and escort duty were recalled from fatigue duty at 10:30 and allowed to rest until the noon meal. After the meal until two o'clock the men were given rest time. At two o'clock the daily routine resumed until 6:30 in the evening when recall was blown and the evening meal served. Retreat was sounded at sundown, which varied from day to day. Finally tatoo was blown at nine o'clock, followed by taps at 9:30.

The O.D. and a corporal in charge of the changing of the guards made their rounds three times during the night at nine, twelve, and one also at two o'clock.

Passes to town were rarely granted. The men who were lucky enough to receive one had few choices to select from. If you were stationed at one of the larger of these desert forts, such as Fort Mohave, you could visit Hardyville or Prescott. Those who were stationed at Cady could visit San Bernardino (a three day trek)—the less fortunate stayed in camp.

Deportment at these posts was typical of that which prevailed at all other desert stations. Usually it was a little more relaxed during the summer heat when shirts could be unbuttoned at the neck and the sleeves rolled up. Often the men were warned of being sloppy in dress and actions.

Desertions were frequent, especially at the smaller forts. In fact, the entire detail stationed at Fort Soda deserted en masse on one occasion. The larger forts had ample men and mounts to pursue such deserters. Deserters had a real problem in just surviving in most cases.

Add to this fact that if the individual headed toward the west from Fort Piute he had to pass Rock Springs, Marl Springs, and Camp Cady. If he was lucky enough to get past these he still had 96 miles to go before reaching San Bernardino. The odds were stacked in the army's favor—a cold deck! Yet a few brave souls did try the almost impossible. As to their success, little is reported in the numerous posts' correspondence.

During 1867 and the early part of 1868, the Indians of the desert took part in several uprisings and burned and plundered the settlements along the Mojave River. Indian problems throughout the desert became so commonplace that hardly a newspaper edition rolled off the press without mentioning the Indian depredations in the Mojave.

Army records speak frequently of Indian problems. Typical problems were cited in the 1867-1868 *San Bernardino Guardian:*

> Station burnt by the Indians . . . We learned the station at the Point of Rocks on the Mojave stage route, was destroyed on last Wednesday week . . . Everything was destroyed . . . Three days before the troops enroute for Fort Mohave were encamped there for a day and a night.

> Still another (Indian fight) . . . The expressman with one soldier as an escort had another fight between Rock Springs and Piute Springs about 100 miles from Camp Cady, on the 28th ult. (The article continues, saying that it was the same expressman and one of the same soldiers who fought at Marl on the 24th. Because of Indian troubles, they had made a dry camp between Rock Springs and Piute Springs. Their animals had been staked out to grass when, after midnight, they were aroused by the snorting of frightened animals. The party reached Camp

Cady without further trouble.)

> Another Indian attack—Hardyville, March 24, 1868. Two soldiers killed, stage mail driver wounded . . . Attacked by 15 armed Indians between Willow Grove and Piute Springs.

For the most part, the Indian attacks were carried out by roaming bands of Piute Indians, the local desert redmen by this time realizing the futility of continuing the struggle against superior forces with greater fire power.

By the end of 1868, the Indians had pretty well been cowed into what almost resulted in semi-surrender. Total capitulation was affected at Fort Mohave when on October 19, 1870, General Price had a meeting of all the chiefs of the various tribes. At this time, the Indians agreed to confinement to the reservations the government had set up for them. Starting in late 1868, garrisons within the redoubt system of the desert were reduced until by 1869 only skeleton crews were left. Then one by one the grand little bastions of the wastelands lowered their colors for the last time. The final end came when Camp Cady, the last post in the long string of forts on this side of the Colorado, lowered Old Glory in March, 1871.

With the final abandonment of Fort Piute, Rock Springs, Marl Springs, and ultimately Camp Cady and Fort Mohave, an era came to an end. The glory of the horse-soldier forts now became legend. They had done their jobs, and now they are only memories. A colorful period of western desert lore had all but faded away.

For the most part, white man himself did what the Indians of the desert could not do. He ravaged his history by destroying the remains of these staunch little strongholds until their remains are hardly recognizable.

In this Bicentennial year it is only fitting that we honor those who settled this great nation of ours, hence, we doff our caps to those unknown desert horse soldiers and their part in this great undertaking. "May their bones rest in peace."

CAMP CADY
by Nancy Ruckstuhl

Along the Mojave River, at a point where the water flows on the surface the year round, lie the remains of Old Camp Cady. The history of this area dates back, at least, to 1776. For it was there Father Garcés replenished his water supply on a trip from the Mohave Indian villages along the Colorado River to the San Gabriel Mission near what is now Los Angeles.

The next recorded visit by white man was that of Jedediah Strong Smith, an American trapper, who was in the area in 1826. Other American trappers and explorers, including John C. Frémont, mentioned traveling the trail and using the area and its water to replenish supplies and get much needed rest.

When gold was discovered in California, the use of the desert trail increased, as did the number of travelers through the area that was to become Camp

Cady.

Between 1850 - 1860, the Indians of the Mojave region grew increasingly restless. They occasionally attacked settlers of the region or travelers of the trails and disrupted the newly organized mail routes. Settlers in California, especially the merchants of the Los Angeles area, who used to trade with the inhabitants of Southern Utah, Arizona and New Mexico, put pressure on the United States government for protection against these Indian uprisings.

Responding to this pressure, Major James H. Carleton of the First Dragoons with eighty of his men established Camp Cady in April 1860.

The camp was named in honor of Major Albemarle Cady of the Sixth Infantry who at that time, was in command of the Army Post at Fort Yuma, Arizona and

Paid in full & $50 Bounty

March 21/66 M. L. Gould

To all whom it may Concern.

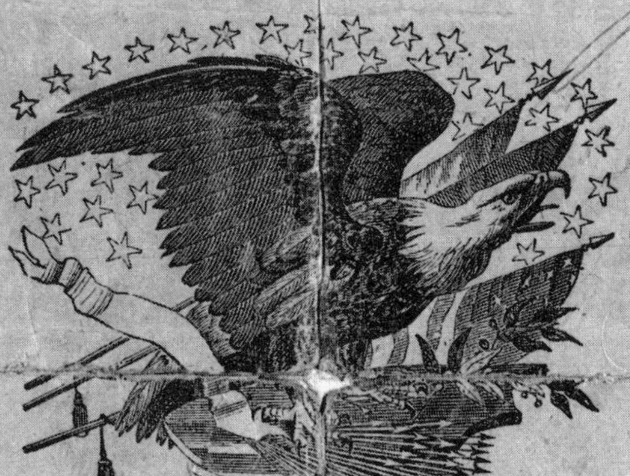

Know ye, That Francisco Rivas a Private of ~~Captain~~ Lieutenant John Lafferty's Company, (D,) First ~~Regiment~~ Batt of Nat Cal Cav VOLUNTEERS who was enrolled on the tenth day of March one thousand eight hundred and sixty four to serve Three years or during the war, is hereby **Discharged** from the service of the United States, this Twentieth day of March, 1866, at Drum Bks Cal^a by reason of being mustered out of U. S Service (No objection to his being re-enlisted is known to exist.*)

Said Francisco Rivas was born in Los Angeles in the State of California, is 23 years of age, 5 feet 3 inches high Dark complexion, Black eyes, Black hair, and by occupation, when enrolled, a Vaquero

Given at Drum Bks Cal this Twentieth day of March 1866.

Alfred Foote

Capt 14 Inft & Bvt Major

~~Commanding the Reg't.~~

a cm

*This sentence will be erased should there be anything in the conduct or physical condition of the soldier rendering him unfit for the Army.

[A. G. O. No. 99.]

John Lafferty

1st Lt Comdg Co

"D" 1st Nat Cal Cav

later commanded the District of Oregon. The site is nine miles from the point known as Forks-in-the-Road.

The first camp was a crude, temporary fort designed to be used only until the Indian uprisings were quelled. The fort consisted of several half-underground adobe huts. Soldiers were responsible for their own food. From this base, Carleton's troops roamed the desert looking for Indians. In July, 1860, a treaty of sorts was signed. Indians would not murder and plunder and Carleton's soldiers would return in the fall with gifts for the Indians. With a signed treaty, Carleton's men made a speedy departure. The camp was completely abandoned the next day.

A relatively peaceful summer followed, but in the fall Indian uprisings began again when it became obvious to the Indians that Major Carleton would not return as promised.

In the 1860's the United States government had more pressing problems. The Civil War began and all available man power was needed in the East. But Los Angeles merchants again set up a cry to have troops once more occupy Camp Cady and other desert forts. During the Civil War years, units of military men were sent on several occasions from Drum Barracks, Wilmington, California, to occupy Camp Cady for short periods. The situation was a serious one. Indians were showing more courage and there was evidence of Confederate activities in the Mojave region, and in San Bernardino. This eventually forced re-establishment of Camp Cady. April 1865 is the date generally agreed to for the second establishment of the base. The troops were California Volunteers, mostly infantry. Since it was impractical to scour the desert on foot, the men spent much of their time constructing post buildings.

The Indian depredations continued. They often came from the mountains on foot with bows and arrows to steal stock from newly established ranches. Indians robbed and burned homes, disrupted travel and mail and threatened lives. Because of the situation, the army sent larger forces to occupy Camp Cady.

But again in 1866, the camp was ordered abandoned. Lt. J. J. Marcher in command at the time, withdrew his troops and returned to Drum Barracks.

Los Angeles was rocked by news of the closure. So vehement were the protests that once again the Camp was ordered occupied. First Lieutenant John Yard, in command of 20 enlisted men, left Drum Barracks enroute to Camp Cady in May 1866. Shortly after Lt. Yard's arrival he was recalled to Drum Barracks to be replaced by Second Lieutenant James Richmond Hardenbergh. Hardenbergh was in command on July 29, 1866, when a crises occurred.

Mr. Crow, a Mormon, living with his family in the area, fired his rifle at a passing group of Indians and then, fearing the consequences of his act, took his family to other shelter and proceeded to Camp Cady to request military aid. Lt. Hardenbergh sent three of his men to Crow's home where they found the house had been rifled of its contents. Hardenbergh had also provided escorts to other desert travelers, as was accepted practice, so Camp Cady was manned with only eight enlisted men. At noon, July 29, 36 Indians were seen passing the eastern bank of the river opposite the post. Hardenbergh decided they were hostile and also concluded they were intending to attack the camp. He gathered his small force and left the camp, traveling up a hill to surprise the band of Pah-Utes. Instead the army was surprised! Three men were killed outright and one

seriously wounded. Lt. Hardenbergh was certain the barely manned camp would be attacked, but it was not. Reinforcements were subsequently sent to the camp and a court of inquiry was held to determine if Lt. Hardenbergh's conduct during the affair was indeed justified.

While troops were never able to subdue the Indians completely, they did manage to quiet them for awhile.

In 1868 the army decided to move the location of Camp Cady. The new location was one-half mile west of the original camp and offered more level land for drill grounds. The new buildings were a decided improvement over the old. Adobe brick, made on the spot, was the primary construction material. Masonry and roofing were completed and some of the walls were whitewashed. Shops, barracks, officer's quarters, a mess hall and kitchens were constructed. Water had to be hauled from the old location, however, due to the salty taste of that at the new area.

But as happened so many times in the preceeding years, forces were ordered reduced: and the Indians increased their raids. In 1870, General Price of Fort Mohave had a meeting with the chiefs of the area tribes and a peaceful settlement worked out which was upheld by most High Desert Indians. During March of 1871 the camp was totally abandoned and sold into private ownership.

In March 1938, the last of Camp Cady was washed away by flood waters.

DID YOU KNOW THAT . . .
by Clifford Walker

Army life has not changed much. The following is a copy of Orders Number 31 (copied exactly as it appears on the records) from Headquarters Post, Camp Cady, California, dated July 20, 1867. It was signed by Lt. Manuel Eyre, Jr.

I. The following are announced as the hours of service at this Post until further orders:

Reveille	Sunrise
Police Call	5:30 A.M.
Breakfast Call	6:15 A.M.
Sick Call	7:30 A.M.
Dinner	12:00
Guard Mount	5:30 P.M.
Drill	6:00 P.M.
Recall from Drill	7:00 P.M.
Retreat	Sundown
Tattoo	8:30 P.M.
Taps	9:00 P.M.

II. At Police Call the men will thoroughly police in and around their respective quarters, the guard relieved the previous evening will attend to the ground around Hd. Qtrs., the Hospital and the Commissary and Quartermasters Store Rooms.

III. There will be no such thing as a Provost Corporal and permanent fatique party as before the arrival of the present Commandant. Details will be made as needed for specific purposes. They will, during hot weather, go to work immediately after breakfast, quit at 11 o'clock, resume work at 3:30 P.M. and cease at 6.

IV. A copy of this order will be posted in the Guard House and the non-commissioned Officer of the Guard will see that the drummer is punctual in sounding the Calls.

Military life on the desert was as interesting 100 years ago as it is now. Here are some letters from Camp Cady in the 1860's.

June 15, 1866

Mr. Dean

Sir, I have the honor to request you not sell my men any Spiritous Liquors it (sic) unfits them for duty, and only brings punishment upon them.

I am Sir very repy.
Your Obt. Ser't.
J. E. Yard
1st Lt. 9th U.S. Inf.

To S. T. Dean

Sir:

I have the honor to inform you, that, after receipt of this communication you will not sell, by charge or barter, give, or dispose of any spiritous, malt, or any kind of intoxicating liquors, to the men in my command with-(out) my written order. Any violation of the above order, I shall exercise the powers invested in me in accordance with the provisions in Act of Congress dated June 31, 1831, Sec. 31.

Jas. Hardenberg
2nd Lt.

Camp Cady (Sutler Dean)

San Bernardino Guardian, Aug. 24, 1867

OUTRAGE BY THE MILITARY. — We have received accounts from different sources, of a gross outrage perpetrated upon the person and property of Mr. Z. F. (sic, F. M.) Deane, living within a couple of miles of Camp Cady, by the soldiers of that post. For some reasons, the soldiers considered themselves ill-used by Mr. Deane, and to get even, a band of them proceeded to his premises, took out what they wanted, held him a prisoner while doing so, and then set fire to the house, leaving him on the desert without food or clothing, or any means of getting away from there. We could scarcely credit that such a fiendish outrage could be perpetrated so near a military post did we not have the most reliable authority for the statement, and moreover, the fact, of Mr. Deane having made his way to town in a most destitute condition. The matter will surely undergo investigation by the military authorities.

Camp Cady   (Sutler Dean)

San Bernardino Guardian, Aug. 31, 1867

TO THE EDITOR OF THE GUARDIAN.

Dear Sir: — On the 8th of August, between the hours of 10 and 11 o'clock A.M., a party of soldiers, some twelve or fifteen in number, of Co. K, 14th Reg. U.S. Infantry, came to my station, two miles from Camp Cady, at which post they were quartered, and commenced shooting at my dog, some twenty rods from the house, then came up surrounding and overpowering me, covering me with three six-shooters held near my breast, at the same time disarming me of my pistol, taking from the house all my arms, breaking open the boxes, robbing the house of its entire contents and literally gutting it. After having secured one hundred and fifty dollars in money, which they found in the house, and searched my person for more, then to complete this hellish villainy, set the house on fire. I succeeded in extinguishing the flames three times; being alone, I became exhausted, and the house, with its entire contents, was consumed, leaving me on the desert without a blanket or a morsel to eat.

During the time that the soldiers were carrying off the goods, the orderly sergeant, second in command, looked on for a few minutes and then retired into the bushes; a government wagon was driven up and all the heavy goods, such as flour, barley, etc., were placed in it, and then started towards Camp Cady. After lying out all night, fearing to go to the post on account of a man named Strouse, having been robbed and disarmed of my pistol the day before, I sent for the Lieutenant who did not come up until the day after, late in the evening; I stated to him my destitution, that the soldiers had taken my blankets, and as it had the appearance of rain, I would like to have covering of some kind; he failed to respond to my request, and gave me no satisfaction. At 9 o'clock it commenced raining and it continued all night; I was without covering and had not a morsel to eat. At the time the men were robbing the house, I asked them what they had against me, and they answered not anything, that they were obeying orders.

The above, Mr. Editor, are the main facts of the outrage, which I can prove by abundant testimony.

F. M. Dean.

San Bernardino, Aug. 29, 1867

San Bernardino Guardian, Sept. 28, 1867

Arrested. "We understand that several soldiers were arrested at Camp Cady, implicated in the riotous proceedings at Mr. Dean's premises. They were brought in here and are now in jail."

San Bernardino Guardian, Oct. 12, 1867

Sentenced. "Five soldiers, who were arrested for participating in the sacking and burning of Mr. Dean's premises, near Camp Cady, were arraigned in the County Court, before Judge Boren, and pleaded guilty.

They were sentenced to imprisonment in the state prison for terms varying from one to three years."

Camp Cady   (Lt. Eyre vs Sutler Dean)

San Bernardino Guardian, June 6, 1868
San Bernardino, June 4, 1868

EDS. GUARDIAN: — The action of the County Court on last Tuesday in granting a nonsuit in the trial of Lieut. Manuel Eyre, Jr., has elicited considerable comment in the community. It is generally thought that the judge ought at least to have let the case go to the jury. The defendant was indicted as accessory before the fact, in advising and encouraging Geo. T. Engle, John Cripp and Thos. Maloney, to commit arson. At the close of the testimony for the prosecution, the defendent's counsel moved for a nonsuit on the grounds of insufficiency of the evidence to prove that Manuel Eyre, Jr., defendant, had advised or encouraged the persons before named to commit the crime. Now it was not disputed but that the crime of arson was committed as charged, by a detachment or party of soldiers from Camp Cady, and that the said Engle, Cripps and Maloney were some of the party who committed it. The evidence against the defendant was that he was the commanding officer at Camp Cady; that in the morning of the day on which the arson was committed, he told the whole company (which was stationed there), in a commanding tone of voice, that they were all cowards unless they 'cleaned out,' or 'burned out' Dean's place, and that said Engle, Cripps and Maloney were in the camp at the time. That soon after and about the time, or just before the burning of Dean's house commenced, the lieutenant ordered a sergeant to go and stop or 'detain' the 'burning' until Strauss' things could be saved. Strauss was living in the house with Dean. That after this, the lieutenant himself went to the place of burning, but sent a corporal before him to tell the boys that the lieutenant was coming. From such testimony, the judge decided that there was no evidence that the defendant had encouraged the crime.

There is no more effectual way of encouraging a soldier to do a deed, than for his commanding officer to call him a coward if he does not do it. It is generally supposed that to encourage a person is to raise his courage, and that to raise his courage you must overcome his cowardice. But in his comments on the motion, the judge seemed to ignore the charge of encouraging, and said the testimony was not sufficient to prove that the defendant had advised the men to commit the crime. From what several of the jury have since said, it is evident the defendant would have been convicted if the case had gone to them, unless he had clearly explained the facts proven against him. It is pretty generally believed, if the defendant had been a private, instead of an officer, that he would have had to take his chances with the jury. But position is everything.

Respectfully,
C. R. S.

Camp Cady   (Lt. Eyre vs Sutler Dean)

San Bernardino Guardian, June 13, 1868

San Bernardino, June 12, A.D. 1868

EDS. GUARDIAN: — There appeared an article in the last GUARDIAN, reflecting on my course in the trial of Manuel Eyre, Jr. The author, I learn, is one Mr. H. C. Rolfe, one of the attorneys for the prosecution, with whose record as an ex-District Attorney, I am familiar. He says 'The court ought at least to have let the case go to the jury.' I regret that I did not let the jury decide the case, not because I did wrong, but, to stop the mouths of those that never have but one idea, and that one generally wrong. The reason I did not let the jury decide, was, the prosecution failed to prove that defendant did advise or encourage Engle, Cripps, or Maloney, to commit the crime of arson as charged in the indictment. The only witness that testified on that point, stated that he could not swear that he ever heard the defendant advise or encourage either Engle, Cripps, or Maloney, as charged in the indictment, and the attorneys having closed the testimony for the prosecution and rested the case, I believed it a waste of time to continue the case farther. The principle of law is well settled that the prosecution must prove the allegations in the indictment, or his case must fail.

Eyre may have been guilty, but guilt must be proved to convict. I did not believe for one moment any juror would convict, until guilt of the accused was proven beyond reasonable doubt. I have conversed with the best legal talent not interested in the prosecution or defense, in the town, who heard the testimony, and some of the jury. All agree that the testimony would not legally sustain a verdict of guilty.

The closing slander in the article is too low and base to notice coming from a man of his record.

Respectfully,
A. D. Boren, Judge.

TRACES CAREER OF FAMED BRITISH PEER
by Helen Graves

Place names and their derivation comprise a study fascinating to most. The Ord Mountains are named for General O.C. Ord who, as Lieutenant Ord, in 1849 surveyed the townsite upon which now rests an important portion of The City of Los Angeles. He also performed the same task for the City of San Bernardino.

Ord came through our desert area and was the first to carry an odometer in his survey wagon. His accomplishments are well documented in many histories.

Ord was the grandson of King George IV of England, according to Dr. James L. Ord, his adopted father, at one time a resident of Santa Barbara. The story claimed documentary evidence and appeared in the *Los Angeles Examiner* on November 12, 1905. His mother, a twice-widowed Catholic, claimed he and two other brothers were born of a clandestine marriage with the Prince of Wales. This marriage went unrecognized because of British statute preventing the Prince from marrying before age 25 and making his succession to the throne impossible by reason of his marriage to a "Papist."

Young Ord, who was born about 1790, assumed the name of the family who reared him, and was educated in Georgetown College and served in the American Navy, seeing duty for two years on the frigate "Congress" during the war of 1812. He resigned from the Navy and entered the Army and later married Rebecca Cresap, daughter of Colonel Daniel Cresap of Revolutionary fame.

Lieutenant Ord and his father came to California with a battery of the Third U.S. Artillery in 1847.

The 1905 story was presented to the *Los Angeles Examiner* by H. D. Barrows, educator and writer-historian of Southern California, noted for his accurate accounts. Thus it is that we learn of the lustre of the name "Ord" in a story more romantic than fiction as we gaze at the Ord Mountains to the southeast of us.

HARVEY GIRLS
by Garland Dittman
(Reprint *Desert Dispatch,* October 7, 1974)

"That's the way Private Pringle likes it," read the World War II advertisement of the Fred Harvey Company. The mythical Private Pringle became a patriotic challenge to the Harvey House employees as they sought to please the traveling servicemen.

Charlie ' B. Willis, of Barstow, has remembered several local stories of World War I. He recalled that soldiers from the troop trains were frequent visitors to the Harvey House in 1917-1918. Charlie spoke of "Dutch" Crooks (Crooks Avenue of Barstow); when the railroad yards were filled with troop trains, "Dutch" would go around telling everyone to call him "Ole."

Barstow's Harvey House fed many troop trains during World War I. The government took over the railroads during this period to facilitate the quick and efficient movement of troops within the United States.

Emotions ran high in Barstow during the war. Charlie further recalled an incident in Daggett involving a giant Frenchman, Pierre LeSage. Following an exchange of remarks in the barbershop, Pierre picked up a German fellow in the next chair and threw him through the front window of the barbershop. Later, fined $10.00 by the judge for disturbing the peace, Pierre handed the judge a $20.00 bill and said, "I'd gladly pay $40.00—it was worth it."

Beginning in 1876, through the World War II years, Fred Harvey's name was found in over 100 Santa Fe depots in the form of hotels, eating houses and newsstands. With ever increasing speed coming to passenger rail travel, more and more trains were passing through the old stops. Fred Harvey dining cars were now taking care of passenger appetites.

By the end of the 30's, over two-thirds of the previous Harvey stops were closed down.

With the coming of WW II, however, many of the old Harvey Houses were reopened, and staffed with grayhaired former Harvey girls to facilitate the feeding of the traveling G.I. Joe.

Mrs. (Addie) Frank Bassett, Barstow Harvey girl from 1927-1967, recalled the WW II days:

> We fed as many as 2,200 servicemen in one day, during the war years. The dining room was called the 'troop' room. The present open front porch area of the building was enclosed on the front, east and west sides. We could then serve 344 at one time. We would, at times, work from 4 a.m. to 11 p.m. to take care of the troop trains.

> We did not feed the traveling public during the war years. The railroad employees ate in the cafeteria—the dining room was for the servicemen. I never thought I'd see the day when we'd have an armed guard at the door to keep the public out.

The Barstow Harvey House was a strategic one. It was the cross roads—a main terminal, for troop travel. One could go northwest to Bakersfield and San Francisco, southwest to Los Angeles, or northeast to the Salt Lake area.

The government paid for the meals, of course, and they only cost 75 cents. There was a ceiling on prices at that time. The servicemen were given all they wanted to eat.

Mrs. Bassett particularly recalled the servicemen's appetite for the Harvey House's freshly baked bread:

> We cut it by hand in those days; a loaf never had a chance to cool. I'd cut bread until I thought my arm was going to come out of its socket. Later of course we bought sliced bread.

> I remember a train load of returning war prisoners. The men said they had been eating worm-filled rice while prisoners. They wanted to eat green vegetables, all they wanted to eat was fresh salad. They couldn't get enough of it.

ARISTO VARGAS

by J.T. Gutierrez

Aristo "Teo" Vargas was born in 1927 on Clark Street in Barstow. His parents, Mr. and Mrs. Valentine Vargas came from Mexico in 1922. Valentine Vargas worked at a rock crusher close to the Mojave River bed near the present State Highway bridge.

During the depression, to supplement family income, they collected firewood along the river using a 1927 Chevrolet pickup truck to deliver the wood to customers in Barstow.

Sixty percent of the population of Barstow was Mexican, about thirty percent Anglo-Saxon, plus several Chinese and a few black families. Dr. Nelson delivered most of the Chicano babies during this time. He was drafted during World War II and never returned to Barstow.

Each year the Mexican section of Barstow would turn out for speeches, street dancing, and parades in celebration of Mexican Independence on September 16 and May 5 (Cinco de Mayo.)

Teo began attending Waterman School in 1933. That school and other buildings in Barstow were built under the W.P.A. program.

There was a big flood in 1938 which did great damage to the old town north of the railroad station and yards. The rock crusher where Teo's father worked, a grocery store, laundry and other buildings were swept away.

In the late 30's the "Okies" began coming into California. Most of these poor people were broke by the time they arrived in Barstow. Many of them had to sell their possessions in order to get gas money to travel on to farming districts.

When World War II began, jobs became plentiful as military bases were opened around the Barstow area. The Navy opened Nebo as a supply depot, the Army opened Camp Irwin for anti-aircraft and tank warfare training; and Yermo was opened by the Army as a supply depot, and later to house Italian prisoners of war. Daggett airport was used by the Army Air Corps to train bomber crews.

The Italian prisoners, housed at Yermo, were permitted to come to Barstow wearing American uniforms with P.O.W. and Italian patches on them. During the weekends the streets were filled with soldiers, even some English soldiers who were instructing the Americans on how to use anti-aircraft guns.

Throughout the war the railroad bridge was sandbagged and had gun emplacements manned by soldiers. Anti-aircraft emplacements were also on "B" hill and the hill east of the railroad yard.

In 1944, Teo enlisted in the United States Army and was on his way to the Pacific when the war ended. He served with the first occupation forces in Japan until 1947, returning to Barstow after his discharge. Around 1948 a National Guard unit, part of the California 40th Armored Division, was formed in Barstow. The majority of Teo's friends were eager to join because it was "easy" money.

In June of 1950, when the Korean War began, the

40th Division was activated. According to Aristo Vargas, the "Fighting" 40th Armored Division became known around Barstow as the "Crying" Division. Many members of this unit tried to resign by contacting Congressmen, draft boards and the Secretary of Defense.

Nevertheless, members of the 40th served in Korea with distinction, returning home to continue their lives on the High Desert.

HISTORY OF THE DAGGETT
INTERSTATE AIRWAY COMMUNICATION STATION

by Department of Transportation, Federal Aviation Administration
Edited by Ronald Johnson

The history of the current Barstow-Daggett Airport may prove more interesting if some of the factors that entered into its birth are known.

Here are some historical highlights in the growth of the small Desert Airways Communication Station, with only an Airways Beacon Site for navigation, into one of the busiest in the nation.

In 1930, the Beacon and its shed were the first structures installed. During the following year, 1931, a well and 40 foot tower were placed in use. Quarters and a flight strip were established in 1932. On January 1, 1932, the facility was established as an Airways Keeper Station. This same year, the marker Beacon was used to establish voice communication with those aircraft that had radios. The following year, 1933, a low-frequency range was commissioned. This was the first of its type in the Sixth Region. The operators would stand 12 hour watches at the station. In their spare time, they pulled a drag over the earthen runways. Starting in 1934, personnel began taking weather observations and relaying this information from Burbank to Kansas City. In 1935, the Northeast course of the range was re-aligned toward Kingman, Arizona.

Starting in 1936, four receivers were in operation and the station guarded the chain frequencies for Trans-Western Air (TWA) and Western Air Express (WAE). Personnel compliment was increased to four men. Also, two teletype printers were installed. In 1937, the teletype printer speed was increased from 40 to 60 words per minute and the weather surveillance area was increased to Great Falls, Montana.

During 1938, electrical power was furnished to the airport by the Southern Sierras Power Company from Bishop. To improve communication, a new 400 watt power transmitter was installed and commissioned in January 1939; in September it was listed as CAA Intermediate Field, Site 10, on the Los Angeles-Amarillo Air-route. In January 1940, a Location Marker Transmitter was put into use as an added navigation aid. In 1941, an Attention Signal was installed on the High Power Transmitter Receiver as a safety measure.

After the Declaration of World War II, various safety measures were instituted and on December 10, 1941, all personnel participated in the first blackout alert. The Fourth Fighter Command issued the radio silence order.

In January 1942, work began to pave the runways under supervision of the U.S. Corps of Engineers. Work was completed and inspection made on May 14, providing Daggett with one E/W runway 6400 feet long and 150 feet wide and a NE/SW runway 5494 feet long and 100 feet wide and one taxiway 5250 feet long and 50 feet wide connecting the two runways. The runways were hardsurfaced and constructed to handle a load of 30,000 pounds, and the field covered an area of 1035 acres. As of March 5 the field was no longer considered a "designated landing area" and landings were restricted to only Air Carrier and Government aircraft.

Shortly after completion of the airport construction, Douglas Aircraft Corporation moved in and utilized this location as a modification center for A-20 Attack bombers, with final destination—Russia.

Numerous buildings, including four nose hangars, three domed hangars, 20 two-story barracks, 20 family cottages, dispensary, administration building, theater, cafeteria and swimming pool were constructed. Several Russian liaison officers were stationed here.

By the end of the year Douglas had assumed full charge of the airport and had constructed a crossing of the Santa Fe Railroad just outside of the main gate to Highway 66.

Prior to Douglas assuming full control, a unit of the California State Guard was detailed to furnish security control. The station garage was utilized as a place to set up cots and any available space in the bachelor quarters was at their disposal. The unit consisted of 12 to 20 men, under the command of a Commissioned Officer.

The nearness of Victorville Army Air Base increased the workload of Daggett by 400-500 percent and a six day week was inaugurated.

On January 9, 1943, the Daggett Tower was commissioned and operated by CAA personnel. It was located on top of the Douglas Administration building.

The field was closed to all traffic except flights on company business with Douglas or the Ferry Command flights, although the field was designated as San Bernardino County airport and was not an Army Air field.

The advent of the Tower aided in easing the Station workload as far as takeoffs and landing were concerned, but added to it by increasing the flight plans, clearances, etc.

In order to give better service to the aviation public, a training program was instituted, consisting of the following subjects: Meterology for Pilots; Pilots Radio Manual; Practical Air Navigation: Civil Air Regulations and Communications Operating Procedures. In addition to these subjects, yearly examinations were given all personnel on Weather Bureau Circular "N"; teletype tests; tape-reading tests; sending and receiving of Internal Morse code at the rate of 20/20 wpm.

Due to the workload in 1944, the Weather Bureau assigned two weather observers to the station.

On July 1, Douglas terminated its activities at Daggett and the U.S. Army Air Force took over the field and utilized it as a training base for P-38 aircraft in gunnery and rockets. Squadrons from as far away as Ephrata, Washington came here to train, due to the outstanding flying weather that prevailed the year around. The airport was redesignated as the Daggett Municipal Airport and the Air Force called it the "44th AAFBU." AAF controllers assumed control of the Tower after CAA left.

With the end of the war, tower operation ceased in October 1945. The airport was closed to all military aircraft and civilian aircraft, excepting those on official government business or in emergencies.

On March 26, 1946, the Army Air Force officially released the base to the U.S. District Engineer who declared everything except the station, as surplus. Arrangements were made through the CAA Regional Office whereby the CAA secured the use of five family quarters for housing. The War Assets Administration assumed control of the installation.

In May, the Weather Bureau removed their personnel and the Communicators resumed responsibility for taking weather observations.

On July 1, the Navy Department obtained the use of the base for the USMC as a storage site for artillery and motor vehicles of the Marine Corps. The area was put into use as an open storage facility and convoys soon began bringing in all types of wheeled vehicles to be picked up and placed on jacks throughout the area.

In 1947, two more frequencies were added to the communication capabilities. On March 5, 1948, one of the first VOR Navigational facilities, in the Sixth Region, was installed on a test basis. In January 1949, a total of 14 inches of snow fell and snowball fights were an everyday occurance. On March 22, the VOR site was put into full operation which greatly facilitated airborne navigation.

On March 11, 1950, the wind began to blow in the forenoon, and reached velocities estimated at 100 mph in gusts, and a steady wind between 75-90 mph. During these hurricane winds, CAA and USMC personnel made "saves" on three different small aircraft on the field with a total of seven people in the aircraft involved. The CAA men did not have time to put on coats or other protective clothing and, as a result, their upper bodies bore multitudes of bruises from the blasting of the sand and rocks.

On August 3, the Commanding Officer of the Supply Depot at Nebo requested the assistance of Electronics personnel of the CAA to aid in meeting a deadline for shipment of military equipment destined for Korea. The USMC was hard-pressed for securing electronic equipment in some vehicles; the Chief Communicator, Maintenance Technician and his assistant volunteered

their services knowing they would not be paid for their labors. These men worked from 16 to 20 hours a day, without rest, for three days, for a total of 152 man hours. The deadline was met and the men received commendations from the CAA Regional Office and from the Commandant of the USMC.

In 1951, monophone communication was installed so airport personnel could talk with maintenance personnel at the VOR Site.

An Air Defense Identification Zone was established in 1952 which still exists.

In 1953, CAA Region Six, which had comprised the States of California, Arizona, Utah, Nevada, Hawaii and the Pacific Islands was redesignated as Region Four, and was made up of 11 western and southwestern States.

On January 22, 1954, the teletype speed was again increased, from 60 to 75 words per minute. Later a "Delta Platform" was erected and all antennaes mounted on it for better transmission.

In 1955, a survey was made which showed that the Daggett Station was the eighth busiest in the nation. This called for the installation of a dual control console. On October 17, 1955, Daggett was assigned as an automatic teletype relay station. In June 1956, a group of Electronic Technicians began installation of Ultra High Frequency equipment for communicating with military aircraft.

During January 1957, five inches of snow fell, the first measurable amount since 1949.

In late July a passenger was blown through the side of a WAE aircraft in flight, and his body was located several miles South of the airport. It was later determined that he had committed suicide. Numerous investigators of CAB and FBI used the station headquarters for two days. Surveys for additional navigation aids continued and sites were selected at Manix, approximately 20 miles East of the airport.

During the summer, the USMC gave formal notice they were abandoning the Daggett Area effective January 1, 1958. The CAA Regional Office prepared to take necessary steps to secure the 20 family quarters, five are presently occupied by CAA families, adjacent recreational area, which includes the swimming pool, playground, water supply system, sewage disposal system and the electrical system.

During the late 1950's passenger service had risen to high levels and people wanted to go further, faster. The jet age was issuing in. The Hector VOR was commissioned May 6, and Manix VOR commissioned July 8, 1958. At the end of 1958, the Barstow-Daggett Airport was being negotiated to be taken over by San Bernardino County. At the close of 1958, the Civil Aeronautics Administration was reorganized and renamed "Federal Aviation Agency."

At the close of 1959, the county was still negotiating for the airport. The Daggett-Gentry Airpot had also moved part of its operations out to Barstow-Daggett in January 1960. The name of this facility was finally changed to San Bernardino County, Daggett Airport. In August, Daggett Airport underwent a second military teletype test which was conducted nationwide, as a prerequisite to assuming military flight service.

The year of 1961 saw the Barstow Airport, operated by Paul Pierce and Russell Riley, abandoned in January and operations at the Daggett-Gentry Airport discontinued on July 1.

A happy note for Daggett was the completion of the much needed voice communication on the Daggett and Hector VORS. Installation of the control lines is finished and voice was commissioned on May 3.

October saw the commissioning of the Las Vegas Radar Microwave Facilities. This carries radar information from Angels Peak Radar to the Los Angeles Control Center.

On May 5 and 6, 1962, the Barstow Chamber of Commerce sponsored a "Fly-In."

Flight Service set up a briefing counter on the ground floor of the old tower building and two tower controllers from Palmdale operated a temporary tower from the old tower cab. The local Buick dealer provided 50 new white convertibles for the pilot's transportation.

Since this is the only active airport near the city of Barstow, the County Board of Supervisors renamed the airport. On June 8, it officially became known as "Barstow-Daggett Airport."

The winter offered a heat of its own kind in what is generally described as the "Cuban Situation." All facilities were moved up to "Defense Condition 3." However, by December the situation was again relaxed.

On January 13, 1963, a record low of eight degrees above zero was recorded. On May 31, the Low Frequency Range was converted to a non-directional radio beacon.

Detroiter Mobile Homes began production during June. A complete renovation of three nose docks and three hangars was accomplished for the production of mobile homes.

On October 31, the Barstow Airport was permanently closed. The Sheriff's Office advised that aircraft landing there in the future would not be allowed to take off from the field but would have to truck the aircraft off the airport.

On December 13, a hygrometer was commissioned for the direct reading of atmospheric moisture.

This station was the second highest in the nation for the delivery of Flight Condition Messages in association with the Flight Following Program.

"Desert Strike," Armed Forces Maneuvers, was held from May through July of 1964, with preliminaries and clean-up from January through September. During May and June the Chief was detailed to Needles to coordinate activities for the Federal Aviation Agency.

The maneuvering area consisted of: Daggett eastward to Kingman, Arizona, North to the California-Nevada Border, South to North of Victor Airway 16. The entire area was closed to civil aircraft surface to 14,500 feet altitude.

There was considerable activity at many of the airports adjacent to the area. A temporary GCA and Control Tower was installed by the Air Force, at the Barstow-Daggett Airport. Interphone lines were installed to Los Angeles Center.

On the afternoon of November 17, a strange occurence for the Mojave Desert began. It had started to snow! Two of the Electronic Maintenance Technicians became snowbound at the Barstow RML site. It was necessary to send a jeep in to tow their vehicle to lower ground. However, the snow was so deep in the area it was necessary for the technicians to walk a portion of the way and meet the jeep. By morning two inches of snow had accumulated on the ground at the airport, and remained for several days.

During 1970, strong gusty surface winds occurred much more than normal, from early spring through September. One of the summer thunderstorms knocked down several telephone poles between the airport and the town of Daggett which caused many hours of teletype and interphone outage. During another thunderstorm a lightning strike on the lines fused some parts in a TD causing an open circuit for a few hours. Fog developed during the early morning hours reducing the visibility at the airport below three miles, and once below one mile. It is becoming increasingly apparent that some of the smoke and haze (smog) is drifting up to the high desert from the Los Angeles Basin.

In March, the FAA Building and Grounds Maintenance Crew established their headquarters at the Daggett Airport. San Bernardino County Airport personnel completed installation of the runway and taxi lights at the Barstow-Daggett Airport in March, and on June 21 the Baker Airport runway lights were commissioned.

As of March 30, the old Apple Valley Airport was closed and the new Apple Valley Airport opened. Also, a study was in process to determine the coverage of Very High Frequency Transmission from the RCAG site (behind the Barstow College) to Lucerne and Apple Valley.

By 1971, air traffic has risen so high that the Daggett Flight Service Station is operating seven days a week, 24 hours a day. They are providing 24 hour weather coverage.

On February 19, one of the worst windstorms in the station's history hit the Barstow-Daggett airport. Gusts were as high as 75 knots. Highest recorded on Weather Log were gusts 55 knots. The 25th of February history repeated itself and gusts were up to 48 knots. Many automobiles had pitted windshields. On April 21, winds were 250 degrees at 53 knots, causing a large military C-130 cargo plane to flip over.

As of December 1971, Total Flight Services increased from 65,649 to 71,866. The increase was due mainly to installation, on June 23, 1971, of a direct line between DAG, FSS and the new Apple Valley airport. The increase was attributed to flight plans and pilot briefings. An Enterprise telephone number was projected in 1972 which will cover Big Bear Airport and Hesperia Airport, and should result in a further increase in services.

Smuggling of dangerous drugs increased with illicit

aircraft activity throughout the area. On October 6, an aircraft was found crashed, pilot dead, 3½ miles south of Barstow-Daggett Airport, in the Newberry Mountains, with 600 pounds of marijuana worth approximately $100,000 in the underground market.

Crossing gates were installed further west of the airport on the railroad. The airport perimeter road was moved to this crossing, removing the danger of low flying planes as a hazard to automobiles, or vice-versa, while aircraft are landing on runway seven.

County hangars and runways were refinished during the year. A new business, that built kitchen modules, was in operation at the airport. Two new ponds landscaped with trees were constructed just east of the swimming pool for the convenience of the general public and visiting pilots. The first fishing derby was held there.

In 1972, a notable "first" took place. The Low Frequency Range Transmitter, which was installed in 1932, the first of its kind for the Western Region, was decommissioned and donated to the Smithsonian Institute. It had been the oldest LF Transmitter in service, bearing serial number 18.

December 1973, total Flight Services decreased from 76,706 to 75,699. This was due to changes in en route frequencies and the fuel crisis.

At the close of 1973, fuel was being allotted on a month to month basis to airports and general aviation was allowed a lower percentage. This, according to the government, was caused by the cutting off of fuel from Arab countries and to no new building of new oil refineries in the U.S.

A new taxiway was constructed in front of FSS joining the main ramp with runway seven. This required moving the weather box and the rain gauge.

In 1974, the Barstow-Daggett Airport gave its hygrometer to the Lemon Grove Fire Department. This was made possible because of the more modern weather gathering equipment installed at the Barstow-Daggett Airport. Also, a National Weather System Facsimile Circuit was installed, thereby providing the Daggett Airport with national weather coverage and national weather maps.

Again, flying count is up, to 83,000, for the month of August. Daggett FSS was designated as a facility for position classification study by NAATS. Representatives from Honolulu, IFSS, TAD, FSS and Washington visited the station. This was for consideration of possible upgrading of the facility, and as the Bicentennial year arrived there have been many fly-ins, increased air traffic and new business environments being added with aviation activity on the national basis doubling every few years. The same growth, or even more, is reasonable to be expected for the Barstow-Daggett Airport.

Barstow-Daggett Airport has grown from a mere beacon and shed, in 1930, to an airport on a major transcontinental air-route capable of being an emergency landing facility for large jets of the 707 and DC-8 variety. It has become an asset to the Hi-Desert community, not only for providing flight service, but recreation as well, namely fishing and swimming. In addition to these recreational facilities, a private enterprise modifying World War II aircraft has come into the Barstow-Daggett Airport.

With the recap of history, it can be seen that the Barstow-Daggett Airport has played an important part in local, national and international history.

DAGGETT ARMY AIR CORPS BASE
by Pat Keeling
(From an interview with James S. Benton)

During the years of World War II at Daggett Air Base, the Army Air Corps tested propeller driven aircraft such as the A-20 and B-26 Bombers; also P-36 and P-38 Fighters. In 1944-1945, P-47 and AP-51's were tested, besides the twin engine split fuselage P-38's. Some of the planes were built at the North American Corporation plant in the San Fernando area and then flown to the desert to add the armaments, such as machine guns and rockets. The testing of such armament was done from the Daggett base.

To test the machine guns and rockets, the Air Corps planes flew over Edwards Air Base, then called Muroc Dry Lake, to the gunnery range. There were outlines of a battleship and wooden structures for pinpoint bombing practice. Bicycle Lake near Camp Irwin was an ideal area for bombing training. Two training P-38's collided over the Bicycle Lake area during the spring of 1945.

During World War II there were many desert training activities for the Air Corps near Camp Irwin. There were emergency landing fields all around the Mojave desert. There was a landing strip at Baker, near the north end of Soda Dry Lake, and remote landing fields at Camp Irwin.

There had been many changes in aircraft through these War Years, but none so great as the testing of jet fighters at Muroc towards the end of the war.

FORT IRWIN
by Celestia Gilliam

Fort Irwin has had a history of activation and deactivation throughout the years. This unlikely spot for habitation covers an area of over 1000 square miles located in the Mojave Desert 37 miles northeast of Barstow.

In the 19th century, Indians retreated there. Later, twenty-mule teams from the desolate Death Valley Borax mines traveled through this same territory on

6 Goffs School remains, used as a Commissary during Patton's desert training, WW II.

2 On Parade Main Street 1941

3-7 Women's Ambulance and Defense Corps - Barstow High School 1942

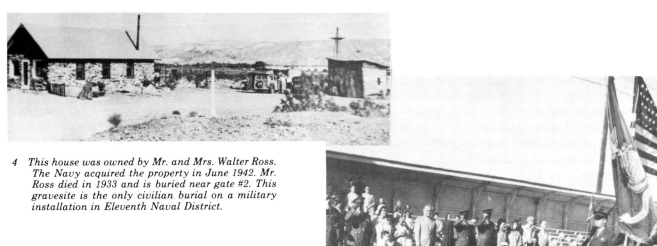

4 This house was owned by Mr. and Mrs. Walter Ross. The Navy acquired the property in June 1942. Mr. Ross died in 1933 and is buried near gate #2. This gravesite is the only civilian burial on a military installation in Eleventh Naval District.

8 Retirement Parade - Sorenson Field Marine Corps 1958

Serving Old Glory

5 Armed Forces Day Fort Irwin 1966

their way to the railroads at Daggett and Mojave. In 1938, the army, needing an artillery and anti-aircraft range, began searching for an isolated spot and sent research specialists to the Mojave Desert. They searched for information about the terrain and water availability. The only inhabitants were miners, camping on their claims.

As plans for military installation advanced, the major problem was with the water supply. They imported geologists who reported that there was no watershed area and if water was found by wells, it would be stagnant and highly mineralized. The project was in danger of being cancelled. Then, someone hit upon the idea of hiring a "water-witch." The "witch" said that water could be found in four locations, which would pump down in twelve hours, but the water would return to its original level within twelve hours. The water originally came from the high Sierras through an underground river-bed. Thus, the plans moved ahead for construction of the installation.

At this same time, miners in the area banded together and opposed the creation of a military reservation because it would withdraw thousands of mining acres. Letters of objection were sent to the War Department and Congressman Harry Sheppard. Nonetheless, the project went ahead and, in August 1940, it was officially designated as MAAR (Mojave-Anti-Aircraft-Range) by President Franklin D. Roosevelt. It was officially renamed Camp Irwin in 1942 after Major General George LeRoy Irwin, a World War I Field Artillery Commander.

During World War II, General George C. Patton, Commander of the First Armored Corps, needed a desert training area for his troops. He was aware of the confrontations to be expected in North Africa. He visited Camp Irwin, inspected the terrain, and as a result, a major training program for "desert commandos" was put into effect.

The influx of the military at Camp Irwin during this period had an impact on the economy of the Mojave Desert. The Post Office had a sub-station at Irwin manned by civilians. One local employee remembers being completely hemmed in, on many occasions, by packages and sacks of letters for the servicemen.

At the end of World War II, in 1945, the Camp was de-activated and was not re-activated until 1951, during the Korean War. Again, because of its terrain and location, it became ideal for tank training and grand scale war games. The firing of the guns and the noise of the tanks would not interfere with civilian industry or residential development.

Full-scale building and staffing took place at this time and the area became a "little city" all its own with housing, commissary, churches, elementary school, library, golf course, bowling alley and swimming pool. It was during this period that Barstow not only enjoyed a business boom with the influx of the military, but many local citizens found employment.

Some of the civilians employed were very young and not used to the grand scale manner in which the army operated. One youth became the Purchasing Clerk for the Post Engineers and was given orders by the Colonel to order all supplies, the Lieutenant, her immediate boss, wanted for building a new tank repair shop. There was no time for bids so the cement was ordered by phone from a local business in Barstow. When the young clerk called and said they wanted to pick up 182,000 cubic yards of cement, the startled businesswoman replied, "All at once?!!"

It was a time of good rapport between the military and Barstow officials and businessmen, an era of an exchange of luncheons and dinners between the commanding officers, their staff and the Barstow citizens. Military appreciation day was well attended at Irwin and they, in turn, participated in local activities. The military band from Irwin was especially enjoyed during parades and other functions which presented a festive air. The only sad moments came from automobile accidents which occurred on the narrow 37 mile road between the camp and town, especially at "Dead Man's Curve."

As with all military bases, single and lonesome soldiers were anxious to get into town. They were welcomed at the USO and invited into homes at Thanksgiving and Christmas time.

The isolation of Irwin provided little entertainment for the soldiers off duty, and many started exploring the rugged North exit by jeep to Death Valley and other places of interest, namely Cave Springs and Saratoga Springs. It was not unusual to see a jeepload of soldiers taking a dip in the swimming pool at Shoshone or the Hot Springs at Tecopa; they were also seen as far North as Ash Meadows, Nevada.

One local enterprising businessman opened a beer bar in the area of Goldstone, near Irwin. He was doing a landslide business until it was not only closed down but his building was demolished. Seemingly, some of his services were less than desirable for a military base!

Camp Irwin became a permanent installation in 1961 and was re-named Fort Irwin through the efforts of Congressman Harry Sheppard. It continued to flourish until 1971 when, to the dismay of the Barstow area, it was closed and all useable material and personnel were moved out. Since that time it has been a National Guard training camp.

Many of those people who came to Camp Irwin in the '50s, feeling they had been sent to Siberia, later decided to make Barstow their home and entered into small businesses or retirement. It is another legendary fact that lends testimony to the lure of our great Mojave Desert.

DEC. 1925—Santa Clause is going to be good to a number of people Christmas morning by leaving them a radio to hear the special program Christmas night. Atwater Kents and Kennedy's seem to be the favorites as their reception for long distance stations and closer to home stations is surprising to all who listen in. Mr. and Mrs. Pence went to visit their twin grand daughters over the Thanksgiving holidays.

WOMEN'S AMBULANCE & DEFENSE CORPS
OF NEEDLES, BARSTOW AND VICTORVILLE

by Pat Keeling

The Women's Ambulance and Defense Corps of America helped in the war effort by mobilizing women into a civilian defense and first-aid group. They were trained by the Army in 1942; Dr. Harry Tyerman of Needles taught them first-aid. Capt. Christeene Welch, a Needles girl now of Sholow, Arizona was the Unit's Army training officer. She later retired from the Women's Army Corps as a Major

One of the Needles Company "L" missions was a passenger train accident, June 25, 1942, between Earp and Calzona, on the Santa Fe. The engineer, E. J. Murray, and fireman F. L. Bentz, were killed and 29 injured when a burned bridge caused the train wreck. It was rumored Japanese internees, detained nearby at Postom, had sabotaged the train. The WADC gave first-aid to the injured, splinting legs, bandaging wounds, and helped remove soldiers and flyers from the wreckage.

The WADC met in Barstow for drill competition and three companies of the Third Battalion were represented. Also at a Needles meeting were Lt. Col. John Cobert of Los Angeles, National Commander and his assistant Commander Rosella Mattmuller of San Bernardino, leader of the Third Battalion, Capt. Ada Henry of Victorville, liason officer, Capt. Clooney of Barstow, Capts. Aileen Watson and J. Henderson of San Bernardino, and Lts. Marie Kelly and Celia O'Neal of Needles. The women gave good area representation in defense on the home front.

The Corps disbanded in the mid 40's. In 1942, General Patton's tank corps troops came into the area to train. Thousands of men were trained over a two year period in Desert Warfare.

THE MARINE CORPS SUPPLY CENTER
BARSTOW, CALIFORNIA

by Lt. Col. James Wilson (Retired)

The Marine Corps Supply Center at Barstow has undergone many changes since it was acquired from the Department of the Navy in 1943. It was first a storage facility, an annex of the Marine Corps Supply Depot at 100 Harrison Street, San Francisco. The General's Flag was retained in San Francisco until 1954 when Major General Roy A. Gulick became the first Resident Commanding General. In the interim, the Center had progressed from storage facility to supply and maintenance facility, and its mission had been increased to carry the major support role for supplies to Marine troops in Korea as well as those assigned to stations west of the Mississippi River in the United States.

During 1958, the electronic supply and maintenance activity was transferred from San Francisco and the center became a complete supply and repair center for all Marine units assigned to the Fleet Marine Force Pacific. Since that time, the status has again changed and the base is currently a major supply and repair activity for the Defense Supply Agency under the Department of Defense. However, support of Marine Corps units continues as one of its major functions.

For most Marines, there are only two good duty stations in the entire corps—the one he has just been transferred from—and the one he will go to next. To many who have served at the Supply Center, on arrival, Barstow was the absolute last choice before direct combat. Some say, however, if a Marine spends one year in Barstow he will return if he can. Only a few get this opportunity while on activity duty, but many do return after their enlistment expires and even more return after retirement. A recent survey has shown that of the many retired military families now residing in the Barstow area, a majority are ex-Marines who have served at the Center since 1943.

The first Commanding Officer assigned to the Center was Major David F. Ross who arrived in Barstow in February, 1943. Since that time, a total of fourteen Commanders have been assigned to the Center, one of these having served two separate tours. The current Commander is Brigadier General Manning T. Jannell who arrived in September 1974.

Fourteen men were in the original complement of Marines assigned to the Center in 1942, when it was known as the Marine Corps Depot of Supplies. The civilian component at that time was 150. The current population of the Center is approximately 700 military and 2,100 civilians. Personnel have always been sufficient to afford Marine Corps combat units with the highest level of supply and maintenance support to assure logistical back-up for the world's finest military force.

The Supply Center is divided into six operating divisions, five located at the Nebo facility and one at Yermo. The Nebo operations include the Personnel and Administrative Division; Comptroller Division; Material Division; Facilities and Services Division; and Plans and Systems Division. The Repair Division is located at the Yermo facility. Operational efforts combine military and civilian personnel, with most in the civilian category. The arrangement provides for continuity of management and technical effort and assures that the latest requirements of field forces are known at the Center, as well as providing up-to-date technical training for Marines. The civilian personnel effort made toward this objective over the Center's history has been monumental and must receive the highest praise from a grateful nation through three wars.

Though the business of the Supply Center is serious in nature, the lighter side of life has played its inevitable roll in the Center's history as well. From early days, a story still told refers to a telephone conversation between a Naval Officer in Washington, D.C., and a Supply Officer at the Center. Desert exercises were being held around Barstow, and a request had been made by the Army Commander for more and faster supplies. The request somehow reached Naval Operations in Washington, and the conversation from there went: "What can you do about this problem?" Barstow—"Very little, all of our transportation is in use." Navy—"We have plenty of landing boats at Long Beach, we will send you as many as you need." Barstow—"O.K., but what are we to do with them?" Navy—"Launch them in the Mojave River, fill them with what the Army needs and float them to locations where Army trucks can pick them up." Somebody had apparently neglected to tell the Navy officials that the Mojave River has been dry since the 1890's except during occasional flash floods.

A Marine Commander, when told that a sufficient number of civilians could not be hired during the Korean War, requested permission to visit the several Indian reservations in the southwest to personally recruit help. He was successful in his efforts and became such good friends with one Tribal Chief that he was made an honorary member of the Tribe. His subordinates at the Center faced a problem, however. His Indian recruits were not used to an eight to five work day and all of the other regulations practiced in the civil service world. When they became tired or otherwise unhappy, they quit and went home. Home for some was as far away as the reservation. This story, however, has a happy ending. Many of those recruits stayed on at the Center and became valuable employees, establishing homes in the community and raising families in our city.

Another Marine was ordered to the Center from a station in the east. His knowledge of Barstow was only that it was east of Los Angeles and that sometime it got a little warm in the summer months. When he and his family arrived in Ludlow in July, his wife asked the Marine whom he had murdered in Washington to be sent to such an awful place. An old timer sitting next to

them in the restaurant overhead the question and remarked, "Lady, there is only thing standing between you and Hell." Taken aback by the remark, the young lady retorted, "And just what would that be, sir?" Slowly turning toward the door, the old man pointed, and with a grin, responded, "It sometimes gets mighty hot on the other side of that screen." What happened to that Marine and his family you ask? Oh, they've been residents of Barstow for more than 20 years now!

COMMANDERS
MARINE CORPS SUPPLY CENTER, BARSTOW, CALIFORNIA

Major David F. Ross, USMC
February 1943 - May 1943

Lieutenant Colonel W.T. Breakey, USMC
May 1943 - June 1947

Colonel C.R. Allen, USMC
June 1947 - June 1951

Colonel H.D. Hansen, USMC
June 1951 - March 1952

Colonel A.J. Davis, USMC
March 1952 - June 1954

Brigadier General Roy M. Gulick, USMC
June 1954 - January 1957

Brigadier General Ralph B. De Witt, USMC
January 1957 - August 1958

Major General George C. Cloud, USMC
August 1958 - April 1963

Major General H. Nickerson Jr., USMC
April 1963 - May 1965

Major General John H. Masters, USMC
May 1965 - November 1967

Brigadier General J.E. Herbold Jr., USMC
November 1967 - February 1970

Major General Harry C. Olson, USMC
February 1970 - September 1972

Brigadier General C.H. Schmid, USMC
September 1972 - May 1974

Major General Harry C. Olson, USMC
May 1974 - September 1974

Brigadier General M.T. Jannell, USMC
September 1974 - June 1976

Brigadier General C.A. Roberts, USMC
July 1976 - present

CALIFORNIA ARMY NATIONAL GUARD
by Captain James T. Biles
Fort Irwin Assistant Administration Officer

The California Army National Guard has trained at Fort Irwin since approximately 1947. Most of the training which occurred here prior to 1950, was anti-aircraft gunnery. Air defense gun units of the 251st Artillery Group and 114th Artillery Brigade came to Fort Irwin from armories throughout the southern part

of California.

After Korea, guard units of the 40th Armored Division, the 111th Armor Group, and the 40th Infantry Division trained at Fort Irwin during both Inactive Duty (IDT) and Annual Training periods. Training included tank and infantry weapons qualifications, tactical operations, and support operations.

A complete list of units of the California National Guard which have trained at Fort Irwin is an impossibility. Due to frequent reorganizations, units appeared and disappeared from the training rolls at Fort Irwin, making an historian's nightmare of the force list.

Units of almost every National Guard in the U.S. have conducted training at Fort Irwin. The Canadian Airborne Regiment parachuted in and trained at Irwin in October 1973. U.S. Army Reserve units of the 86th Arcom, 63rd Arcom, 124th Arcom, 91st MTC, 75th MAC, 416th ENCOM, and 351st CACOM have conducted evaluations and training at Fort Irwin. These USAR units have also come from all over the country.

A "RETIRED" ARMY WIFE
by Germaine L. Moon

What was the life of an Army wife? She was married to a bigamist, her husband, who was also married to another entity named the U.S. Army. When duty called, she became wife number two and, until she accepted her rival, her life was miserable.

An Army wife was international. All ethnic groups were represented. She was an Iowa farm girl, a Southern belle, a Japanese doll, a French mademoiselle or an Ex-Army nurse, but when chatting together Army wives spoke the same language.

An Army wife usually came in three sizes: petite, tall, and pleasingly plump. Above all, she was a woman, although there were times when she wondered . . .

In the middle of the night, her husband answering the phone exclaimed: "Alert!" He left her side, laced his boots, grabbed his field jacket, hastily kissed her and hurried down the stairs. Gone anywhere from a few hours to months, his destination was a field exercise, the Berlin Wall, Lebanon or Viet-Nam. During his absence she would give birth to a baby or break all speed limits driving their ailing child to a military hospital miles away. Then she found herself mowing the lawn, servicing the car, painting the house and clearing quarters.

The word "move" brings kaleidoscopic memories to her mind. If she purchased new curtains the phone was sure to ring and she knew her husband would say: "I am being transferred overseas right away, you will have to pack!" Ready for such an emergency she would scurry through the house for his traveling gear. He would find her winded, sitting on his duffel bag stuffed with neatly folded uniforms, handing over his AWOL bag.

Shortly after the moving company arrived, she began to suspect her husband had a secret pact with the Army . . . In spite of having spent hours sorting, piling and labeling their possessions for storage, household goods and luggage, the "John Doe" movers packed their traveling clothes, leaving behind a battered footlocker containing Christmas decorations! Or they had sent into storage the borrowed coffee pot, complete with grounds, and stained cups while she picked up the children's school records.

She really had little time to grieve over the home she was selling, and the lovely plants she abandoned. She had just broken her children's hearts when she gave their pet away! How difficult it was to explain that international regulations, and too often money, prevented them from keeping it. They would be in tears as the passport pictures were taken and cry again biding goodbye to their friends; smiles returned as they boarded the plane.

She gained the wisdom of a scholar before reporting to any Port of Embarkation. She had the patience of an angel when, harnessing the children to 400 pounds of suitcases and bags, she searched for transportation in freezing rain and haggled over the fare with a New York cabby! Soon she would brandish orders, passports and immunization records and, kids in tow, crossed the gang plank.

Welcome aboard! She sat cheerfully through indoctrination and heard blithering talks against consuming products grown in her native land. To spice her cruise, a storm inevitably broke. Leaving her cabin located on the lowest level, they bumped along interminable corridors and skipped over the results of sea sickness to report for meals upstairs. She was lucky at least, her family wasn't sick; it was another story when hubby traveled along! En route to the new assignment and filled with high spirit of adventure, she knew it was worth it. Tired, coming down the ramp with a smile on her lips and glowing with love, she found refuge in his waiting arms!

She had the flexibility of putty and the stamina of a horse to survive the many roles of an Army wife. He offered her the permanency of a gypsy's life, the miseries of loneliness, the frustrations of conformity and the security of love.

Once, fresh from Paris, France, she faltered and cried, when exhausted, they finally reached Camp Irwin on her first introduction to American life! She knew it was in a Californian desert and shunned the tales of rattlesnakes, black widow spiders and tarantulas, but she had no idea how isolated and primitive it was. To add insult to injury, they were informed that housing wouldn't be available for months. Barstow had little to choose from, and they gladly shoveled sand from a rented duplex on Radio Road before shopping for furniture . . . A year later came the "Berlin Crisis." She was stranded alone with three kids to feed, a new home and unpaid bills. A sergeant's pay did not allow for residences apart! She joined him 13 long months later.

Eventually she fell in love with the desert and years later suggested retiring in Barstow, where they had found lasting friends. It offered a civilian job and, God willing, a permanent home. The children grew and they have gone; but we are still here.

As she hears the reassuring steps and cheerful voice

of the guy who gave her this . . . her heart tells her she was happy being his Army wife, now she delights being his "retired" Army spouse.

APOLLO-GOLDSTONE
MANNED SPACE FLIGHT NETWORK STATION

"TRANQUILITY BASE HERE. THE EAGLE HAS LANDED." "THAT'S ONE SMALL STEP FOR A MAN, ONE GIANT LEAP FOR MANKIND."

The Goldstone Prime and Wing Stations had the proud distinction of being the active link in the Manned Space Flight Network when those historic statements were made.

Leading up to this event were two other Manned Space Flight Projects: The Mercury project and the Gemini project.

The success of each mission of the man-in-space program depends on the reliable contact between spacecraft and earth, which is provided by the worldwide chain of tracking and communications centers comprising the Manned Space Flight Network (MSFN). The Goldstone MSFN Station is one link in the chain and is representative of the highly sophisticated techniques and equipment developed by the Goddard Space Flight Center to meet the expanding demands of spacecraft tracking and communication at lunar distances.

The Goldstone Station, a part of the worldwide Manned Space Flight Network is maintained and operated by the Goddard Space Flight Center,

National Aeronautics and Space Administration (NASA). The primary mission of the Goldstone Station is to provide tracking, communications and data support for the spacecraft of the Apollo and other NASA programs.

The stations of the Manned Space Flight Network are placed strategically around the world in locations calculated to provide optimum tracking coverage. In those areas where land-based stations could not be constructed, one instrumented ship and several high-altitude aircraft are available to augment the network as required.

Land-based stations are of two types: those equipped with 30-foot diameter antennas and those equipped with 85-foot diameter antennas. Twelve MSFN stations are equipped with 30-foot diameter antennas. Basically, the smaller antennas are more suitable for the near-earth phases of the Apollo missions (parking orbit injection, insertion into translunar trajectory, etc.). The Goldstone MSFN Station is one of three land-based stations, equipped with 85-foot diameter antennas. The other two 85-foot diameter antennas are located near Madrid, Spain and Honeysuckle Creek, Canberra, Australia.

GOLDSTONE DEEP SPACE NETWORK
by Community Relations Office
Goldstone Deep Space Communications Complex

This document describes the history of the Deep Space Network from its beginning to January 1976. The DSN is a facility of the National Aeronautics and Space Administration (NASA), Office of Tracking and Data Acquisition (OTDA) under the management and technical direction of the Jet Propulsion Laboratory (JPL), California Institute of Technology. The DSN is capable of two-way communication with spacecraft at inter-planetary distances and provides the control and data-handling capability to support deep space missions.

The historical evolution of the DSN is traced from its early beginnings at JPL with the U.S. Army through subsequent developments after transfer to NASA in 1958. Deep space stations were constructed, and the communication capabilities of the networks were developed along with computer applications as data processing requirements became increasingly more extensive. The DSN advanced from a single-mission support capability to a multiple-mission capability. Research and advanced development activities continuously improved the technical capabilities of the DSN and its support for other programs, such as Earth-based radio science.

DSN Systems

Although the DSN evolved as a consolidation of facilities, its primary function in supporting spacecraft in flight can best be described in terms of its three primary data systems: the DSN Tracking, Telemetry and Command Systems.

The DSN Tracking System provides the configuration that permits the generation of radiometric data at each of the deep space stations and the formatting and transmission of these data to the Control Center for validation. These data—consisting of angle, two-way doppler, and range—are used for trajectory-related computations. The deep space stations generate these data types while radio tracking the spacecraft in angle and frequency.

The DSN Telemetry System provides the confiruration that permits the reception of the engineering and science information generated aboard the spacecraft. The information is telemetered to Earth, formatted and transmitted to the Control Center, and provided to the mission control analysts who control the mission. The data are received on a subcarrier of the same carrier that is used by the DSN Tracking

9   Hadec Antenna, parabolic dish, used for hour angle and declination, 26 meters (85 ft.) diameter. Echo Site Dry Lake

System.

The DSN Command System provides the configuration that permits the transmission of commands from the Mission Control Center to a deep space station and then to the spacecraft in flight. The system accepts coded commands that are processed by a central computer for transmission to the deep space station. The command is then sent to the spacecraft by modulating the same basic carrier used for transmitting tracking and telemetry information. The command signal is received by the spacecraft, decoded, and used to operate equipment on board.

The primary use of the DSN has always been the direct support of deep space flight project requirements for tracking and data acquisition.

The primary purpose of the DSN activities has been the development of an instrument for the scientific investigation of deep space, primarily through communication with, and control of, unmanned, automated spacecraft. The end result of the DSN functions is the placing of reliable scientific data in the hands of scientists—to provide new knowledge about our solar system and the universe beyond.

At JPL, research into the tracking and communication requirements for lunar and deep space probes had been in progress for some time. A large-diameter, steerable, parabolic dish antenna was determined to be the necessary ground adjunct for the Pioneer lunar missions and for the support of expected follow-on deep space missions. To meet the year-end launch dates scheduled for Pioneer, the antenna had to be built and operable in approximately 6 months, and at the same time should represent an advanced and reliable design. An antenna that met a great majority of these requirements was fortunately already in existence. It had been designed for use as a radio astronomy antenna and was being fabricated for a number of scientific institutions. The antenna was a 26-m (85-ft) diameter parabolic dish.

Of equal importance with the choice of the antenna design was the selection of the antenna site. To obtain the full benefit of the extremely sensitive ground receiver, the site had to be remote from man-made electrical and radio interference, that is, away from metropolitan centers but still close enough to be practical.

JPL engineers considered the Mojave Desert, approximately 160 km (100 air miles) north of Pasadena. During March, 1958, a JPL survey team made a series of radio interference tests and selected a remote natural bowl-shaped area near Goldstone Dry Lake on the Fort Irwin military reservation. In April, a construction company was selected, access roads were started, and in early June steel workers began construction on an accelerated basis to meet the scheduled Pioneer launch dates.

During November, construction of the new 26-m antenna at Goldstone was completed. A communications system consisting of voice and teletype circuits was installed connecting Goldstone, the Atlantic Missile Range, and Mayaguez with JPL in Pasadena.

Goldstone

Dr. Eberhardt Rechtin, who led the proposal team and later became the Assistant Laboratory Director for Tracking and Data Acquisition at JPL, had already assembled and was leading the team that designed and built the first antenna at Goldstone, California, to support Pioneers III and IV. The station was subsequently named the Pioneer Deep Space Station.

The antenna was patterned after the radio astronomy antennas then in use by the Carnegie Institute of Washington, the Associated Universities, and the University of Michigan. There were significant differences, however. First, the Goldstone antenna incorporated a closed-loop device for automatically pointing the antenna at the space probe. The electrical simplicity of a steerable parabolic reflector made this a good choice for maintaining continuous contact with the spacecraft. Second, to track the space probe automatically, the antenna had to possess an electrical feed capable of utilizing the space probe signal for driving the servo control system. Third, the antenna had to be able to operate without failure for many continuous hours without being impaired by wind or temperature. The single significant feature borrowed from the radio astronomy antenna was the design of the gear system that moved the antenna. The axis of the polar, or hour angle, gear wheel was parallel to the polar axis of the Earth and pointed precisely at Polaris, the North Star. The declination gear wheel was mounted on an axis parallel to the Earth's equator, which enabled the antenna to move up and down. Since the spacecraft moved much like a celestial object in space after traveling several thousand miles away from the Earth, it was natural to choose a mount that would steer the antenna from one horizon to the other at a sidereal rate, thus simplifying the mechanical complexity. All of these design features were successfully incorporated into the construction and operation of the Goldstone 26-m antenna.

June 1958 - Construction began at Goldstone on the first 26-m (85 foot) diameter antenna station, built initially to receive signals from Pioneer spacecraft; later named the JPL Pioneer Deep Space Station.

November - Construction of the Pioneer Deep Space Station was completed.

December - The first JPL 26-m-diameter antenna deep space station, Pioneer, became operational.

July, 1959 - Construction began on a second JPL 26-m (85 foot) diameter antenna deep space station at Goldstone. This station was to be equipped with a 10-kw transmitter.

December - Construction of the second Goldstone deep space station was completed. Built initially to support the Echo II Project, it became known as the Echo station.

April, 1960 - The JPL Goldstone Echo Deep Space Station became operational.

March, 1961 - First use of Goldstone antenna for radar astronomy experiments; signals were bounced off Venus, providing a more accurate determination of the astronomical unit. Radar range to Venus was measured to within ± 500 km, permitting an accurate target designation for the upcoming Mariner II mission to Venus in 1962.

May, 1962 - Construction started on the buildings at the Venus Site.

June - 26-m AZ-EL Antenna moved from Echo Station to the Venus Station.

October - Venus Station commenced to function. 9-m AZ-EL Antenna constructed at the Venus Site.

January, 1963 - The first radar contact with the planet Mars was made by the 26-m-diameter antenna at the Goldstone Venus Station. Return echoes indicated both rough and smooth surfaces.

October - Construction began at Goldstone on the Deep Space Network's first 64-m (210 foot) diameter antenna deep space station, which was to be known as the Goldstone Mars station.

April, 1964 - Construction began on an interim MSFN S-band control room at the Goldstone Pioneer Deep Space Station.

June - Construction was completed on the interim MSFN S-band control room at Goldstone Pioneer.

September - Construction was completed on the permanent MSFN control room facilities at the Pioneer Deep Space Station.

June, 1965 - The Goldstone Echo station was converted from full L-band operation to full S-band operation.

February, 1966 - Construction of the 64-m-antenna Mars Deep Space Station was completed at Goldstone.

May - The 64-m-antenna Mars Deep Space Station became operational at Goldstone. With this event, the operational range of Earth-to-spacecraft communication became immensely extended.

October - The MSFN S-band control room facilities at the Goldstone Pioneer Deep Space Station became operational.

1969 became the year of great hope and wild excitement in the scientific community. Mariner IX had reached its target—Mars. With its cameras turned on, the incoming data to the Mars Antenna at Goldstone seemed to be distorted. The images were not showing a planet potmarked with craters, but rather an obscure ball. Were the cameras on board malfunctioning? Was the long voyage going to be aborted at the very moment the probe had reached its objective? Hardly! The planet surface was hidden; the cameras were recording and operating correctly and Goldstone was receiving the good data. The data was in fact a windstorm covering the planets. Winds velocity in the storm, 200 mph plus. A Giant Windstorm; a Giant Wind Dust storm.

As the storm started to subside two objects appeared. Tops of mountains was the first opinion; but rather than mountains, the summits were in final reality tops of volcanoes. The largest volcano found in our solar system; named Nix Olympica. The volcano is some 315 miles across its base and stands 15 miles above the valley floor.

Another discovery later appeared. The appearance of what looks like dried up river beds, some several hundred miles in length and with the meandering effect of erosion cut by running water.

Also as the photos were put together another unusual surface feature came together. A Giant Rift Valley; so long it would span the entire United States and our Grand Canyon would fit into one of its smaller tributaries. Its impressive dimensions—3000 miles in length; 75 miles across; and 4 miles deep.

These discoveries answered and at the same time raised several new questions; but the one question in the minds of many is life. Life on Mars! With Mars the nearest planet and with the best chance of supporting a life form, it was inevitable that the question needed to be addressed. The Viking Project launch in August 1975 attempted too answer that question. In 1976, a lander separated from the orbiting spacecraft on command from the Goldstone Complex and landed on the planet surface. There it began its prime objective: "The scientific exploration of the planet Mars with the special emphasis on the search for life."

The 64 meter Mars antenna sent the command to the Viking spacecrafts which released the landing vehicles and initiated the ultimate descent to the planet surface. The lander performed its life-seeking experiments and video photos of the Marscape.

Currently, Goldstone through Pioneer, Echo, and the Mars station is providing tracking support for Pioneer X and XI, Helios I and II as well as Mariner X spacecrafts.

The future of the Goldstone Complex will include updating major control room equipment subsystems and antennas for future Deep Space Missions.

Chapter IV

The Lure of Riches

Burdens on burros
Searching for El Dorado
Over the next hill.

SETTLING THE MOJAVE TRAIL

by Clifford Walker

The Mojave Desert is still a frontier—an outpost of civilization—as it has been ever since the trek of Father Francisco Garcés in 1776. The reality is that this desolate area was settled before much of the good farmlands in more favored parts of California were occupied. The ancient dry lands of the Paiute, Chemehuevi, Serrano and Mohave Indians were rich in the minerals that new Californians coveted. The new Anglo owners of New Mexico and California were more vociferous in their demands for roads, communication, and commerce than their Spanish and Mexican predecessors had been. Desert Indians were pacified early. Finally, the demand for agricultural products helped establish agricultural communities in the desert. When Solomon Carvalho's "fairyland" bloomed with hay, barley, and alfalfa, the desert became truly settled.

Successful prospecting gave the impetus to early Anglo settlement in the desert. The forty-niners who rushed through the desert to seek gold in California ironically passed within a few yards of a rich gold area—Salt Springs—located a few miles south of the great bend of the Amargosa River. The first recorded discovery of gold occurred when the seven Mormon wagons with Jefferson Hunt in 1849 camped at the mesquite-covered brackish creek called Salt Springs. James Brown recalled that the discovery was made in the narrow pass at Salt Springs, and that after leaving there he and several others could not resist going back to find more gold. Addison Pratt entered the discovery of gold in his diary of December 1, 1849. He said Hunt, Rowan, and a son of Mr. Forgs (Forbes) made the discovery.

When the Hunt train straggled into San Bernardino and the Mormons talked with Isaac Williams at Rancho Chino, their news initiated a gold fever in Southern California. The *Los Angeles Star* of May 17, 1851, summarized the activity that followed. After the discovery was made by Mr. Roan (Sic), B.D. Wilson (later mayor of Los Angeles) outfitted a party for a gold hunting safari on the Mojave River Trail. Isaac Williams hurriedly sponsored his own party to the desert. Shortly afterwards San Francisco entrepreneurs organized the Desert Mining Company, and Southland citizens formed the Los Angeles Mining Company. The rivals laid out their claims and worked side by side in the desolate desert. One company made an arrastre for gold crushing at Salt Springs, and located a smelter somewhere on the Amohave (Mojave) River. The *Star* mentioned brackish water at Agua de Tamoso (Bitter Springs) as being unpleasant to the miners at first, but later fresh water had an "insipid and flat taste." The *Star,* or its informants, probably meant the brackish water at Salt Springs, since both springs have saline-tasting water.

No record exists of the exact time when mining started at Salt Springs; but Cheesman noted in his diary, during the winter of 1850, that miners were working a quartz ledge one-eighth mile from the road. He recalled that one of the men was a sheriff of San Jose, and another a Mr. Yount. While camped at Bitter Springs, the exhausted emigrants with Cheesman were surprised to see a rider gallop up from the south, jump off his horse, and let it loose to drink. Without saying a word the rider rushed to the shade of a mesquite tree, yanked out a copy of the *New York Herald* and began reading. Cheesman ascertained that this man, a nephew of Aaron Burr, was an employee of one of the companies at Salt Springs.

At least one of the companies prospered. On June 10, 1851, the Board of Trustees for the Desert Mining Company ordered one dollar per share to be paid each month for the next four months. Others intended to exploit the treasures in the desert. On November 8, 1851, the *Star* announced that a party of 30 men passed through Los Angeles with enough provisions to last all winter, and that they were going to make a prospecting tour of the Mojave River and the desert. The mining rush that brought wealth for over a hundred years was on.

Though mining was a continuous asset to the desert, it had the characteristics of a bright flame that quickly died out in one area, only to be kindled in two or three other desert locations which also subsequently died out. This process has continued until the present, with the total effect of bringing wealth to cities like Los Angeles, San Bernardino, and Bakersfield, as well as establishing key settled areas in the desert, namely Daggett, Barstow, Victorville, Mojave, Needles, and Lone Pine.

The mining at Salt Springs was short-lived. At least one of the companies stopped operations in July of 1852. According to a report in the *Star*, the Salt Springs Mining Company, probably a branch of the Los Angeles Mining Company, planned to negotiate a transfer to foreign capitalists. The editor chided Los Angeles citizens for not capitalizing the enterprise so that a proper type of ore-crusher could be purchased. The Desert Mining Company had suspended its operations by August 15, 1853, when Gwinn Heap and Edward Beale found the remains of houses and the abandoned Mexican quartz crushers (arrastre) there. Some mines reopened, however. The *Star* of September 29, 1860, reported three arrastres operating at Salt Springs. The ore in the area yielded $2,500 per ton. Mrs. J.A. Rousseau, coming through the Mojave Trail in December, 1864, noticed what she called a dilapidated-looking place—four houses by a quartz mill, destroyed by Indians. She heard that three men had been left to take care of the operations and that they were supposedly killed by Indians two months before.

In the meantime other mines were being worked. In 1857 San Bernardino County issued deeds for lead and silver mines on the desert side of the San Bernardino Mountains. But, the wealth of the San Bernardino

Mountains lay uncovered for three years. In May, 1860, William F. Holcomb discovered gold in these mountains and a flood of miners soon combed the area. Then, for a short time, activity blazed. Individual miners extracted up to $50.00 worth of gold a day in 1860, and they took a total of over $350,000 in gold from the aged mountains in 1861. In 1861 Bellville became the largest voting township in San Bernardino County. More than 40 people were shot there, most of them in retribution for crimes, alleged and real. The mountain mining continued for a decade, but the operations dwindled, involving only 40 men in 1868, whose wages varied from two to six dollars a day.

At the other end of the Mojave Trail, Peg-leg Smith unsuccessfully prospected on the Colorado River in 1854. Peg-leg unfortunately explored the wrong spots, for in 1853 Francois Xavier Aubry, looking for a railroad route, had discovered gold in the coarse sand and in the heavy black sand on both banks of the Colorado River about 50 miles south of the present Hoover Dam. The Mohave Indians, however, were too numerous and too dangerous for Aubry to concentrate on prospecting. Since Aubry's diary was published by the *Santa Fe Gazette* on September 24, 1853, perhaps Peg-leg Smith made his prospecting excursion as a result of hearing or reading about Aubry's discovery.

As early as April, 1861, miners were prospecting along the Colorado River in Southern Nevada. In January, 1862, when gold was discovered on the Colorado just seventy miles north of Fort Yuma, the rush to the Colorado River Basin began. Soldiers in western Arizona panned gold, one making $60 a day near Camp Whipple. Some prospectors found nuggets worth from $3 to $40.

Other desert areas in the 1850's did well. *The Wilmington Journal*, September 28, 1866, reported that the Argus District and Slate Range were rich in silver. The lodes were well defined. On the 1868 Bancroft Map of California, four mining districts had been established on the Mojave Desert: Argus and Slate Range between Death Valley and Walker Pass, Salt Springs near the Amargosa River, and the San Bernardino District encompassing the San Bernardino Mountains and Lucerne Valley. Five districts existed just east of the Colorado River in Arizona.

Although prospectors were busy in the 1870's with mines in the Panamint Mountains, Owens Valley, and Arizona, mining operations soared to ever greater heights in the 1880's. Jacob Rentchler opened the Oro Grande Mine and worked it with Chinese coolies. The Watermans—R.W. Waterman, J.S. Waterman, W.S. Waterman, and T.A. Waterman—were finding good mines almost every year. They found eight in 1881. R.W. Waterman and John Porter started near Barstow what became one of the leading silver mines in California. They built a complete town including stores, boarding lodgings, houses, a school, and offices. On the Mojave River, just four miles south of the mines, a 10 stamp mill, driven by an 80 horse-power engine, operated 24 hours a day in two shifts of 12 hours each.

Also in the 1880's the famed Calico miners began their operations, creating a town of over one thousand. The town supported the *Calico Print*, a weekly newspaper, from 1882 to 1887. This informative and amusing paper had advertisements from Los Angeles, San Bernardino, and San Francisco, as well as from the local mining areas. It served the once proud communities, or company towns, of Providence, Ivanpah, Mescal, Alvord, Oro Grande, Grapevine, Death Valley, Daggett, and Barstow. It featured such articles as how a woman kisses a tobacco chewer, a contest between two drunks in bed who were shooting at a door knob, and a felonious assault in the street where the victims were struck by a volley of eggs. The mining wages, according to the *Calico Print*, were a healthy $4.00 a day in 1882.

Prospectors exploited other areas and minerals during the '80's. The Amboy and Bonanza King mines started in the eastern part of San Bernardino County. Crude cement and lime kilns were established at Oro Grande in 1887. Borax mining spread from Searles Lake to Death Valley and then to the East Calico Mountains.

In 1888, San Bernardino County produced more silver than all other California counties together— $1,200,000, out of $1,700,000. Even when the low silver prices caused mines in Calico, Daggett, and Victor to be idle in 1892, the county mined $47,037, in gold and $67,022, in silver. The following year it increased to $148,000, for gold and $447,020, for silver. Mohave County in Arizona Territory also produced more silver than all other counties in Arizona.

Although the settlement of the entire length of the Mojave Trail was laid on a mineral foundation, the vicissitudes of mining fortunes sounded the death knell to community after community. Of the township of Bismark, east of Calico, only foundations, bed springs, and rubble give any clue that many workers lived and sweated in the roasting mines near the now cavernous and undermined hills. Not one building remains at the site of Marion, a settlement between Daggett and Calico where the Pacific Coast Borax Company built a crushing and drying plant. Marion was the center of a railroad (which has also disappeared) that ran from Daggett to the Colemanite beds in the Calico Mountains. Each year hundreds of deer hunters and picnickers traipse over the site of the once-populous city of Belleville in Holcomb Valley without even knowing it existed. Salt Springs is only a few hundred yards from the Baker-Shoshone road, but not even a sign marks the spot of this desert mine—just debris, rock foundations, and brackish water.

Throughout all the desert mining activities, year after year, came demands for freight, supply stores, transportation and finally agriculture products closer to the mining communities. The mining helped settle the Mojave Desert.

GHOST TOWNS AND CAMPS OF THE MOJAVE DESERT

by Jack Wright

Today people can travel over 100 miles across the Mojave Desert without seeing one shack, but this has not always been true.

From the 1860's to the 1900's, especially in the 1880's, this desert had quite a large population. Most of those old settlements are now ghost towns, and in some cases only general locations are remembered; others have been forgotten entirely. Yet, in these towns and camps, people lived and died, had hopes and dreams, and helped build our country.

There was a railroad—The Tonopah and Tidewater Railroad which ran from Ludlow north, up past Death Valley. The towns and stations along it from south to north were: Ragtown, Stedman, Broadwell, Mesquite, Crucero, Rasor, Silver Lake, Riggs, Valjean, Dumont, Sperry. There were numerous towns and camps not served by the railroad. In the Mountain Pass area there was Mescal, and on the Ivanpah-Lanfair road there were Ivanpah, Vanderbilt, Barnwell, Hart, Lanfair and Von Trigger Springs. The mining camp of Providence was in the central eastern Mojave. Some of these towns, or at least the sites, still remain. In the Alvord Mountains, near the Old Spanish Trail, is the old mining camp of Alvord; in the Calico Mountain area

there were: Calico, Borate, Marion, Bismark, Goblerville.

North of Barstow one can find the sites of: Coolgardie, Crutts, Goldstone and Copper City; in the Randsburg-El Paso Mountain areas, there are: Randsburg, Goler, Garlock, Cuhady Camp and Holland Camp. Between Baker and Halloran Springs, on the north side of the freeway, is located Cree Camp; in the Avawatz Mountains is the town of Crackerjack. The 29 Palms area had a town named Dale that moved three times.

In addition to the towns and mining camps there were several military posts. From east to west they were: Fort Paiute, Camp Soda Springs, Camp Marl Springs, Rock Springs, Soda Springs (Hancock redoubt) and Camp Cady.

Many of these towns and camps have long since been abandoned and all traces of them have vanished. Some remain as recognizable, even viable places. Relics of others may exist, but they are off the present day main highways. To some history buffs, these old names may evoke a sense of nostalgia strong enough to bring them out onto the trail of rediscovery.

THE DISCOVERY OF THE SILVER KING MINE IN CALICO MOUNTAINS

by G. Frank Mecham

(Reprint from *The Pioneer Cabin News*, San Bernardino Society
of California Pioneers, San Bernardino, California 1968)

Foreword by Harold B. Mecham

There have been many and varied accounts of the discovery and locating of this famous mine—some of them, of course, fairly accurate—but erroneous versions have been given such wide publicity that I now write the entire account, as the leader of the locators— my father—told it many times, and wrote it, in the simple, direct language of the pioneer, without embellishment. His memory of people and events, of desert scenes and trails, he retained like living pictures . . . the desert he loved and knew so well.

We know that pioneers, in general, were a rather silent people, seldom even taking time to record events; treating their discoveries and accomplishments in a humble, matter-of-fact way. We have lost so much by their silence. When we were young, most of us did not realize fully, how important a part in history our parents and grandparents had lived. And so, we did not listen with the attention we should have, and many accounts were lost with their passing.

If we have what we believe is a true version of an episode in that history . . . and don't tell it . . . we have only ourselves to blame, if a different version gains general acceptance. And so, I present this brief account.

THE ACCOUNT

When my father, Lafayette Mecham, first established the Fish Ponds station, in 1865, he had a contract to supply hay to Camp Cady, the military post 15 miles down the river from Fish Ponds. He had neither a horse or wagon, so at first he cut the hay with a butcher knife, stuffed it into sacks and carried them out to the road, where passing wagons took them to Camp Cady. (A few years later, he purchased one of the first mowing machines in this part of the country.)

The native gayote grass (pronounced Guy'-o-ty) grew in great patches over hundreds of acres of the river bottom land, especially up the valley from the Grape Vines (where Barstow was later built.)

With hay selling at $80 a ton, it wasn't long before he had made enough to buy a horse, which simplified the hauling problem.

But it was only a month later, with the horse staked out in back of the house, that Indians slipped up in the night and made off with him. When father got up in the morning and saw the Indian tracks, he started in pursuit right away. The Indians were giving quite a bit of trouble at that time, and one always carried a gun whenever he left the house, and always kept a sharp look out all the time. He followed the tracks across the river and up over the Fish Ponds mountains, across the dry lake to the foot of Calico mountain. (It had not been named at that time.) The trail led into the mountain and up over the summit. When he could look over into the valley beyond, and could see nothing of the Indians, he turned back.

In coming down the mountain, he crossed over the big red ledge that was later to become famous as a great silver producer of the 80's and 90's.

He often spoke of going back to work the vein. He tried to interest others without success. One, a prospector by name of Dan Ingersoll, whom he had met on one of his trips to Arizona, said he didn't think much of the mountain for prospecting . . .that 'they were all burned out' . . . So he went into what are now the Ord mountains, where he located several claims. A few years later the Ord Mining District was formed, and my father was the district recorder.

In 1881, R. W. Waterman, later Governor of California, relocated the old Lee mine. Lee had located it as a quick-silver mine, but it proved to be rich in silver. (It was said that a traveler came upon Lee one day, sitting on a rock at his 'quicksilver' mine, whittling shavings from a specimen of pure silver, unaware that it was anything of value.)

This Waterman discovery brought a new interest in mining, so, when a man by name of Potter, and his partner Loveland, made a new strike, which they thought was the lost Alvord mine, my father and I went to look over the country. But we soon discovered the prospects were not extensive enough to bother with.

Returning, father told me to get Uncle George Yager to go with me and prospect the red ledge he had so often spoke about . . . he was 'getting too old for prospecting.'

Back in San Bernardino, I went to see my Uncle. He said, "Yes, I'd like to go; let's see Huse Thomas, and get him to go with us." We found Huse in the Sheriff's office, along with Tom Warden and the sheriff, John King. They all said they wanted to be in on it, the sheriff offering to finance the trip, if we needed it, and also furnish provisions for our families while we were gone. So that was the way the King Mine Company was formed.

Four of us—Huse Thomas, Tom Warden, George Yager, and myself—started out as soon as we could get things together. We established our camp at The Grapevines (later, it became Waterman—then Barstow.)

It was here that we heard a man by name of John Peterson refered to the mountains we were headed for as "that calico-colored mountain," and that name stuck. That was the first time we had heard the name used.

The ledge we were going to locate was about eight miles from our camp. We started out early in the morning, "Doc" Yager driving the team. Huse Thomas remained in camp at The Grapevines. When we got within a mile-and-a-half of the ledge, Tom Warden and I got out of the wagon and walked on ahead. Reaching the ledge we constructed the monuments and put in the location notice, naming it the Silver King. (This was in the Spring of 1881.)

The mine proved to be very rich, the ore milling at about $200 a ton. We had ore that assayed as high as $16,000.

(Later, Frank's brother Charles, working as a miner in the King Mine, uncovered a rich vein that led to making it the biggest silver producer in the State, during the mid-80's . . . H.B.M.)

I hear, and read, a good many stories now (in the 1930's) as to who discovered the Silver King. There is no one of the original King Mine Company living now, except me, to tell the true story of its discovery and location.

THE WATERLOO MINE
by Greg Morris

The town of Calico is situated 12 miles east of Barstow and four miles north of Yermo, in the Calico Mountains. The silver boom of 1881 was the reason for Calico being built. People of all kinds came from everywhere to find their fortune in the silver strike. Others came, not because of the silver strike directly, but to open businesses. There were store-keepers of all sorts, bartenders and adventurers.

The actual discovery of silver was credited to three miners, John McBride, Larry Silva and Charlie L. Mecham. The original discovery was made at the head of Wall Street Canyon. These miners were looking for the other end of the Comstock Lode. Little did they realize the immensity of the rich silver deposit that was to follow their discovery.

The Southern Pacific and Atlantic and Pacific Railroad played an important role in the silver boom. Without rail transportation, the miners had to take their silver by wagon to Oro Grande, some 40 miles away. The railroad ran to within 5½ miles of the Waterloo Mine.

The Waterloo Mine was owned and operated by the Oro Grande Mining Company. The mine was located two miles west of Calico. A description of the mine comes from the 1888 - 1889 report of the State Mineralist of California:

This mine, with all the tunnels combined, was 1900 feet long by 600 feet wide. It ran nearly east and west, but dipped south 60 degrees, varying in width from 10 feet all the way to 85 feet. This mine opened with a 350 foot shaft, accompanied later by a 604 foot tunnel. For the men to reach the vein, they had to drill 120 feet straight down. In all their drilling they found no water. The mine contained a smooth hanging wall which ran for several hundred feet. It was of a bright red color from the iron oxide in the rock. The foot wall of the mine was of a rough surface. There were four

1 J.B.'s Prototype Traction Engine built in San Francisco, 1889

4 J.B.'s wife,

Libbie Osborn - Daggett

2 Jonas Bertram Osborn

5 Daggett's New Arrival - Osborn's self propelled wagon

6 Permanent resident at Alf's Shop no match for the desert sand

3 Osborn Grader

7 Bill La Montain and Markie Garinger dismantling the "vision" for scrap iron in WW1

levels to the mine. The first was 625 feet long, the second was 509 feet long, the third was 690 feet long, and the fourth was 120 feet long. At each level, ore was found. There were developments made involving each level. The fourth was to be 120 feet, the third 500 feet, the upper level 200 feet, with 200 feet cross cutting with three winzes of 85 feet each (a winze being a small inclined shaft from one level of the mine to another).

The work done on the mine was by a Baker horse power hoist, single hand drilling, using Giant and Safety Nitro powder. The hand drilling was at the rate of one to four feet per day.

The men who worked the mine used stopes (three sides of a square used to hold up the roof of the tunnel when ore is removed) made of pine from Flagstaff, Arizona. The plan for removal of ore was to stope every other block, leaving immediate blocks standing. To stope is to excavate up or down from a level in steps. This lowers the expense of using timber. The other blocks were removed and the space was stoped.

Only 25 feet of the width of the vein was being mined, yielding $25 per ton. Two men could break enough ore to keep 15 stamp mills crushing about 30 tons a day. The ore was jaspery quartz. The quartz was of a heavy spar, compact siliceous rock containing alumina. The rocks all contained horn silver. In some of the rock they found up to 1000 ounces of silver per ton of rock. The rock also contained carbonate of lead and silver in the form of chloride.

The Oro Grande Company, in order to haul all the silver the Waterloo Mine produced, had to build 6 miles of wagon road and 5½ miles of railroad to Daggett. Before the wagon road and railroad were built, they had to haul the silver 40 miles to the stamp mills in Oro Grande.

All the ore produced in the Calico Mountains had to be treated. The silver produced by the Waterloo Mine was treated in the mine by the Boss Continuous Amalgamation Process, costing $4.50 per ton.

The miners had 9 grinding pans, 27 pans for amalgamating and 2 pans for cleaning up. There were 12 miners who used these pans. The stamps, pans and the settlers (or miners) were arranged in 3 parallel rows. There were pans and settlers at the end of the line of stamps. Each row contained 4 batteries of 5 stamps, 3 grinding pans, 9 amalgamating pans and 4 settlers.

The pulp was conveyed by iron pipes, instead of wooden troughs. The mine was illuminated by incandescent lights. The lights were driven by a magnificent coal-fueled steam engine. The transmission of power was by grooved pulleys and ropes. When the mine opened, it employed 26 men, but before it shut down, the number rose to 100. The wages for miners and millers were $3 per day; the timberman received $3.50 per day.

The Waterloo Mine contained a very small vein, which was referred to as a vein for convenience only. It was a good mine, but not a rich one.

Walter Alf, of Daggett, said, "In 1894, the Waterloo Mine shut down for good."

In the 15 years the silver boom lasted, some 86 million dollars worth of silver ore was brought to the surface. The strike was so big that the population of Calico rose to 3,500 inhabitants. The Waterloo Mine, like all other mines, helped to attract more people to the Calico area.

It seemed, with this strike, that Calico would become a permanent town, even though it had burned to the ground 2 or 3 times. But, as the strike came to an end, so too did the mining town of Calico.

Appendix A Statistics

Length of shaft on incline – 350 feet • Verticle depth reached in mine – 125 feet • Length of ore shoot – 600 feet • Width of vein – 10 -85 feet • Character of hanging wall - Smooth slate • Number of men employed - 26 • Wages paid in mine – $3 per day • Length of wagon road – 6 miles • Length of railroad – 5½ miles • Method of treating ore - Boss process • Number of stamps in new mill – 60 • Weight of stamps - 850 pounds • Drop of stamps – 6½ inches • Drops - 100 per minute • Duty per stamps – 3 tons in 24 hours • Kind of shoes and dyes - Steel • Cost of shoes and dyes — 9¢ per pound Kind of screens – No. 30 brass wire • Kind of pans — Boxx • No.of pans for grinding – 9 • No. of pans for amalgamating - 27 • No. of pans for cleaning up — 2 • No. and kinds of feeders — 12 Hendy • No. of men required in mill - 21 • No. of stamps in old mill — 15.

MINERS IN POLITICS
by Pat Keeling

Several mill and mine owners from the early days of the Mojave River Valley became politicians and governors of the State of California.

John Daggett, owner of the Pioneer Quartz Mill (referred to as Hawley's Mill) at Forks in the Road, was Lieutenant Governor from 1882 - 1886 under Governor George Stoneman. He was also owner of the Sioux, Bismark and Odessa Mines. He sold the businesses in 1883. In prior years, Daggett was in the California Assembly, and became President Pro Tem of the Assembly in 1882. He later became Superintendent of the San Francisco Mint from 1893-1897.

Robert W. Waterman, owner and operator of the Waterman Mine and Mill, and founder of the town of Waterman, was elected Lieutenant Governor in 1886. A Republican, he served under Governor Bartlett, a Democrat. When Bartlett died, Waterman completed his term as Governor.

In 1890, Henry H. Markham was elected Governor and served until 1894. Markham was operator of the Oro Grande Mill at Halleck and later the Oro Grande Mill at Daggett. He first ran for Congress in 1884 when he was at Calico.

The springboard to politics from Calico collapsed when the price of silver dropped.

Under the terms of the Bland-Allison Act of 1878, authorizing the coinage of silver, the U.S. Treasury was buying 4,500,000 ounces of silver a month. It gave silver an inflated value, the silver dollar being worth approximately 70 cents in gold. Powerful "sound money" forces demanded the demonetization of silver and repeal of the Silver Purchase Act. In 1893, President Cleveland and the Democratic Party supported the repeal, and the Sherman Act, devaluating silver, became the law of the land. It dealt the silver mining industry of Calico a death blow.

Most of the silver mines in Calico were closed by 1896 when the price of silver dropped from the 1894 price of $1.13 to .57 cents a troy ounce. Since that time, no governor has been elected from the high desert!

DIX VAN DYKE LEDGER
Ben Hays Scraps in Bancroft Library Vol. 3, 1874

" . . . After the exodus from Panamint City, a gang originating in Pioche, Nevada: Silas Pearson, John Taylor, and John Mowbray located at Quail Springs and called it Tecopa. Others followed and J.B. Osborne came in 1876 and acquired much property, Tecopa was laid out 20 feet above the creek. It has 2 stores, 3 saloons (1 that would not disgrace any town in the State) 1 blacksmith shop, 3 stables, 2 restaurants, several dwellings, 7 white ladies fullgrown. The Indians, especially the female portion of them, are very friendly."

In 1876 J.B. Osborne surveyed 160 acres at Resting Springs and filed a map together with a squatters claim in the County Recorders office at San Bernardino. (It was there in 1925, in 1949 could not be found).

ROBERT WHITNEY WATERMAN
by Martha Burnau

Robert Whitney Waterman was born in Fairfield, New York November 15, 1826. When he was a small boy, the Waterman family moved to Illinois. In 1850, at the age of 24, young Waterman, like countless other men lured by riches, moved with a team of oxen across the country into the Feather River Canyon area of California. He prospected for a while, but decided the merchandising business offered better and more profitable chances for advancement.

Waterman opened a general store in Oroville and sold all of the usual items needed by the residents and roving prospectors. Despite the fact that he refused to sell whiskey in his store, he did a thriving business.

Waterman was a known friend to the miners. When the snows and waters prevented them from working their claims he could be depended upon to advance supplies on credit. Despite the roving ways of prospectors, Waterman did not lose money on his credit accounts.

After a few years in California, Waterman returned to Illinois, arriving there in time to take an active part in the 1856 formation of the Republican Party. Illinois called a convention that was made up of a group calling themselves the "Anti-Nebraska Party." Waterman attended this convention held in Bloomington on May 29, 1856, which adopted the name "Republican" for the party and a strong series of resolutions which were supported, in debate, by former Congressman Abraham Lincoln. Illinois sent a delegation of two men to the first National Convention held by the Republicans; one was Waterman, and the other was Lincoln. The Convention chose Lincoln as its leader. The first Republican candidate for President was John C. Fremont, but he was defeated at the polls by James Buchanan. Although disappointed that his party had lost the election, Waterman continued his active part as a member and was one of the first men to urge Lincoln to run for office in the 1860 Presidential Election.

In 1873, Waterman and his family (wife, the former Jane Garder, three sons and four daughters) moved to California. A popular book that year authored by Charles Nordhoff was *"California for Health, Pleasure and Residence."* A complete chapter was devoted to San Bernardino and its surrounding valleys. Nordhoff pictured San Bernardino as California's agricultural paradise.

Waterman and his family arrived in the Sacramento Valley and headed to the agricultural region that Nordhoff had described. As a result, Waterman bought a large farm east of San Bernardino. He is credited with bringing the first herds of Holstein cows into the area. Since San Bernardino was the source of supplies used by miners in the desert mining districts, all the talk in every store and on the streets was of mining. Waterman listened and his interest in mining returned.

In June 1880, Waterman and his partner John L. Porter, a geologist, both experienced miners, made their initial visit to what was later to become the Grapevine Mining District. The formation was negative and considered a volcanic pile, but the two men gathered up a sack of the ore and returned to San Bernardino. When the ore was finally assayed after December 1, it indicated good silver content. On December 9 Waterman and Porter returned to the property where they located nine claims and recorded them legally.

Development of the mine was a tremendous expense. The fuel and water for the steam hoist had to

8   Calico's Zendia silver mine 1932

11   A.J. Laswell, Sr., Calico Miner 1886

9   Alvord Gold Mine in the Alvord Mts. 1935

90 years of Mining

12   Alvord Mine 1935 - note stone house and water tanks

10   R.C. Shaffer at Jack Moore Mine 1935

13   A 1976 photo of Vanderbilt Mine, Providence

be hauled five miles up hill. The ore had to be hauled to the mill five miles below. Wood fuel for the boilers was costly and hard to get. Until the railroad came through the area in 1882, freight and supplies were hauled by wagons from San Bernardino. The Waterman Mines, as they were known, were still a profitable venture. The production of silver between May 1, 1881 and March 15, 1887, amounted to $1,611,429.30 @ 1.29 or 1,249,170 ounces of silver for approximately 40,000 tons of ore per mill.

Once involved in a profitable mining business, Waterman kept looking for other properties. One that appeared rich, though poorly exploited, was located near the little town of Julian in San Diego County. The Julian property was known as the "Stonewall Jackson" mine. Waterman promptly changed the name to "Stonewall." The name "Stonewall Jackson" on the Julian property had a bit too much political flavor to suit the staunch Republican buyer. Waterman paid $45,000 for the mine and immediately invested $50,000 more for a new mill, shafts, etc. The improvement turned a losing property into a bonanza.

In developing the mine at Julian, Waterman became convinced of the future of San Diego. He helped to finance the San Diego and Cuyamaca Narrow Gauge, a little railroad, with visions of providing an eastern rail connection. He also bought a mountain empire for a cattle ranch, the present Cuyamaca State Park.

At the 1886 Republican State Convention held in the Los Angeles area, a delegate from Mendocino County, George Knight, nominated Waterman for lieutenant governor. In the November election the Democratic candidate for governor, Washington Bartlett, won by some 2,000 votes, and Waterman, a Republican, became lieutenant governor by a like margin. Waterman's popularity in the traditionally Democratic mining districts is said to have elected him. Bartlett died September 12, 1887, after less than a year in office, and Waterman served out the remainder of his term as governor of the state. Due to poor health, Waterman refused nomination for another term. While serving as governor, Waterman signed a bill declaring September 9, as California Admission Day, a legal holiday.

As governor, Waterman did not forget his home town of San Bernardino. Plans for the state hospital located at Patton, as well as other improvements, had their initiation during his administration.

Robert Whitney Waterman died in San Diego on April 12, 1891.

WATERMAN SILVER MINE

by Jo Park—Barstow Women's Club 1938

The patented silver group, "Alpha and Omega," better known as the Waterman Mine, was located by Robert Whitney Waterman of San Bernardino in 1878 (sic 1880).

A man named Lee had located a ledge many years before believing that he had a vast cinnabar deposit. Lee put in a small tunnel and dug pits along the vein into which he expected the metal to drip and accumulate, erroneously thinking that quicksilver came free in its commercial form. Lee abandoned the claim and went into other fields.

Waterman and J.L. Porter, a mining engineer formed a partnership which was one not only of a successful business enterprise but of rare friendship also.

There was no railroad leading into the desert beyond Mojave at this time. All materials and supplies for opening and maintaining the mines and camps had to be freighted by teams from San Bernardino, by way of Cajon Pass and desert roads. Materials were shipped from Los Angeles or San Francisco to Mojave, and then freighted by teams 65 miles further to Waterman.

From lack of water at the mines, Mr. Waterman bought School Section 36 from the Government and established his mill and little town four miles below the mines on the north bank of the Mojave River, opposite the present town of Barstow. The great ore teams came down into town laden with ore from the mills, and went back with barrels of water and supplies for the camp on the hill. There were over 100 men employed in the mill and mine. Wood to keep the furnaces going was cut from the great supply of trees along the river. When the Southern Pacific railroad came through in 1882, the Watermans' were able to ship in coal which was a tremendous savings.

It should be said of the Waterman community on the river, as well as the mining camp, that no liquor, gambling, or "bawdy" houses were allowed. The wives of the miners liked their husbands to work there because they could save money and the men got fair treatment.

The success of these mines, which were of high grade silver and produced abundantly, brought people to the desert hills. When the price of silver dropped it was no longer profitable to work the mines. Mr. Waterman closed them, and the town was abandoned.

MILL SITES OF THE CALICO MINING DISTRICT

by Dolores Leroux and Virgil Collins

The Calico Mining District is northeast of Barstow and comprises an area 10 square miles having a southwest angle at a point near Little Red Butte, two and one half miles west of the Waterloo mills on the

Mojave River, the boundary lines running with the cardinal points of the compass. The district includes Township 10 West, Range 1 East and the west half of Township 10 North, Range 2 East.

The first mining discovery in Calico has been credited to a Mr. Lee in 1875, who found ore in such richness it was believed to be quicksilver or mercury.

It was not until the fall of 1880, that E.L. Porter, a partner to R.W. Waterman, relocated the idle claims.

By the year of 1882 over 1000 people lived in the town of Calico and in the canyons surrounding it and there were several mills operating in the area.

The first ores to be processed were taken by wagon to Oro Grande, 40 miles away. The procedure being so slow and costly that the mining companies decided to have their own mills in the immediate area.

By 1889, there were four mills operating in the Calico district and vicinity: "Silver King-Garfield" mill; "Oro Grande-Waterloo" mill; "Pioneer Quartz;" and the "Barber" mill. The California State Mining Bureau of 1953 states the following:

> Following the bonanza operations of the first few years, mining activity was strongly influenced by fluctuations in the price of silver. In the period 1883-85 San Bernardino County yielded nearly 6 million dollars in silver, about 85% of the states total, obtained mostly from the Calico district. In 1890, at the peak of activity, mills totaling 150 stamps were treating the ores, and about 700 men were employed in the mines and mills. The monthly output of bullion was valued at about $200,000. By 1892, however, diminishing production forced the closing of two mills, one with 60 stamps, the other with 15 stamps, both at Daggett. A 30 stamp mill owned by the Silver King Mining Company remained in operation at Calico until 1896. The drop in the price of silver from $1.13 per ounce in 1894 to 57¢ in 1896, together with the exhaustion of the known high-grade bodies, led to virtual cessation of mining. Several factors, including the richness of the ores, the belief that the bodies were shallow, and the unrestricted activities of lessees, led to improper mining practices at many of the properties. The leasing was of a type commonly known as "cloriding" in which only high-grade ores are sought and methods are unsystematic. Ore mined by lessees were treated at a custom mill, the claim owner receiving one-sixth to one-fourth of the return.

SOME MINES—THE CALICO DISTRICT

Alabama, Argentum, Backdoor No. 1 prospect, Baltic, Bismarck, Blackfoot, Barcham (Total Wreck) (Gold-lead), Burning Moscow, Carbonate group, Cisco, Cuba, Dietzman, Gale Group, Galena King, Garfield, Grandview, Grant, Humbug, Falls, Le Montain (Silver-lead barite), Lamar, Langtry, Lead Mt. (Silver-barite), Leviathan, Lone Star group, Mulcahy group, Occidental, Odessa, Old Oriental, Oriental, Possibility group, Red Cloud, Revier, Runover, St. Louis Consolidated, Silver Bow (Silver-lead barite), Silver Tip (Silver-lead barite), Silver King, Silverado, Sioux, Snowbird, Thunderer, Union (Gold), Voca (Washington), Waterloo, Waterman and Zenda.

MILLING PROCESSES

There are many ways of processing the ore after it is mined. One of the earliest was the simple 'arrastra.' The word arrastra is Spanish and means "a crude Spanish-American ore-crushing mill with vat and rollers worked by a horizontal beam."

When mining began in the Alvord Mountain District the process first used was arrastra. The remains of an arrastra could still be seen outside of Randsburg on highway 395, in Kern County, in the late 1950's.

A round pit was dug into the ground and lined and floored with flat stones. An upright beam was set in the middle of the pit and crossbeams were attached to the upright, from these crossbeams dragged huge rocks, held by chains. A long pole, extended from the upright and reached far out, at a height of about four feet off the ground. The principle of operation was to revolve the crossbeams and upright post, dragging the heavy rocks around and around the pit, crushing the ore.

Power to revolve the crossbeams was usually a mule, but sometimes a horse was used, fastened to the long pole that extended from the upright. The animal walked around the pit turning the crossbeams and crushing the ore, which was taken out and spread over a courtyard or patio in low heaps. It was then sprinkled with mercury and chemicals (common salt and copper sulphate) and mixed by mules which were driven over every part of the heaps. Complicated chemical reactions took place, the effect of which was to free the silver from its intractable compounds and enable it to be taken up by the mercury. The heaps were trodden by the mules every day or two until amalgamation was complete, which might require a month. Lastly the material was agitated with water in large tubs and the mud run off through the plug holes. The amalgam found at the bottom was collected and put into filter bags and squeezed to remove the surplus mercury. The liquid mercury passed through, containing a minute quantity of silver dissolved in it, and pasty amalgam containing from 25% to 50% of silver remained in the bag. The amalgam was heated in retorts, the mercury driven off as vapor, only to be condensed in a cool chamber for use again, and the silver now nearly pure is melted down and cast into bars.

Another way to process the ore was with the 'Boss Process.' The 'Silver King-Garfield' mill used this method.

The *Encyclopedia Britannica* has this to say about Boss or 'Pan Amalgamation' process:

> The process was used for silver ores, especially in the United States, in the later half of the 19th century and was superseded by the cyanide process and by smelting. Silver ore was ground to a fine paste with water in iron pans by rotating iron shoes. The shoes were then raised a little, so as to agitate the pulp without further grinding,

and mercury was sprinkled into the pans. The agitation was continued until amalgamation was completed, and the end in view as assisted by heating the pan with steam and by the addition of chemicals, especially common salt and copper sulphate. The amalgam was separated by dilution of the pulp and stirring and finally by running off the charge into large settling tanks. The amalgamation pans were about five feet in diameter and the charge was 2,000 or 3,000 pounds.

Complex silver ores containing minerals not amenable to amalgamation (such as arsenical and antimanial sulphides, galena and blende) were roasted in furnaces at a red heat with common salt as a preliminary, when silver chloride was formed, a compound from which the silver ore can be extracted by mercury.

SILVER KING-GARFIELD MILL

The remains of this mill can still be seen. All that remains are a timbered wall and the ore tailings. The King mill was located on the south side of the Calico mountains between Wall Street canyon and Odessa canyon (Doran Drive).

The Silver King Mining Company (limited) of London, England, owned the King mill as well as three groups of mines in the area. The Odessa, Oriental and the Occidental mines were among the richest group of mines in the district. Ore from the Garfield mines, which was part of the Occidental group, was processed by this mill. Mr. W. H. Storms had this to say in his book, *"Old Mines of Southern California":*

On December 1, 1891, the King mill was enlarged by the addition of ten stamps, making thirty in all. The Boss process of continuous amalgamation was also adopted.

In the year of 1896, due to the low price of silver which had dropped to 57¢, it was no longer profitable to mine the silver, so the King-Garfield mill closed its thirty stamp mill.

ORO GRANDE-WATERLOO MILL

In 1882 there was a 10 stamp mill at Calico station (to avoid confusion the name was changed to Daggett in the spring of 1883) across the Mojave River on the south side of what is now known as Elephant Mountain.

Big business took over in 1884 when the Oro Grande Milling Company (the second firm with this name) bought the Oriental and shortly after the Silver King mine and mill. Principal of this new company was a Milwaukee capitalist. D. Bahten was the Superintendent. The mill expanded to 15 stamps. The company paid its fourth dividend in September, 1884. In 1895 it bought the Snow Bird mine and later acquired the Waterloo mine in west Calico, some two miles west of the Silver King property.

Cost of hauling ore to the Waterloo was $2.50 per ton by mule team and the charge for custom milling was $11 to $14 per ton. The cost of milling ran from $3 to $5.

Shipments from the mill generally averaged 40 to 50,000 dollars a month. The output of ore amounting to 200 tons every 24 hours, this quantity being reduced by the two mills.

By 1887 the Oro Grande Mining Company started building a new 60 stamp mill ($250,000) along side their old mill at the river when on August 17, just as it was almost finished, the new mill caught fire and burned to the ground. Col. Sanger immediately started upon a second mill on the same site, utilizing the old boilers from the burned out units.

A narrow gauge railroad was built in 1888 between the new 60 stamp mill and the Waterloo mine.

In 1889 the Waterloo Mining Company bought out the Oro Grande Mining Company, a Wisconsin corporation owned by the same interest.

For years, the Waterloo mines had kept the 15 stamp pan and the 60 stamp Boss process mills, on the Mojave at Daggett, busy night and day. In March of 1892 the Waterloo Mining Company could no longer make ends meet. The mills and mines owned by the company were closed down and 130 men were out of work.

BARBER MILL

The mill was located in the Calico area, the remains of which still can be seen as three concrete tanks.

Coal for the fuel was brought from New Mexico and salt for the chlorination came from south of Danby (100 miles east of Calico).

Between the years of 1883-1885 the Garfield mines sent a large amount of unassorted ore to the Barber mill.

PIONEER QUARTZ MILL

This mill was located on the north side of the Mojave river, just east of where Minneola road is now.

The mill was built by the man who was to later become Lt. Governor of the State of California, John Daggett. During the year of 1883 the Silver Odessa Mining Company purchased the mill. It was more commonly known as 'Hawley's Mill,' as Mr. Hawley had a stage stop on the Old Spanish Trail and the Government Road about one mile west of 'Forks in the Road.'

Ore from the Cuba mine was processed at Hawley's mill. Also the "Alvord mines took their ore there to be milled after their mill burned in 1891."

NUMBER STAMPS PER MILL

Silver King-Garfield Mill
     20 stamps, enlarged in 1891 to 30 stamps

Oro Grande-Waterloo Mill
     10 stamps, enlarged in 1884 to 15 stamps
     and in 1889 to 75 stamps

Pioneer Quartz (Hawley's) Mill   10 stamps

Barber Mill   10 stamps

4 Waterman 10 stamp Silver Mill

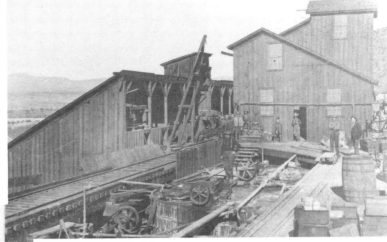

18 Bagdad Chase Mill - slope of "B" Hill

5 Calciner Plant under construction at Marion

19 Waterloo Mill at foot of Elephant Mt.

Mills

16 Ore crusher at Daggett

20 Waterloo Mill Crew

17 Waterloo Ore Train 1888

21 Hawley Mill

CALICO

San Bernardino City and County Directory 1886
(Reprint)

One of the principal mining towns in the county, is about 88 miles east of San Bernardino and six miles from Daggett, its station on the Atlantic and Pacific railroad. The first discovery of mineral in this region was made in 1881, about three miles north of Waterman and Porter's mill and Grapevine Station, by an old man named Lee. In the spring of 1881 John McBride and others discovered and located numbers of claims in this section and on Calico mountain. The first work was here done some four miles northwest of the new town of Calico.

In April, 1882, Thomas Warden and Hues Thomas discovered the great King Mine, the richest and largest in the State.

In July, 1883, rich deposits were located on the Burning Moscow.

In 1881 there was not a single house where Calico now stands.

The great King Mine immediately overhangs the town.

The fanciful name of Calico was given to the mountain on account of its varied and fantastic colors.

The town of Calico is six miles from Daggett, by which it is connected by an excellent stage line conducted by Messrs. Barrett and Greer, which leaves Calico daily at 11 o'clock a.m., and connects with the express trains at Daggett at 2:30 p.m., returning to Calico after the arrival of the trains.

The elevation of Calico is about 2,600 feet above sea level.

It has a present population of about 1,200.

The town exhibits all the usual vim and bustle of a mining town.

Calico supports an excellent weekly newspaper, ably edited by the proprietor, Mr. John G. Overshiner, who has ingeniously christened it the *Calico Print*. It has a good circulation and is much prized as an exchange for the full and reliable news which it contains in its mining reviews.

The place has a good school with average attendance of about 50 scholars. There are regular church services every Sabbath.

There are telegraph and telephone offices; Wells, Fargo and Co's. Express; post office (E.E. Stacy, P.M.); a regularly-ordained minister; two doctors; two lawyers; a justice of the peace; five commissioners; deputy sheriff and two constables.

There is a fine public hall for entertainments, several good stores, markets, etc. etc.

The town is located on the south side of the mountain and is provided with such excellent natural drainage that sewers are almost unnecessary.

The climate is dry and healthful, and good water is provided by the water company.

The approximate amount of silver bullion shipped from the mines during the last two years is $2,500,000.

There are extensive and very valuable borax mines close to Calico, which are owned and worked with profit by Mr. William T. Coleman, of San Francisco.

CALICO

a story from handwritten notes of Alice Salisbury
Barstow Womens Club 1938
Compiled by Pat Keeling

Calico first attracted attention in early 1880. The colored rocks and hills gave the Calico area its suggestive and unique name. The mining district was on the southern slopes of the mountain. At first there were no shafts or tunnels built, but surface ore was used. This ore was sacked and dragged down from high levels by rawhide and steel cable, with burros hauling it to Oro Grande some 40 miles away. Later, tramways, ore chutes, bins and stamp mills were built, followed by a narrow gauge railroad to Daggett.

With all this activity and excitement, a town was growing on the plateau. The town site was never laid out, no lots were sold due to govenment ownership. Claimants to lots had to build fast or relinquish to someone who would. There was one main street with frame buildings, until they all burned down. After the fire, adobe houses were built and yards were fenced, but there were no sidewalks. Some of the houses had foot boards 12 inches wide along the base of the building. A few two story buildings were constructed. Alladin houses were also built; in 1901 they were

moved to Barstow. The ruins of several adobes may still be seen in the Calico area.

The town boasted of having a general store, assay office, shoe shop, hotel, lodging house, restaurants, dance halls, the newspaper called *Calico Print*, saloons, Post Office, telegraph, telephone, express offices, school house, many dugout pits and tents, Chinese quarters, and a cemetery, also many breeds of animals like burros, and a pet calf. Cock fighting was a common sport. Calico was unfortunate in not having a jail or church. It boasted seven quartz mills to grind the ore. There were small trees such as cottonwoods and peppers.

The water supply was carried from the valley by steam engines fired with creosote brush.

The social life of the town depended on everyone joining in and cooperating. The town's people had friendliness, cooperation, charity, and sympathy. A big "to-do" was made over weddings and funerals, everyone turning out in his best bib and tucker.

Dances were given regularly and occasionally a

22 The Lane family in front of general store

25 Silver King Mine crew

Calico!

26-27 Mr. and Mrs. M.H. Ball owners
(H.L. Drew, partner) of freight
teams at Calico 1880's

23 Frank Denning -
Calico miner 1880's

24 Calico 1890's

28 Mr. and Mrs. Walter Knott donating Calico to S.B. County w/Supervisor Ross Dana

minstrel show with local talent. Local regulations were accepted by all, with little drinking or gambling. At dancing parties, music was by guitar, violin, or an organ was played and guests sang songs. Emma and Eugenia Oliver were young belles of the camp.

The men of the community followed the code of the West in their conduct: prejudiced against violence, debts were paid, laziness was laughed upon, secret go-getters held in high respect, their word was as good as a bond, respect for women, collections when someone got hurt or died, no cut-throat stuff; thieving was a rarity.

Women of the community valued home-life and encouraged young people to have home parties and picnics. Some of the girls were quite popular and a bit uppity.

Many nationalities were represented in Calico: Irish, Cornish, Greek, French, Dutch, English, American and Chinese, all contributing to its growth and colorful history.

MARCUS PLUTH
by Walter Alf

Marcus Pluth, one of our most successful miners, came to Calico in 1884. Miners in those days carried their beds with them. One morning when several of them had their beds spread on a hillside, Pluth got up early and started to prospect around where his bed was. He found some float, but before prospecting further to find where it came from, he discovered that the ground had already been located by two parties. He took a lease from both of them and continued prospecting to find the ore body. It later proved to be the property known today as the Silver Cliff. Pluth was the discoverer of the first ore and worked this property for some time. One of the parties he leased from was the Barber Milling and Mining Company, and I have among my relics, in Daggett, the company's old bullion stamp.

Pluth, a man of great foresight, located the first iron, known at the time as the Bitter Springs iron deposit, which he sold in 1900 to the Colorado Fuel and Iron Company.

He also prospected for iron properties for the Merritts and recommended that they buy the property at Eagle Mountain for approximately $100,000. His recommendation was turned down, and in less than 8 years the property was purchased by the Harrimans for $1,250,000. This is the property Kaiser is working today.

The lime deposit now being worked by Southwestern Cement Company, one of the largest deposits in Southern California, was located by Pluth in 1906.

In about 1909, Pluth located a lime deposit in Riverside County, known to the old-timers as "Whitewater

Marcus Pluth, pioneer mining man and dreamer, died in 1939 and sleeps in the little Daggett cemetery. lime deposit." This property was sold in 1923 for $95,000.

OPERATIONS OF THE PACIFIC COAST BORAX COMPANY 1883 - 1907
Daggett, Marion, Borate, and the Borate-Daggett Railroad
by June Zeitelhack and Jan Zeitelhack La Barge

The story of borax has not caught the attention of historians and fiction writers as have those of gold, silver and gems, Thus, there is little recorded history on borax operations. (The one exception is the legendary "Twenty-Mule Team Borax" story originating from the Harmony works at Death Valley 1883-1888.) For years, radio and television productions publicized this five-year segment of the borax story. Harmony owner, Francis M. "Borax" Smith, recognized such romantic possibilities when he adopted the "Twenty-Mule Team" as the trademark of his company, and the present U.S. Borax and Chemical Company continues to market borax under the "Twenty-Mule Team" trademark. Further evidence that the neglected story of Borax could well tickle the imagination of fiction writers and intrigue the historians comes from research into the operations of the Pacific Coast Borax Company on the Mojave Desert.

Legend has it that the ancient Babylonian goldsmiths obtained borax from the Gobi Desert. The Egyptians used it to preserve the dead. The Romans may have obtained it from a deposit near Panderma in Asia Minor to spread on the floor of the Circus Maximus as a deodorizer or antiseptic after gladitorial combat. Marco Polo brought some tincal (a borax ore) back from China to be used by Venetian goldsmiths as flux. The Chinese had been using borax for 900 years in glazing. An Arabian chemist mentioned borax in 600 A.D.; but the western world had no knowledge of the source of it until the sixteenth century when deposits were found in the bottom of Tibetan Lakes having no outlet. The first borax discovered in the United States was also from such lakes. In the early nineteenth century deposits around hot mineral springs were found in Italy and in 1836, borax was discovered in Chile.

Dr. John A. Veatch's discovery of a form of borax in Clear Lake (or Borax Lake), California, in 1856, was the first in North America. (Veatch and a friend, Dr. William O. Ayres, formed the Borax Company of California in

29 Borate early 1900's - L. Chinese cook, and J.W.S. Perry, Supt. of Transportation

32 Watering the teams at Borate

30 Miners at Borate boarding house

Borax Replaces Silver

31 Miss Pearl Perry and "Dolph" Navares (92 years young) 1962

34 Ore train entering Waterloo Mill

33 Ore chute - Borate 1910

35 Borax Mill at Marion

1864, moving to Hachinhama or Little Borax Lake in 1868. Their operations reduced importation of borax and the price dropped from 50 cents to 30 cents per pound.)

Francis Marion Smith entered the story when William Troup of Virginia City, Nevada, found cotton ball (ulexite) at Columbus Marsh in 1871. Since 1867, Smith had been surviving by working at anything he could get while searching for a good mine. At the time, Smith owned several wood camps supplying wood and timber to mines and mills at Columbus. Smith investigated Teel's Marsh near one of his wood camps, taking his samples to the assayer at Columbus. Smith was prudent enough to outfox the assayer, who sent an agent to follow Smith to jump Smith's rich claims. Smith had trouble obtaining the sole rights to Teel's Marsh after he had first located 160 acre claims because of a change in interpretation of mining laws. As Smith told the story to John R. Spear for his book *Illustrated Sketches of Death Valley and Other Borax Deserts*:

> Borax lands had heretofore been located under the saline laws of the State, one locator taking 160 acres. Soon after the date of my discovery— the fall of 1872—Commissioner Drummond had decided that borax land should be located as placer claims, allowing only 20 acres to the individual.

Because of the remoteness of the area, the high cost of fuel and transportation, and falling prices, it was necessary for Smith to locate his claims very carefully to obtain the richest deposits. News of Smith's discovery reached the coast and there was a rush to Nevada and Teel's Marsh. Smith, determined to own the whole deposit, had to fight claim jumpers and buy out claims until he had acquired the entire deposit. He sent for his brother, Julius, and to start production they founded the firm of Smith and Storey Bros. They hired John Roach and John Ryan. Many years later, when Smith was bankrupt, he left the company but Ryan and Roach remained.

Smith's company was beset with marketing problems and he engaged William T. Coleman of San Francisco as his agent. The industry was suffering from high taxes, low prices, difficulties in obtaining labor, production costs, and limited use. Boldly deciding it was a good time to expand, the Smith brothers built a refinery in Oakland. Smith also opened offices in New York to set up an advertising campaign.

In 1884 Smith's brother, Julius, left the company and F.M. Smith became sole owner. He also acquired acreage, lots, and a store in Columbus. He hired the Wells Fargo agent from Candelaria, Nevada to operate the store. In 1885, when Smith established Pacific Borax Salt & Soda Company at Columbus Marsh, he made Christian Brevoort Zabriskie, the ex-Wells Fargo agent, superintendent. The Teel's Marsh operation was reorganized and named Teel's Marsh Borax in the same year and Smith became the largest borax producer in the country.

Another chapter in the borax story was developing in Death Valley. About 1880, an itinerant prospector had stopped at the Ash Meadows cabin of Aaron and Rosie Winters showing them samples of cottonball borax. Aaron thought he knew there was a large deposit of the material. After the man left they went down to Death Valley, gathered some samples, and as soon as it was dark performed the test for borax. They poured a mixture of alcohol and sulphuric acid on the mineral, and set it afire. It burned green—it was borax!

Thus in 1881, William T. Coleman received samples sent to him by Winters, and he immediately dispatched an agent, William Robertson, to Ash Meadows. Coleman bought out Winter's claim for $20,000. Winters and his wife took $15,000 and made a down payment on the Pahrump ranch of Charles Bennett, and contracted a mortgage of $5000 for the balance.

Hearing of the Winter's discovery, Isadore Daunet in Darwin, remembered other white marshes in Death Valley. He and his partners, Gilbert Clemons, J.M. McDonald, Myron Harmon, and C.C. Blanch located claims on 260 acres near Bennett's Well and formed the Eagle Borax Company. They beat Coleman into production in 1881, but their operation became defunct when Daunet committed suicide the following year. They had produced a total of 130 tons.

Philander Lee, Harry Spiller, and Billy Yount discovered the Monte Blanco deposit in Furnace Creek canyon. They sold out for $4,000. Philander used his share in developing a ranch at Resting Springs. Philander settled his Indian wife and their children at the ranch. In later years one of the Alf sisters of Daggett went to Resting Springs to teach the Lee children. It was Lee's son who was killed by Bert White as related in the story *Life on the Mojave River Valley-Freight Teams 1905* by Dix Van Dyke. Philander had three brothers, Leander, Salamander, and Meander. Leander was caretaker at the Amargosa works in 1896 when Spears journeyed to Death Valley. Although they have not been heroes of Death Valley lore their names are mentioned in many stories of the area.

Coleman's Harmony works in Death Valley began production in 1882. The borax would not crystalize there during the summer months, so Coleman bought other borax claims at Amargosa where the temperature was low enough to operate during the summer months. The Amargos claims were purchased for $5,000. from Aaron Winters and two men named Parks and Ellis.

The Harmony Borax Mining Company, (Death Valley) incorporated in May, 1884, operated during the winter months. The Meridian Borax Company, incorporated November 1884, operated during the summer months. A. Neuschwander was Superintendent at Amargosa (Meridian). The first year's production was hauled by Charles Bennett, former owner at the Pahrump ranch. When summer work began at Amargosa, the company purchased an outfit from J.P. McLaughlin, and hired teamster Ed Stiles, who put together the first 20-mule team. Stiles made three trips from Amargosa to Daggett, driving the 20-mule team.

After that, J.W.S. Perry was assigned the task of

organizing a system of transportation over the desert from Death Valley to the railroad at Mojave. He designed the 10 wagons which were to make the hauls to Mojave 165 miles away and had them built at a cost of $900. each. He determined the route, making use whenever possible of known desert roads. He planned for the dry camps and set up a system whereby water and feed were replenished by the returning wagons. The wagons were so well built and so sturdy that they never broke down during their five years of travel over the grueling route. Ed Stiles said that one reason the wagons held together so well was that Perry had followed his advice in having the wood seasoned and dried in the desert before building the wagons. Some of the wagons are still in existence today and are on display at Furnace Creek Ranch in Death Valley. In 1937 two wagons retraced the route from Mojave to Death Valley. Mrs. Gertrude Alf, daughter-in-law of Seymour Alf, Daggett contractor, believes these two may have been the ones built by Alf to Perry's specifications for the Borate operation. For some years a borax wagon and water trailer were on display at the Santa Fe Station, Barstow. The 20-mule team route went from Mojave, past Castle Butte and Cuddeback Dry Lake to Granite Wells, to Blackwater well at the base of Pilot Knob. It joined the San Bernardino and Daggett road to Post Office Springs (Ballarat), then followed the Panamint City Freight Road 26 miles north to Lone Willow Springs. Six miles north of Lone Willow, the route turned east through Windy Gap (Wingate Pass), down Long Valley (Wingate Wash) into lower Death Valley. From there the road turned north up the west side of Death Valley to Mesquite Spring (Salt Wells), then to Bennett's Well, past the eagle works and Tule Well, across the "Devil's Golf Course" to the east side of Death Valley to Greenland Ranch (Furnace Creek).

The 20-mule teams were used on the Borate-Daggett haul until a railroad was built, and later in the Colemanite mines in Death Valley, though never again were they used commercially on such long hauls. The use of the long mule teams to haul borax came to a halt with the completion of the Tidewater & Tonopah Railroad August 16, 1907. (The mules were called upon when machines failed in the construction of the Los Angeles Aqueduct which was begun in 1907. Fifty-two mules were used to haul a 26-ton section of pipe to Jawbone Canyon.)

The Mojave Valley portion of the borax story began in December 1882, when one of Coleman's men discovered a new ore in a canyon in the Funeral Mountains above Death Valley to the east. It was a quartz-like mineral occurring as an out-cropping in the canyon walls. It proved to be borate of lime and was named Colemanite after Coleman. This started a borax rush, and prospectors scattered over the deserts looking for Colemanite.

The borax rush hit Calico in May 1883. The men deserted the town in their eagerness to locate claims in Mule Canyon. A reporter for the Calico Print went along and had this to say in the next edition of the paper:

Men start out from town on a dog trot, leaving in their wake rows of monuments (claim markers), and do not slacken their pace until the shade of night prevents further operations. Inside a couple of days two men located 96 claims, and one, was lame at that. If the men work the silver mines with the same energy that they expend to cover the country with monuments the camp would soon be booming.

Coleman's firm acquired a great number of the claims. After the company failed, Coleman's associate, F.M. "Borax" Smith and his Pacific Coast Borax Company acquired the Coleman properties.

Hugh Stevens and Bill Neel were the prospectors who found the great lodes of Colemanite at Borate, five miles as the crow flies from Calico across barren twisting canyons. There seems to be no extant record of the price Coleman paid for their claims and very little is known about these two men, only that they were comparative newcomers in Calico. It is not known whether they were the two mentioned above who staked 96 claims. Hugh B. Stevens, a merchant at Calico, was listed in the San Bernardino City and County Directory of 1889.

Little was done with the Calico discovery until after 1888. Until that time, the 20-mule teams were hauling ore out of the Death Valley and Amargosa works. Smith's interests were centered in Teel's Marsh, and Columbus Marsh, Nevada. In the spring of 1888 Coleman went bankrupt. Some of his banks had called in loans unexpectedly and he was unable to meet their demands for cash.

In 1890, Smith, thinking of colemanite as the ore of the future, acquired the entire assets of the Harmony and Meridian borax mining companies. The deal included all the Death Valley and Amargosa claims, the ranch property in Death Valley, the Alameda refinery, and the Calico mine. Smith filed incorporation papers September 5, 1890 and the Pacific Coast Borax Company was born. The future of the company lay in its colemanite properties, as the marsh deposits were near depletion.

The Calico deposits were favorably situated, only 12 miles by crooked canyon road and across the flats to the railroad at Daggett. This made the Calico deposits more valuable than the richer Death Valley colemanite deposits, as the transportation problem was infinitesimal compared to the other locations. W.J. Stormes stated in Report of the State Mineralogist Old Mines of Southern California of 1893:

The borax vein is from seven to ten feet in thickness where it has been exposed in the underground workings. The material when hoisted to the surface is loaded in great wagons hauled by 20 animals and taken to Daggett, where it is shipped to the works in Alameda.

Little is known about activity at the Borate mines between 1888-1891. In 1891, the Pacific Coast Borax Company was assessed for a total of $7,107, in property as per the San Bernardino County Book of Assessments for that year. Besides the 282 acres in the mining claims the company owned six lots in Daggett. They had 17 mules valued at $1,275; five half-breed horses and 19 harnesses. This was enough for one team of 20 and a team of horses for the use of the company officials. The record gives no indication of the assessment ratio of that time to the actual market value.

By 1892, the company was taxed for 39 "old harness," 24 horses, a colt and 17 mules, enough animals for two teams and one spare, and ten wagons. The following year (1893) the company had only five horses and 16 mules, harness for 11 of them, and seven good wagons and 11 "old wagons." The company also owned 17 lots in Daggett, tools and machinery at the mine. They paid taxes of $28.99 on assessed valuation of $7,035.

The company did not choose to use all its capital on wagons and animals. Seymour Alf, of Daggett, contracted to haul ore, building two borax wagons to the same specifications as the original Death Valley-Mojave wagons. Since Alf was partial to horses rather than mules, his teams were mostly horses. It took a total of three days to make the trip to the mine and return; Camp Rock, part way up Mule Canyon, was the overnight stop. The wagons hauled supplies and water to Borate and Camp Rock on the uphill trip.

In those days, as today, there were vandals. According to Spears:

> Even on the short trail nine and one-half miles between the Borate mines in the Calico Mountains and Daggett, where there is but one way station, the water has been run to waste by these desert tramps.

Spears said it cost the first Death Valley borax manufacturer (Eagle works) eight cents per pound to freight supplies from San Bernardino 250 miles away. The company was looking for a less costly way to haul from Borate to Daggett. In 1894, they tried using "Old Dinah," a huge steam tractor, which is now on display at the Furnace Creek Ranch in Death Valley. The men coped with the tractor for one year, but in the end it was back to mule power. The mechanic who came with Old Dinah worked most nights so that the tractor could be operated for the next day's hauling. The tractor worked well on comparatively level hard ground, but it dug itself a hole in soft ground. In going up a steep hill the single steering wheel in front would rear up and the machine would lose steerage and block the road. Sandbagging the front end did not work. The mule skinners had feared the tractor would put them out of work, but they spent a lot of time with the mules hauling it out of its predicaments.

After some years in storage in Daggett, Smith and Ryan tried Old Dinah on the traction road they constructed from Ivanpah to the Lila C. in Death Valley. (This road still shows on topographical maps of that area.) The tractor was shipped to the end of the Santa Fe at Ivanpah, unloaded there, and started out to Death Valley via Stateline Pass. It blew up on the way and was eventually dragged down to Furnace Creek. This tractor may have been a pet project of John Ryan.

Wash Cahill, an office man, became an expert at making it run when the blacksmiths could not, and this impressed Ryan. Ryan had just returned that year from a three-year prospecting trip to South Africa and was Smith's right hand man in the Mojave desert operations.

San Bernardino County assessment records show no assessment in 1894 on the steam tractor. In 1895 the assessment was $375 for machinery. The 1894 assessment did include $150 for half-breed horses, but no mules. Previous assessments indicate a value of $50 placed on each horse.

Construction of the Borate-Daggett railroad began in 1898 and it was completed the same year. A calciner plant was built about four miles north of Daggett on the northeast side of the Calico dry lake. The plant site was named Marion after Francis Marion Smith. Spears describes in *Illustrated Sketches of Death Valley & Other Borate Deserts of the Pacific Coast* the chemical factory at Alameda, which the company used before the Marion plant was constructed, as follows:

> Some idea of the extent of this factory may be had from the dimensions: thus, one part is of concrete 40 x 230 feet; another is of frame, 80 x 170; a third is 26 x 110, and all three are three stories high. There is a one-story building 80 x 145, and a shed 30 x 110.

There were no concrete buildings at Marion, but some concrete foundations still remain. The buildings were of wood and the furnace chimney was brick. The process used at Marion may not have been the same as at Alameda. *The Story of Borax* says: "The calcining process dehydrates ore through the application of intense heat." This makes us wonder what fuel was used to stoke the furnace. Thomas O. Williams says, in the Coke's book, *Mining on the Trails of Destiny* that Indians living along the Mojave River made their living cutting wood which was hauled to the plant at Marion by Bill Bateman and Jack LaFergie. Since the silver mills had also been using wood, could this have been the only fuel supply? Wood or coal were probably shipped in by rail to Daggett, then hauled to Marion on the newly built Borate-Daggett railroad.

The company was assessed for the railroad and the plant at Marion in 1899. The assessed value of the company holdings jumped from $5,790, in 1896 to $32,690 in 1900. The railroad of 11 miles was valued at $16,000; the furnace at Marion $5,000; buildings at Marion $1,000. The value of the mines had increased from $2,500 in 1895 to $7,100 in 1900. The Pacific Coast Borax Company holdings at Marion, Daggett and the railroad continued to increase in value as per the San Bernardino County assessment books until 1906 when the value of the company holdings reached $135,275. The taxes that year were $2,698.22. The peak of production had been reached in 1902, as from then on the mines were being depleted. In 1906 the company showed property in Yermo valued at $16,000. (This may have been the plant at Marion.) The end came in 1907 when the company was assessed for less than $2,000 for 160 acres, improvements and personal property. The mines at Borate were all but depleted, but the Lila C. (Ryan) and New Ryan in Death Valley were much richer than the Borate deposits had ever been. The earnings of the borate mines provided the money to construct the Tidewater and Tonopah Railroad which made it profitable to develop the mines at Death Valley.

The Borate and Daggett Railroad was torn up and sold; the plant at Marion was torn down; Alex McLaren wrecked the buildings at Borate and shipped salvaged building materials to the Lila C. mine. At the Daggett Ranch a house was built from the reclaimed lumber from the Marion mill, and Bill Swartz, a ranch hand, his wife and two children lived in the house. Mr. O.A. Russell, owner of the Calico Motel, said he formerly surfaced the motel driveway with slag from the Marion site. The roads at the United States Marine Base at Yermo were originally surfaced with the same material, according to Russell.

Field surveys were conducted to determine the exact route of the railroad and where it entered Daggett. Remains were found of a right-of-way grade between Daggett and the United States Marine Corps Base, Yermo. The railroad joined the present tracks between the Fouts garage at Fourth and Santa Fe Streets in Daggett and the Union Pacific tracks. A faint trace of raised road-bed is in line with a grade behind the houses next to the Daggett baseball field. It runs intermittently from there to the Marine Base fence. Railroad artifacts in the area indicate that this is all that is left of the Borate-Daggett Railroad.

A survey of the old Mule Canyon Road to the Calico-Yermo road revealed artifacts along the side of the road indicating that the railroad right-of-way became the road. O.A. Russell has a picture in his collection showing four ties imbedded in the Mule Canyon road just as it enters the mountains. The railroad followed the present Mule Canyon road to the summit, then veered off in a southeasterly direction to the Borate mines. In the Alice Salisbury papers, at the San Bernardino County library, in Barstow, there is a manuscript quoting Mary Van Dyke Golden and Frank McShane, former Daggett residents, as saying that the railroad had three rails from Daggett to Marion and that it entered at the east end of Daggett, terminating at a spot just west of where the Union Pacific now rounds the bend towards Yermo. This seems to verify survey conclusions.

The Fouts garage at Santa Fe and Fourth streets was originally a roundhouse at the Waterloo mill which stood near the present Daggett-Yermo road bridge. The building was later moved to its present location.

The Francis, one of the two Heisler engines used by the railroad was sold to the Nevada Short Line after it was used in the construction of the Death Valley Railroad. From there it went to the Terry Lumber Company at Round Mountain, California. The fate of the Marion is unknown. The narrow gauge engines had pulled standard gauge ore cars from Marion on the three-rail track to Daggett, thus avoiding an additional off-loading for shipment on the standard gauge Santa Fe.

From Marion to the Borate mines the railroad was narrow gauge.

Little is left of the Marion plant today—a few foundations, much rubble, (many square nails, pieces of fluted terra cotta, broken glass, pieces of kegs and their hoops, a piece of a conveyor bucket and other pieces of metal) scattered over quite an extensive area on both sides of the road.

The canyon leading into Borate bears south just east of Tin Can Alley. At present there is almost nothing left at the site of Borate, (a few pieces of broken crockery, a timber here and there sticking out of the side of the hill, bluegray tailings from the mines.) It is hard to imagine the hustling, bustling mining camp it must have been when viewing the site of Borate now. According to the company publication *The Story of the Pacific Coast Borax Company* the 120 men who worked there lived mostly in dugouts in the sides of the canyon. (Two dugouts can still be found, one of which would be large enough for one or two men, the other about eight.) The foreman, Perry, had a house, as did the storekeeper, W. W. Cahill. Next to the store was a reading room. A third house on top of the hill was called "Smith House," and was used by Smith when he visited Borate. A picture in the *Story of the Pacific Coast Borax Company* indicates a total of eight structures. The date given is "about 1900."

Before the railroad was completed Borate had no post office; the miners each paid a girl, Fanny Mulcahy, one dollar a month to ride horseback from Calico two or three times a week to bring the mail. Since this was a stag camp, they enjoyed the sight of her! There are three Mulcahys listed in the 1889 San Bernardino County Directory—Ed.D., miner; John D., miner; and Mrs. M., widow.

The Borax operations had a profound effect on the town of Daggett. Dix Van Dyke said that in 1902 three borax mines employed 200 men, this supported the town, since it was the shipping point. At that time Daggett had three stores, three saloons, two Chinese restaurants, a drug store and a lumber yard. It was larger than Barstow and Victorville. After the borax companies moved in 1907, the town consisted of one store, one saloon and one restaurant.

Other Borax operations in the area included the American Borax Company with its plant at Daggett and its mine at Columbus, and another company, Borax Limited, of London. Tax records of San Bernardino County also included the Palm Borate Company.

Little information was found as to wages paid Pacific Coast Borax employees in this area. The following letter gives some idea as to the wages and working conditions at the time. In 1883 William T. Coleman wrote to the D. W. Earl Company in Daggett as follows:

San Francisco March 14

Mesr. D. W. Earl & Co.
Daggett, San Bernardino Co.

Dear Sirs

Mr. Neuschwander my Supt at Amargosa & Death

Valley told me that he may need some men soon & I think if they can be had at Daggett it would be better to send them out from there. However, I would rather reject offers of men, concerning whom there is not reasonable assurance that they are good men, & will probably stick.—I want nothing to do with tramps, as you can appreciate the inconvenience, extra expense of hiring men who only remain a short time & leave—If you can find a few around Daggett, who in your judgement would be suitable, you will please forward them by the teams going out. In every case inform the men that they must take out their own bedding & although we have clothing at the store out there, they had better supply themselves if possible before going out.—Tell them they will be required to do any kind of work usual around works & that no men for special positions are needed; that they must expect to rough it if necessary until we get our buildings up. They may be sent to Death Valley where they must expect hot weather—I am trying to make my employees comfortable, but everything out there except Amargosa, is in a state of preparation. Several men have gone forward who pretended when they got there, that jobs were misrepresented to them, in order to have a pretext to be discontented, hence a caution to you to fully inform them of what they must expect. In each case please give the man a note to the Supt. say that he has been employed to do any kind of work which the Supt may see fit to put him at & that you have informed him fully of the state of affairs & what he is to expect—On the road out, transportation will be furnished for a reasonable amount of baggage, but the men will be expected to walk, whenever the head teamster requires it & they will be subject to his orders in everything of that sort & will be expected to help take care of the teams & cooking & c—kindly provide grub for them, but their wages will not commence until they are put to work at the works—You may engage six men besides the teamsters already engaged—The wages of those whom you engage will be $50.00 per month. Please write to Mr. Neuschwander informing him of the exact terms, on which men are engaged and ask him to inform you from time to time when he may need men—The men whom you engage, on reaching the works, will be subject entirely to the orders of the Superintendent & his Foreman—The Supt of course has power to discharge all employees who fail to suit—Address communication on subject to Mr. Neuschwander & also to J.W.S. Perry, so that, in Mr. N's absence, Mr. Perry may attend to the matter when they reach Amargosa. Eight mules & ten horses will probably go forward tomorrow & our Mr. Renner will accompany them & assist you in rigging out the teams. Kindly wire what success you may meet in this matter.

Hoping to have an early reply

I am dear Sirs

Yours truly

Wm. T. Coleman

In 1885, the Chinese coolies who built the road across the Devil's Golf Course in Death Valley were contract labor at $1.25 per day per man. If they returned the next season the pay was increased by 25 cents per day. Chinese laborers would apparently take jobs that no one else would take, however there is no indication that they were employed in the local borax operations.

Dix Van Dyke states in a manuscript in the Salisbury papers that the highest paid man in Daggett was Henry Blumenberg, Manager of the American Borax Company, at $150 per month. Superintendent M. Bouldin earned $125 a month, and his assistant, Newton Millett, made $110. Millett worked for American Borax seven days a week for seven years. White mill workers worked a 12 hour day for $2.50. Negroes from Louisiana earned 15 cents an hour. Miners earned $14 and board for a 70-hour week. The railroad paid Navajo and Mexican Indians 10 cents an hour for track labor. The section foreman earned $65 per month, plus free ice in summer and a house to live in. Some of the workers at the Marion mill were Lane Marshall, Frank Tilton, Dennis Coyle, Frank LaMantano, "Cottonball" Gray, "Klondike" Cook, Billie Burt, Enyon Timmons, Dick Hall, and H. E. Bouldino.

The San Bernardino City and County Directory (1889) lists a "Smilie" Tilton, farmer in Barstow and Thomas Gray, miner in Calico. In Daggett there were three Cooks: Henry H., mason; Joel, mason; and Warren, laborer. William P. Burt is listed as a Daggett farmer. The others do not appear in the directory in the three local towns listed. The nicknames of two of the men give us a clue to where they had been before coming to this area. "Cottonball" may have worked the cottonball deposits in Death Valley or elsewhere. "Klondike" may have come from Alaska. "Dolph" Nevares was a company employee; there is a Nevares Mountain in Death Valley. Frank Tilton is mentioned in books about Death Valley region. Tilton drove 20 mule teams between Amargosa and Daggett. He was afraid "Old Dinah" would put him out of work in 1894. In 1899 Tilton hauled supplies from Daggett to Jimmie Dayton, caretaker at the Furnace Creek ranch. He also figured in the story of Jimmy Dayton's death. He and "Dolph" Nevares, were sent out to look for Jimmy who was overdue coming in from Greenland Ranch (Furnace Creek). In 1940 he was a carpenter in the Tonopah & Tidewater shops at Death Valley Junction. It appears that Frank Tilton was a long time employee of the borax related companies. Mrs. Eda Henderson stated Frank Tilton built the Henderson store at First and Main in Barstow in 1924.

Jimmy Dayton was also a Pacific Coast Borax employee. He was a caretaker of Greenland Ranch, Furnace Creek, after the Borax operations moved to the Calicos. He appears in the 1889 County directory as a teamster in Daggett and was a swamper for Ed Stiles on the Death Valley-Daggett route. He died coming out of Death Valley in 1899 and is buried there. The story is one which adds to Death Valley lore.

Other teamsters working on the Amargosa-Daggett route were Charley Button and George Plant, and swamper, Bill Pitts. Pitts was lynched in Daggett for killing his driver. Ed Stiles drove the first 20-mule

OFFICES
39 J Street, SACRAMENTO.
RENO, NEVADA.
BATTLE MOUNTAIN, "
CARLIN, "
HAWTHORNE, "
LUNING, "
BELLVILLE, "
CANDELARIA, "
END OF TRACK, C. & C. R. R.
CALICO, CAL.

D. W. EARL & CO.
Forwarding and Commission Merchants,
WHOLESALE DEALERS IN
FLOUR, GRAIN, SALT, COAL, LUMBER,
Mining Timbers, Etc.

Calico, Cal. _____ 188__

Cash	13.06	DW E & Co.	4701.73
Mdse	1048.73	Duane	548.32
Frt	568.60	M T&T	274.35
Ibex Mines	512.02	A. Warden	87.07
Lot Co. C	114.60	A. Winters	14.77
DC & Co	91.87	Bennett	143.44
Delaney	151.15	Van Brasur	78.68
Bartlett Mfg.	820.00	Waters	203.06
AE Titus	223.86	Dunlap	4.43
HS Drew	1244.81		
HS Drew & Co.	215.88		
E. Borax wks	158.79		
McLaugh	268.71		
Osborne	229.36		
Howell	199.84		
Wixom	100.44		
Odessa	7.82		
Max	15.60		
O. Lamb	36.35		
A. Lamb	34.36		
	6055.85		6055.85

team from Daggett to Amargosa. In 1883, teamsters who freighted for Coleman and Smith were Charles Bennett, who owned three teams; Mr. Carter, J.H. Delaney, Mr. Crouch, and Joseph Cook carried mail and express to Amargosa and Death Valley for Coleman and Smith.

Seymour Alf was not an employee of the company, but did contract hauling for them. Ed Pitcher, husband of Ella Pitcher, well known Barstow pioneer, was an Alf employee. Pitcher was well liked and was considered an expert mule skinner. Judson Stickney, whose parents were Antelope Valley pioneer homesteaders, had an uncle, Russell Stickney, who was a 20-mule team driver.

Jerome Connelly worked as a fireman on the Borate-Daggett railroad and later became an engineer. According to the 1889 county directory Jerome Connelly was a laborer in Daggett that year. A man named Timmons was also engineer on the railroad, perhaps the Enyon Timmons mentioned above as a Marion employee, or a relative of the Virgie Timmons quoted in the Alice Salisbury papers.

John Ryan, Clarence and Lew Rasor, J.W.S. Perry, Wash Cahill, Christian B. Zabriskie, were all long time employees of Smith in his various operations. Ryan, the Rasors, and Cahill loomed large in the borax story after operations were closed in this area. Later Zabriskie became president of the company. All remained with the company and were involved with the construction of the Tonopah & Tidewater Railroad and the development of the Death Valley colemanite deposits. When a new ore was found at present day Boron it was named Rasorite for the Rasors. Perry seems to have dropped out when the Borate mine closed. Mr. and Mrs. Walter Alf of Daggett and Perry's daughter, Pearl, were long time friends. According to Mrs. Alf, Pearl Perry died in 1967.

John Roach, superintendent at Marion, was succeeded by Frederick William Corkill, whose father, Frederick Corkill, was a foreman at Borate. Three generations of Corkills held responsible positions in the United States Borax and Chemical Corporation, which succeeded the Pacific Coast Borax Company.

"Borax" Smith continued his rise in the borax business after operations were moved back to Death Valley. In 1896 he joined Pacific Coast Borax with a British Chemical firm to form Pacific Borax and Redwood's Chemical Works, Ltd. This gave the American firm new outlets and the chemical firm a source of supply. In 1899 Borax Consolidated, Ltd. was founded. Smith was the largest share-holder and became Managing Director in America.

Smith and a partner, Frank C. Havens, ventured in real estate in Oakland in 1895. Smith was also buying interests in transportation systems of the East Bay area. United Properties Company, a $200,000,000 firm was formed by Smith and associates in 1912. It was a great holding company and became the instrument of Smith's bankruptcy in May, 1913. He followed the unhappy lead of his former associate William T. Coleman and lost his borax holdings. Smith subsequently tried to recoup his fortune in another borax company, West End Chemical at Searles Lake, but did not quite succeed. He died August 27, 1913 at the age of 85.

Smith was an entrepreneur of great talent. He became a "king" in the borax business in part through his ability to choose dedicated, talented employees who grew with him. He was a rags to riches product of his times, and as long as he stayed with the borax industry he was successful; when he diversified it brought on his downfall. He must have been an admirer of Theodore Roosevelt, as his pictures indicate that his mustache, hair, and glasses were worn in the Rooseveltian style. Indeed there was a strong facial resemblance. He must have been a fairly regular visitor to the Mojave Valley as there was a house built for him near the mines at Borate, and his presence is noted in letters to D.W. Earl Co. in Daggett in 1883.

The production of borax in San Bernardino County was at its peak in the year 1902 when the total value was $2,198,100. Production exceeded $1,000,000 in the years, 1897, 1898, and 1899. It has been estimated that the borax taken out of the Calico hills amounted to an aggregate of more than $9,000,000.

Borax kept people employed here after the Calico silver production had waned. The borax era lasted longer than the silver era and ensured the prosperity of Daggett and Calico until 1907. The people worked long hours for small pay, but that was not unusual in the late nineteenth and early twentieth centuries. They were hardy souls who ate dust riding behind their teams—who had little water—and who had not the luxury of air conditioning. They played hard, too. They found their fun picnicking, dancing, drinking, and gambling at the saloons. As at other mining camps the men may have enjoyed the charms of the "ladies of the evening," that story remains untold.

LETTERS TO DW EARL & CO.

Messrs DW Earl & Co.

March 1883

Calico, Cal.

Dear Sirs:
Herewith S. R. for 1 sack seed sweet Potatoes 3 Bxs Plants & Trees (open)

Please forward at first opportunity & arrange for watering the Trees and Plants occasionally.

Yours

Wm. T. Coleman
Per Townsend

Also inclosed is receipt for 5¢ WMC for R.M.

37 *Rest stop on the Borax Trail*

Borax—The Green Flame

38 *"Old Dinah" Pacific Coast Tractor Wagon 1894 with Eng. Harold Grey, fireman Jerome Connely, Mr. and Mrs. Saunders and Hutchinson*

39-40 *Locomotives used to haul ore to the mills*

41 *(L) Nettie Mulcahy, Frank LaMaintain, (L) Ed Mulcahy, Jim Mulcahy, (L) Ed LaMaintain, Maurice Mulcahy*

42 *Evaporation Vats at Borax works - Daggett*

43 *Old Waterloo Mill - foot of Elephant Mt. - Daggett*

Messrs D.W. Earl & Co.   March 12, 1883
Daggett, Cal.

Dear Sirs:

Herewith S. R. for—6 Half Bbls Sugar, 2 Chests Tea, 6 Bx Candles, 1 Sk okra, 3¢ crackers, 1 Bx Soda, 1 Bx Cocoanut, 3 Kegs Syrup and 2 Bales Bags.

Which please forward by first opportunity to R.M. Amargosa. We will probably ship tomorrow 10 Head of Horses and a Teamster with Harness etc for the new wagon so you can hold all of our freight for loading it

. . . with Bill & S. R. Wagon Cover to replace stolen one $17.00.

        Yours
        Wm. T. Coleman & Co./Townsend

Mesrs D W Earl & Co.   Amargosa, Febr. 22, 1883
Calico Station

Dear Sirs

Enclosed please find card of McLaughlin which I omited to forward to you by last mail. I hope Mr. R. M. Smith has made some arrangements with you to send a lot of Provisions through to Coleman (Coleman is now the name of our Camp at Death Valley,) by McLaughlins Team upon his return to RR. Mr. Robertson, Agent of Wm. T. Coleman will perhaps be down on his way to S.F. and may then make definite arrangements. I shall order a general supply for Coleman by this mail in order to reach the Station in time for McLaughlin to load.

        Respectfully yours
        R. Neuschwander, Supt.

AMERICAN BORAX COMPANY– 1900's
(Reprint — *San Bernardino Weekly Times Index*)

On or about September 15 the American Borax Company of Daggett will be in the market to furnish patents in the desert with bricks made from its borax tailings, after the boric acid is extracted. The brick will be sold at such a price that it can be used in preference to lumber at the present selling price.

This working up of the by-products of the American Borax plant has taken several years of experimenting, and now they are utilizing everything that they mine. In other words, their ore is ground to 60-mesh then treated to extract the boric acid; then the residue is composed into bricks—of which they make two kinds, common red brick and Mexican adobe . . . and will give consumers along the line a brick which will cost them less than the brick has ever cost heretofore on the desert.

The American Borax company expects later on to make pressed brick roofing tile, or any fireproof material that can be used on the desert. The advantages

brick or adobe houses have over wooden houses on the desert are well known for they are cooler in the summer and warmer in winter, and they can be built absolutely fireproof.

The only reason heretofore that lumber has been used mainly in the Mojave desert was that the price of fireproof material such as brick, was excessively high. This is now overcome by utilizing the by-products.

It is believed any one who will investigate before building, will find they can erect a fireproof house as cheap as a wooden house on the desert, which will be safer and far more comfortable for the householder or storekeeper.

The American Borax company has exceptional facilities for making this brick and has put in modern and up-to-date machinery. The company . . . can load the bricks direct to the cars from the spur, thereby giving the consumer every possible advantage.

DAGGETT TAX ROLLS

Lot Book 14, San Bernardino County Mountain and Desert 1904 - 1907

American Borax 1905, 1906, 1907	3469	
American Borax 1905, 06, 07		3466½
American Borax 1905, 06, 07		3462
Pacific Coast Borax 1905, 06, 07		3464
American Borax Company 1905, 06, 07		3463

PERSONAL PROPERTY TAX
March 1903 — San Bernardino County

NAME	ASSESSED	TAXES		
Assessor W.A. Mc Elvaine			Page 9	
1903				
March				
20 American Borax Co.	5000	100.00		
Seymour Alf	955	17.10		
17 D.W. Earl Co.	2100	42.00	P-11	
			Manvel	
20 Alex Falconer	600	12.00	P-13	

NAME	ASSESSED	TAXES
D.W. Earl Co.	220	4.40
23 J.J. Lefurgey	400	8.00
May		
14 J.C. Mulcahy	100	2.00
1904		
March		
22 Seymour Alf	900	18.90

106

	Earl & Co.	2100	44.10	Manvel
31	Earl & Co.	225	4.72	Daggtt
	Alex Falconer	800	16.80	
	American Borax Co.	5000	105.00	

April
8	J.J. Lefurgey	400	8.40	
	Mulcahy	100	2.10	

1905
March
15	Earl & Co.	2100	50.40	Manvel
18	Alf	550	13.20	
	Earl & Co.	225	5.40	Daggtt
	American Borax Co.	7400	180.00	
19	Falconer	800	19.20	
	Lefurgey	400	9.60	
	Mulcahy	100	2.40	

1906
March
6	Mulcahy	80	1.84	
	Falconer	800	19.20	
	Earl & Co.	225	5.17	Daggtt
	Lefurgey	560	12.88	
	Alf	550	12.65	
	Alf	45	10.35	Yermo
	Earl & Co.	2100	48.30	Manvel

1907
March
7	Falconer	750	16.50	
	Lefurgey	350	8.25	
	Alf	550	12.10	
	Earl & Co.	225	4.95	Daggtt
		1100	24.20	Manvel
	Alf	450	9.65	

1908
	Alf	250	4.75	
	Falconer	750	14.25	
	Alf	550	10.45	
	Earl & Co.	225	4.25	Daggtt
	Alf	200	3.80	Wtrmn

1909
March
	Earl & Co.	250	5.50	Daggtt
	Falconer	750	16.50	
	Alf	550	12.10	
	Alf	250	5.50	Yermo
	Alf	200	4.40	Wtrmn

1910
April
18	Alf	600	9.90	Yermo
11	Earl & Co.	350	5.75	
11	Falconer	1450	23.90	
18	Alf	1200	19.80	
	Alf	300	6.00	

MINING CLAIM

The following is taken from an 1893 mining report on San Bernardino County, written by W. H. Storms, Assistant in the Field:

Twenty-three miles northeast from Daggett are the Alvord Mines. The property has changed hands several times, but is now owned by a party of Pasadena capitalists who have under consideration the reconstruction of their mill which was burned in September, 1891.

The property consists of six full claims located on one mineral-bearing zone . . . The mine is well equipped. The company also owns a millsite at Camp Cady, on the Mojave River, 9 miles distance from the mines, as well as valuable water rights at Paradise Springs 11 miles northwest from the mines; and a spring about one and one-half miles east of the camp which is used for camp purposes only . . . To Mr. Burnham's report I am endebted for information concerning the value of the rock, tonnage and bullion out to date. He has given arbitrary figures for shipments aggregating $37,000 and an estimate on $13,000 more, making a total of $50,000. This ore was milled mostly at the Camp Cady mill and at Hawley's Mill.

DEATH VALLEY SCOTTY

A FAMOUS BARSTOW VISITOR
Barstow Womens Club Members 1938

For more than 30 years an outstanding figure in the news, Walter Scott, traveled in and out of Death Valley —one time broke—the next time with pockets full of money. The source of his wealth, it is said, not even his wife knows. Scotty tells various glamorous tales about it which he does not expect anyone to believe.

In the early days he and his wife made regular trips to Barstow, their headquarters being the L.J. Henderson store. They and their pig were well known in the little desert town. Finally the pig grew up and had to be discarded as a traveling companion.

Scotty over sensationalized Los Angeles when he zipped down Spring Street in a buckboard filled with money which he strewed along the way.

In 1905 Death Valley Scotty chartered a Santa Fe Train to Chicago from Los Angeles for himself and party. It was one of the miracle times when his pockets were full of money which he spent with a lavish hand and threw to the children along the way. What a good time the newspapers had writing up the trip of the

"Coyote Special."

About 15 or 20 years ago Scotty met up with A.M. Johnson, a Chicago banker, in Death Valley for his health. A friendship sprang up resulting in a $1,800,000 castle for Scotty. It is a magnificent place with a cooling and heating system, fountains, marble halls, pipe organ and every luxury money could buy, including a storehouse full of the choicest of food stuffs.

Since then Scotty claimed to be broke but says that he knows where there is plenty of gold to be found His greatest delight is to go to San Bernardino and Los Angeles and be interviewed by reporters.

BARSTOW GOLD BEGINS TO SHOW
by Beth Pinnell

"Barstow Gold Begins to Show" so reads a headline from the January 1, 1906 issue of the *San Bernardino Sun*. The day before articles of incorporation for the Barstow Mining and Milling Co. were filed with the Los Angeles County Clerk. Capitol stock was listed at $1,000,000 in shares of the par value of $10 each.

"The property owned by the company is located opposite Barstow, near an old cemetery," states the article. "The first locations were made by C. W. Reach, a special officer for the Santa Fe, who claimed to have discovered gold galore. Soon all manner of startling accounts of rich strikes were in circulation and a stampede was created."

The news article reports that there was also a "systematic effort to jump the claims" and that the first attempt was thwarted by two of the company's stockholders. Then it was "alleged" that one of the stockholders had been found alone and was "brutally beaten by the jumpers, who secured temporary possession of the property, but were soon arrested by the special officers of the Santa Fe."

COOLGARDIE PLACER MINES
by Nellie Payne
1938—Barstow Womens Club

The Coolgardie placer mines are located about sixteen miles north of Barstow. They were discovered by Dick Duncan and called the Black Nuggett, named after a famous mine in South Africa. The mine produced over $100,000 in free gold. Duncan made his discovery by picking up a handful of black sand, the free gold remaining in his hand.

Robert Greer owned a mine in this area about 1900 called The Yucca; it was nothing for him to take out $75.00 per day in free gold. Greer had the first scales and weighed all the gold for the miners.

GEORGE B. PARKS, BARSTOW PIONEER
by Joseph Randolf Duarte

George B. Parks was one of the early pioneers of Barstow. He came to the area to settle in 1899.

He was born in Urbana, Illinois on December 2, 1879, of German-Dutch parents. After living the first 18 years of his life on the farm with his parents, he enlisted in the Fourth United States Cavalry, Troop E with the rank of Private. He saw action in the Philippines as the orderly of General Funston and later was honorably discharged.

After being discharged, Parks came west and worked for the Southern Pacific Railroad in Sacramento, California. When his job was finished with the railroad, he went to Silver Creek, near Oroville, California, where he located his first placer diggings. When winter came he left his claim and started down state.

Parks arrived in Barstow in the winter of 1899 and found work as a carpenter. He built many of the houses on First Street in the old town. One of them was for Ed Pitcher, an early pioneer of Barstow.

He knew many of Barstow's old timers. Among them were: Arthur Doran, Lubin Henderson, Thomas Carter, Mrs. Ella Pitcher, White and Platt, the Fogelsongs, Sturnacles, Dolphs, Griffiths, DeWolfs and Cunninghams.

In 1920, Parks began mining at the Calico Silver Mine and the old Waterman Gold Mine. When he learned more about mining and prospecting, he began to explore for himself in the desert area. He did most of the work on his mines himself. He prospected for gold, silver, nickel, tungsten and turquoise, Parks sold some of his mines in the 1920's for as much as $40,000, which in those days was a small fortune. He was a very generous person and often grubstaked miners less fortunate than himself. In the early 1930's he sold another mine and was working as a professional prospector for out-of-town people.

In 1934 he located the Conceback mine, and started the Desert King Mining Company, which was located about 10 miles out of Barstow on Fort Irwin Road. The Desert King was a low-grade gold mine and did not pay very well. In 1936 he located the Mary Nickle mine also on Irwin Road. He worked the mine with two hired men, but was unable to promote enough capital to work on a big scale. He held this claim until 1946. In 1938 he located a small gold mine between Barstow and Yermo. This mine he called "Coyote Wells." In 1939 and 1940 he prospected between Barstow and Baker and found tungsten deposits, but they were of low-grade ore and not worth working. In 1945 he located the Golden Reward in the Ord-Bellville mining district.

Much of the mining Mr. Parks did is classified as dry placer mining. There are three types of placers: residual, transported, and dry placer. Residual placer mining utilizes bearing rock broken down by disintegration of chemical alteration. Transported placer mining involves moving the gold and rock fragments from their source. Dry placer methods of mining employ the use of air instead of water to separate the gold and other rock particles.

Mr. Parks was married twice, both times to Barstow women. Little is known about his first wife except that her first name was "Lovie." His second wife was named Julia Soliz, they were married on January 21, 1930, in Las Vegas, Nevada. Prior to Julia's death November 7, 1941, her granddaughter, Mary Soliz, came to live with the Parks'. When Julia died, Mr. Parks continued to take care of Mary and saw that she finished school.

On July 13, 1942, Mary married a local boy by the name of Joe Duarte and shortly thereafter Joe left for overseas. Parks lived with Mary until Joe returned in October of 1945.

Parks kept up his mines in the months that followed, until he became ill. He had a military funeral on November 8, 1946 and is buried in Sawtell Memorial Cemetery.

George B. Parks was truly a pioneer. He displayed the characteristics that made small mining camps grow into towns and towns develop into cities. With his work on the mountain sides, he and others like him left untold memories of an era not quite lost in the minds of men.

A STUDENT INTERVIEWS KEN WILHELM—1962
submitted to "Frankie" Simon
(Barstow High School Teacher)

As I walked into the huge yard it looked as if it were some kind of auto graveyard. But as I looked closer I observed that they were not ordinary autos, but crude looking creations equipped for the rugged terrain which surrounded them. Some were fenderless freaks and others had special gadgets and seats welded on for the comfort of the occupants. Each was a shaggy masterpiece. But they all had one thing in common: they were all very tired.

I stood for a moment wondering if I had come to the right place to talk with the man the local residents had told me would know more about the desert than anyone else. I glanced about until my eyes fell on the most hideous wreck of all, an old touring car with balloon tires. There, toiling over the miserable looking thing, was a short, stout grumbling man with head thrust into the engine compartment. I began to walk toward the old car, noticing that this was the hottest place I had been in my life. Upon my approach the stubby man turned, I noticed for the first time that he was wearing a grease stained, dust caked hat that was badly wrinkled and pulled down over his ears. His little round beet red face was streaked with grease and sweat. The skin was drawn tightly over the face in evidence of many summers of exposure to the hot desert sun. He held a stub of a cigar tightly in his teeth and his little blue eyes danced merrily.

He stuck out his hand and said: "Wilhelm's the name. What can I do for you?"

I told him I was new to the desert and the people of the surrounding area told me that he could give me some interesting information and tell me some of his fascinating experiences on the desert. He suggested we go into the house.

Entering the house I found a large collection of guns and various types of archery equipment. The house was simple but comfortable. Being quite inquisitive, I asked him to give me a brief history of himself. He explained that he had come to the desert in 1922 with his older brother, Walt, and his father, Sherman. Liking the area they leased about 30,000 acres for the purpose of oil speculation. Their land started about 13 miles east of Yermo, bounded on the south by a Union Pacific R. R. stop named Manix.

I was astonished to find that this Manix stop was used to unload Texas longhorn cattle for Sidney D. Smith, who owned the Fort Cady ranch in the early 1900's.

Asking about the weird cars I had observed, I was told that they were used for wild desert escapades, such as roping coyotes with his good friend Erle Stanley Gardner who visited him often and wrote books of their adventures. He also told me that the car he was working on was a 1912 Reo with a special seat mounted on the front for an archer to shoot rabbits. Shooting rabbits with a bow and arrow?!

He told me that he had shot a collar button off of his brother's head on the "YOU ASKED FOR IT" T.V. program a few years previous. In addition to being an expert geologist, and a mining engineer, he was also a world famous archer. I was beginning to realize that Ken Wilhelm was quite an extra-ordinary individual.

I asked if an oil well had ever been drilled? Ken stated there had been two drilled, one in 1924 the other in 1930. Neither one was successful.

Wilhelm's latest activities have been the drilling of a third small well which produced in 1960, and the leasing of the Fort Cady Ranch in 1960. In addition to this he has many mining operations going all over the desert area.

I have related to you, to the best of my ability, the story of Kenneth Wilhelm—Mining Engineer, Geologist, world famous Archer and Master Mechanic, and certainly an asset to the Mojave communities. I think you will agree that Ken Wilhelm is a most exciting and colorful character.

CHARLIE WILLIAMS
(as remembered by ROY ELLIOTT)
by Louella Bishoff

We came to Barstow in 1937. That year and the next we ran around all over the desert looking for pretty rocks. In 1938 we wore out one set of tires doing just that.

When I was over in the Opal Mountain district looking for opals, I ran into a monument (a prospector's claim marker) with Charlie Williams' name on it. After I came back into town, I met Charlie at the pool hall and said to him, "I bet you can't guess what I found out there in Opal Mountain district?"

He replied in his distinctive nasal twang, "What was it, Roy?"

"Well, I found a monument out there with Charlie Williams' name at the top."

"Well! By golly! It just takes a Missourian to find somethin' like that. I've been huntin' for three years for that thing. Will you take me out there tomorra?" And I did.

Charlie was quite a rock hound. He had one of the biggest rock collections in the state, at that time. A black light display brought out all the unseen beauty of the seemingly colorless desert rocks. One of his specialties was geodes. Charlie told the following story to me one day when we were talking about the value of his collection:

> One day a lady came into the Gem Store, picked up a half a geode that had been polished, and asked me what it was worth. I replied: " Well now I'll tell you. You get into your jeep. You take your dinner with you, your lunch, and water. Go out there in the desert and look all day. Maybe you'll find one, maybe you won't. Well, you go out the next day, and let's say you find one eventually. You bring it in here, and you saw, and saw, and saw until you get it sawed in two. Then you polish it and polish it. Here, you're lookin' at both of them, one in one hand, and one in the other, and you drop one and break it all to pieces. Now, what's this other one worth?

He was quite a character.

Early on in the history of Barstow, Charlie Williams had homesteaded some property south of the present Main Street. After the town began moving south from the tracks, he started selling it off. He told me the following story about one of his sales of property on Main Street, near the corner of First and Main, for which he received $10,000.

He went down to San Bernardino to fill out the papers. Charlie was drinking pretty heavy about that time. He told them if they got the papers made out in time to get to the bank before it closed, "I'll just knock off a thousand dollars." They did.

He went to the bank, got the money, in cash, put it into a paper sack, threw it in the back of his Ford, and came home. He spread it out on the table at home and was counting it when the fire siren blew. Charlie was a member of the volunteer fire department, so he threw a newspaper over the money and went to the fire, leaving his door wide open. When he came back the money was still there.

He then said he had to hide it, " 'cause that's too much money to leave lyin' around." He had a little lean-to garage next to his house with a floor made of brick just laid in the sand. He took up some of the bricks, dug a hole, and put the money in it. Then he covered it back up.

"One day," he told me later, "I wanted some money, and you know, Roy, I forgot where I hid that darn stuff. I think I tore up every damn brick—it was under the last one, anyhow."

Many years later, after Charlie had been drinking rather heavy and was broke, his wife who lived up north somewhere wanted to get him home. I think it was some of the businessmen in town who bought him a ticket on the train, and even took him to the depot and put him on the train. Later that day when one of them; went into a local bar, there stood Charlie. They said to him, "I thought you left on that train."

"Well," he said, "I'll tell ya. You guys are pretty smart. You put me on that train, but I just got off on the other side and came back to town. When I want to go somewhere, I guess I'll know when I want to go!"

Charlie was a pretty witty ol' boy. In his younger days, before he got married, he was in the Navy and traveled all over the world. He told me about being in China, Japan, and all over the South Pacific. I don't remember any of those stories he told me, only that he said he had a good time.

He not only told the townspeople a story or two, but one time he even roped in a tourist passing through. It seems Charlie was standing on a corner downtown one day when a car pulling a boat came from the west and stopped in front of Charlie. The driver asked, "Which way is the river?"

Charlie said, "Well, see that gas station there across the street? You go in there and fill up your tank until it can't take any more. Then, you turn east and keep going until you think you don't have any more gas in the tank. You go to the top of the next hill and look down, and there it'll be. But we don't do our fishing there."

"Where do you fish, then?" asked the driver.

"Well," said Charlie, "We go out to one of the dry lakes nearby."

"What on earth could you catch there?" replied

the driver.

Charlie retorted, "Dried cod fish, you fool!"

He was a great pool player, a real good one. Charlie played, a lot of times for money. I played with him some, but of course I didn't play for money because he usually had more money than I did.

I don't think Charlie had an enemy in the world. If he did, it was himself, for he liked to drink. As a man his word was good. Everybody liked him. Sober or drunk he was always joking with you. "A very good guy!"

THE STAUDINGER FAMILY
by Miriam Staudinger Oxsen,
edited by Germaine Moon

Land around Newberry Springs was already homesteaded by 1910. Few people lived in the area because of the scarcity of jobs other than the employment available at the railroad.

In the 1930's the situation improved when bentonite mining began operations. Land was selling then for one dollar per acre but no one could afford it for lack of money.

The bentonite claims were originally discovered by Oscar L. Hoerner who filed and named each claim after a kind of fruit. The main claim which Percy Staudinger worked for the next 27 years was called the "Lemon" mine located about three miles west of Pisgah Crater and seven and one half miles north of Hector siding on the Santa Fe railroad.

Percy, an enthusiastic young man, came to the desert to seek a new life. He obtained a contract to mine bentonite from the California Talc Company. When Percy first began to develop the mine he lived in a tent at Hoerner's gasoline station and drove a Model T back and forth from Mojave Water Camp to the mine. Later on he moved closer to the Lemon mine, still lived in a tent, and had to haul all the necessary water supply.

Bentonite is a rock composed of clay minerals formed by the alteration of minute glass particles that once composed volcanic ash. The name was derived from the Fort Benton series of Cretaceous rocks in Wyoming where it was first found.

To extract and mine the bentonite, Percy, and other miners, dug underground tunnels and blasted the clay ore loose, a hazardous and difficult task. To operate safely they braced the tunnel walls with wood posts and headboards. As timbering progressed, lighting was provided by carbide lamps worn on the miners' hats and larger carbide lanterns hung on the bracing posts. Underground the temperature was constant at 60-65 degrees Fahrenheit. The bentonite was loaded into ore cars, hoisted to the surface and emptied into dump trucks, then transported to Hector where it was spread on drying platforms. Afterward the bentonite was loaded into box cars and shipped to Los Angeles on the Santa Fe railroad.

In 1930, Percy acquired a Model T pickup to drive but from the $125 monthly pay promised, he received only $100 because the California Talc Co. claimed they couldn't afford so much.

About 1932 Karl Diehl was hired and later promoted foreman of the Lemon mine where he worked many years. The company employed from six to fifty men, their pay varying from 40 cents per hour in 1932 to 75 cents per hour in 1948. Mining operation being the main support of the community, almost everyone in Newberry has worked at the mine at one time or another.

In 1932 Percy was promoted supervisor, but the best event of the year was when Dorothy, his wife, and Miriam, their daughter, joined him from Los Angeles where they had been living. At first, desert life was a challenge for Dorothy, especially their first home, a one room shack with steps made of railroad ties. She built a warm and cozy home wherever they lived.

Once a week she drove to Highway 66 to meet Dad Crowel's ice truck and "refrigerate market." Along with blocks of ice, he sold meat, vegetables and fruits. In addition to other purchases Dorothy bought ice which lasted but one day or two.

Time passed; California Talc Co. became Baroid Sales Division of National Lead Co. The company built a two bedroom house for the Staudingers at a new location west of Hector where they lived until 1945.

The "Mine House," as they called it, was an improvement over the shack. A "REO" truck, equipped with a 500 gallon tank, hauled the water from the Santa Fe railroad. Only coal oil lamps and coleman lanterns lit the home until a very exciting venture, the purchase of a "Light Plant." The house was wired, sockets and bulbs installed and the big night came. The generator was cranked up and in an instant electricity illuminated the room.

In the 1930's, traveling on newly completed Highway 66 which had replaced the old six or seven feet wide road, Percy, Dorothy and Miriam went to Daggett. They bought all their supplies at Homer Ryerson's store and stopped at Milletts' Cafe which served "all you can eat" dinners for 50 cents.

By hand augering and churn drilling prospectors brought the discovery of another bentonite mine, west of Hector. Mining started by digging an open pit until the ore vein was located, then tunneling began. This new mine operated 24 hours a day on eight hour shifts. In 1935 a sudden flash flood inundated the tunnels, ruined all the equipment and filled the open pit. However, there was no loss of life but further mining was impossible at this site.

In 1936 a second daughter, Ann Staudinger, was born in Barstow at Sarah Thornburg's Nursing Home. Barstow had no hospital then.

Miriam and Ann attended Newberry's Fairview grammar school and both graduated from Barstow High School. They rode the bus driven by Dutch Dorrance to grammar school. Going to High School they caught the bus at 7:30 a.m. and returned at 5:00 p.m.

The Staudingers and Newberry's residents joined in recreational activities. PTA meetings, school plays and Saturday night dances were held at Fairview school. Everyone brought his own lanterns as there was no electricity. Mothers took along their children; this was before the babysitter invention. School desks were pushed together and covered with blankets and pillows for the children to sleep on. Kathryn Dorrance was the only one who could start the coal oil stove to make coffee: she knew the precise "bang, kick and shove" to get the stove going. They all danced to the sounds of Cliff Barnes on the guitar and jazzbo, Dutch Dorrance on the banjo and jazzbo and Vangie Hoerner McCoy at the piano.

Outdoor games and get-togethers were also held. The softball field was where the Continental Telephone Company Substation is now. At community picnics the people gathered at the Cliff House (now Newberry Market) where huge cottonwood trees shaded the picnic tables. Each family brought food and drinks which were shared by all. The men played horseshoes and everyone cooled off by jumping in the pool. The pool was the highlight of the day for the kids. Afton Canyon was another site for community get-togethers.

In 1945 the Staudingers moved from the Mine House to build their own home on Ft. Cady road. On their property was the water well which ended 16 years of drudgery-hauling water! Through the efforts of the Farm Bureau, and at the cost of $100 per pole, electricity was conducted to the house.

American Tansul and Inerto Co. hired Percy to oversee their experimental pilot plant, located at Newberry Springs. The new plant developed the refinement of bentonite making it usable for cosmetics, lotions, juices and liquors purification, and pharmaceutical purposes. Under Percy's supervision the pilot plant proved so successful that it was made permanent. National Lead Co. purchased American Tansul and Inerto Co. and they modified and enlarged the plant which is still in operation today.

In 1975 the Staudingers celebrated their golden anniversary at the Newberry Springs Community Center. Friends from far and near attended their reception. The Staudingers took part in community activities and helped to organize many worthwhile projects since they first came to the desert.

Percy loved the desert and his favorite pastime was prospecting. He said that this area was the best place to live, and he lived a full life until his death on October 13, 1975.

SHORT FUSE CHARLIE

by Bill Mann

In 1962 a colorful old miner came in off the desert to get some explosives. His eyes were black and blue and one side of his face was a massive, nasty bruise with an ugly cut stitched up through the middle.

I said, "What in the world happened to you?" and he told me the following story:

He was alone in the Silver Peak mountains west of Victorville, blasting boulders one Friday afternoon when he found he was running out of fuse. He had only about 10 boulders left and it was 56 miles to our powder magazine, so he took what fuse he had and divided it into the number of boulders he had and cut it into 10 or 12 very short pieces. He then plastered the dynamite on top of each boulder. He said he figured that if everything went all right he would be far enough away when they went off. He had all but the last one lit when the first one went off and a big rock chip hit him flat on the side of his face. It knocked him down and stunned him. He remembers the explosions getting closer and closer to him, so he managed to crawl far enough away from them to keep from getting killed.

He lay still until he got enough strength to crawl over to his old pickup and drive to the hospital at Victorville.

From that day to this, he is known out on the desert as "Short Fuse Charlie." Incidentally, he carries plenty of fuse with him now.

Chapter V

Rails Upon The Sand

*Riding over rails
Laid upon old desert trails,
Through the ages past.*

THE RAILROAD EXPLORERS

by Pat Keeling and Clifford Walker

So desolate does the region look that the traveler unfamiliar with the desert scene often feels a sense of insecurity and a vague wish that one could see something reassuringly green. As one travels on the railroads leading to Barstow, he sees the large expanse of endless desert, mountains, valleys and dry lake beds. At different times of the year, one beholds an awe inspiring sunset of pinks, reds, purples, golds and silvers playing on the cloud formations. At night millions of stars shine out from the black velvet sky and at moonrise the beauty of the honey gold sphere above the mountain tops bathes the desert in a pale glow. The traveler always has many sights to behold within the vast desert. In the mid 19th century, the explorers, surveyors and the railroad builders came into this country.

The Indian trails were used by Spanish traders, then by Jedediah Smith, William Wolfskill, Joseph Walker, Antoine Leroux, and other "Mountain Men" who discovered new routes to Spanish communities on the California coast.

The United States sent many survey parties into the upper Mexican Republic, and direct trails were established from Santa Fe and Albuquerque, New Mexico, westward to the Pacific Ocean. These are called "The Spanish Trail," a northern route; "The Gila Trail," a southern route; and "The Mojave Trail," a middle route. These formed a path for the later coming of wagon trains, horse-soldier forts and the railroads.

One of the first early U.S. Army explorers was Brevet Captain John C. Frémont, who usually managed to find something attractive in every California panorama, but in 1844 could only see the desert as a glaring scar. He was stunned by the ugliness of the Mojave Desert from the heights of a Sierra mountain, where everything behind was lush and green. He saw the great expanse of plains, without water or grass—without anything . . . "Every animal that goes out there dies," he was told. Frémont could not believe the great change in the landscape in so short a distance.

When he at last reached the Spanish Trail, he commented in his journal:

> A general shout announced, that we had struck the great object of our search, The Spanish Trail, which here was running directly north. The road itself and its course were equally happy discoveries to us . . . The course of the road, therefore, was what we wanted, and once more we felt like going homeward. A ROAD to travel on and the right course to go were joyful consolations to us; and our animals enjoyed the beaten track like ourselves . . . Between us and the Colorado River we were aware that the country was extremely poor in grass and scarce for water, there being many days journey 40-60 miles, without water, where the road was marked by bones of animals.

(Report of the Exploring Expedition to the Rocky Mountains in the year 1842 and to Oregon and North

California in years 1843-1844, Sen. Doc. 166, Washington 1845 by John C. Frémont, Brevet Captain.)

Fremont descended the Mojave River, which to his amazement, "Instead of growing, dwindled away, so it was absorbed into the sand."

John C. Frémont later returned to live in California, serving briefly as the Military Governor of the state, and later in the United States Senate. He was the first Republican candidate for President, running against Buchanan in 1856.

With news of the gold discovery in California in 1848, a new era began for the state. The gold fever had drawn pioneers westward and Californians and New Mexicans were no longer satisfied with the government roads and monthly mail services. They wanted an all-weather route from the Atlantic states to California, railroads to allow communications and transportation between Salt Lake, Santa Fe, and all points east and west. At that time the desirability of constructing a trans-continental railroad was the subject of discussion in all parts of the country, even though Congress did not authorize a survey of all available routes until later.

In 1851 Brevet Captain Lorenzo Sitgreaves took a military survey party along part of the 35th parallel route. He made a safe trip from New Mexico, via Zuni, the Falls of the Little Colorado and Bill Williams Fork to the Colorado River. Above The Needles Sitgreaves visited the Mohave villages where brisk trade ensued. The Sitgreaves party included 35 soldiers, five American and 10 Mexican hired hands, ably guided by ex-trapper Antoine Leroux. Several years before Leroux had traveled as far west as the Mohave tribes on the Colorado River enduring great hardships. On February 4, 1853 Leroux wrote a letter to William Seward recommending the 35th parallel route for a railroad. He stated in the *Daily Missouri Republican* on February 17, 1853:

> I have crossed from New Mexico to California by four different routes, namely: Cooke's Sonora route, the Salt Lake Route, that recently followed by Capt. Sitgreaves party, and the Old Spanish Trail . . . I have trapped on nearly every stream between Cooke's route and the great Salt Lake, and am well acquainted with the region of country between these places.

Because of Leroux's recommendations and others Congress approved the 35th parallel route.

In 1853 Captain Joseph Walker submitted a railroad report to the California Senate Committee on Public Lands about a pass he discovered in 1834. The route Walker favored in his recommendation was substantially the same as he later called Walker Pass. On January 13, 1834, he departed from Mission San Juan Bautista, and may have utilized the Indian trails through Pacheco Pass to the banks of the San Joaquin River. A railroad could start from Monterey and cross the coastal range through Pacheco pass. It could follow the San Joaquin river down the valley and head across the continent through Walker Pass. Walker recommended three possible railroad routes across the desert after leaving the Walker Pass. One was the Mojave River eastward to the Colorado, a second along the Owens River and east by the Humboldt River and the third directly east to Las Vegas and the Muddy River. In 1853, the Walker Pass was easily accessible and traveled by many convoys bound for California in search of land or gold. Since the Walker route was obviously practical, it is difficult to comprehend why it was not selected.

At this time the Benton-Frémont alliance in Congress was the most powerful force in the development of the Western routes. Their influence used against a 32nd parallel route prevailed and expediency was substituted for practicability. Thus more explorers closely examined the 35th parallel route.

Although traversed in part by trappers before and immediately after the Mexican War in 1848, and for some distance by Capt. Sitgreaves, the 35th parallel route was first examined from New Mexico to California by Francois Xavier Aubry. He made two trips with his sheep from New Mexico to California. On his return in 1853 and 1854 he also wanted to find a practical route for an Atlantic-Pacific Railroad. Aubry entered the Mojave desert via the Tejon Pass, followed the Mojave River past the present Camp Cady, then headed northeast. He reached the Colorado River below Black Canyon and crossed the river a short distance south of the present Hoover Dam.

When he returned to Albuquerque, Aubry met Lieutenant Amiel W. Whipple, who took along a copy of Aubry's journal for his survey team. After his second trip Aubry still thought the 35th parallel route was the best one for a railroad although he now recommended that it be constructed through the Tehachapi instead of over the Cajon Pass.

Lieutenant Robert S. Williamson, Topographic Engineer, explored several passes between the San Joaquin Valley and the desert. In September, 1853, at Tejon Pass, he noted in his *Report of Exploration in California for Railroad Routes to Connect with routes near the 35th and 32nd Parallels of North Latitude:*

> Near the eastern extremity of the Tejon is a break in the mountains, known as Tejon Pass. Through this break a wagon raod has been made leading to Los Angeles, and it is one of the worst roads I ever saw. This pass has been much and favorably spoken of as a railroad pass . . . The Tejon Pass is a peculiar one. The altitude is quite great; but the ascent and descent appear to be gentle, except near the summit. It was hence supposed that, by means of a tunnel, the pass might be found to be a good one.

Williamson skirted the northern slopes of the San Gabriel Range through the Cajon Pass and down the Mojave River. A part of the expedition then proceeded along the river to its sink at Soda Lake and northward to the Salt Lake Road about five miles north of dry Silver Lake.

In 1854 Lieutenant Amiel W. Whipple reached the Mohave Villages on the Colorado River to begin the last leg of his railroad survey along 35th parallel. He obtained a sub-chief Cai-rook to guide the party to the watering holes, and show the way to the Puenta del Agua, the point where the branch road from Santa Fe and Salt Lake strikes the Mojave River. As the Indians guided Whipple over the mountains, the party was divided into three groups to insure enough water for the animals. This route later became the old Government Road, following Piute Creek, Rock Springs, Marl Springs, Soda Lake and the Mojave River. The Union Pacific Railroad now travels on part of it. Lt. Whipple, however, recommended that the railroads take the dryer, more direct route between the Mohave villages and present day Barstow, which is now used by the Santa Fe Railroad.

In 1857 Lieutenant Joseph C. Ives, Corps of Topographical Engineers was ordered to explore the Colorado River from the Gulf of California upstream for possible navigation for steamboats. Accordingly, Ives designed and had built at Philadelphia a steel steamboat 54 feet long of a form believed to be practicable for navigation of the Colorado River. Naturally, this had a very shallow draft. The boat was shipped, dismantled, aboard the steamer Monterey to the mouth of the river where it arrived on November 29, 1857. The material was not unloaded until December 2, but the boat was shortly reassembled and on December 31, 1857 the trip upstream began. In Ives' comments in *Report Upon the Colorado River of the West, Explored in 1857-1858:*

> Fort Yuma was reached on January 5, 1858, . . . the Mohave Indian villages on February 11, · · · the mouth of Black Canyon on March 8 . . . (Further ascent proved difficult.) The boat then struck a submerged rock and the concussion was so violent that some of the men were thrown overboard.

He found the head of navigation to be a point which was located at the foot of Black Canyon. (This area was flooded by Lake Mead when Hoover Dam was built in 1933.)

Ives concluded that the lower end of the canyon was the end of practicable navigation. It was shortly after this trip that Fort Mohave was established in 1859. From that time, until 1917, river steamers hauled freight and passengers regularly from Yuma to Ft. Mohave.

In 1866 Brevet Brigadier General James F. Rusling explored the region and visited Fort Mohave on the Colorado River. He wrote in support of the railroad:

> . . . The great drawbacks to Arizona overshadowing perhaps all others, not excepting the Apaches, was the perfectly frightul and ruinous cost of transportation. To reach any mining district there from California, except those along the Colorado, you had to travel from three to five hundred miles through what are practically deserts; and for every ton of freight carried into or out of the Territory, you were called to pay from three to five cents per pound per hundred miles, in coin . . . The patent and palpable remedy for all

of this is either a railroad or the speedy and regular navigation of the Colorado . . . All attempts to develop herself except from that, in the absence of a railroad, seem likely to end like the efforts of the man who tried to build a pyramid with the apex downward. History declares it was not a success. *(The Great West and the Pacific Coast.)*

General Rusling's writing seemed to have had a great influence on Washington, and in 1868 the Army sent another general to look at the 35th parallel route.

General W. J. Palmer visited Fort Mohave in January 1868, for President Andrew Johnson's recommendation of a railroad subsidy for the 35th parallel. "This was the best route across the continent," said Palmer. "And it will be quite a change for the customers to buy watermelon at Christmas and tomatoes raised by the Mohaves in January," (*San Bernardino Guardian*, April 25, 1868.) Palmer's impression of the route was that a gradual descent to the Colorado River had been found.

It was 14 years after this statement that the railroad dream of the early pioneers became a reality.

RAILROAD AND OTHER LAND GRANTS
(Encyclopedia Americana 1955 edition)

After 1850 and the admission of the State of California into the Union, a strong agitation developed for the construction of a railroad to the Pacific Coast which resulted in the acts of July 1, 1862 making grants of lands to the Union Pacific RR Co., the Central Pacific RR Co. and other roads. There were many subsequent land grants to railroads up to 1871.

The land grants to the states and railroads for railroad purposes provide usually for a grant of odd sections with six to 10 miles on either side of the line of road. In some cases the grant was 20 miles in width on either side. In addition the roads were authorized to select indemnity lands where any portion of the main grant had been otherwise disposed of. As of June 30, 1918, the area patented to railroads was 85,927,123.63 acres or 65 percent of all grants to states for easement purposes, wagon roads or railroad grants.

In addition to this, the granting acts authorized the issue of U. S. 6 per cent bonds in aid of the construction of the Pacific railroads on the basis of $16,000 per mile in the Great Plains east of the Rockies; $48,000 per mile for the portion crossing the Rocky Mountains; $32,000 per mile for the line through the Central Plains with similar grants to the Central Pacific for the western part of the line. These bonds of the U. S. were a second lien against the property of the companies.

The total bond issue for the Pacific roads was $64,623,512. All have made settlements except the Central Branch of the Union Pacific, which still owes the principal of the bonds, $1,600,000 plus interests which amounted to $1,977,000 to March 31, 1919. This debt is being very slowly reduced by credits due to the transportation of public property.

RAILROAD GIANTS INVADE THE MOJAVE DESERT
by Germaine Moon and Pat Keeling

A huge area of seemingly empty space stretched from the Mississippi to the shores of the Pacific Ocean. The railroad's giants were playing a mammoth and new kind of monopoly game. The Big Four in California, Holliday and Frémont in the Midwest and all the eastern magnates were at war! Behind them, townsmen, farmers, miners and merchants were lending capital, voting on bonds, voicing desires, trying at best to enter the game themselves.

Everyone had the railroad fever, even Washington officials. Their objective was to unite the country. First they sent surveyors, Frémont, Whipple, Sitgreaves, Beale, Ives, Williamson and others, and bickered over their reports. Finally, on May 20, 1862, Congress passed the "Homestead Law" and on July 1 the Pacific Railroad Act, sweetened by the "Railroad and other Land Grants," thus launching the construction of the railroads heading west.

With the California railroad delegation returning from Washington were two heroes, the state junior Congressman Aaron A. Sargent and Theodore D. Judah, a railroad delegate from Sacramento. Both men had prepared and moulded the "Pacific Railroad Act"

adopted by both houses of the 1862 Congress.

Previously Theodore Judah (1826-1863), a young engineer, surveyed and projected the Sacramento Valley railroad, the first built in the state, which opened its 22 mile line to Folsom, February 22, 1856. At the Pacific Railroad Convention held in San Francisco, in September, 1859, and after years of fruitless discussion, Judah was able to convince Californians that a line over the Sierra Nevada was feasible from an engineering and fiscal standpoint. It was during this convention that Judah met and impressed the future Big Four who, with Judah's technical cooperation, organized and built the Central Pacific railroad. It began at Sacramento in 1863 and on May 10, 1869, linked with the Union Pacific at Promontory, Utah. It was completed December 31, 1885.

From the Central Pacific, the mother company, emerged the Big Four: Collis P. Huntington, Mark Hopkins, Charles Crocker and Leland Stanford. None was rich at the start. Their total worth in 1862 was less than $112,000. Yet, by every means conceivable, they built an empire. They jumped upon the country with their Chinese laborers and mutated into a gigantic

Politicians

1   John B. Daggett, California's Lt. Governor-1882-1886.

3   Gov. Waterman's youngest daughter, Miss Abby Lou: early School Board Member, Active in forming the Barstow High School.

4-b   Robert Withney Waterman, California's Governor 1887-1890.

And
Railroad Giants

2   Cyrus K. Holliday, the "Dreamer," Incorporator and first president of Santa Fe Railway

4-a   Thomas Nickerson, the "Organizer," Santa Fe's 8th president,

4-c   William Barstow Strong, the "Executor," Santa Fe's 10th president.

117

dragon. Their rivals and Santa Fe labeled them "the Octopus." Individually or together, the Big Four formed other railroads and contracted to build them with their own construction companies or companies in which they had interests.

The Big Four looked around and couldn't resist expansion. Twenty years before the completion of their first venture, they fathered a most promising gamble, the Southern Pacific Railroad Company of California. It was incorporated in December, 1865. The company pledged to build a railroad and telegraph line from San Francisco Bay south through all the coastal counties except Santa Barbara and from San Diego east to the boundary of the state at Yuma, there to connect with a railroad from the Mississippi River. This description indicates a linkage on the 32nd parallel. But, in July 1866, the Congress granted the Southern Pacific another route, roughly along the 35th parallel. It was to meet the Atlantic and Pacific at the Needles on the Colorado River.

On the 32nd parallel route, speeding eastward, the Southern Pacific reached Colton in 1874 and immediately established freight yards, depot buildings and a round house. San Bernardino citizens made strenuous efforts to have the line routed through their town on its way south. To negotiate with the company they promptly appointed a blundering committee whose members missed the chance of a lifetime by greedily underbidding Phineus Banning.

> . . . The railroad demanded a grant of land in San Bernardino suitable for a station and freight yard. The City refused to provide free land. Phineus Banning and a group of Los Angeles businessmen saw an opportunity. They not only offered free land but a bribe of six hundred thousand dollars if the railroad would come through Mint Canyon to Los Angeles.

The oversight was fine for Ellis Spackman who wrote this comment in the May 19, 1972 San Bernardino Sun-Telegram, entitling his article, "Why San Bernardino is not L.A. Hooray!" The railroad certainly guaranteed Los Angeles tremendous wealth.

As a result of Banning's action, the Southern Pacific raced down the San Joaquin Valley, paused long enough to establish the town of Mojave in 1876, and on September 6 provided Los Angeles their much awaited trans-continental connection.

Oh yes! Between the railroad giants were shady deals and politicking in Washington, in Sacramento and other state capitals, and in local government. Transcontinental steel roads were big business and profits the stake of the game. The rules were that the railroad company which laid its tracks first reaped land grants and other federal aid after securing state and local approval and subsidies.

Huntington's Southern Pacific, busy with its 32nd parallel linkage, met Jay Gould's Texas and Pacific at Sierra Blanca, near El Paso, December 1, 1881. It didn't stop at Yuma or the Colorado, but pushed aside faint hearted competitors along the way and by January

1883, reached New Orleans. The Big Four-Jay Gould Alliance had boxed rival interests out of California. But, in the process, Huntington antagonized an equally ruthless and determined opponent, William Barstow Strong of the Atchinson, Topeka and Santa Fe Railroad. Santa Fe lost its chance on November 28, 1878, when Strong and Nickerson decided to use the Atlantic & Pacific 35th parallel charter instead of following Robinson's urging to build on the 32nd.

The Rollins Bill recognized the original charters of transcontinental roads including the Leavenworth, Pawnee and Western Railroad of Kansas. In 1863, Frémont and associates acquired control and made a ridiculous attempt to launch a railroad under the name of Union Pacific Railway, Eastern Division!

Samuel Hallett, the builder, was murdered July 27, 1864, by O.T. Talcott, the chief engineer. Frémont, the principal owner, sold out, but kept the Kansas franchise. By the end of 1864 he lost control of his Mariposa estate in California and in 1870 everything else.

On December 11, 1865, Frémont and a handful of speculators introduced a bill in Congress to charter a railroad from Missouri and Arkansas to the Pacific, along the 35th parallel. The milestones began in Springfield, Missouri, reached Albuquerque via the Canadian River valley, proceeded across the western states, snaked up the San Joaquin Valley and ended in San Francisco. The line was to be completed by July 4, 1878, thus creating the Atlantic and Pacific Railroad. A clause in the law authorized a portion of the line from San Francisco to the Needles, to the Southern Pacific.

Frémont sold securities in the Atlantic & Pacific as it progressed slowly toward California. By 1872, the A & P had grown to 361 miles and extended from Pacific, Missouri, near St. Louis, to Vinita, Oklahoma.

On April 26, 1872, Atlantic & Pacific interests in St. Louis accepted an invitation from San Francisco businessmen to discuss the possibilities of a transcontinental connection between the two cities using the A & P franchise. After investigating the A & P charter at St. Louis, the San Francisco delegates were dismayed to discover that a portion of the route fell into Indian Territory. They resolved to build a road owned entirely by California capitalists. The financial depression of 1873 and the pressure of its enemies, crushed Atlantic and Pacific; by 1875 it was bankrupt.

In Arizona between 1878 and 1883, John C. Frémont sat in the governor's chair financially destitute as his railroad dream encircled the territory. He must have conjured up the devil against the sadistic forces that had combined against him. His former railroad now the St. Louis and San Francisco known as the "Frisco," emerged on September 11, 1876. It held the lion's share of the 35th parallel charter with possession of the A & P's enormous land grant. Until 1879, it built aggressively from Aurora, Missouri, westward invading the Atchison, Topeka and Santa Fe realm in southern Kansas. Strong and Nickerson seized half of the Atlantic & Pacific charter in negotiations with James D. Fish, President of the Frisco. They signed the Tripartite Agreement on November 14, 1879. The Frisco stopped construction at Wichita and was to use Atchison, Topeka and Santa Fe rails being built to Santa Fe and Albuquerque. From this point, A.T. & Santa Fe, Frisco and A & P would jointly build and sponsor a company called the Atlantic and Pacific Railroad to California.

Early in 1880, Nickerson became President of the Atlantic & Pacific. The agreement was ratified between the Frisco, A & P, and Santa Fe. By this time Strong, Nickerson, and Robinson had already started their newest projects, the Atlantic & Pacific's Isleta-Needles road and the California Southern, San Diego to Barstow, meanwhile strengthening their system with the Mexican Central to Guaymas.

Before the Atlantic & Pacific could span the Little Colorado 26 miles west of Winslow, with a bridge over Diablo Canyon, the Southern Pacific's Colorado Division had sent its dragon across the Mojave Desert and was the first to brace the Mojave-Needles route with iron.

In August 1882 William Hood, Chief-Engineer of the Southern Pacific, landed from the company steamer "Mohave" at the Needles. S.P.'s Colorado Steam Ship Company ran vessels on the Gulf of California and the lower Colorado. After the trip upriver from Yuma, Hood, with 30 men and 35 animals, departed westward to survey the line. Working in reverse, a large construction crew and 60 Chinese had started from Mojave on February 20, 1882. As they labored eastward incessantly digging and laying tracks they were expected to gobble up the Atlantic & Pacific scales, tail and fins.

On October 23 the tracks reached the settlement and silver mill of Waterman & Porter on the north bank of the Mojave river. The Waterman section house and tool shed was 70 miles distant from Mojave.

Southern Pacific's rails crossed the river at the base of "B" hill, turned eastward and followed the Mojave southern bank to the site of Fish Pond, an area settled earlier as a way station. In 1867, ranch owner Lafayette Meacham called his station the "Accidental" Hotel. He provided shelter, food and necessities to weary travelers.

Emerging from Fish Pond, October 1882, S.P. passed Elephant Mountain and built its facilities, a coaling station for locomotives, a telegraph and ticket office, and passenger accommodations at Calico Junction, after 1883 called Daggett. Since December 1880 and the filing of Waterman's claim, the silver craze raged in the Mojave Valley and the Calico hills sprouted with "bonanza" strikes. S.P.'s arrival in 1882 opened the area to throngs of promoters, miners, merchants, professionals, and various adventurers.

Southern Pacific was past Ludlow as 1882 ended; at Amboy by February 12, 1883, and at Goffs by March 19, 1883. The railroad already supplied isolated mines with necessities, including water at two cents a gallon from Newberry Springs.

At Needles the Southern Pacific built a 14-stall roundhouse, a large depot accommodating 500 people, a "magnificent" hotel and numerous buildings. At Mojave, Calico Junction (Daggett) and Needles meals and telegraph service were available. Amboy and Fenner just had section houses and the telegraph.

By April 19, 1883, with the last spike hammered in place, Southern Pacific's Mojave-Needles road was completed. The Atlantic & Pacific finally arrived on the east bank of the Colorado in May, immediately building a bridge. On August 8, Santa Fe's puppet enterprise, A & P, crossed the Colorado after completing the Isleta-Needles road. A & P land grant of 14,325,760 acres was almost untouched, two (2) million acres had been sold and 8,000 acres were used for rightaway (when the line went into receivership in 1897). Behind the scene was Santa Fe moving on to California's financial paradise!

On September 13, 1883, another Atchison, Topeka, and Santa Fe enterprise arrived at San Bernardino battling its way out of San Diego. The California Southern Railroad was organized February 2, 1880, chartered on October 12 and had absorbed the California Southern Extension, chartered May 23, 1881, by consolidation. The Extension was to build their part of the San Diego road from San Bernardino to a point 81 miles northeast (Barstow-Daggett) there to link with the Atlantic and Pacific. But the Southern Pacific had already built their Mojave-Needles line and held the junction point and the road in between.

California Southern Chief Engineer, J. O. Osgood, surveyed the route through the Temecula Canyon and was fired for overspending in 1882. He was replaced by F. T. Perris, surveyor of Cajon Pass. J. N. Victor was appointed the Road Superintendent in August 1882 and remained until 1888.

Presiding over the California Southern was Thomas Nickerson, "the Organizer," flanked by Boston capitalists and supported in San Diego by Frank Kimball, the Chamber of Commerce and the town citizens.

San Diego was the western seaboard of the 32nd parallel charter, Frémont's Texas Pacific scheme. In 1872 Thomas A. Scott, president, changed its name to Texas & Pacific. Gaining sufficient support in San Diego, Scott constructed 10 miles of tracks to National City. The completion date was to be July 5, 1876. Unable to terminate the project, Scott offered to relinquish the line, but San Diego refused. However, in 1879, Kimball and associates contacted Santa Fe officials in Boston, who naturally jumped at the chance. Release of one-half of the lands and terminal facilities was effected December 11, 1879. Thus 27 days after the signing of the Tripartite agreement Santa Fe gained their western seaboard and the Southern Pacific the southeast counterpart, New Orleans for their Sunset line (32nd parallel).

In 1875, Los Angeles built a railroad to Santa Monica and grading commenced in Cajon Pass. Los Angeles and Santa Monica R.R.'s principal projector and president, U.S. Senator John P. Jones, hoped to build the line all the way to Independence in Inyo County, which was in the midst of a mining boom. In 1878, S.P.'s Big Four bought Jones' interests and apparently Santa Fe acquired that road for their California Southern Extension.

In January and February 1884, storms washed out tracks, trestles and bridges in the Temecula Canyon, destroying 30 miles of line and arresting the California Southern for nine months. In July the company defaulted. Very convenient, since the "Big Trade" was taking place. On August 20, 1884, Southern Pacific "sold" their Mojave-Needles branch to Atlantic & Pacific, and on October 25, 1884, Atchison, Topeka & Santa Fe officially bought the California Southern.

For constructing the 242 miles of Mojave-Needles road, the Pacific Improvement Company, a Southern Pacific subsidiary, received in stock and bonds an average of $24,000. per mile. The Atlantic & Pacific paid S.P. in cash and bonds, an average of $30,000. per mile. A terrific trade considering that S.P. still owned the road's original land grant.

> " . . . Southern Pacific railroad Co. for example, owned 2,043,651 acres of "outlying lands" in California. The term refers to property which is not included in railroad rights of way or lands otherwise used directly in rail activities.
>
> This land, incidentally returned to Southern Pacific $2.4 million in oil and natural gas rentals, $2.7 million in agricultural leases, $149,000 in grazing fees, $2.3 million in timber sales and $321,000. in mining lease fees . . . " *Los Angeles Times,* August 27, 1967.

In 1885 Chinese and Mexican crews toiled from Cajon summit as grading progressed in opposite directions. Then, rails were laid and the last spike driven on November 15. The first eastbound passenger train departed from San Diego on November 16. The first Pullman from Kansas City, arrived in San Diego on November 26.

By the time the California Southern reached the junction behind "B" hill, south of Waterman, the railroad was in Santa Fe's hands although Atlantic and Pacific remained the legal owner's until May 4, 1897. Scant railroad facilities were built by California Southern east of the junction. Families settled and business interests moved close to the track. A post office was

established in May 15, 1886 and the budding town was named Barstow in honor of William Barstow Strong "The Executor" of Atchison, Topeka and Santa Fe's western achievements.

Literature and newspaper reports depicted the California Southern and the Mojave-Needles roads as a battleground for control between Strong and Huntington. Because Strong opposed entering into Pooling Agreements with other railroads once he had reached San Diego and Los Angeles, he began to cut passenger fares. Within a short time, rates from Kansas City to the West Coast dropped from $24, minus a $3 rebate, to $16. For a brief period, passenger fare sank as low as one dollar. Having had the foresight to purchase speculatory land, Strong most opportunely created a real estate boom and additional revenues.

On December 23, 1894, Atchison, Topeka & Santa Fe went into the hands of receivers . . . and on December 10, 1895, the railroad died. Edward King, representing the Atchison, Topeka, and Santa Fe "Railway," bid 60 million dollars . . . The Frisco and the Colorado Midland (Union Pacific link to Salt Lake) were abandoned. On May 4, 1897, the A & P from Albuquerque to Needles was foreclosed and returned to Atchison, Topeka, and Santa Fe Railway, with a 12 million dollar debt and the land grant. From all the lines west of Isleta, New Mexico, a new corporation was created, the Santa Fe Pacific Railroad, which remained until 1911 when all titles were cleared. Thus the Mojave-Needles route changed its name from Atlantic & Pacific R.R. to Atchison, Topeka & Santa Fe R.R. in 1897.

Meanwhile, C.P. Huntington had died (1900), and his empire fell into the hands of Edward Henry Harriman, the Union Pacific's "Law and Master," until 1909. The last railroad giant to wage battle for a route ownership through the Mojave desert was Harriman versus U.S. Senator William Andrew Clark. Both contestants co-owned the San Pedro, Los Angeles and Salt Lake railroad in 1905. The route was purchased in 1921 by the Union Pacific.

THE DREAMER: CYRUS K. HOLLIDAY
Father of the Atchison, Topeka and Santa Fe
by Germaine L. Moon

At the age of 28, Cyrus K. Holliday arrived on the Kansas scene during the fall of 1854 with two dreams. Founding a town and having it named the state capital, the other, building a railroad over the old Santa Fe Trail and beyond. His first objective was realized in 1859 when Topeka became the state capital.

On February 1, of the same year, Holliday, then a member of the Territorial Legislature, introduced his

own one-man Atchison and Topeka railroad charter bill. The bill sailed through both the House and the Senate and was approved by the Governor on February 11, 1859.

When construction began at Topeka in October 1868, Holliday predicted that the railroad would reach the Pacific Coast and the Gulf of Mexico.

THE ORGANIZER: THOMAS NICKERSON
by Germaine L. Moon

In 1870 Atchison, Topeka and Santa Fe was a mere infant, of less than 60 miles, verging on the threshold of bankruptcy, when the Nickerson family and their

financial magicians took over. Nickerson, as Santa Fe's eighth president, 1874-1880, was their Grand Wizard. He re-organized the company's shaky finances and sought investors even among his friends. If Nickerson was elected president of a rival or new company, it soon succumbed and fell into Santa Fe's fold.

Although cautious, Nickerson yielded to long range investments when, as Atlantic & Pacific's president, 1880-1881, he engineered the birth of the Frisco following the Tripartite agreement, giving Santa Fe opportunity for western expansion, as well as trackage into St. Louis.

Unable to circumambulate Jay Gould's new empire in Kansas and in Colorado, he advocated building to Guaymas, Mexico, and transacted the San Diego's capture. While those two ventures were taking place, he served as president of the two railroads, the California Southern and the Mexican Central, 1880-1884.

Behind Thomas Nickerson were his brothers all powerful railroad businessmen, Joseph was Atchison, Topeka and Santa Fe's director; nephew, Albert was AT & SF's board member; and Frederick was Union Pacific's director . . . Yes, in the bosom of "the" rival company!

THE BUILDER: ALBERT ALONZO ROBINSON

by Germaine Moon

Albert Alonzo Robinson came to Atchison, Topeka and Santa Fe in 1871. He was William Strong's "right hand" and a major asset in enlarging the company. Promoted to chief-engineer in 1876, during the cattle trade rush to Dodge City, he supervised 5,000 miles of construction during his career with the company.

Strong and Robinson were firm expansionists, not easily thwarted by obstacles. In 1877-1878, together, they contrived, seized, and conquered the 8,000 ft. Raton Pass in a triumphal victory over William J. Palmer's Denver and Rio Grande Railroad.

In 1893, Robinson, then vice-president and general manager, disagreed wholeheartedly with the shady accounting practice of Atchison, Topeka and Santa Fe. Having been passed twice for promotion, he resigned to become president of the Mexican Central, which had been used as a trade-in for the Southern Pacific's Mojave-Needles road, a chicanery concealed until 1897. Thus in 1893, A.A. Robinson joined the enemy camp, the Southern Pacific Railroad.

THE EXECUTOR: WILLIAM BARSTOW STRONG

by Germaine Moon

William Barstow Strong Esq. was drafted by Atchison, Topeka and Santa Fe, in 1877, when he appeared as a vice-president and general manager. He had gained insight into railroading by ascending from station manager and telegraph operator to general superintendent of different railroads. He is worshipped by the Santa Fe Railroad's historians and they credit him for some 6174 miles of its growth. He executed the dream and desires of the company creators.

Historians also depicted Strong as the gladiator, forever defending and protecting Atchison, Topeka & Santa Fe against the hated Southern Pacific baron C.P. Huntington and ally Jay Gould, the Kansas Pacific mogul. Strong gained a victorious foothold in California but nothing in Colorado or in Kansas in his fight against Gould. On the contrary, because of his agressive policies, Strong was blamed for the Atchison, Topeka & Santa Fe financial debacle of 1888, when he lost the presidency (10th president) and was demoted to menial tasks. In 1889, he resigned and abandoned railroading altogether.

EARLY COMMUNITIES ALONG THE RAILS

by Pat Keeling

The locations of early communities followed the expanding railroads.

Stations along the lines existed for various lengths of time, some acquiring facilities and developing into permanent thriving communities. Some smaller stations were short-lived but still provide a colorful part of desert history.

"Needles" is the initial example of the expanding stations and opens the story of early communities along the rails.

In 1883, as a terminus of two railroads, the Southern Pacific Railroad and the Atlantic and Pacific Railroad, "The Needles" was destined to be of more than passing importance to California. It had many natural advantages, plentiful water, level land, and a good river crossing, and some disadvantages, the intense heat and scant population.

In the first year of 1883, the Southern Pacific depot, providing accomodations for 500 people, impressed many sight-seeing passengers. Meanwhile the Southern Pacific Railroad built a roundhouse and utilized a mechanical department consisting of trainmen and track crews. It employed many men and paid large sums of money in salaries every month. This steady work, along with monetary abundance, attracted many families to the area.

The A. & P. acquired the Colorado Division (Needles-Mojave) from the S.P. line. The first train over the new A. & P. division from the east on May 4, 1884, was driven into "The Needles" by Engineer Robert M. Watson.

5 Railway Pass

Rails Across The Mojave

6 First Train in Barstow?

7 Sept. 13, 1883 - California Southern enters San Bernardino
County

9-10 Engine #11

11 Waiting on the siding between Victor(ville) and Hesperia,
Nov. 1886

8 First California Fruit Express 1888

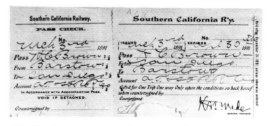

12 Mr. Brown's pass - Barstow to San Diego

The Colorado division opened many new job opportunities along the 242 mile route and the population began to increase.

The San Bernardino City and County Directory of 1889, published by McIntosh, Flagg & Walkens, had this to say about Needles:

> There is perhaps no village in San Bernardino County which has sprung so suddenly into notoriety, and which has such an assured future of prosperity as Needles. At the last census, the population of the town scarcely figured up to 150, but within the past few months it has rapidly gone up to 650. New dwellings have been erected, new stores built, a newspaper established, and bustle and activity have taken the place of graveyard quiet and dullness.
>
> The town is on the line of the Atlantic & Pacific Railroad. The Colorado River, a stream navigable by boats partially encircles it from the north and east, and affords fine facilities for the transportation of ores from the valuable mines adjacent. A daily mail from the east and one from the west, together with a tri-weekly mail each way from Fort Mohave, place it in thorough communication with the world. Besides four large flourishing merchantile establishments, Needles has three saloons, a hotel, two lodging houses, six restaurants, an express and telegraph office, a flourishing public school, and a hospital of the Santa Fe Railway Employees Association. Being headquarters for the California division of the A. & P. Railroad, here are located large machine shops, roundhouse, a store house, and the offices of division officials of the company.

Stations along the right of way between The Needles and the junction point at Daggett included Hartoum, Java, Klinefelter, Ibis (Ibex), Bannock, Homer, Goffs (Blake), Piute, Fenner, Essex (Edson), Arimo, Danby, Siam, Cadiz, Bolo, Bengal, Saltus (Bristol), Amboy, Bagdad, Trojan, Siberia, Klondike, Ash Hill, Ludlow, Argos, Lavic, Pisgah, Hector (Haslett), Troy, Watson, Newberry (Water), Minneola, Gale and Daggett.

In 1882, when the Southern Pacific Railroad built at Daggett, there were wagon way-stations and feed lots, adobe houses, and the Stone Hotel.

The San Bernardino City and County Directory of 1886 gave a glowing account:

> This is a station on the Atlantic and Pacific Railroad about ten miles east of Barstow. It is the railroad station for Calico, which is six miles north. The elevation of the town is about 2000 feet above sea level; the present population is about 300.
>
> There is a fine passenger depot and commodious freight house. The Railroad Eating House kept by Mr. Seymour Alf is said to be one of the best hotels and an excellent lodging house; there is a post office, Wells, Fargo & Co.'s express, telegraph and telephone, and all modern advantages.
>
> The place is provided with good public schools and three general merchandise stores. There are two Justices of the Peace, Messrs. J. A. Johnson

and J. A. Owen. There is one lawyer, Mr. C. J. Perkins, a graduate of the State University of Wisconsin and a man of fine ability. The fine stables and stage line of Messrs. Barrett & Greer are located in Daggett.

> The large forewarding and commission house of D. W. Earl & Co. is doing a fine business. They also deal in mining supplies, hay, grain, etc.
>
> There are reducing works and two quartz mills, one of 20, and one of 5 stamps located here. Northeast from Daggett are the Providence Mountains gold mines. The Mojave River passes near the town.

On the south side of the Mojave River, from Daggett, the Southern Pacific Railroad ran past Fish Ponds (Nebo) and Grapevine stage station on the north side of the river, past a station across the river at Waterman. Connections with the Central and Southern Pacific Railroad Line at Mojave were possible. Along the S.P. right of way, stations were located at Mace, Hinckley, Eades (Harper) (Hiawatha), Hawes, Jimgray, Kramer, Boron (Amargo), Rich, Solon, Muroc (Rodriguez) (Rodgers), Hut, Bissell, Yucca and Mojave.

In 1885, the California Southern Railroad Company connected with the then Atlantic and Pacific Railroad line on the Mojave River creating Waterman Junction, and built the first facilities there.

A railroad Engineeer, Frank Hutt, who retired in 1940 after serving Santa Fe for 53 years, reminisced to the *Printer-Review* of April 12, 1951, about Barstow's past and its facilities:

> Before the founding of Barstow, there was a railroad station named Waterman on the northwest side of the Mojave River, across the railroad bridge. It was named for Governor Waterman who owned a mine nearby and a mill also. All the facilities, first built at Waterman siding, were inaugurated and completed by the California Southern Pacific Railroad Company, which manned the station and yard and ran the junction for some time. The California Southern Railroad, a separate company but backed by Santa Fe capital, built north from San Diego through San Bernardino to Barstow, arriving there in November 1885 . . . In those days, the coaling station for locomotives in this locality was at Daggett. Trains and engine crews of the A. & P. would eat at section houses anywhere between Needles and Mojave.

Those railroad yards, station and turn-table were destined to become a community named Barstow in 1886. The Atlantic and Pacific put in a roundhouse, steam generating plant, a freight house and other facilities.

The San Bernardino City and County Directory of 1886 tells of Barstow:

> Formerly called "Waterman" is the terminus of the California Southern branch of the Atchison, Topeka and Santa Fe railroad and the point of its junction with the Atlantic and Pacific railroad. It is 82 miles from San Bernardino and 12 miles from Daggett.

13 Atlantic and Pacific Railway 1896

17 Southern Pacific Railroad station - note double roof - 1890's

Barstow Grows

14 Before 1900's, tracks ran north of Stockyard Hill. Old Harvey House still standing. Railroad depot disappeared.

15 Wagon bridge over the river at Buzzard Rock - 1905

16 Million dollar construction, the new Harvey House - rails run south of Stockyard Hill. Note Dillingham's new apartments in lower left.

Early 1920's.

ATLANTIC & PACIFIC RAILROAD—WESTERN DIVISION.

WESTWARD No. 1. Pacific Express. Daily.	Distance from Mo. River		STATIONS. See Main Line time table page 9.		EASTWARD. No. 2. Atlantic Express. Daily.	
3.30AMWe	887	Lv	†Albuquerque	Ar	12.50AM	
3.35AM	895	Lv	Barr	Ar	12.25AM	
3.40	897		Isleta		12.20	
3.50	900		A. & P. Junction		12.11AM	
4.20	911		Luna		11.45PM	
4.45	922		Rio Puerco		11.15	
5.20	934		San Jose		10.44	
5.50	947		El Rito		10.15	
6.10	953		Laguna		9.55	
6.25	959		Cubero		9.41	
6.54	970		McCartys		9.20	
7.26	983		Grants		8.45	
7.55	994		Bluewater		8.20	
8.34AM	1009	Ar	Chaves	Lv	7.50PM	
†9.10AM	1023	Ar	†Coolidge	Lv	7.10PM	
9.30AM	1023	Lv	Coolidge	Ar	6.45PM	
9.51AM	1033	Lv	Wingate	Ar	6.20PM	
10.17	1045		Gallup		5.55	
10.35	1053		Defiance		5.19	
10.54	1061		Manuelito		4.41	
11.30	1074		Allantown		4.08	
11.50AM	1087		Sanders		3.35	
12.15PM	1100		Navajo Springs		3.00	
12.45	1113		Billings		2.28	
1.15	1125		Carrizo		1.50	
1.50	1140		Holbrook		1.25	
2.43AM	1151		Hardy	Lv	12.56PM	
†3.10AM	1172	Ar	†Winslow	Lv	12.30PM	
3.45AM	1172		Winslow	Ar	†11.59AM	
4.20PM	1185	Lv	Dennison	Ar	11.25AM	
4.59	1198		Canon Diablo		10.55	
5.44	1209		Angell		10.29	
6.10	1215		Walnut		10.15	
6.25	1220		Cosnino		10.03	
7.15	1231		Flagstaff		9.35	
7.57	1243		Bellemont		8.55	
8.40PM	1255	Ar	Chalender	Lv	8.18AM	
†9.15PM	1265		Williams		7.45AM	
9.45PM	1265	Lv	Williams	Ar	7.15AM	
9.54PM	1268		Supai		7.05AM	
10.12	1273		McLellan		6.43	
10.31	1278		Fairview		6.15	
11.05	1288		Ash Fork		5.30	
11.25	1296		Pineveta		5.05	
11.59PM	1306		Crookton		4.35	
12.25AMTh	1315		Prescott Junction		4.05	
12.57	1326		Aubrey		3.32	
1.26AM	1338		Yampai		3.00AM	
2.00AM	1352	Ar	†Peach Springs	Lv	2.00AM	
2.30AM	1352	Lv	Peach Springs	Ar	1.40AM	
3.05AM	1364	Lv	Truxton	Ar	12.55AM	
3.37	1375		Hackberry		12.10AM	
4.15	1387		Hualapai		11.30PM	
5.00	1402		Kingman		10.40	
5.30	1413		Drake		9.35	
6.05	1426		Yucca		8.52	
6.45	1439		Franconia		8.09	
7.15AM	1453		Powell		7.28PM	
†7.30AM	1461	Ar	†The Needles	Lv	7.00PM	
8.00AM	1461	Lv	The Needles	Ar	†6.15PM	
8.20AM	1468		Java		5.52PM	
8.49	1475		Ibex		5.33	
9.21	1484		Homer		4.58	
9.42	1492		Goffs		4.27	
10.02	1502		Fenner		3.45	
10.21	1509		Edson		3.12	
11.10	1518		Danby		2.39	
11.10	1531		Cadiz		1.54	
11.45	1539		Bristol		1.27	
11.45	1545		Amboy		1.07	
11.59AM	1553	Ar	†Bagdad	Lv	12.45PM	
12.15PM	1553	Lv	Bagdad	Ar	12.15PM	
12.45	1560		Siberia		11.52AM	
1.29	1570		Ash Hill		11.23	
1.45	1577		Ludlow		11.00	
2.07	1585		Lavic		10.32	
2.30	1596		Haslett		10.00	
3.00	1609		Newberry		9.30	
3.30	1621		Daggett		9.05	
†3.50PM	1630	Ar	Barstow	Lv	8.45AM	
4.30PM	1630	Lv	Barstow	Ar	†7.45AM	
4.34	1641		Waterman		7.40	
5.01	1640		Hinckley		7.18	
5.23	1650		Harper		7.00	
5.58	1663		Kramer		6.20	
6.38PM	1681		Rogers		5.35AM	
7.30PM	1691	Ar	Mojave	Lv	4.45AM	

Barstow is the point on MAIN LINE (A. & P. R. R.) where passengers, through or to Southern California, take the California Southern Line. See Map.

Mojave is junction point on Southern Pacific R. R. for passengers who do not go by the way of Southern California. See Barstow as above, and map.

CALIFORNIA SOUTHERN R. R.—BARSTOW DIVISION.

SOUTHWARD. No. 39. Daily.	No. 1. Daily.	Miles	Time changes One Hour. STATIONS.		NORTHWARD. No. 2. Daily.	No. 38. Daily.
5.20 AM	3.30PMTh	1630	Lv	Barstow	Ar	6.30AMTh	11.30 AM
6.05	3.49	1642		Cottonwood		6.05	10.50 AM
6.38	4.04	1651		Point of Rocks		5.45	10.12
7.18	4.34	1661		Oro Grande		5.24	9.45
8.00	4.50	1667		Victor		5.13	9.15
8.42	4.59	1675		Hesperia		4.53	8.43
10.12	6.07	1692		Summit		3.58	7.45
11.07	6.37	1703		Colon		3.08	6.42
11.42 AM	6.55PM	1711	Ar	†San Bernardino	Lv	2.45AM	6.10 AM

13

18 Time tables - October 1888

19-20 *Mohave Indian Village—two civilizations meet—early 1900's.*

24 *Atlantic & Pacific Roundhouse, Needles, 1890. Square water tank, built according to Southern Pacific style. Elevated track was at the east end of the coal chutes.*

People Are The Heart of Needles

21 *Eugene Watson, first engineer to cross the Colorado River bridge in 1884*

25 *High Fashion - 1910*

22 *Railroad bridge at Topock built in 1888*

23 *1907 Transportation*

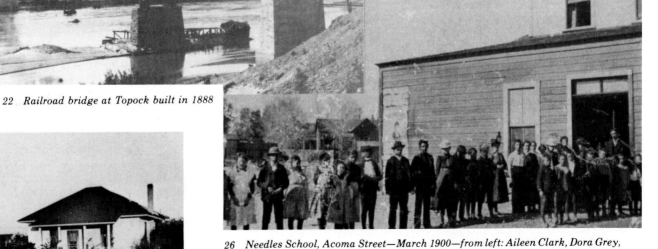

26 *Needles School, Acoma Street—March 1900—from left: Aileen Clark, Dora Grey, Irene Cubbage, Alice Fraser, Gertie Robie, Bessie Harrison, Susie Rhodes, Paul Booth, Treasure Heister, George McCabe, Mable Taylor, Murry Higginson, Addie McCollough, James Clark, Alfred Williams, Frank Testerra, Floy McCollough. Addie Carpenter. Irene Lamar. Leoleta Clark. Wesley Carter, Violet Diffenbaugh, Eccie Hartagan, Lily Obsfelder, Mable Snyder, Charlie Barber, Mr. Perry (teacher). Front: Arthur Burke, Leland Driver, Roy Gunnusen, Flora Obsfelder, Gladys Snyder, Earle Clark, John Tuck, Willie Wing, James Williams, Eric Cohlhauer, Frank Amans or Arnans.*

The town is yet young but thrifty and promising. There are several stores, post office, Wells Fargo and Co., express, telegraph and telephone offices.

A daily stage line from Calico connects with trains by the eating station for both the Atlantic and Pacific and the California Southern railroads. Connection is also available with trains for San Francisco, Los Angeles, San Diego, and all points east.

The famous Waterman and Porter quartz mill is located just north of the town and across the river, which turns out $15,000 in silver bullion per week.

By 1888, Barstow had a population of 300. The city's first business directory in the *California State Gazeteer and Business Directory of 1888* included:

G.R. Gooding, agent for Wells, Fargo & Co. and S.P. Railroad; L. Gooding, Grocer and Postmaster; J.M. Beatty, general store; P.M. Bugbee, saloon; Mrs. H. Curley, dry goods and notions; Dean Issac, stock raiser; Alex Gibson, barber; Leslie Gilbert, teacher; I.C. Moodie, dairy and stock raiser; Mrs. R. Nichols, restaurant; Robert Puelty, saloon; I.R. Ross, restaurant; George Shepard, stock raiser; The Southern Pacific Railroad Hotel; O.K. Strong, Western Union Telegraph Company; T. Twaddle, clothing; Waterman and Porter, silver mine and stamp mill.

As the California Southern Railroad steamed and whistled outbound the small communities and stations between Waterman Junction and San Bernardino were Lenwood (Todd), Cottonwood, Hodge (Hicks), (Point of Rocks), Helendale (Helen) (Judson), Bryman, Oro Grande, Victor, Hesperia, Lugo, Summit, Al Ray, Camp Cajon, Keenbrook, Devore, and others.

The railroads of the 1880's needed telegraphers for single track train orders every five miles to prevent train collisions. Every twenty miles of track was maintained with repair and construction sites called "section houses" to facilitate the people in the small communities.

Many of these stations still existed when the last steam powered helpers were used in 1952; but by 1968, the railroads had torn down most of the unused stations for tax relief.

DEAR THELMA
by Margaret Fouts

February 1, 1976

Dear Thelma:

Let me tell you of the 97 wonderful old letters I found in a drawer at our folks' house here in Daggett. They include five post cards, five telegrams and a train order too. All are dated between July 8, 1890 and July 12, 1896. Ben Butler wrote 94 of the letters to his parents, the John R. Butlers, and to his brother Nate and sister Mary of Marburg, Ontario, Canada. For a while, the question of how these letters got to Daggett, California, was quite a mystery, but, will tell you of that later.

Ben Butler, though five years younger, and my grandfather, Frank Ryerse, were boyhood friends in Canada where they grew up on farms. A few years after grandfather came west to "get rich quick" ($60 a month) telegraphing for the Atlantic and Pacific Railroad, Ben Butler did likewise. In fact, several other telegraph operators from the same area in Canada already were employed by the A & P Railroad in Arizona Territory and California, including Fred Brooks of Daggett in the 1890's or earlier. In his January 1, 1891 letter, Ben said he often talked "over the wire" to Fred and that he was a fine operator.

While Ben Butler was day operator at Ludlow, from May 1 to September 7, 1891, he wrote of buying all his groceries from Fred in Daggett, so Fred Brooks ran a market in addition to his railroad job. Ben wrote of Frank Brooks too, but I haven't been able to determine whether he was Fred's brother or his father. Fred and Frank Brooks had a cattle ranch in Arizona and brought carloads of cattle to Daggett. At various points, where Ben was agent or operator for the railroad, he would see either Frank or Fred traveling through with the cattle. Their corrals and slaughterhouse, located in Daggett by the old dirt irrigation ditch, were the same ones still being used in 1928 when your family moved from Needles to Daggett.

What I want to know is where are your cousins, Lenora and Francis Brooks, the two children of Marion and Ethel (Imel) Brooks? In 1894, or perhaps late 1893, my grandfather Ryerse began work for their grandfather, Fred Brooks, at the Pioneer Meat Market in Daggett. Later, my grandfather bought the market, corrals and slaughterhouse. I was nearly nine in November, 1923, when we (the Earl Kenney family) moved from Canada to Daggett. Grandfather was operating the market all by himself.

In January, 1924, Ben Butler came from somewhere to visit. We later learned he lived in Los Angeles. Being so busy getting used to this new country, it didn't register with me until his later visits, that Ben Butler was grandfather's former business partner in the meat market. The market burned November 30, 1926 and what a sad day it was.

Ethel Brooks, Lenora and Frances' mother, passed away, but I have never heard about Marion, their dad. Marion, his brother Lionel and sister Vera are pictured in a Daggett School photo dated 10-11-1897, along with Alice (Fox) La Mantain, Walter Alf, Art McCuistion and others. Helen Brooks, a younger sister, is shown in a later photo, which includes Bert Osborne. In his July 11, 1892 letter, Ben wrote "Fred's wife in San Jose. New Baby. Makes four." That baby was Helen Brooks.

Only wish I had known Ben's letters existed while my

folks were still living. Ben's parents, the John R. Butlers, were the people who raised my mother and Aunt Hazel, on their farm in Canada. After their mother, Hettie Belle Ryerse died in Daggett in June of 1896, grandfather sent his two little daughters to board with the older Butlers.

Aunt Hazel Ryerson passed away January 22, 1975. I learned from her diary that these most precious letters were given to her by Ben's nephew, Willard Butler, during her July 1958 visit to Canada. Hazel read very few of the letters, brought them to Daggett to my mother, Myrtle Kenney, who didn't read them at all. I'll always believe that Ben Butler's letters were placed in the drawer to wait for me.

Lots of love,
MARGARET

P.S. As you may have guessed, Ben Butler's letters are my favorite subject today. In my opinion, they are truly fabulous! To most people it would be enough just seeing that the letters were written between 80 and 85 years ago. Some are on Wells Fargo stationery and others on A & P Railroad stationery, and the letterheads show at least 12 differences. The descriptions of several of the 10 or 12 places where he and Grandfather Ryerse worked are interesting—Yucca, Hackberry, Ludlow, Bagdad, Peach Springs, Mellon, Danby, Fenner, Kingman, Goffs, Blake (new name for Goffs); also Albuquerque and Needles railroad hospitals when he was sick, or visiting his aunt and uncle in San Jose where transportation for his sight-seeing trips was by horse and buggy. He told of how fine the city of Santa Clara looked at night lit by electricity and that the street cars ran by electricity.

During his stop-over at the Chicago Worlds Fair in 1893, he decided, after his first day, that "a person doesn't know anything about what is going on in the world until he sees the things that are here." Ben stayed two days and had a nice room for $1.25 a night, which he felt was very reasonable. He warned his father that should he go to the fair, to "be sure to take a lunch as it would cost 50¢ a meal if a fellow should eat much."

The letters also told of the early day mines increasing the railroad freight business, new wagon roads to mines, short railroads, the strikes, bad working conditions, wrecks, washouts, and hardships of daily living.

The particular six years during which Ben wrote these letters was a most important period in the history of our family. My mother (Myrtle Ryerse Kenney) was born in Fenner depot where grandfather was agent-operator for the A & P Railroad.

From Ben, I found out that grandfather had store businesses besides his job at both Hackberry and Fenner, and that he was good at baking bread and washing clothes too. When I knew him, cooking and laundry was woman's work.

Reading Ben's letters is very like an 1890's introduction to friends and relatives that I never really met until they were in their 50s and 60s. The letters were a peek into the past.

Atlantic & Pacific Railroad Company.
(WESTERN DIVISION.)

Ludlow Station *Aug. 13th* 189-1-

Ludlow, California
May 18, 1891

Dear Friends at Home:

Received you letter, also the papers. Was very glad to hear from home again & hear you are getting along with the work so well. I am fine here, am getting to be quite a cook. I can make flapjacks to perfection. I suppose you never heard of condensed milk. That is what is used out here. You thin it with water. Of course, it is not as good as cow's milk but fills its place very well. I cook rice & prunes & with all kinds of canned fruit & fish & meat. I live very good. I get good butter from Daggett for about 30 cents per pound. I buy my bread for I don't think I would make a very good baker. I think I can live for $10 or $12 per month without any trouble.

This is a soft job & no mistake. All I have to do is take 2 or 3 train orders a day & report the trains as they pass. I get rather lonesome sometimes. Then I say this is better than farming & so content myself. The pumper and I are good friends and afford quite a lot of company for one another. He is a man about 25, unmarried & lives in back part of the pump house, batches himself. I call him brother batchelor. One of the Section Foremen has his wife here & she gets awful lonesome, she says. I guess they are going to pull out June 1.

I have a nice little cook house right beside my office so I can hear them when they call me. I sleep in the office which is a fine cool place to sleep. Sometimes I have to get up in the night to get orders, although I have been up only twice since I came here. Business is very dull now on the road. I hear they have laid off 6 freight crews at Needles.

I have given up the idea of going Braking, for a year or so at least. I intended going on freight as I can make as much at this business as braking on passenger. I know brakemen on freight that made as high as $135 & $140 per month. So you see that beats this business.

About boys learning this business & coming out here, I don't know what to say about it. I think there are very few boys could stand it in this country. It is a good place to make money, fine climate & that is about all I can for it. Whose boys are thinking about it?—We are having the finest weather a person could wish for now. It is about 80 degrees in the shade & a fine cool breeze blowing. I hope it stays this way but am afraid it won't. I am glad that you got the Wringer Mother. I think you had better get a sewing machine now. Perhaps, though there is something you need worse. Whatever you want, get it.

I suppose you got the $40 I sent from Hackberry. I don't know how much I can send June 1. I guess $50, perhaps more.—Mary, I want you to tell George's girls to write, if they haven't, tell them I would like to hear from them, & I will bring you a nice present when I come home. I guess I won't dare to ask for a lay off to go & see Uncle Ben until about August, being as I have taken this office. I guess one time will be as good as another to go up there though.

Are you taking Comfort now? If you are, send me a copy of it as I like to read. I have subscribed for the Examiner for 3 months so I will have something to read. Well this is all for this time, so I will close hoping to hear from you again soon.

Give my respects to all my friends there. Be sure and address to Bagdad, California P.O. now.

Good Bye.
Ben.

Ludlow, California

July 28, 1891

Dear Friends At Home:

Your letter and Papers received, glad to get them. I wrote YOU July 13, but have been waiting to hear from Uncle Ben before writing again, so I could tell you whether I was going or not. I asked the Chief Dispatcher for 15 days lay off, not heard from him yet. Am sure He will let me off as he has other Operators. Expect to leave Sat. 1st & get back Aug. 15. Guess this is my last letter until I'm back. Will write a good long letter & tell you all about my trip.

The Section foreman's wife is going away for a month, account of the heat. If he doesn't hire a cook, I will have to batch again when I come back, but I can stand it if I have to.—That must be quite a lodge you have down at the school house. I will join it when I come home & that will make another member. No I won't then.—Was surprised to hear Jack & Mima were married. Has she given up her teaching? What does Miss Lemon think of It, I wonder?

Am glad you are getting along with the work so well & hope wheat will be a good price as it is a good crop.—Pa, I am glad you are getting along so well with your agency & think it will be a good job for you.—What kind of a time did you have at Niagara Falls Nate? Was it a pleasant day?—I will tell you all about my trip when I get back. Want you to send me a picture of the house soon as you get them finished. I will send one of my pictures soon as I get them. Well, this is all for this time. Good Bye.

Ben.

Ludlow, California

August 13, 1891

Dear Friends at Home:

Your papers received yesterday. Glad to get them. Am well & hope this finds you all the same. Haven't been able to get away yet, but will go tomorrow if nothing happens. They are sending a lady Operator here to work while I am away. I think she will find it rather lonesome here as there are no women here at all. Her sister is working at Newberry, the first office west of here. I think they have lots of grit to work on this desert. It is bad enough for a man, I think.

This road is going to change hands on the 15th. The General Manager resigned his position & don't know who is to be the new Manager. I sent a message to Chief Dispatcher & told him that unless he could guarantee me my job on my return, I wouldn't go now. He said my job would be all right so I am going.

So do you have a new binder. Well that is a good thing to have to tie up the crops & you got a good bargain too. That was fast work George Ryerse did for Dick Lampkin. I saw it in the paper.

Business is rather dull on the road yet but guess it will pick up again in a month or so.—Why don't Nate write some to me? Is he mad at me or is he too busy? I haven't had a line from him in a long time.

You rememeber hearing of Thompson, the Engineer out here related to Thompson at Nanticoke? Well, he is running right here on this Division pulling passenger. I was out and had quite a long talk with him one morning. Says he is going back East next summer.

I wish I could have been there & gone to the picnic at the Glen. Suppose you had a good time Mary? Is Jack Mc and his wife living in Woodstock? Tell Georges girls to write. I haven't heard from them in a long time.

Well, this is all for this time.

Good Bye,
Ben.

Goffs, California

Dec. 22, 1892

Dear Friends at Home:

Your papers & note of the 2nd received last night. It was sent up here from Fenner & taken out to the mines, which accounts for it being so long on the road. I kept waiting to hear from you to see if you got the money before I wrote. Besides, have been so busy this month that I have scarcely had any time to write. Hope you won't be worrying because you don't hear from me oftener. I got Nate's and Martha's letter & picture some time ago. Was glad to get the picture & know they are getting along so well in their new home.

Well I am getting along all right in my new home but of course it is not so pleasant as theirs, I guess.—The freight business is rushing here now. I have done over $700 worth so far this month, so you can imagine how busy I am kept.—The express Co. opened their agency the 10th, & the business isn't so bad either for a new office. I have to get up at half past six in the a.m. & hardly ever get to bed until 9 or 10 at night and am busy most of the time, but I don't mind that at all as long as I can make $100 a month.

I am well and satisfied so guess that is all that is required. The mines North of here are splendid ones, so I am told. They strike a fine vein of ore as they go down, every now and then and they think they will have quite a town there in a short time.

They are still surveying the new railroad which will run out to one of the mining camps, a distance of 28 miles. They talk of commencing work about the 1st of the New Year. They will probably get it completed about spring.

The express Company sent me a safe with a combination lock on it but I could not work it. I think they sent the wrong combination or else the lock is worn out. I will know in a few days though.

I wrote to Uncle Ben a while ago but haven't heard from him yet. I am glad you have the Post office at Victor again. It will make it so handy in getting and sending mail. Who is running the Post Office and store, or haven't you got the store yet?

How is Tom McBride making out with the livery and is Nellie Corbett and he going together again?

I think I will be able to send about $50 more the latter part of this month or first of next. Will write you when I send it. I wish I was there to eat Christmas dinner with you but you will just have to eat my share, that is all.

Well this is all for this time so will close, wishing you all a Merry Xmas and Happy New Year. Will write when I can.

Good Bye.
Ben.

Yucca, Arizona
July 22, 1894

Dear Friends at Home:

Your letter of June 26 reached here a few days ago. Was delayed somewhere on the road account of the strike. Got the papers of June 22 & 29, yesterday morning. Got your July 15 letter today & was real glad to hear from you again. I am real well & hope this finds you all the same. I sent some papers to Nate last week & will send some more this week.

The weather has been pretty warm all this month, but isn't near so warm out here as it was 2 years ago. I think the weather is getting cooler every year. It is 106 today. One day was 112, the hottest this summer. We had quite a rain about 2 weeks ago. It wet the sand down so I could ride my wheel pretty. I made 4 miles in 15 minutes one a.m. Is too hot to ride in daytime. Cloudy today & first to speak of since the first of the year. This would be poor farming country if we depended on rain for water, wouldn't it?

I guess the strike is over now. It was a great strike and lots of good men lost good jobs through it. A great many older men on this road were discharged, mostly firemen though. One fireman got 8 months in jail for interferring with the running of trains, although he didn't use violence. Only made some threats, I heard. I think Courts in this country are very unjust in some ways.

I was going to see Uncle Ben next month but will wait. Haven't been paid for May yet but expect it soon. Besides, a railroad job is uncertain now. Some at Needles, who had no connection with the strike were fired. If I am to be let out, I would want to be here, not away on a visit. So guess I will wait and see how things look by Christmas or next summer. I need some clothes but can send for them.

Today, a letter from Edith Stafford says her folks sold their business & will move to Los Angeles, August 1. She has a school at Gilroy, near San Jose and commences teaching Sept. 1st . . .

Did Clare Lampkin make up friends with Mathewe's folks? I would like to hear news of all Marburg affairs.— Glad you have prospects for a good crop & hope prices will be good too. Don't work too hard & make yourselves sick. Better hire man than do that. Yes, we ought to make quite a payment this year.

This is all for now, so will close hoping to hear from you again soon. Hope everything is alright at Nate's.

Good Bye to all
Ben

P.S. Here are some of my cards. Give them to my friends. O.R.T. means Order of Railroad Telegraphers.

Ben Butler was born August 29, 1871—he was a telegrapher and freight agent for the Atlantic & Pacific Railroad, and later for the Atchison, Topeka and Santa Fe.

BARSTOW IN THE '90's

by Louella Bishoff

Memories of her childhood were brought back to Winifred White when she heard of my son's illness on the radio. She sent the following letter to him along with a get well card and we would like to share it here with you:

San Diego, California
Aug. 25, 1965

Dear LeRoy:

I was born on a ranch near the small town of Fallbrook near here. Frank Capra has owned the Red Mountain Ranch next to the one I was born on a little over 75 years ago. He is an actor and movie director.

We moved to Barstow when I was two years old for my mother's health. My father was a switchman on the Santa Fe until a train crew "kicked a string of cars" down on him before he had given a signal and his foot was caught, or partly so, in the frog on the track. That is where the switch throws the track over so the cars will go on another track. He was injured and off work for some time. Then he operated the pump house that furnished the only alkali free water for the boilers on the steam engines. Sometimes father would take me down with him when he went to work. I had two older sisters.

Barstow was a very small place at that time. There were perhaps a half dozen houses up close to the hills. To the left, quite a ways over, was a school house; down towards the railroad tracks were a few more houses, the depot, Harvey House and library; also Guy Goodings General Store. Next to our house was the bunkhouse where some of the railroad men slept—also the office of the Division Superintendent and his son. They used to bring me candy, cookies, fruit and pictures from San Bernardino. Uncle Hank Newhall, an old railroad man, and his daughter 20 years of age, and his son Ralph lived in the duplex with us. Uncle Hank had charge of the library for the railroad. There used to be dugouts in the side of the hills to the right as you walk up the tracks. Some of the railroad men slept there in the summer as the dugouts were cooler than the bunkhouse. We used to have picnics down by the railroad bridge. Near there were the remains of an old Stagecoach Depot. We used to find fern rock near there. There used to be a garden at one end of the depot. When I was about four my father let me ride the large turtle that was there. One time a cow got stuck in the quicksand out near bird-rock. Dad used to take me to the store and put me in a large wooden box when I was about four and carry me home on his shoulder.

I have a small red and clear glass which I guess is of hobnail design and has my first name and the date of the Fair of 1894 made into it. I also have one card from my scrapbook. One of the miners who used to come to our house brought four gold nuggets, one for my mother, two sisters and myself. One sister kept them.

We went to Barstow in 1892. I have lived like Death Valley Days. I was hit by a car and walk with a rock and roll, but some of the patients I helped care for couldn't walk at all.

Winifred White.

DAGGETT
Barstow Womens Club 1938
by Gertrude Northup

The first A. & P. railroad agent, T.C. Brazelton, checked in on October 1, 1884. From this Daggett station, he shipped goods to and from Borate, Oro Grande, Hawley, Armagosa, Hassayampa, and Death Valley. The station receipts from Daggett made it the second heaviest shipping station west of Albuquerque to Mojave, and receipts were exceeded only by Ashfork (the transfer point to Phoenix, Arizona).

SMALL RAILROADS AND MINING FEVER
by Pat Keeling

The dream of every man to find a great bonanza of wealth and a fortune at track's end gave momentum to the buiding of several branch railroads.

Few miners got rich, many eked out a meager existence, while mill and mine owners, politicians, con men and bankers became wealthy.

THE CALICO RAILROADS

The discovery of rich, silver-bearing ores on the slopes of Wall Street, Odessa, and Mule Canyons provided the initial incentive for the early settlers to stake and work their claims.

The Calico railroad started in 1888 to haul ores from the rich Calico silver strikes to the Oro Grande Milling Company, across the river from Daggett. The railroad was sold to the Waterloo Mine and Milling Company and the name was changed to the Daggett-Calico Railroad in 1889.

John R. Spears, who came to California to write about borax, described the area in 1891 in his book *The Great Borax Deserts of the West:*

> On the morning of December 1, 1891, we drove out of Daggett heading across the Mojave River bed. The interest of the tourists is aroused from the first. There is a river to begin with. It has but a slight depression for a channel and no other sign of water about it . . . Near this dry ford, a gang of men worked on a bridge that was suspended 15 or 20 feet above the sand. It was a curious thing to see a bridge there, but the need of one is unquestionable, for floods coming down the channel, sweeping (sic, swept) everything but the deepest set piles before them, and there is plenty of teaming across from the men up in the mines of the Calico Mountains some six or seven miles from the stream . . . Off to the left is a little narrow gauge railroad belonging to a mining company. It runs from a quartz mill with 70-75 stamps to a little camp called Calico.

In 1891 there was over 100 tons of ore from the Silver King and 50 tons from the Waterloo mine hauled daily by two small saddle tank steam locomotives and ore cars to be processed at the mill near Daggett. But the railroad was closed in 1892 and the mine shut down in 1896. A real tragedy had struck the flourishing Calico Silver mines when the price of silver bottomed out, in 1896.

28 Aileen McCue Powell

31 Daggett Depot - 1899-1904

The Daggett Bunch

29 George Lingenfelter, Santa Fe R.R. agent.
Wells Fargo agent lived upstairs

32

30 Cloudburst - August 14, 1914

33

30

34 Rain again!

THE BORATE-DAGGETT RAILROAD

The borax mines at Borate located in Mule Canyon were first developed by William T. Coleman and Company, previous developers of the Harmony Works in Death Valley. When Coleman went bankrupt in 1883, his holdings were bought by Francis "Borax" Smith, who had the ability to recognize the romance of the "Twenty Mule Team."

As a narrow gauge railroad, the Borate-Daggett Railroad started in 1898, and it ran from Daggett, past the mill town of Marion, then on up Mule Canyon to the camp of Borate. The railroad had three tracks between Daggett and the Calciner plant at Marion. Three tracks were required for the narrow gauge locomotives and the standard ore cars. The processing mill was located at Marion and was reached by two Heisler geared engines, named Francis and Marion after Francis Marion "Borax" Smith. The railroad reduced the cost of hauling ore from $2.50 to 12 cents per ton.

Calico's borax deposits far to the east at Bartlett, and to the west at the Columbia mine in the Calico Mountains, were to become the important factors in the economy of the Calico region. This led to the building of another railroad.

THE A.B.C. RAILROAD

In 1894, the American Borax Company had a mine called the Columbia four miles west of the Calicos. The ore was mined there and the milling done at the company's plant in Daggett. The A.B.C. built a seven mile long narrow gauge railroad between the mill and the mine in 1901. From the Columbia mine, the rails headed to a connection with the Waterloo Mine Company Railroad before branching off short of the Oro Grande Mill, then continued across the Mojave River to the plant at Daggett.

Mrs. L.C. (Aileen McCue) Powell moved to Daggett in 1906 when her father went to work on the Borate-Daggett Railroad. She said: "The fumes from the evaporating tanks of the American Borax Company killed all the pepper trees in Daggett, and the citizens had to replant all of them . . . "

In 1904 the Tonapah and Tidewater Railroad was built and Smith moved to richer deposits near Death Valley Junction.

Mining operations continued until 1907 when the price of borate dropped.

The American Borax Company plant was moved to Los Angeles when borax was discovered in other areas.

More than nine million dollars in borax was taken out of the Calicos during the 15 years after the discovery of colemanite. The town of Calico and the borate camps became a part of the past when large borate deposits were discovered at Boron in the 1920's. Borate ore kept the Mojave desert mining industry active for over a century.

The railbeds can still be traced through the Calico dry lake past the long forgotten town of Marion, up into Mule Canyon, through the area where the rail trestles and bridges have long since vanished. The memory of train whistles are only known and remembered by oldtimers.

THE NEVADA SOUTHERN

In 1870, the Providence and New York Mountains had bonanza strikes. Until the 1880's and the coming of the railroads silver, gold, and other minerals were brought out by wagon trains, and many loaded freighters threaded, and traded, into the area.

The Nevada Southern construction began January 1893 by Issac C. Black. By September, from the Goffs junction on the Atlantic and Pacific Railroad line, the railway extended north to the mining community of Barnwell. The railroad ran through Lanfair Valley and served the many mining men, homesteaders, and ranchers along the route. Mines in the New York Mountains were owned by New York financiers who built the California Eastern from Barnwell to Ivanpah Station. The California Eastern (the re-organized Nevada Southern of 1895) was opened in 1902 to bring ore

shipments from the gold mines between Ivanpah and Goffs. The line ran from Barnwell, via Vanderbilt, to Ivanpah, across the dry lake that closely parallels todays Interstate Highway 15.

In 1907, the Atchison, Topeka & Santa Fe Railroad took over the operation of the California Eastern and they completed a 23 mile route from Barnwell to Searchlight. The Santa Fe-Searchlight branch was a busy railroad, hauling ore from Searchlight and freight from Goffs where it joined the main line of the Santa Fe. A daily passenger service, except Sunday, consisted of a mixed train (freight and passengers) which traveled from Goffs to Searchlight in two and one-half hours. Instead of going to Searchlight on Sunday, the train traveled to Ivanpah.

THE MOJAVE AND MILLTOWN RAILROAD

The Mojave and Milltown Railroad Express, built in 1902, operated from the ferry, located on the eastern side of the Colorado River at Needles, to the mine near Oatman, Arizona. The railroad consisted of a little train with a passenger coach, freight cars, and a steam engine. The train hauled supplies from the ferry to the

RANDSBURG DISTRICT

WESTWARD First Class 93 MIXED	Capacity of Sidings	Fuel, Water, Turn Tables and Wyes	Distance from Kramer	Ruling Grade Ascending	TIME TABLE NO. 54 May 9, 1920 STATIONS	Ruling Grade Ascending	Telegraph and Telephone Offices and Booth Phones	EASTWARD First Class 94 MIXED
Leave Tuesday Thursday and Saturd'y only	No. Cars		Miles					Arrive Tuesday Thursday and Saturd'y only
PM 4.15	82	WY		105.6	**KRAMER**		P	PM 7.05
				14.4		122.0		
f 4.45	6		14.4	125.1	FREMONT	62.3		f 6.30
				8.1				
f 5.05	10		22.5	132.0	ST. ELMO	0		f 6.10
				1.5				
f 5.10	13		24.0	132.0	ATOLIA	121.4		f 6.05
				4.5				
5.25 PM	30	Y	28.5		**JOHANNESBURG**		DP	5.50 PM
Arrive Tuesday Thursday and Saturd'y only					(28.5)			Leave Tuesday Thursday and Saturd'y only
(23.5)					Average speed per hour			(22.9)

BARNWELL DISTRICT

WESTWARD First Class 91 MIXED	Capacity of Sidings	Fuel, Water, Turn Tables and Wyes	Distance from Goffs	Ruling Grade Ascending	TIME TABLE NO. 54 May 9, 1920 STATIONS	Ruling Grade Ascending	Telegraph and Telephone Offices and Booth Phones	EASTWARD Second Class 92 MIXED
Leave Monday and Friday Only	No. Cars		Miles					Arrive Monday and Friday Only
AM 8.30	166	WY		116.2	**GOFFS!**	0	P	PM 2.40
				9.1				
f 8.55	5		9.1	118.8	VONTRIGGER	0		2.10
				3.7				
f 9.05			12.8	105.6	BLACKBURN	0		f 2.00
				3.2				
f 9.15	3		16.0	105.6	LANFAIR	0		f 1.50
				6.2				
f 9.35	7		22.3	112.5	LEDGE	0		f 1.28
				2.6				
f 9.43	3		24.8	118.8	PURDY	158.4		f 1.20
				4.7				
s10.00	18	Y	29.5	52.8	**BARNWELL**	132.0	B	s 1.05
				5.9				
f10.15	6		35.4	52.8	HITT	132.0		f12.45
				5.0				
f10.30	19		40.4	52.8	JUAN	132.0		f12.30
				11.7				
11.00 AM	29	WY	52.1		**SEARCHLIGHT** (52.1)		DP	12.01 PM
	18	Y	29.5	53.1	**BARNWELL**	158.4	B	
				4.7				
	6		34.2	0	VANDERBILT	158.4		
				4.2				
			38.4		IVANPAH			
Arrive Monday and Friday Only					(8.9)			Leave Monday and Friday Only
(20.8)					Average speed per hour			(19.6)

THIRD DISTRICT

SECOND CLASS 33 FREIGHT Leave Daily	First Class 93 MIXED Leave Tuesday Thursday and Saturd'y only	9 The Navajo Leave Daily	Capacity of Sidings No. Cars	Fuel, Water, Turn Tables and Wyes	Distance from Albuquerque Miles	Ruling Grade Ascending	TIME TABLE NO. 54 May 9, 1920 STATIONS	Ruling Grade Ascending	Telegraph and Telephone Offices and Booth Phones	2 The Navajo MIXED Arrive Daily	First Class 94 MIXED Arrive Tuesday Thursday and Saturd'y only	SECOND CLASS 34 FREIGHT Arrive Daily
AM 3.45	PM 2.40	AM 8.15	Yard	FW TY	747.0	34.3	**BARSTOW**	0	P	PM f 1.55	PM 9.00	
							5.0					
	f 2.52	8.23	70		753.0	5.3	MACE	7.7	B	f 1.45	f 8.45	
							5.0				8.35	
	s 3.05 3.15	f 8.30	82	W	757.0	31.7	HINKLEY	24.5	P	f 1.36	s 8.25	
							5.2					
	f 3.27	8.37	81		758.2	34.3	EADS	0	B	f 1.27	f 8.10	
							4.5					
	f 3.37	f 8.44	82		766.7	34.3	HAWES	12.2	B	f 1.20	f 7.55	
							5.6					
	f 3.50	f 8.51	81		772.3	28.1	JIMGREY	12.2	B	f 1.11	f 7.40	
							7.8					
	4.05 PM	s 9.01	82	WY	780.1	24.3	**KRAMER**	29.0	P	s12.58	7.20 PM	
							4.2					
		9.06	82		784.3	0	AMARGO	35.4	B	f12.45		
							4.4					
		f 9.11	81		788.7	0	RICH	34.8	B	f12.38		
							4.7					
		9.17	82		793.4	23.2	SOLON	6.6	B	f12.30		
							4.5					
		f 9.23	82	W	797.9	21.1	MUROC	0	P	f12†23		
							5.0					
		9.30	82		802.9	21.1	FLUHR	0	B	f12.15		
							4.3					
		f 9.36	82		807.2	29.6	BISSELL	0	B	f12.08		
							5.7					
		f 9.43	81		812.9	50.2	GAMBA	0	B	f11.59		
							5.3					
		s 9.50 AM	Yard	FW TY	818.2	124.2	**MOJAVE**	136.2	P	s11.50 AM		
							67.0					
		PM 12.33	59		885.2	11.6	KERN JUNC.	15.8	P	AM 8.30		
							2.5					
5.05 PM		f 12.40 AM	Yard	WTF	887.7		**BAKERSFIELD**		P	8.20 AM		PM
Arrive Daily	Arrive Tuesday Thursday and Saturd'y only Arrive Daily						(140.7)			Leave Daily	Leave Tuesday Thursday and Saturd'y only	Leave Daily

mill and returned to the landing with gold ore.
According to Frank Madden:

> I remember the ferry when I first came. The ferry
> was operated by Bill Sweeney. My Indian friend
> Tom McDowell, who was born in Needles in
> 1903 . . . tells me that the ferry was pushed
> across the low water with poles and pulled across
> the channels with a rope attached to a tow boat.

The gold ore was processed in Needles at the smelter
built next to the river bank, close to the brick factory.
The Needles Mining and Smelter Company employed
many men and a few women. The smelter milled ore
from the Oatman and Searchlight mines until ore veins
were expended. Thousands of gold bars were shipped
from the mills to the mint in San Francisco.

In 1913, after numerous wash-outs, the rail line of the
Mojave-Milltown Railroad was abandoned. After the
1924 flood, the smelter and the brick factory were so
badly damaged that their remnants were sold for scrap
and the rail route from Searchlight closed.

In 1924, when the gold mines were exhausted, the
need for the freight wagons and railroads passed; only
the homesteaders and cattlemen remained in these
remote areas.

THE RANDSBURG RAILROAD

In the 1890's the Mojave River flowed almost to
Daggett and water was plentiful around Barstow.
During the early mining boom, Mojave became the
headquarters for men and materials arriving and departing by rail. During the 1880's the Southern Pacific
railroad (later owned by Atlantic & Pacific and Atchison, Topeka and Santa Fe railroads) was extended
across the desert and a new type of transportation was
used. Gold strikes in the Randsburg area required
shipment and milling.

In 1897, J. M. Beckley, Albert Smith and A. A.
Daugherty, founders of the Randsburg Railroad, decided that the line should run from Kramer Junction
north to the town of Johannesburg. Leaving the Santa
Fe Railroad tracks at Kramer the trains traveled 28½
miles north along the relatively flat plain into the
mining country. Construction started in October 1897
with a 200 man crew, built a standard gauge railroad.
By Christmas Day, 1897, the line reached Johannesburg. The first train to arrive caused much celebration.
It made one trip daily. Initial plans were to take the
railroad on into Death Valley but Johannesburg was as
far as it went.

In 1896 the Randsburg-Santa Fe Reduction Company owned by J. P. Beckley, B. E. Chase, and J. H.
Steadman built a 50 stamp mill in Barstow on the west
side of "B" hill along the California Southern Railroad
route from San Bernardino. A contract for milling was
signed with the Yellow Aster Mine of Randsburg for
reducing their ore.

The Yellow Aster stopped using the mills at Garlock.
Yellow Aster's ore was shipped to the Barstow plant,
processed, and gold sent to the San Francisco mint via
the railroad. When the contract expired in 1899, the
Yellow Aster built its own 130 stamp mill. The railroads
carried many millions of dollars in gold to market from
the rich ore strikes in the Randsburg area.

The railroad was sold in April 1903 to the Atchison,
Topeka and Santa Fe Company and the service was cut
to three weekly trips to haul bullion bars to the mint.

The Reduction Company mill was later called the
Bagdad Chase Mill.

THE LUDLOW-SOUTHERN RAILROAD

While scouting for indications of water John Sutter, a
roadmaster of the A. & P. in the 80's and 90's, found
a cropping of gold ore south of Ludlow. His discovery
led ultimately to the 1901 founding of the Bagdad-
Chase Mining Company with the resultant extensive
development of the properties, including a rail-line
from Ludlow to the mines.

Ludlow was a water stop for engines on the A. & P.
Railroad in the 1880's. At that time Ludlow had no
permanent water supply, so all water had to be hauled
by rails from Newberry. The first water tanks were built
of wood slats in the manner of straight sided barrels.
The vat's diameter commensurate with the width of the
flat car upon which two of them were positioned, just
atop each "truck" (axles and wheels).

A group of financiers headed by Chauncey DePew
(former president of the New York Central Railroad)
and the mill owners looked for mining prospects and
found the claims of John Sutter. These and other
claims became the Bagdad Chase Mine. The mine
located at the town of Steadman (named for one of the
stockholders), was served by a wagon road before the
seven mile rail line was constructed. In 1902-1903, the
Ludlow-Southern Railroad completed construction
south from Ludlow. DePew's private railroad car was
put on a siding at the mine. The trains were operated
from the mines, connecting with Santa Fe at Ludlow.
Because Ludlow had no water, all ore was hauled into
Barstow to the reduction mill for processing. The
Bagdad Chase Mill operated until the late 1920's.
During the first decade of the Twentieth century, the
Bagdad Chase mine became the largest single source
of copper and gold in San Bernardino County.

Fire and floods took their toll and the Ludlow
Southern ceased to be a common carrier in 1916; the
Randsburg line was abandoned in 1933; and by 1935
the rails were taken up and sold for scrap.

Learn along the way
  And on to a brighter day,
    Ideas grow up.
      Learn along the way

A bonanza of wealth in salts was dreamed of at tracks end. A curious monorail line that ran from a spur out of Magnesia on the Trona Railroad, (south of West End) became the Epsom Salts Railroad. It traveled east across the southern end of Searles Lake, over the Slate Range, through the Panamint Valley, on through Wingate Pass, and along Wingate Wash to end at the epsom salt works near the Owlhead Mountains.

When the line started in 1922 from original patents, the road was to be 16 miles long, but some 28 miles was built by 1923. Construction of the line was completed in 1924, some of the grades were as great as 12 per cent. The mine was closed down in 1926 and in the 1930's the single rail was removed. Nearly all traces of the line have vanished like the salts the railroad once carried.

Only the dream for the great bonanza of wealth and fortune from tracks end signal the beginning and the end of the small branch railroads.

THE SANTA FE SEARCHLIGHT LINE

by Arda M. Haenszel

Travelers had several ways to get from southern California to Searchlight, Nevada, in 1919. One could drive from San Bernardino through Cajon Pass and over the unpaved Highway 66 to Arrowhead Junction, 15 miles northwest of Needles, then turn north on the Arrowhead Trail, which ran somewhat to the east of the present Highway 95, passing through Searchlight.

Or a traveler could take the Union Pacific transcontinental train to Nipton, if arrangements had been made for someone to meet it and carry the passengers 21 miles by automobile to Searchlight.

Or he could board the eastbound Santa Fe train and change at Goffs to the little branch line that ran twice weekly through Lanfair and Barnwell to Searchlight.

My mother chose the latter route, by far the easiest, for us to join my father, who had preceded us by a few weeks as the new Searchlight doctor.

On that first trip on the Searchlight Branch, I remember how intrigued my mother and I were with the car in which we rode. It was half a passenger and half a baggage car, coupled to the end of a train of mostly empty cattle and ore cars and one refrigerator car with supplies for residents and the general store. The passenger section had a pot-bellied stove at one end bearing the usual pot of coffee for the crew. The horsehair seats, upholstered in red plush, were rounded and hard. The walls were decorated with painted scrolls and other designs, and mounted between the windows were fancy coal-oil lamps with big reflectors. The car was definitely an antique even then.

Another surprise of our first trip on that Searchlight line was the casual disregard for the time schedule. Suddenly the train stopped right out in the middle of the desert, and several of the crew walked away from it with guns in their hands. Were there bandits out there amid the creosote bushes? But it was not long before they returned, each carrying a couple of limp, dead cottontails dangling by their hind legs. When all were back on board, the engineer started up the tall-stacked locomotive again, and we were on our way. The crew on that run were accustomed to furnishing meat for their family skillets in this manner.

In moving to Searchlight my father had assumed responsibility for the medical care of residents in an area of almost 2500 square miles. His patients were not only residents of Searchlight but workers and their families at the scores of isolated mines and employees of the Rock Springs Cattle Company, whose animals ranged from the Mid Hills to the Colorado River. He had also been hired, at a salary consisting of little more than an annual pass, by the Santa Fe, whose stations at Goffs, Lanfair, and Barnwell, as well as Searchlight, were still active. In fact, lacking a Nevada license to practice medicine, the railroad arranged for the doctor to be nominally assigned to Barnwell for a few months where he could use his California license until the next medical exams were given at Carson City.

Remote, at the end of the line, and in the midst of a vast mining and cattle country, Searchlight in 1919 retained some of the features which characterized the old west, as well as some of the conveniences of modern civilization. One of the advantages my father enjoyed, along with the Searchlight station agent, was the privilege of buying ice very cheaply from the refrigerator cars. It was pretty snowy, but the only other source in the hot summer was via the Cashman stage from Las Vegas. The ice started out from there in nice, clear, big blocks, but though it was insulated with layers of newspapers and a thick canvas tarp, the 60-mile trip in the back of the truck considerably reduced its size, and the price of the ice was F.O.B. Las Vegas.

On another occasion my mother and I made a trip "inside" to Los Angeles on the Searchlight Branch and were involved in an accident. As I think back now, it must have happened near Vontrigger, where the tracks were laid practically in the wash between the Vontrigger and the Hackberry Hills. The present Lanfair road goes through this pass.

It was a summer afternoon, and when the train stopped at Lanfair, the crew bought some local watermelons to take home at the end of the run. Then it began to rain. Torrents of water flowed down the car windows. Soon, rushing streams began to run along the ground outside, parallel to the tracks. Anxious to complete his run, but aware of the danger, the engineer slowed the train to a crawl, inching along over the tracks now almost awash. Suddenly we felt a violent jolt as the train stopped. Our car remained upright. Out of the window we could see the locomotive standing on the track ahead, steaming and panting, and the tender tilted to one side. All the other cars between it and our lone passenger-baggage car had fallen onto their sides into the wash, with the flood waters swirling around them. Miraculously no one was injured in the wreck. The doctor's wife was called on to render first aid. The engineer and fireman, feeling the tracks give under the locomotive, and expecting it to capsize, had jumped— right into a clump of catsclaw.

The cloudburst was soon over, the flood subsided, and we climbed back into the comfort of our car. The brakeman immediately hiked back up the track to a telephone pole, which he climbed in order to tap the line and summon help from Goffs. It was a long wait. Darkness fell, and we had nothing to eat for dinner except the Lanfair watermelons. I'll never forget how good they tasted. Toward midnight several automobiles arrived with men to assess the damage and to rescue the passengers and crew. It had taken all that time to make the trip out from Goffs because the road had also been badly washed out. I don't remember the rest of the drive. At that hour, and after such an exciting day, a little girl could be expected to fall asleep in the back seat of the Hupmobile.

DAGGETT STORIES
by Aileen McCue Powell as told to Pat Keeling

Mrs. Powell recalls some incidents of the community of Daggett and the surrounding areas:

My family went to Daggett in 1906. The girls that I went to school with had pigtails and bonnets; the boys were just boys. They would walk by Mike Walsh's saloon. At that time he had a billy goat. The boys would let the goat out and the goat would butt at the door to get in. You should have seen us with our pigtails flying!

My father was a brakeman on the Borate-Daggett Railroad, and sometimes we would get in the train and go up to the mine at Borate and visit Francis Cluney and Mrs. Albert Johnson. Her dad was the foreman at the Borax Company. Women of the community of Daggett would get dressed up and would go to visit all the surrounding communities. They would go to Marion for tea, as there were nice homes and there were trees planted all around them. And sometimes they went on the hill—west of the highway—there was a silver mine with homes—and the ladies would go for lunch and a game of croquet. Sometimes they went across the dry lake in the carriages with the fringes on top and had lunch with those ladies.

BUILDING A RAILROAD THROUGH THE MOJAVE
by Allan Krieg
Union Pacific Railroad, Public Relations

It was a brisk end-of-January afternoon in 1905 some 20 miles into Nevada from the California line when chief engineer E. G. Tilton sheepishly fished a tiny gold replica of a railroad spike from his pocket and pushed it into the tie. There were a few hurrahs from the track layers—one of them set a desert shrub afire to mark the occasion.

That was as much ceremony as there was to mark the completion of the third transcontinental railroad to Southern California. The little spike was a token to tradition, provided by the wife of an official of the new road. This binding of the rails between East and West meant that through trains of the Salt Lake Route would soon rumble down the Mojave River Valley.

The project began in 1901 when Sen. William Andrews Clark, Montana/Arizona copper magnate, philanthropist and art lover, formed San Pedro, Los Angeles & Salt Lake Railroad and started construction eastward from Los Angeles.

Clark anchored his line on a small local railroad which he bought and which tied Los Angeles with Pasadena, Glendale and the new harbor at San Pedro. He also organized Empire Construction Co. to do the building.

Clark's goal was Salt Lake City and a connection with transcontinental lines there. The route would be 400 miles shorter than any other between Utah and Southern California.

His plan was not new. As early as the 1880's, Union Pacific had seen the value of a line from the Utah capital through rich mineral regions to deepwater in the Southwest and had surveyed a route extending from its lines already built into Southern Utah. However, the company had been frustrated by tight money during the financial panics of the '80s and '90s, and eventually filed bankruptcy. It forfeited to taxes, the roadbed and tunnels that it had constructed from Milford, Utah, into Nevada as far as Clover Valley Junction—Caliente.

Furthermore, Collis P. Huntington of Southern Pacific had threatened Union Pacific with unfavorable action on traffic interchange at Ogden should it extend to California.

By the turn of the century, UP had been rescued from fiscal doldrums by Edward H. Harriman, a railroad genius who took up the Southern California project anew. By this time Harriman also had acquired control of Southern Pacific.

136

Clark, however, resolved to push on independently. He quickly claimed the abandoned UP grade in Eastern Nevada. Fists and shovels flew along the right-of-way and a battle in the courts was joined. Further exacerbating conditions arose when both companies determined to drive track through confining canyons where there was a practical route for but one line.

In 1902, Clark and Harriman announced a series of agreements that settled the conflict.

Simply put, the Salt Lake Route (SP, LA & SL) acquired all UP tracks south of Salt Lake City; UP obtained half-interest in SP, LA & SL. Clark's people would be the operators of the new line.

In 1916, the name was shortened to Los Angeles & Salt Lake Railroad (in corporate existence today) and in 1921, Union Pacific acquired complete ownership of the line.

At the California end, track reached Pomona in October, 1902; Ontario, March 1903; and Riverside in February 1904.

Union Pacific had been running trains from Milford to Caliente since July 1901.

Negotiations with Southern Pacific made that company's track from Riverside to San Bernardino available to the new road, and Salt Lake Route trains began running between Los Angeles and San Bernardino, in July 1904.

Beyond San Bernardino, surveys run up Lytle Creek may have encouraged Santa Fe's agreeing to trackage rights for Salt Lake trains on the Santa Fe line over Cajon Pass. Today, UP trains operate over Santa Fe rails between Riverside and Daggett.

Meanwhile (July 1903) construction on the now jointly owned line was begun south from Caliente, and (August 1903) east from Daggett where the new route diverged from Santa Fe steel.

Seymore Alf, Daggett businessman and borax teamster, subcontracted to "build, construct and in every respect fully complete all the grading, excavating and filling required for a single track railroad . . . from Railroad Survey Station O (Daggett) 6.2 miles, more or less," to Otis (now Yermo) where the Salt Lake Route would build a roundhouse and other facilities.

Alf was allowed 60 days to complete the job and was paid from 12 to 35 cents a cubic yard for material excavated or filled.

Alf's crew set up two camps, the second at the present site of Yermo. After completing the grade, they levelled a yard from which track and other materials were dispatched.

"The name, Otis, was tacked on the first telegraph shack and it stuck," said Alf's son, Walter, "until former railroader George Swartout was appointed postmaster and changed the name to Yermo."

In the fall of 1903, when the yard was finished, Alf's crew spent another seven months on 15 miles of grading in the Calada-Nipton area.

Arthur L. Doran of Barstow was another grader.

By mid-December 1903, 30 miles of rail were down. The grade extended another 12 miles through difficult

Caves (Afton) Canyon. Survey crews worked far ahead of the graders and steel gangs.

After isolation in the hard, hot desert, the railroad builders would sojourn periodically at the three-saloon community of Daggett, which, until the rail men trooped to town, thought it had seen everything in hell-raising.

There were no towns along the proposed route and not many people—mostly cattlemen and miners. "If one man should die at Afton," said the *Los Angeles Times* shortly after the line was connected, "half the population would be destroyed. One is the operator who sleeps alongside the telegraph instrument, in his tent; the other is an engineer in charge of the pump station."

"A week ago, a train of flatcars came by, shunted off lumber and cement barrels, then came a gang of workmen who erected a section house exactly like a dozen others that decorate the way, and built a bunkhouse exactly like some dozen others."

April 1904 saw the tunnel at Afton 40 percent complete, the grade pushed to Siding 21 at Kessler summit (today's Cima).

In November, trains from the North were whistling into Las Vegas and from the South were halting at Cima.

Cima became the construction force's nerve center on the California side. Orders and materials were dispatched from the administration train parked on a freshly laid siding.

At Kelso, Siding 16, the road would build a depot, and for crews assigned there to operate helper locomotives needed in those days of steam power to assist trains up Cima hill, a hotel. Wells were drilled to supply the locomotive boilers.

At this time 650 men, mainly Mexicans and Americans, were manipulating steam shovels, following Fresno scrapers and driving braying mules.

The Times correspondent described the scene:

Following (the graders) came the track layers, with the great engines tumbling out ties in enormous bundles, rails shooting out with incredible swiftness; then the ballasting crews, surfacing gangs embedding the ties in firm earth.

Behind these the trains bearing pile drivers to replace the temporary bridges, each gang a class, a stratum of society, a little world unto itself.

Came the commissary department dropping kitchens and dining rooms in the wilderness; came the operating department, drawing complete little railroad office bureaus in condemned cars to be switched onto sidings with telegraph lines, trainmasters, stenographers, clacking train orders, flimsy train slips, filing cases, boyish clerks, detail maps, train dispatchers.

Came after these the drawling freights, the gangs to dig wells, the carpenters to erect section houses, the painters and the plasterers. And at last the ubiquitous drummer bearing samples of the finest articles for sale on this earth.

Progress was about a mile and three quarters a day. The year turned to 1905.

Halfway into January, a man atop the track laying machine, inching south from Las Vegas, spied a puff of smoke over the hill and shouted to his mates: "The California crew is coming up the slope."

A new enthusiasm prevailed and progress spurted to two miles a day by the time the rails met.

The last tie was tamped on temporary track—a shoofly—laid across relatively easy country while difficult rock work was completed over against the hills at Sloan on the permanent line around Goodsprings summit.

It was all over but the puffing—of steam engines that soon would replace the clanking and shouting of the builders.

J. Ross Clark, the senator's brother and vice-president, along with general manager Ralph Evans Wells and other railroad officials, inspected the entire line on the first through train leaving Salt Lake City February 9. On April 15, a special excursion was laid on for the Woodmen of the World. The road's founder, William A. Clark, toured the route a few days later. Regular train service south from Caliente to Los Angeles would shortly begin.

On the evening of May 1, the whole line was formally opened for public service with passenger trains leaving at each end of the route.

"Mid Cheers and Red Lights First Train Opens Regular Service on Salt Lake Line," hailed the *Times'* banner May 2, and T. E. Gibbon, SP, LA & SL vice-president, remarked to a reporter, "Well, the baby is born," as the departing train's red marker lights mingled with glimmering green switch lamps down the First Street yard on the east side of the Los Angeles River.

Conductor E. P. Jones had just called "All aboard!" and waved the "highball" to the engineer at the throttle of the big Baldwin "Pacific" engine which easily wheeled the 10-car Salt Lake Express with 400 or more aboard out of the old Los Angeles Terminal depot.

So, with cheers and best wishes began a new railroad service, but other than telegraphers on duty at lonely desert stations, there probably were few wakeful enough to hail the train as it rolled through the early morning hours along the Mojave.

The puffing steam engine was replaced a quarter century ago by the growling diesel locomotive, still a symbol of modern railroading.

Today, Union Pacific Railroad is considered one of the most efficiently managed and practically operated railroads in the world.

Although the 220-mile route between Victorville and Las Vegas is one of its most sparsely populated territories, the stretch across the Mojave is an important link in the 9500-mile rail system.

Union Pacific moves a diversified array of farm products, minerals and manufactured goods into and out of the fast-growing West. Its well-maintained track connects key Missouri River gateways with inland consuming and producing areas in 11 western states and major West Coast ports.

Over the past decade, the road has spent more than $1.5 billion for equipment and plant to insure highly competitive, dependable operations now in the future.

The company got something for its money: one of the youngest car and locomotive fleets in the nation, high speed repair and servicing facilities, intermodal trailer and container terminals, microwave communications and electronic data processing systems and track and signaling systems—all among the most up-to-date in the industry.

UP management feels that it is only by such continual upgrading that rail operations can combat the cost/price squeeze caused by today's inflationary economy so that customers' freight can be moved for an average of about a cent-and-a-half a ton-mile.

Union Pacific's principal operating point between Victorville and Las Vegas is Yermo. This is the meeting point of the road's first and second subdivision of the 330-mile California division. Here is the change point for crews of up to a dozen main line freight trains.

Yermo, also, is the home terminal for the crew of a local train which serves the territory between Dunn and Barstow, interchanging freight cars with Santa Fe at the latter station.

The Yermo station and employees' sleeping and recreational quarters, built in the early '20s, are scheduled to be replaced in 1976 by a modern facility. In addition to railroad offices, the building will include accommodation for 53 railroad personnel.

Besides its other customers, the road serves the cement plants at Victorville and Oro Grande and numerous desert industries—principally mineral traffic—along the route to Las Vegas.

The railroad is a subsidiary of Union Pacific Corporation, a transportation-based enterprise which also includes natural resources and land development.

Another UP subsidiary operating in the area is Calnev Pipe Line. This petroleum products pipe line, first laid as an 8-inch carrier from Colton to Las Vegas in 1961, was enlarged to a 14-inch line with a 60,000 barrels a day capacity in 1973. At Victorville the line serves George Air Force Base, at Barstow it serves the Santa Fe Railway, at Daggett four major oil companies and at Coolwater, near Daggett, the electric generating plant.

Upland Industries, also a UP company, is active in assisting new industries seeking to locate along UP lines in the region.

FEB. 1926—Almost half of the navel crop of California has been shipped and this holds true of that of the Redlands district, San Bernardino County. The shipments here have reached almost 1,900 cars and this is fully half the navels to be shipped, according to the estimates. The total shipments include navels, Valencias, sweets and seedlings from this district.

CONSTRUCTION OF THE SAN PEDRO, LOS ANGELES & SALT LAKE RAILWAY

by Walter Alf

In going through my father's old papers June 13, 1953, I found a copy of a contract entered into on June 13, 1903, with the Empire Construction Company, a subsidiary of the old San Pedro, Los Angeles and Salt Lake Railroad Company, as follows:

The party of the second part agrees that he will construct, build and in every respect fully complete all the grading, excavating and filling required for a single track railroad with side tracks on what is known as the Daggett Branch of the San Pedro, Los Angeles & Salt Lake Railroad situated in San Bernardino County, State of California, from railroad survey station 0 to a connection with the Santa Fe Pacific Railroad Company's tracks in Daggett, upon the located line of the San Pedro, Los Angeles & Salt Lake Railroad Company, a distance of six and two-tenth (6.2) miles, more or less, in accordance with the general contract stipulations marked Exhibit A, signed by the parties and annexed hereto, and the specifications marked Exhibit B, signed by the parties and annexed hereto, said general contract stipulations and specifications being made a part of this agreement and are hereby declared and accepted as an essential part of the same."

(Signed) Seymore Alf (Signed) The Empire Construction Company
By J. Russ Clark, President
Ross W. Smith, Secretary

With the beginning of this construction, we had miners and boys as drivers of these Fresno teams. They thought it would be fun to drive a team, but it did not take the miners long to go back to the mines after working one-half to three days. The boys, only 15 years of age, stuck with the job until completed, one being, Bert Osborne.

After completing the grading between Daggett and the Mojave River, we established our first camp on the north side of the river. The nearest water to the camp was at Daggett. As work progressed we moved our second camp to where the town of Yermo stands today. All grading was completed as far as where the Inspection Station now stands. Then we returned and graded for a month what was known at that time as the Material Yards.

In 1905, after the railroad had laid the steel, a little shack was built for a telegraph office and was given the name of OTIS.

Water at that time was quite scarce on the desert, and the nearest point from which we hauled water for the camp was at Marion, where the Pacific Coast Borax Company was located.

Just about the time our contract was completed the Empire Company brought in some men who started digging a well by hand with picks and shovels. This was the first water developed at the Material Yards. An old-time miner, Henry Hart, was one of the employees and knew how to set the well cribbing so that the sand would not come in. Later he worked on the first shaft put down at Boron, about 1912.

The completion of the new railroad had little effect on Daggett. It was the supply point for all the Death Valley area and Daggett had three borax plants operating which employed many men, providing a steady payroll. These did much to develop the town of Daggett.

HISTORY OF YERMO UP TO 1915
by a student of Clifford Walker
Edited by Clifford Walker

The history of Yermo is quite sketchy. Besides the Indians who lived near the Mojave River, many other men passed by the present site of Yermo, usually along the river trail to the south. Two of the men were Fray Joaquin Pasqual Nuez and Lt. Moraga. Nuez passed south of Yermo in 1819 on his way to Santa Ana y San Joaquin, which is either Camp Cady or Afton Canyon. Moraga tried, in vain, to punish the Mohave Indians.

In 1830, Antonio Armijo wrote in his diary about stopping at an Indian village, Hayatis Arroyo, near Yermo for water.

Another man who passed by the present site of Yermo was Ygnacia Palomares. As he and others were chasing horse and mule thieves near Minneola Road, they were ambushed by the thieves, and two men were killed.

Besides the names Hayatis Arroyo in the 1830's, the name Punta Del Agua (Point of Water) was also used by the New Mexican caravans. Los Alimos Altos (Upper Cottonwoods) was a name used by the Mexicans in the late 1840's on the Old Spanish Trail, and Forks of the Road by the Americans in the 1850's, as part of the Salt Lake-Los Angeles Wagon Road.

Towns near Yermo sprang up, namely Calico and Marion, in the 1880's and 1890's. They died away after the mines in the Calico Mountains were worked out.

Not very much happened around Yermo until 1903, when Seymore Alf of Daggett acquired the rights to all the grading, excavating and filling required for a single track railroad from Daggett to Yermo, then northward, for the San Pedro, Los Angeles and Salt Lake Railroad Company. Before the grading could be started, the local people and Alf had to find water for their teams and personal use. After four or five wells had been drilled and failed, they finally found one suitable for their needs. This was the beginning of the town of

35 Whistle stop by President Hoover 1932

38 Union Pacific depot - Yermo

Otis

To Yermo

39 Boy Scouts greet President Hoover: flag bearer, Dick Coyle, Herbert and Eddie Brimmer, Gary Lee, Ted Wallin

36 1941 freight train From steam . . .

40 First Union Pacific streamliner into Barstow

41 . . . to diesel

Yermo.

The first name for Yermo was Otis, but there was also a town in Colorado called Otis and the Post Office got the mail mixed up. In 1907, the Post Office changed Otis to Yermo, meaning "desert."

In old Yermo, people lived in tents until they could build cabins. Most of the people who lived there were employees of the railroad. Other families in the area were dry farmers.

In 1905 the railroad completed the roundhouse and the depot. Before this time, Yermo was only a material yard for the railroad.

In 1906 there were very few buildings in town: homes, a school and two stores. One of the stores was Alf's General Store, located near the depot. At first Mollie and Emma Alf ran the store and Post Office. Later, the store building (which still stands) was rented to various parties. The other store was owned by Bruce McCormick.

The first school in Yermo was held in a tent near Alf's General Store. Only six children attended the school; one boy was Seymore Alf's son Walter. When the town grew larger, a cabin was erected for the school. After 1910, Yermo steadily grew.

FAMILY LIFE IN EARLY YERMO
by June Zeitelhack

Edward and Chloe Brimmer arrived in Yermo on Christmas Day 1918. Edward was a stationary engineer with the Union Pacific Railroad. Yermo was still a new town, owing its existence, since 1907, to the railroad line to Salt Lake.

Mrs. Brimmer described life in Yermo for a young housewife and mother. Her family was dependent on the railroad for water, coal, delivery of food, clothing and medical care, as well as the family livelihood. Her husband worked eight hour shifts and earned $100 per month—which was good wages at that time. The water used by the family was provided by the railroad and was piped to a faucet outside the house. The railroad also hauled the coal. The first community church was housed in a building that had been moved into Yermo from the railroad yard.

Mrs. Brimmer relied on Doctor McKenzie, the railroad physician, for medical care. Dr. McKenzie was from out of town and had moved to the desert because he suffered from asthma.

There was a small store in Yermo. However, most of the family food came in on the train. Each payday Chloe sent her grocery list, by train, to Los Angeles. She also ordered clothing, yardage and other house-hold necessities the same way.

In the early days there were only three automobiles in Yermo and few people had horses and wagons or buggies. The Brimmers did not travel much as they were dependent on other folks who had cars or horses for their transporation.

The housewife in Yermo's early days heated water and washed their clothes in the back yard. She sewed her family's clothing on a treadle sewing machine and at night, used a gas light. The yardage was brought in by train. She made all the family clothing except overalls, which were ordered from the catalog.

Sixteen children attended Yermo School in 1918. The Brimmer family had five boys and three girls, all attended grade school in Yermo and graduated from Barstow High School. The School District provided their transportation to Barstow, at first in a small car, later by bus. They traveled the road from Yermo nearly to Daggett, around Elephant Mountain on the north side of the river to Fish Pond and on to Barstow.

Mrs. Brimmer recalled that the depression years brought little change to their life in Yermo. When people were out of work they left town. She also stated that the big flood of '38 did no damage at Yermo.

RAILROADS IN THE CHANGING DESERT
from
IRON RAILS ALONG DESERT TRAILS
by Andrew F. Kitts

The Southern Pacific Railroad moved out of the Tehachapi Mountains to a new terminus, aptly named Mojave, on August 8, 1876. Mojave was the railhead only briefly; rails were pushed across the desert and through Palmdale, only to disappear into Mint Canyon for the descent into Los Angeles, which was reached on September 5, 1876.

The half century following the Southern Pacific's appearance at Mojave saw a network of rails built across the desert.

Silver was discovered in the Panamints and at Old Ivanpah (near Valley Wells Station, on I-15) during the 1860's, but it was not until 1880 that the fabulously wealthy Waterman and Calico silver strikes were made. Desert mining never contributed much to the financial success of the transcontinental railroads, but the railroads were of paramount importance to desert mining ventures.

The Tonopah and Tidewater Railroad was built between August 1905 and October 1907, between Ludlow and Gold Center, Nevada. Trackage rights on the Bullfrog Goldfield Railroad permitted T&T trains to operate to Beatty, a rail distance of one hundred sixty-nine miles. The bonds of the railroad were guaranteed by the Pacific Coast Borax Company, as the main reason for the construction was to provide an outlet for the Lila C Mine near Death Valley. In 1913, when it became apparent that the ore at the Lila C would soon be exhausted, the Pacific Coast Borax Company decided they would open the Biddy McCarthy, about twelve miles northwest in the direction of Death Valley. The California Railroad Commission would not approve additional bonds to permit the Tonapah and Tidewater to construct the branch to the new mine. A new corporation, set up by the borax company, had no difficulty in issuing bonds to build the narrow gauge Death Valley Railroad from Death Valley Junction to the new mines. The line was completed by December 1915.

The Southern Pacific built a branch line from Mojave to Owenyo, in the Owens Valley during 1908. The line was built to carry supplies for the Los Angeles water project in the valley. The line connected with the narrow gauge line, then the California and Nevada, but better known by the original name, Carson and Colorado.

The short nine and three quarter mile railroad to the Gunsight and Noonday mines east of Tecopa was completed in 1910. This little mining railroad had an average grade of over six percent and the small saddletank locomotive could hold only two loaded cars on the downgrade.

The Trona Railway from Searles Lake to Searles, a station on the Owens Valley branch of the Southern Pacific, was completed in 1915.

In the Victorville area, two short railroads were built in 1915. The Golden State Portland Cement Company built a one and three quarter mile line to their quarry, which used the only Shay geared locomotive in the desert. The Southwestern Portland Cement Company built the longer Mojave Northern, to their quarry.

The last major precious metal strike was at the Kelly Mine in 1919 in the Red Mountain area, already served by the Randsburg branch of the Santa Fe.

The nation suffered a mild recession following the first world war. This was followed by the wild boom of the twenties and the great depression of the thirties which ended only after the start of the second world war. The Mojave Desert, however, underwent a depression during the two decades following the first great war. Small cities became ghost towns as mines became unprofitable. Declining business and the increasing use of the automobile and motor truck caused the short lines and branches to be abandoned.

The twenties and thirties were exciting years for rail fans. Steam locomotives were built which dwarfed earlier locomotives in size and performance. The desert lines of the Santa Fe, Union Pacific and Southern Pacific carried some of the largest and fastest steam locomotives ever built. Through the years of World War II steam was still king of the rails. A new competitor however appeared in 1934, as the diesel powered streamlined train on the Union Pacific broke the Chicago to Los Angeles record time established in 1905 by Death Valley Scottie's "Coyote Special." The fact that the record was broken is not too surprising, but the single locomotive made the entire trip com-

pared to the 19 engines required by Scottie's special.

In 1936 the Union Pacific "Cities" trains, diesel powered, streamlined speedsters, were put on regular schedules. In the same year the Santa Fe used a diesel to pull its crack "Super Chief." Today Rail fans treasure photos of diesel powered passenger trains being helped over Cajon Pass by steam locomotives. More prophetic was a photo, taken in 1941, at Cajon Summit of the Santa Fe's red ball freight with a four unit 4500 horsepower diesel locomotive ahead of 110 reefers and other high cars, on its initial trip East, without a steam locomotive in sight.

In the middle years of the 1920's, the Pacific Coast Borax Company opened their open-pit mine at Boron. Following the completion of the three mile spur to the new mine, the operations in the Death Valley Area were terminated. The Pacific Coast Borax Company attempted to maintain a viable econony in the Death Valley area. A luxurious hotel, the Furnace Creek Inn, was built north of Ryan. Accommodations were also available at the Amargosa Hotel, while for the more adventurous, there were the corrugated sheet iron buildings of the Death Valley Hotel at Ryan. New motor cars were purchased for both the Tonapah and Tidewater and the narrow gauge Death Valley Railroad. These railroads offered the only practical method of travel to Death Valley as existing roads were only for the most venturesome. Still, lossess were too great and the Death Valley Railroad ceased operations on March 15, 1931.

The Pacific Coast Borax Company had continued to pay the interest on Tonapah and Tidewater bonds, and after 1927, they picked up the operating deficits as well. During the 30's, operating costs were often double the road's revenue.

The shops were moved to Death Valley Junction and operations were discontinued from Ludlow to Crucero, where the line crossed the Union Pacific. Flood damage in 1938 brought matters to a head.

It was estimated that the Pacific Borax Company, by the end of 1938 had paid five million dollars to keep the line operating. The principal of the bonds would be due in 1960, and the accrued interest and principle would constitute a sum in excess of another four million dollars. In December 1938, an application was filed with the Interstate Commerce Commission to cease operations. Protests held up approval until June 1940. The tracks remained in place until requisitioned by the War Department in 1942. The steel was removed during 1942 and 1943. Part of the bridge timbers ended up as framing for the Apple Valley Inn, while a large number of cross ties were used in construction of the El Rancho Motel in Barstow.

In 1941, the Shay locomotive and rails of the Golden State Portland Cement Company were scrapped. The Oro Grande plant was reopened in 1943, but trucks are used to haul the limestone from the quarry.

On the eve of World War II, the Trona Railway was the sole surviving short line common carrier in the Mojave Desert. The line discontinued passenger service in 1937, but operated a special school train, from

Tonopah and Tidewater R. R.
Bullfrog Goldfield R. R.

via

Union Pacific—Santa Fe—T. & G. R. R.
Connecting Trains Between
Los Angeles, Riverside, San Bernardino
and
Tecopa, Death Valley Jct., Beatty, Goldfield, Tonopah

GOING NORTH	Tues., Thur., Sat.	Mon., Wed., Fri.	Elevation
STATIONS	No. 26	No. 4	
UNION PACIFIC			
Lv Los Angeles	6 05 PM	11 00 PM	....
Lv Riverside	7 49 PM	1 05 AM	....
Lv San Bernardino	8 20 PM	1 40 AM	....
Lv Victorville	10 08 PM	3 20 AM	....
Lv Barstow	11 10 PM	4 20 AM	....
Lv Daggett	11 25 PM	4 35 AM	....
Ar Crucero	12 40 AM	6 00 AM	....
SANTA FE	No. 18	No. 22	
Lv Los Angeles	5 15 PM	11 00 PM	....
San Bernardino	7 35 PM	1 05 AM	....
Barstow	10 15 PM	3 55 AM	....
Ar Ludlow	11 23 PM	5 06 AM	....

STATIONS	Sun., Wed., Fri.	Tues., Thur., Sat.	
	No. 9	No. 11	
TONOPAH & TIDEWATER R. R.			
Lv ‡Ludlow	1 30 AM	7 00 AM	1774
Broadwell	1 57 AM	7 27 AM	1294
Mesquite	2 15 AM	7 45 AM	1246
Ar Crucero	2 30 AM	8 05 AM	1013
Lv Crucero	2 45 AM	8 05 AM	976
Rasor	3 01 AM	8 25 AM	934
Soda	3 12 AM	8 35 AM	921
Baker	3 32 AM	8 54 AM	906
‡Silver Lake	3 59 AM	9 20 AM	969
Riggs	4 21 AM	9 45 AM	1076
Valjean	4 36 AM	9 58 AM	1042
Dumont	4 55 AM	10 16 AM	827
Sperry	5 10 AM	10 29 AM	1005
Acme	5 26 AM	10 44 AM	1315
‡Tecopa	5 46 AM	11 03 AM	1368
Zabriskie	6 00 AM	11 16 AM	1566
Lv ‡Shoshone	6 15 AM	11 30 AM	....
Gerstley	6 32 AM	12 10 PM	....
Evelyn	6 56 AM	12 30 PM	1870
Ar§‡Death Valley Jct.	7 30 AM	1 00 PM	2037
Lv Death Valley Jct.	8 00 AM	....	
Bradford Spur	8 17 AM	....	2300
Scranton	8 35 AM	....	2330
Jenifer	8 50 AM	....	2350
Leeland	9 05 AM	....	2380
Ashton	9 29 AM	....	2663
Carrara	9 42 AM	....	3240
Ar ‡Beatty	10 05 AM	....	3344
BULLFROG GOLDFIELD R. R.			
Lv Beatty	10 20 AM	....	
Hot Springs	10 39 AM	....	3640
Pioneer	10 53 AM	....	3920
Ancram	11 12 AM	....	3990
Bonnie Clare	12 01 PM	....	4010
Stonewall	12 45 PM	....	....
Ralston	1 02 PM	....	....
Red Rock	1 51 PM	....	....
Ar ‡Goldfield	2 15 PM	....	5 00
TONOPAH & GOLDFIELD R. R.			
Lv Goldfield	6 40 AM	....	....
Ar Tonopah	8 05 AM	....	....

Standard Pullman Sleeper leaves Los Angeles for Beatty, Tuesdays, Thursdays and Saturdays, via Union Pacific Train No. 26.

§Meals.

‡Telegraph stations.

Connecting Trains
BETWEEN
DEATH VALLEY JCT. AND RYAN

DEATH VALLEY R. R.

STATIONS			Motor Coach
Lv Death Valley Jct.	Daily Except Tues.		8 30 AM
Ar Ryan	" " "		9 45 AM
Lv Ryan	" " "		3 45 PM
Ar Death Valley Jct.	" " "		5 00 PM

BETWEEN
CRUCERO AND LAS VEGAS, SALT LAKE CITY
GOING EAST

STATIONS		No. 4	No. 26
UNION PACIFIC R. R.			
Lv Crucero	Daily	6 00 AM	12 40 AM
Ar Las Vegas	"	11 25 AM	5 10 AM
Ar Caliente	"	4 00 PM	9 10 AM
Ar Salt Lake City	"	5 00 AM	8 30 AM

GOING WEST

STATIONS		No. 3	No. 25
Lv Salt Lake City	Daily	11 35 PM	8 55 AM
Lv Caliente	"	11 50 PM	5 55 PM
Lv Las Vegas	"	5 30 PM	9 40 PM
Ar Crucero	"	10 19 PM	1 49 PM

BETWEEN
LOS ANGELES AND SAN DIEGO
GOING SOUTH

STATIONS		No. 72
SANTA FE R. R.		
Lv Los Angeles	Daily	9 15 AM
Ar San Diego	"	1 00 PM

GOING NORTH

STATIONS		No. 71
Lv San Diego	Daily	9 00 AM
Ar Los Angeles	"	12 50 PM

BETWEEN
SAN FRANCISCO, STOCKTON, BAKERSFIELD
AND
BARSTOW
GOING WEST

STATIONS		No. 21	No. 9
Lv Barstow	Daily	2 30 PM	4 50 AM
Mojave	"	4 20 PM	6 35 AM
Ar Bakersfield	"	7 09 PM	9 15 AM
Lv Bakersfield	"	8 35 PM	9 45 AM
Ar Fresno	"	11 21 PM	12 35 PM
Ar Stockton	"	4 35 AM	4 23 PM
Ar San Francisco	"	8 00 AM	8 00 PM

GOING EAST

STATIONS		No. 22	No. 2
Lv San Francisco	Daily	1 15 PM	10 30 PM
Stockton	"	4 08 PM	1 42 AM
Fresno	"	7 45 PM	5 00 AM
Ar Bakersfield	"	10 45 PM	8 00 AM
Lv Bakersfield	"	11 00 PM	8 30 AM
Mojave	"	1 55 AM	11 20 AM
Ar Barstow	"	3 30 AM	1 00 PM

Corrected to May 1, 1927

1936 to 1941, from West End, South Trona and Boro-solvay to Trona. The motor car used for this train is still in use by the California Western Railroad between Fort Bragg and Willets as one of the "Skunks."

World War II strained the facilities of all major railroads to the extreme limits, the great transcontinentals of the desert were not excepted. New diesels allocated to the desert roads played important roles in this effort.

Following the end of the war steam locomotives vanished from the rails with astonishing speed. The diesel's low water consumption was of great interest to desert railroads.

Since the war, Santa Fe has built a new spur from Hesperia to Cushenberry in Lucerne Valley to serve a new cement plant. The Southern Pacific completed a new seventy-eight mile cutoff from Palmdale to Colton through Cajon Pass to connect the San Joaquin Valley route to the Sunset route.

Railroads today carry the bulk of the freight to and from Southern and Central California across the Mojave Desert. The desert industries provide cement and chemicals for the nation's industries, which are moved to markets by the railroads. The railroads provide, probably, the desert's largest payroll.

Railroads have been in the desert for one hundred years in August of this bicentennial year. The rails have been one of the most important factors in shaping the history and life style of the desert.

CLINTON FRAZER
by Pat Keeling

As a young man working as an apprentice machinist for the Tonopah and Tidewater Railroad, Mr. Clinton Frazer, who retired as a Road Foreman in 1961 after 41 years of service with the Santa Fe, tells of working in 1914 for wages of 20 cents per hour:

The shops did everything that was done in San Bernardino except turning the tires on the drivers on the steam locomotives, as we didn't have a lathe big enough—and we even put on the new fireboxes . . . and gave them a complete overhaul. We had the finest machinist in the world working there, even if it was a boomer job. There were about 80 men working there. We worked 10 hours a day—starting at 7 a.m., had an hour for lunch and quit at 6 p.m. The apprentices got 20 cents per hour and the machinists got 42 cents per hour—this was 1914 and I thought if I ever could get to where I could make 42 cents per hour, which was $4.20 a day I really would be able to "live high on the hog."

When I first went to Ludlow I roomed at Mrs. Preston, whom some called the "Desert Queen." She was a character and never wore anything but her Mother Hubbard—she was a rough, tough customer but had a heart of gold. Her ability to help people who were down and out was well known, but she could give you a cussin' in two different languages that I know of. She had this store with rooms above it and all the bachelor men from the shop roomed there, and it would be funny if I told you what a small price we paid for the room. The railroad company ran a boarding house to feed the men, so Ma Preston did not cook for the men. I don't know where she picked up her husband, but he was rough and ready and we had heard that she previously had run a house of ill repute at Daggett when the Borax was going in there. When the railroad was built in Ludlow, she moved here.

There were many houses and homes in Ludlow, and at that time was much larger than Barstow. The T and T maintained several houses for the management even though they would only be there several times in a year.

TONOPAH & TIDEWATER MEMORIES
by Celestia Gilliam

The Tonopah & Tidewater Railroad shaped the destinies of my family.

When the railroad was completed in 1907, it put my grandfather, R.J. "Dad" Fairbanks, out of business at Ash Meadows, Nevada. He had had a freight business hauling water and supplies to the Death Valley area from the Las Vegas and Tonopah Railroad. Before the T & T was built, Death Valley had no transportation or communication to speak of from the south. After the T & T was completed, "Dad" Fairbanks was asked by the Pacific Coast Borax Company to go to Shoshone and open an eating establishment for the convenience of passengers and crew. It was not exactly a Harvey House operation. Wooden benches and table covered by a tent were presided over by a Chinese cook, "cue" and all. The sign inside read, "All You Can Eat for 50¢."

My mother, as a girl of 17, made this move with her father. She was in love with a handsome miner from Greenwater, Charlie Brown. To be near her, Charlie obtained a job at the Noonday Mine at Tecopa. Lacking funds and transportation to court his sweetheart ten miles away he managed to borrow the handcar from the track-walker on many occasions and would pump the 10 miles to do his courting. Love will find a way! In 1910 this couple got on the T & T in Shoshone and traveled to Goldfield where they were married.

Many memories of my childhood in Shoshone relate to the T & T Railroad. I still remember my excitement when the train came in carrying mail, groceries, tourists in "dress up" clothes, gossip from the other stops and, best of all, cold pieces of ice thrown from the refrigerator car. The train was the lifeline and the

47 *Zabriskie Point on T & T R.R. 1910*

43 *Old Store — Ludlow 1916*

48 *Murphy's new store built by John Denair in 1908*

Once Busy Center of Life—
Today's Ghosts

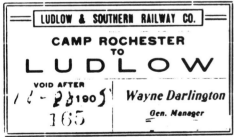

44 *T&T Shop and Repair facility west end of Ludlow*

45

49

50

46 *Music Time. Do you know where it was?*

51 *T&T Roundhouse crew 1914*

"happening" for every little town along the way. The townspeople gathered "en masse" for the arrival and you could hear the old-timers say, "Here She Comes!" After the flat wagon was pulled up to the sliding door of the baggage car and all our necessities were taken care of, the big steam engine would huff and puff and continue on to Death Valley Junction and the excitement for the day was over. After all the townspeople left the tracks, we children would run to see what the train had done to our nails and occasional pennies which had been carefully placed on the rails.

The T & T didn't have hoboes; after all it didn't go anyplace. But a few of the locals were not above hitching rides without a ticket. One time, my cousin and brother were visiting in Tecopa and decided to sneak a ride to Shoshone. They successfully hid in the bottom of an ore car as the train pulled out. After a short ride, however, they found themselves side-tracked and all alone at Zabriskie, and had to resort to walking the six miles home. Perhaps the ore car was needed at Zabriskie, but it is more likely that there was a sly smile on the face of the switchman as the train puffed on down the tracks.

I remember, too, that the little hand cars and later motor cars were used not only for checking the tracks. They were used for shopping trips and even borrowed for joy rides and courting purposes. Riders had no worry about running into a train once the T & T had made its scheduled run.

During prohibition, some of the local citizenry found a batch of still whiskey. Not being sure of what its quality would be like, they waited for the little old Mexican track-walker to come by. They asked him if he'd like a few snorts of good whiskey and, of course, he happily obliged. They watched him carefully to see if he developed any tremors, nausea or went blind and when he didn't, they waved goodby to the happy section hand as he pumped on down the track and promptly divided up their great find.

We had our tragedies with the T & T also. When one of the famous desert flash floods washed out a bridge, the engine plunged down and exploded, killing the engineer and fireman. We children walked to the scene and found a single, scalded thumb lying on the sand as a macabre testimony to the horrible deaths.

In many ways, transportation was better by train in those days than on the modern roads of today. If it wasn't better, it was certainly more fun. For a trip to Los Angeles, you could get on the T & T at Shoshone. It was like joining your family. You were sure to know everyone on the train, including the crew. At Ludlow, you would get the fancy part of the trip on the Santa Fe: dining car, finger-bowls, and all, to reach your destination.

The T & T Railroad, from 1907 to 1940, provided contact for all the little towns along the 250 mile line and the people enjoyed a social life never to be forgotten. They had no problem attending a dance or a party as long as it was on the T & T line. The men who operated the train contributed much to the color and history of the desert. They included Blacky Meier, Micky Divine, Heavy Green, Bill Trenkle and Paddy Miles to name a few. Sometimes as I stand near the now abandoned grade of the old tracks and look south—just for a fleeting moment I am sure I hear a voice of yesteryear saying, "Here She Comes!"

LUDLOW

by Phyllis Couch

The year of 1882 saw the founding of the town of Ludlow, brought about by the establishment of the Southern Pacific Railroad until May 4, 1897 when it became the Santa Fe Railway. This line was the main line and connection with Los Angeles.

Nearly a quarter of a century later, in 1900, the Bagdad Chase mine was discovered about 10 miles to the south. The railroad to the mine, rich in copper and gold, was called the Ludlow-Southern. The train traveled the road from Ludlow to the mine in about 40 minutes. The living area at the Bagdad-Chase mine was known as Camp Rochester. This camp was often nicknamed "Copenhagen" due to the fact of numerous Danes and Swedes who gathered there to find employment.

Ludlow became the hub of a thriving community. Workers from the railroads, plus the miners at Camp Rochester soon chose Ludlow for their amusement and entertainment.

Ludlow was the "water stop" for all steam engines. Water was found here but proved to be too salty for overall use. So water was hauled by train tank cars from Newberry (later known as Newberry Springs) to permanent tanks in Ludlow. A water train would run about every eight hours. A complete railroad shop was built in Ludlow with housing for the employees. Later a school and church was constructed.

In 1905, the Tonopah and Tidewater Railroad was started mainly for transportation of ore from Beatty, Nevada. Also, this line transported mixed baggage and included a passenger car. W. W. Cahill was superintendent and lived aboard his private car located on a line in Ludlow. He used this car for administrative offices.

The presence of Cahill and his crew, plus all the railroad workers and the miners from Bagdad, created much activity around Ludlow. Ludlow was the Junction and headquarters for all the surrounding area. Cafes and rooming houses sprang up. These were used as meeting places for business as well as entertainment. One of the more popular gathering places was known as "Ma Preston's." She had moved from Calico after marrying Tom Preston. He had discovered a silver lode there but moved to Ludlow for the construction boom.

The first school contract was signed August 10, 1905. Cliffie Hoffman, the first teacher, received a salary of $60.00 a month. A tent structure, with board walls half-way up was the first schoolhouse. This was heated in winter by a wood burning stove and had canvas sides which could be lowered in winter for warmth and rolled up in summer for the cool breezes. There were six original pupils. Later the attendance reached 40, with two teachers.

A United States Post Office was founded in 1902. Originally called Stagg, in honor of an engineer on the Tonopah & Tidewater Railroad, this office was officially changed to Ludlow in 1926. There have been 5 Postmasters during the time of Postal Service: B. C. Higgins 1902-1907; Lena E. Reed 1907-1929; Verna E. Sherridan 1930-1961; Helen Kinderman 1961-1968; and Phyllis Couch 1969-1974.

The post office was discontinued in 1974.

Lee Yim was the only oriental businessman located at Ludlow. He was a cafe owner and operated a barber shop in the same building. He raised a family of 9 children, 8 of whom were graduates of the Barstow High School.

In 1913, Ludlow consisted of 2 blocks of business establishments. Contained within this area were 2 general merchandise stores, 3 cafes, 1 pool hall, 1 barber shop and 2 rooming houses. The Murphy brothers were prominent Ludlow residents. Tom had a store and cafe in Ludlow while Mike conducted a like business in Tonopah.

In 1915, there was a cross-country automobile race from Los Angeles to Phoenix, Arizona. People from Death Valley came to Ludlow to view the race. Barney Oldfield was the main attraction, being the top auto racer in our country. The entire day was like a country fair.

Ludlow continued to prosper and through World War I, the Tonopah & Tidewater Railroad remained in operation on its now 250 mile route. However, on June 14, 1940, it ceased all runs.

During its peak years, Ludlow population was around 500 people but after the T & T ceased operating the population dwindled to a mere handful of permanent residents.

In 1962, the Cameron Friend family purchased the townsite. Lack of water still made living in Ludlow very costly. So, Cameron Friend "water-witched" the area. A well was drilled and good water was found at 650 feet down. Today, there are three wells producing good water in Ludlow.

The Friend family continues.

CAMILO, PEDRO AND FRANK DURAN

by Frank E. Duran, Jr.

In 1904 Camilo Duran (1877-1945) arrived in Barstow with his wife Guadalupe and son Pedro by way of El Paso, Texas, after leaving the village of San Christobal in the state of Jalisco, Mexico.

Pedro recalls that many other persons crossed into the United States at the same time. Contractors for railroads and other industries seeking workers met the people who had just crossed. Camilo had signed to work for the Santa Fe Railroad. He was told he would be going to a place called Waterman in California, later to be renamed Barstow. The Duran family boarded a train at El Paso. Along the way individuals and families who had signed on in El Paso were dropped off at various water stops and towns that would be their new homes.

Pedro recalls that the Barstow depot was a wooden building with one small room. Two stores in the town, Dillingham's and Gilham's, were general merchandise stores.

Camilo leased a parcel of land from Santa Fe and built a house which is still standing today at the corner of Hutchison and Sixth Street, a distance from the main town at the time. He sold the house after the influenza epidemic of 1918, purchasing a lot at today's Sixth and White Street to build another home, which is also still standing.

The only two homes in that area up until the late twenties or early thirties belonged to a railroad engineer and to a Mrs. Cook, who was a piano teacher.

Before Pedro could start school in 1908, his father, a laborer in a section gang for Santa Fe, had to get permission from school officials for Pedro to be admitted. Camilo asked his section foreman and road foreman to use their influence. Barstow schools admitted Pedro Duran in 1908 as one of the first Mexican students. Pedro recalls that a year later he was followed by Donaciano Varela. Now there were two, instead of just one, in the numerous fist fights.

Pedro went to work for Santa Fe about 1914, retired in the 1960's and is still residing in Barstow. Donaciano retired in the 1960's as well and is also still residing in Barstow.

Camilo Duran had three other sons born in Barstow. Paul, born in 1907, died in the 1930's; John, born in 1910; and Frank, born in 1915.

Shortly after the youngest son, Frank, was born, Guadalupe Duran died. In 1918, Camilo went to Mexico and brought back Guadalupe Lopez with her children, Jesusita, Francis, and Joseph, to Barstow. Camilo and Guadalupe Lopez were married by Judge Carter, who was a judge for many years and was also employed by Santa Fe as a roadmaster.

Frank Duran was young at the time, but he remembers that the "old town" burned twice. The town had no fire department or engines, but was close to the tracks. To fight a fire, they just moved a locomotive to the area, rolled out water hoses and pumped water from the locomotive tank to the flames. When one locomotive ran out of water, another was rolled up behind it to take its place.

For years the depot at the "old town" had a big dog as a mascot. The dog finally died of old age. Where today's depot is now, a retaining wall kept the river back when it flowed. The old bridge spanning the Mojave was constructed similar to the one that crosses the railroad tracks today, and it had wooden planks for the road.

"Mexican town" was near today's Santa Fe diesel shop. The Mexicans called this neighborhood "La Verija," a name best not translated. Some of the houses were moved in the late 20's and 30's to the area of today's Williams Street between Sixth and Seventh Streets. All the people gathered to move one or two homes a day to their new sites.

Frank recalls that when he started school in 1923 or 1924, one had to be between 8 and 9 years old in order to start the first grade. The school at the time was a large wooden structure, divided into different rooms for each grade. Some of the teachers he remembers are the Smithern sisters, Mrs. Colby, and Mrs. Johnson. Mrs. Johnson's husband, Donald, worked for Hillis, the owner of the Barstow Ford Motor Products garage. Mrs. Leak was a part-time teacher. Miss Crealy, also a teacher there, later changed here name to Mrs. James C. Thomson, and in the 1950's a Barstow school was dedicated in her name.

Frank remembers that the cemetery was located next door to McDonald's funeral home, the area of Seventh and Main Streets. After the fires, the town moved south to the present Main Street. In the area of today's Cunningham's Pharmacy were located the local bank, post office, and theater. In the 1930's, the bank manager was Ed Demerest. After the post office moved to Second Street in the late 30's, the postmaster was Alfred True.

Frank remembers that his family kept the same post office box number of 213 from the early 20's through various moves of the post office—Cunningham area, Second Street, and the building that the Barstow Academy of Beauty now occupies. Postal home de-livery service was instituted about 1950.

Frank remembers that up to the 40's, the only real police force was the Santa Fe police agent, who also policed the town when needed. In the late 30's, a California Highway Patrolman moved to Barstow.

Frank worked as a bellhop after school and on weekends at the Beacon Hotel, which was built in the early 30's. The owner was Tom Wilson whose wife, Edith, was an English teacher. Many people stopped there on their journeys across country. Many were movie stars.

When Ginger Rogers and her first husband were on their way to be married in Nevada, Frank picked them up at a private air strip in Daggett and brought them to the Beacon to spend the night. Rex Bell, a star of the 30's (later governor of Nevada) and four friends stopped at the Beacon and asked if they could get some "booze" and if there was a "house" in town. Frank told them directions to the "house," which was located on the east side of today's Fifth Street. They asked him to drive them there in their car. Frank remembers the car as being huge. After returning from the "house," each of the men gave him a big tip, five dollars each. That was a lot of money at the time.

The bellhops, and other people, acquired liquor from various bootleggers in town. (This was during the prohibition of the 30's.) The closest bootlegger to the Beacon was a man named Tom, located about the corner of Fredricks and 7th Street. The Beacon owner sold mix for drinks to the bellhops for 20 cents a bottle. The bellhops, in turn, sold it to the people for 35 cents.

He remembers that "Death Valley Scotty," when he stopped at the Beacon, never tipped. Instead, he gave out red ties, exactly like the one that he wore. In the early 30's, Emilio Portes Gil, the President of Mexico, stopped at the Beacon while on a tour of the country. The governor of California, Frank Merriam, had come down from Sacramento. A big, beautiful fiesta was held at the Beacon with mariachi music and all the trimmings, and attended by many dignitaries.

DEATH VALLEY SCOTTY SPECIAL
by Pat Keeling

T. E. Gallagher was the engineer who took part in the sensational dash across the country on the Death Valley Scotty Special train on July 9, 1905. Mr. Gallagher, then a resident of Needles, engineered Scotty's famous train between Barstow and Needles on the cross country race in three hours and 15 minutes. He was then one of the youngest engineers assigned on the run.

Engineer Gallagher performed his portion of the trip on engine 1005, a vavelain compound steam locomotive. The fireman was Ed D. Nettleton of Needles. Both of these gentlemen engineers, from 1910 on, worked with my father, Daniel E. Jernigan, in Mojave, Bakersfield, Needles and Barstow. They all retired with over 50 years of service to the Santa Fe railway.

The Scotty Special was engineered from Needles to Seligman (as shown on the train order #16) leaving Needles at 7 p.m. and arriving at Seligman at 10:05. The Arizona Division First District-Eastward, through Needles, Beal, Topock, Powell, Franconia, Havilan, all the other communities, into Seligman, broke all records for steam engines and transcontinental trains. The record held up until the railroad began using diesel locomotives.

———

Needles Nugget 9-4-42 Commercial Ad:

52 Tom Gallagher was engineer of Death Valley
Scotty's special run to Chicago July 9, 1905

55 Harvey House Employees Sept. 1930. Front row: (L-R) News stand employee,
Ralph Barker, Paul Durhan, Minne Leutjen, Phyliss - Gertrude Flarety -
lunchroom manager, Annie McUmare - housekeepter, Sam Goldber,
Herman Horndoff - chef, Jim Carter - news stand mgr., Vernon Hallock
- office, S.A. Arnold - office and Riley Whitty - mgr. 2nd row: Peggy Botts,
N.I., Jewell, Sylvia, N.I., Covis Crow, Ruby Boles, N.I., Hattie, Jane Clark,
Hazel Poe - main dining room mgr., Alice, Beulah, Anna Lou Snyder -
dining room girls. 3rd row: 3 hotel maids N.I., Kate, N.I., Opal Cole, Mollie
Anthony Saunders, Ester, Beatrice English, Flo, Ethel Gray, Gladys
Baker, Ors Bassett - soda foundain mgr. 4th row: N.I., 2 house-men, asst.
chef, Frank Kauirama - chef, Cruz - head pantryman, Shorty - head dishwasher lunch room, Felix Cruz - main dining room head pantryman,
chef, head bus boy - lunch room, head bus boy main dining room, Pasqual -
head bell hop.   (N.I.-not identified)

They Were Needles

53 Reading Room and
Harvey House

56 Showing off her "new"
Desert Cooler 1930's

57 Front Street
early 1920's

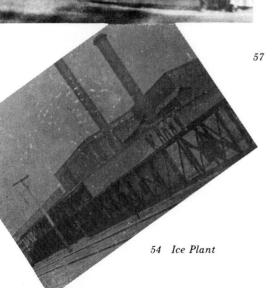

54 Ice Plant

THE JERNIGAN FAMILY

by Pat Keeling

I remember my father, D. E. Jernigan, carrying his oil can along side the big steam locomotives during the 1930's. He would stop to check the large steam pistons, oiling them along each fitting, making ready for the long trip away from town.

How he loved to use the whistle on his steam engine, with a special long sound only he could make. We always knew when Dad was coming into town. He would lay on the whistle, "Woo, woo,———woo, woo!"

For over 47 years he ran engines over the two strands of rail in and out of Barstow. The Arizona Division of the Santa Fe was Seligman-Needles; Needles-Barstow; Barstow-Bakersfield with interchangeable seniority rights to the employees.

Dad's first contact with desert railroads came when he became a fireman for the Santa Fe in 1910. He borrowed a train pass from a friend to ride a passenger train from Pittsburg, Kansas, to Bakersfield, California.

His 100 miles of travel was a long days work, and usually lasted over 16 hours. Enginemen furnished their own cushions and oil cans. The fireman, besides his regular job, had to oil the pistons and valve stems, and tighten loose nuts. The steam engines were all coal burners until 1912. The cinders from the coal fed the dust down to the ash pan, much of it settling over the engineer and fireman; this necessitated the traditional overalls and cap.

Dad moved his wife, Lillie Heston Jernigan, and four children, Opal, Clifford, Floyd and Jesse, to Bakersfield in 1911, however Dad was soon transferred to Needles. There, a home was rented on Broadway and "D" Streets, near Claypool's store.

Needles, as usual, was quite warm on that 1911 August day, when they arrived. The children were treated to a trip to the depot where ice, stored in small carts on the platform, disappeared into waiting hands.

The focal points of entertainment in Needles became the Santa Fe Harvey House, "El Garces Hotel and Restaurant." Santa Fe employees also enjoyed the reading room and recreation center which included a swimming pool, library, dance pavilion and stage. Concerts, dramas, and parties presented additional entertainment during the intervening years.

In 1912, Dad was assigned to Bagdad, in the middle of the Mojave Desert. A community of some size, Bagdad consisted of eating houses, railroad houses for employees, a grocery store, telegraph and telephone for Santa Fe, Western Union, and Wells Fargo & Co. The family would ride the train to Needles to visit friends, shop, attend birthday parties, or go on picnics.

Dad moved to Bakersfield, away from the heat in 1912, he ran engine service from Bakersfield through the 57 tunnels in the Tehachapi's via Mojave to Barstow. He was promoted to Passenger Engineer in 1917.

In 1924, Lillie was killed in a tragic automobile accident; Dad was left with two teenage sons, Floyd and Jesse; his daughter, Opal; and two small grand-

daughters, Aretha and Francis. Opal kept house for the family in the interim year at Barstow, Needles, and Bakersfield. Dad later took a helper job from Bakersfield to Mojave.

In Mojave, 1925, Dad courted and married my mother, Opal C. Shumaker, a young auburn-haired Fred Harvey Girl from Kansas. After the family welcomed Opal, they packed to brave the trip by automobile, as Dad had been transferred back to Needles. It took three days to cross the desert, via Barstow. There were few roads, none kind to automobile travelers. Flat tires, broken springs, radiators without water and many crank starts were the rule of the day.

In Needles, as a bride with a young son, Phillip, and two teenage boys, Opal found house keeping rather challenging. Teenagers gathered at the Jernigan household on Acoma Street. Mother's favorite story was about a Mohave Indian princess called "Indian Georgia." One of Georgia's habits was looking in windows to see what was going on. She would stand outside the house, cup her hands against the glass and peer in. One day, in 1927, all the boys in the neighborhood were gathered in our living room. My brothers, and friends, including today's San Bernardino County Sheriff Frank Bland, were there. When Georgia saw all of those boys, she just backed away from the window. That afternoon, when Mom went grocery shopping, Georgia came down the street. As Mom approached, Georgia stepped into the street, waving her arms and bowing to Mom saying, "Squaw HEAP MANY BOYS!!" She thought all of those young men belonged in our family.

The years passed. Floyd and Jesse graduated from High School. I was born in Bakersfield in 1929, and Don in Redondo Beach in 1931, due to the non-existent maternity care in Needles.

The stock market crash and the depression created another era in Needles. In 1932 my folks decided to build their own home. Our house on Cibola Street had a large screened-in porch across the back just for sleeping. The house also had a large basement for Dad's daytime sleeping quarters. During prohibition he brewed his own liquor and the basement was filled with vats, bottles, bottling equipment and various paraphernalia. The capping machine was a favorite plaything, "Snap! Click! Clack!" pulling the handle was lots of fun . . . until Dad wanted to use the equipment! "Who used all of my caps?" he hollered. It wasn't until I married and moved away from home that I finally realized not everyone had a bottling "works," complete with wine vinegar, in their basement! These were days of wine, friends, and music from the old piano.

Mom, Don and I would wait until we heard Dad's whistle from the crossing, then hurry to the Depot and sit on the cement pillar bench 'till he arrived. The family would always greet him before he signed the register and reported on his trip. Hidden in his pockets would be "goodies" for us, coloring books, toys, lifesavers,

58   Opal Jernigan Porikas, Lillie Heston Jernigan, D.E. Jernigan - 1911

59   Ray and June Henderson Wallin, Floyd
Henderson - Hinkley 1948

63   Road to Bakersfield 1925

62   Mojave Harvey Girls 1925—
front: Opal C. Jernigan

A Railroad Family.

60   Opal C., Donald and Patricia Jernigan - Topock 1937

64   Double header Troop Train - D.E. Jernigan, engineer

61   Phil in the new family car - Needles 1933

65   Clifford, Thelma and D.E. Jernigan

jaw breakers, or a package of gum. It was always a treat to get dressed up to meet his train. As a little girl, wearing a yellow dress, with long curls flying behind, I would run and hug my Dad.

We took trips on the train to visit the rest of the family throughout the country and spent the summers out of town because of the unbearable heat in Needles. Many families, including Nell Pyeatt, May Lobough, Hettie Barnum, Bess Brewer and others would leave Needles to go to various places in California and Arizona to keep cool. It was during the '30's that Bill Smart and Dad worked on Bill's new invention called the "cooler." It became a tremendous help to us during that summer.

Train trips to visit telegraphic agents Floyd and Lorayne Henderson and daughter June, at various stations along the railroad, would take us to Yucca, where we stayed in a caboose; Hackberry, in a company house with no electricity; Goffs; Kramer; Rice; Barstow and Topock. When Floyd was agent at Topock, during the depression, there would be days of playing baseball, hide-and-go-seek, kick the can, dress-up in old clothes, Chinese checkers, and cards. We picked dates from the tall palms, and fished in the Colorado River; the nearby Sacramento Wash provided space for picnics and baseball. Following World War II, Lorayne became a woman railroad agent at Hinkley.

In the depression years, Mother helped many people. My cousins, Luther and Jack Jernigan, found part-time work in the mechanical department at the roundhouse. They prospected the hills for new mining claims, while staying with us. Our folks were always working on a new building project. When hoboes came to the house for a meal, Mom would say to them, "If you want to work I'll fix you something to eat." One day she fed 25 men. There were no Welfare Agencies in those days!

The memories of a Christmas long ago recall the warmth and tenderness of a family together.

One year we were too poor to buy a tree, but Dad surprised us with a big piñon pine to adorn our living room. Cut above Peach Springs, Arizona, it arrived tied to his great big steam engine. With my brothers, Phil and Don, he made its stand and brought it into the house. How regal and magnificent it looked in the corner! Then Mother gave us corn to pop and cranberries which we strung together on long threads; we merrily twirled these garlands around the tree. Then, out came colored papers which we folded, cut and twisted into chain rings, the shades of a rainbow, suspending them among its branches. The biggest thrill of the day was when, with Dad's help, we topped our creation with a gold star. Now, tired, but delighted, we hung our stockings by the potbellied stove in hopes Santa Claus would be there. With the fragrance of pine floating in the air, we went to bed, our hearts bubbling with the spirit of Christmas.

When morning came, there was a book and harmonica for Phil; a toy whistle and gun for Don; a tiny doll and book for me; and for all shiny red apples, golden oranges, walnuts and hard candies. As we enjoyed the glow of fire Mother told of past Christmases in Kansas, at her Grandmother's house filled with children . . . Oh! What a grand time we had!

During World War II Dad held various jobs as an Engineer on freight and passenger engines over the entire route; on helper engines to Cadiz and on double headers to Ash Hill. He made as many as three trips each day, to help in the war effort. Every conceivable type of equipment was pressed into service then as passenger trains were filled to overflowing; freight trains made up as long as allowable; and troop trains whisked through the area.

I remember how proud my dad was in 1944, when he was "called" to make a passenger run on a brand new diesel locomotive. William White, now Superintendent of the Barstow Diesel shops, worked his diesel maintainer on many trips during the war. Dad said "Bill is the best maintainer on the railroad."

Dad worked 25 years, from Needles to Barstow, 1932-1957. As a part time resident of Barstow, he built apartments on Cottage Street and enjoyed watching the changes that the city made throughout the years. "The Shack," the name of his apartments, was a resting spot every other day as a home away from home. Dad walked everywhere; a three mile jaunt over the bridge to visit his friends was just a short stint for him. His favorite place on October 31 was Main Street watching the Kiwanis Mardi-Gras parade.

The end of the war brought about many changes on the railroad. Diesels transformed working conditions to and from Needles. The new shops built in Barstow brought radical changes to the communities and people along Dad's route.

In 1957, Dad made his last trip on a silver streamliner with its red and yellow diesel. After the Korean War, my brother Don attended college. Later he returned to his father's calling, and became a Conductor in 1957.

Bill Keeling and I were married in 1946; we moved to Barstow in 1947. Bill went to work in the diesel shops and is now a Santa Fe supervisor. We are the parents of four children, Pam, Judy, Candy, and Tom. Our son Tom followed in his grandfather's footsteps, and became an Engineer in Needles in 1976.

The Jernigan family returned time and time again to visit Needles; a camaraderie is always there.

Today, while listening to the roar of diesels going on their way to distant places, I shall always remember the long low whistle only my Dad could make on the steam engine . . . "Woo, woo—woo, Woo!"

Needles Nuggett 2-7-41: Ad

THE BIRTH AND GROWTH OF NEWBERRY

by Charles McCoy

Many desert towns have lived and died over the past century. Although some of those that remain are declining, most have prospered economically. One such town that is building up rapidly is Newberry Springs. Sometimes, amidst the prosperity, the people who founded the community, and the reasons why Newberry Springs survived while the other small towns died, are forgotten.

The first settlement at the present town of Newberry Springs was founded about 1911. The Santa Fe Railroad used the water from Newberry Springs for its steam engines and for the water cars that were hauled to Ludlow and Bagdad. For this reason the town was renamed Water. Later this name was replaced by Wagner, after the first postmistress. This name lasted only a few years. When Mrs. Wagner moved away the town was again called Newberry.

The first homestead claims were filed for the parcels along the Valley Center Road. Land was homesteaded in 160 acre sections under the provisions of the Homestead Act. They located their quarter-sections following the original mesquite stakes used by the early surveyor who was sent by the land office to lay out the official boundary lines.

Dutch Dorrance, one of the first residents, walked to Newberry from Minneola in 1910, to stake his claim. "When I first came here there was nothing, just the desert . . . there got to be sort of a settlement in time down along this road (Valley Center) . . . all of the available homesteads were taken." Mr. Dorrance lived in a dugout until he built his home of adobe brick. All of the early homes were constructed of adobe brick because the adobe could be found almost anywhere by digging away about a foot of topsoil. Ray McCoy said, "If constructed properly these buildings required no reinforcement."

One of the first improvements for a claim was the digging of a well. Since there was no machinery in those days, wells were dug by hand. Dutch had to dig thirty feet to find water. He then planted alfalfa for animal feed.

There was another settlement on the other side of the tracks, known as the "South Settlement." This area was founded by Christopher Burckhardt and his partner George Schaefer. Charles Van Doren and a fellow named Hannon also settled there. The four men helped each other improve their property. The remains of these homesteads can still be seen on Fort Cady Road east of Newberry Springs.

There were only two teams of horses in the Newberry area around 1911. The team owned by Walter Knott was used for light work. The other team by John Burden was used to do the heavy work. The men gave Burden a days work for the use of his team to do their own work.

Prior to 1923, Dutch Dorrance was the only one in the area with fresh fruit. During the summer everyone bought fresh apricots, peaches and grapes from him. Besides his fruit stand, Dutch was a sales agent for Chicago Airmotor Co., which manufactured windmills. Everyone in the area ordered through him. The mills were delivered from Oakland by train.

Many of the first homesteaders had children, and so a school was needed. The first schoolhouse had only one room and a single teacher. It was built of adobe brick by Dutch Dorrance and Ray Pickering. The 600 square foot building was constructed in six days and each of the men was paid $12 for his work. This building was used until 1923 when an addition was built. Grades one through eight were taught in the Newberry School. Since there was no High School in Barstow until 1915, those who could afford it went to school in San Bernardino.

After a hard days work the people were ready for a little relaxation and entertainment. Dutch and Marvin McCoy recall:

> The people had fun in simple ways. They would all load up in a wagon, drive down to the lake for dinner, then come home. The women of Newberry had a Literary Society that put on plays which were given at John Burden's place. The dances held at the schoolhouse were the biggest social events of the time. People came from as far away as Ludlow. They enjoyed the music provided by banjos, guitars, sax, jazbos and the violin. On Sundays the people gathered together at the Dry Lake for a softball game.

As the town grew, several businesses opened to serve the needs of the community. The general store for the area was run by John Burden. The ruins of Burden's store may still be seen on Fairview Avenue, just north of the Santa Fe Railroad tracks in Newberry Springs. The store sold just about everything that a person could want. It sold the only fresh beef in the Newberry district. The meat was shipped from San Bernardino by train and stored in the brine tank to keep it cool. The only ice machine between Barstow and Ludlow was also located at the store. All the supplies for the store arrived on the train. Trains carried special cars known as "peddler cars" which served the desert communities like a warehouse. The men who worked these trains received extra pay because the train crews were responsible for the unloading and delivering the goods.

The other store in Newberry, The Cliff House, received its name because of its location below the cliffs at Newberry. It was built by Holly Douglas who later sold out to the Sischo's. The Cliff House catered more to the travelers since it served as a rest stop for the Yellow Way Bus Line. There was also a garage there. People came from as far as Barstow to splash in the refreshing waters of the area's only swimming pool located to the rear of the Cliff House.

Burden's store also served as the Newberry Post

66 Water train over Diablo Canyon Arizona

67 Fort Cady remains in the '20's

70 The well at Newberry Springs

68 The mules hauled their own water

Water Is Life

71 The lost one, 1909, died within 2 miles of water

69 Goffs' desert graves

72 Vandalized desert grave

Office. C.B. McCoy was paid $20 a month to carry the mail from the depot to the store. Before the Post Office was established, the mail was just dumped off at the depot. Someone from the settlement was supposed to be there to pick it up. Occasionally, if this person was delayed, the mail scattered along the tracks all the way to Ludlow. Whoever picked up his own mail also picked up his neighbor's. The mail was distributed along the lane until each family received theirs.

Denny Womack had the best service station in Newberry. His station, located in "Cozy Cove," was known for its large inventory of spare parts. The quality of a service station was rated by the kind and number of parts in stock. The largest item Womack had in stock was auto coil springs. Since there were many makes of automobiles on the road then, he had quite a supply. The gasoline which arrived in 50 gallon drums from the Standard Oil Refinery in El Segundo came by train.

One of the less known but more popular businesses of Newberry was that conducted by the bootleggers. A real old timer, C.B. McCoy said:

> The women folk could make the best beer, oh brother! And then we had some Old Tennessee boys back in the hills there, who knew how to make moonshine. If you could take the third drink you was in. That was the biggest farce. There was a honey of a still down in the river. Boy, it was the real thing . . . nobody went short after the country went dry.

The fact that Newberry was located on Route 66 was another reason why the town grew and prospered. The highway, built around 1925, was a one-lane dirt road constructed using a drag, a piece of iron rail drawn behind a horse used to smooth the ground. The highway followed the railroad as closely as possible so that stranded motorists could flag down the trains for help. The highway between Barstow and Ludlow was so rough that a person wasn't able to travel it without breaking a coil spring. All service stations kept a good supply. Motorists were also warned not to travel without a spare tire. The highway through Newberry was finally paved in 1930.

In 1925 the first bus of the Yellow Way Bus Lines, which ran from Los Angeles to Denver, arrived in Newberry. It was a memorable event because there was now a new form of transportation for the desert people. One bus from each direction arrived daily. The fare from Los Angeles to Denver was $21.

Newberry's prime importance to the railroad was the water from the spring. Marvin McCoy recalls that during the 1920's, water was hauled to Ludlow and Bagdad. Everyday a special train of 33 water cars left Newberry. Eleven of these cars went to Ludlow while the remaining 22 went to Bagdad. Each car held 10,000 gallons and was sold for $65 a car. At Ludlow the cars were emptied into a cistern and then pumped into a tank. The town's water supply came from this tank.

The well at Newberry produced approximately 500,000 gallons of water a day for the water cars as well as the engines on the 25 to 30 trains which ran through Newberry daily, as recalled by Raymond McCoy.

By 1930 the Newberry settlement had grown from the desert to a quiet community. However, during the depression days times were hard for all. Tom Garb, a fireman for the Santa Fe who had been laid off, had the job as Head of Relief for Barstow Area 33. He had government surplus food available—butter, flour, fresh meat and canned goods. Tom came to Newberry everyday to see C.B. McCoy who distributed the goods to the Newberry people. Mr. Garb could write food and clothing orders. Clothing included such articles as overalls, shoes, boots, dresses, and stockings.

Mr. C.B. McCoy summed up the depression for Newberry in these words, "The people were starving and I was appointed in the Newberry district to get food and clothing; that was the great depression in Newberry." . . .

Bentonite was the one mineral discovery in Newberry that paid off. Oscar Hoerner, who owned a service station east of Newberry, found some interesting looking mud on his tires one day after becoming stuck on a remote dirt road. When he discovered it to be bentonite he rushed to San Bernardino and filed his claim. Hoerner sold his mine to California Talc and received a royalty on each ton mined. California Talc sold out to National Lead, which operates the mine today. Many of the people in Newberry now work for National Lead either in the mine or at the mill.

MEXICAN WORKERS FOR SANTA FE

by Richard R. Lemus

(As told by Encarnacion Martinez, Salvador Hernandez Flores, Donaciano Varela, and Senon Ramos.)

Mexican personnel employed by the Santa Fe Railroad have contributed much to the growth and expansion of the Barstow community as a whole. Many of the workers migrated from Mexico in the early 1900's. Some came because of job opportunities and others for adventure or a different life. They stayed to become permanent residents and are among the oldest "old timers" in Barstow. Today their families point with pride to providing a third generation of employees for

Santa Fe. Senon Ramos, Encarnacion Martinez, Salvador Hernandez Flores and Donaciano Varela are four of the Mexicans who came to Barstow more than fifty years ago to work for the railroad. Their personal histories give a unique view of Barstow as it was in the early 1900's.

SENON RAMOS

Senon Ramos was born on January 13, 1880 in Penjamo, Guanajuato, Mexico. Barstow was not a very big town when Ramos came in 1911. The only industry was the Santa Fe Railroad. Ramos remembers that one could walk the length of town and back in 15 minutes. The only store was owned by Dillingham, located where the Santa Fe wrecker is today.

Barstow had no automobiles nor did El Paso, Texas, as he remembers. The horse, mule, and buggy were used for transportation. The first Mexicans to have automobiles in Barstow were Julio Gonzales and Ramon Carrancos.

Ramos recalls the census of 1912. The Mexican population was 99 out of about 250 overall population. Tom Carter was the first judge for Bastow and he served for 25 years.

Daggett was a main point for the railroad then, because that is where people got off to go to Death Valley. Daggett was just a housing section for the track gang. Ramos said that 10 men worked that area and each had his own small room. The men cooked on a wood burning stove. When they were out of groceries, one or two men going to town in Barstow would get the items needed for everyone.

At times it was necessary for men to move from one section to another. It was important in one case as Ramos remembers. Men were laying track in Hodge and had no means to store water. Ramos and several others were dispatched to Hodge to dig a well. Using pick and shovel the men broke through the hard ground and dug 20 feet. The Indians working behind them dug the last five feet. The diameter was nine feet. After cement was applied around the inside, the depth was 24 feet and the diameter was eight feet six inches. The well was constructed so precisely that only one bucket could be dipped in. It had a lid with a canvas around it so that no dirt nor insects could get in. The well held two tanks of water brought from Newberry for the railroad.

Ramos remembers that the pay was one dollar a day for each track gang employee and that all Santa Fe employees were given the day off to celebrate July 4 and Mexican holidays on May 5 and September 16.

There was no Catholic Church in Barstow but almost every Sunday a Priest came from needles to give Mass and to baptize.

Friends who helped Ramos get settled when he first came to Barstow were Encarnacion Robles, Luis Lozano, and Manuel Casteneda. These men all worked for Santa Fe.

DONACIANO VARELA

Donaciano Varela was born May 24, 1895 in Guadalajara, Mexico. In 1913 he came to Barstow with his father Calixto Varela as part of the gang laying railroad track. He then worked at the old Round House as a laborer, machinist helper, and machinist and retired after 56 years service in 1966 at the age of 72 years. He began his railroad career at the age of 16.

Shorty, as his friends call him, was an amateur photographer and also a carpenter. He built several cement block houses, making the blocks himself. He made the blocks for the old Forum theatre, now Sears, and for his own house.

In 1915 Donaciano lived by the riverbottom but because of the floods and damage to the house, he and his family were forced to move to the section homes where the diesel shop is now located. In 1924 Donaciano moved to his present address on Sixth and White Street.

Donaciano remembers going to school to learn how to read and write in English. His teacher was Ruth Thomson. Shorty says that even the Valley Hotel was used for school purposes.

SALVADOR HERNANDEZ FLORES

Salvador Hernandez Flores was born on April 13, 1890 in Santa Eulalia, about 12 miles from Chihuahua, Mexico. Flores came to Barstow in 1921 and was hired by the Harvey House as a dishwasher shortly after. He was paid $40 a month. In 1923 he became a porter and was paid roughly $65 a month. A few years later he transferred to the rip track. In 1970 Flores retired with 48 years of railroad service.

Flores remembers that there were no paved roads from Needles to Barstow, nor to Victorville. A horse dragged a flatbed loaded with heavy rails to make the roads driveable. Because of the rough roads, one had to carry his own tire patches and air pump to make any repairs. Barstow had few cars at that time but needed mechanics. Julian Flores, Salvador's brother worked part time as a mechanic and worked full time for the railroad.

The Mexican holidays of May 5 and September 16 were celebrated more then than they are today. Flores remembers that everyone took part in the fiestas. Beginning at Seventh and Main, the people marched to the Henderson's Clothing Store at First and Main. After hearing talks by the judge and other speakers they then marched back to the "barrio" where they had permission to fire guns, drink, and enjoy themselves. There was a dance hall on the southeast corner of Seventh and Clark Street that they used on these occasions.

His very close friends were Tomas Arroyo, Marcos Renteria, Brijido Montana, Tomas Diaz, Francisco Vasquez, Julio Sanchez, Juan Gomez and Senon Ramos. These men were all employees of the Santa Fe Railroad.

ENCARNACION MARTINEZ

Encarnacion Martinez was born on March 25, 1916 in Quitzeo de Abasolo, Guanajuato Mexico. Soledad Negrete, his uncle, arranged for him and his mother, Brajedes Martinez, to come to Barstow in 1919. Soledad came to Barstow in 1913 and was a section gang employee.

Martinez went to school here in Barstow. He remembers some of his school friends, Lupe Sanchez and Ernesto Puente who attended school in the bungalows and high school where the El Rancho Hotel is today.

Martinez worked at the Harvey House while going to school and so did Ernesto Puente. He recalls that in the 1930's the wages were very low. The monthly pay at the

Harvey House for some jobs was as follows:

  Cook — $65
  Cooks helper — $35
  Pantry-man — $35
  Storekeeper — $50

The Harvey House manufactured its own ice cream, he remembers.

In 1938 Martinez went to work for the track gang. He was paid $2.66 for eight hours work. About 1940 the union came into effect and the pay was raised to $3.04 for eight hours. He remembers that in 1946 a laborer working for the Santa Fe Railroad was paid four or six cents per hour more than a laborer at the Marine Base. At that time the hourly rate of pay was $1.24. Anytime a man was hired by the Santa Fe he was issued a card. With this card he was sent to the Holmes Supply that was owned and operated by the Santa Fe.

There one could buy shoes, clothing, groceries, and miscellaneous items. The bill was deducted from the employee's pay check.

MRS. HUGH "NELL" PYEATT
by Pat Keeling

Mrs. Hugh (Nell) Pyeatt went to Needles as a bride on July 4, 1916. She says this about early Needles:

In 1916, when I arrived there, it was about 118° and there were hardly any sidewalks, and we had to walk in the street. There were not many cars because of the non-existence of roads in Needles. Almost everyone did their traveling by passenger trains. When I had my first child, I pushed him everywhere in a big wicker baby buggy which was easy to push. The only amusement in town usually was to go to the depot and see the passenger trains and the Indians selling bead work. There was recreation at the Santa Fe Reading Room once a week, or church shows, or side shows that sold patent medicines. Once in a great while there would be a circus that would delight the children. The Colorado River was not a great place for recreation like it is now because of the quicksand, the rapid change in water level, sand bars, etc., and we would never let a child swim in it. I did go down and sit on a rock and put my feet in the water just to relax and cool off. At night we would have to sprinkle water all over our beds to keep cool, or sleep out in the yard under the grape arbors. We would spray water from the houses over sheets hung from the trees to get a cool breeze. This was prior to the invention of the desert water cooler. The youngsters of today do not realize how hot it really was. I have seen it 118° at midnight, in August.

When Mrs. Pyeatt moved from Needles in 1941, she sold her maternity home (the only one in Needles at the time) and brought her family to San Bernardino. As a native daughter of California, she had seen many changes, including the railroads. Her father, David Neale, was an emigrant from England. In 1906, as an engineer on a Santa Fe steam engine, he had a run from San Bernardino to San Diego through Colton, Fullerton and Oceanside. It was a long haul for an engineer at that time.

EARLY BARSTOW MASONS
by Clarence S. Crooks, Jr.

In 1921, the Santa Fe Masonic Club was organized consisting of Masons working for the Santa Fe Railroad in California and Arizona for the purpose of fostering and cultivating good fellowships; and to form a closer acquaintance among the employees.

A Benefit Fund was established to assist the family of deceased brethren. At the time of a death, each member would be assessed $1.10 to be put back in the fund. At the earliest moment, the treasurer would give the family of the deceased $250. In those days that was a lot of money.

Since Barstow didn't have a Masonic Lodge at this time, the Masons would get on train No. 7 (Mail & Express) in late afternoon and go to San Bernardino to the Phoenix Lodge No. 178. After lodge, they went to the Santa Fe Depot and went to bed in a Sleeping car. Early the next morning the car would be attached on the back end of train No. 8 (Mail & Express), arriving back in Barstow in time for the men to go to work by 7:00 a.m. Some of the members were: William Askren Roy Canady, Oscar Collins, H.G. Crawford, Clarence Crooks, Abner Cunningham, Roby Damerell, Harvey Davis, Samuel Davis, Arthur Doran, F.E. Dunlop, Newton Henderson, Bernard Merrill, Roy Parsons, Ludlow Powell, Royal Pray, Lorice Rice, Frank Smith, Charles Springer, Bernard Stafford, Udall Tenney, George Weaver and Harold Wilson.

RAILROAD STRIKE 1922
by Pat Keeling

Working conditions for the railroads were not always the best. In 1922 there was a nationwide strike called by the shop forces against the Santa Fe. Mrs. Nell Pyeatt remembers:

The strike called in 1922 was an effective

measure of stopping trains but really never settled. There were fellows that came out from the East to take over the jobs of the strikers. The men who went out on strike—never got back to work—and went on to work in other places. The families of the men who came in to work on the strike, you couldn't associate with them because they were strike breakers. If you talked to the strike breakers the other people would all be down on you, so I just didn't go anywhere that I could see them. The wages were next to nothing, at about $100 per month. When payday came, the women would go and set up tables and beg for donations for the strikers but I wouldn't go out and do this. Almost every woman who did this—got their husband fired. After the jobs were replaced by someone else, many people left Needles and found jobs elsewhere. The strike had been forgotten to some extent by some, but still remembered because of the bitter feelings and resentment it caused over 50 years ago.

This was a big strike action for our country, but it was not the last. There have been many other railroad strikes for changes in working conditions during the past 50 years, but perhaps none so bitter as this one. Many people involved in the 1922 strike never spoke to one another again.

MRS. OLIVA McCONNELL
by Sachiko Kitts

Mrs. Oliva (Robison) McConnell was born in Bagdad in 1916. Her family consisted of her father, mother, two sisters and three brothers. Her father worked for Santa Fe as a locomotive hostler. Later, he was injured when he was switching a box car.

At that time, Bagdad was a good sized town with a Harvey House, a large hotel and homes including those for the track crew. Oliva went to Bagdad School for the first grade (early 1920's).

They raised a garden using the old grain doors for a sifting screen to get the rocks out. They planted vegetables, poured water on them, and they grew.

It was hot, 125° at night. They put wet sheets over them to let the breeze go through to cool them.

Water came from Newberry, as it does today. There was no fresh water.

There was no power, at that time, and wet gunny sacks were placed around a screen box for an ice box.

Oliva's father and brother went to Twentynine Palms to shop for groceries. They would build a fire at the top of the hill on the return trip to let the mother know they would be home the next day.

The most fascinating play was to cross the railroad back and forth until the train came, counting how many times they could cross. There was a candy store at Amboy.

The family moved to Long Beach and San Diego—a few months each, and to San Bernardino. They went to Saltus and the ranch in the Granite Mountains for summer vacations, staying at her sister's. Her father came and worked at Saltus Mill, driving a Dinky there.

Bagdad vanished when in the 1950's the Santa Fe changed from steam to diesel and no longer stopped for water and coal. Today, only the graveyard remains.

Oliva came back to the desert in October, 1963 and married Frank E. McConnell in December. Their house in Cadiz is surrounded with trees, grass, grapes, tropical plants, cactus, vegetable gardens, fish pond, pool and a green house which they built all by themselves. People call it desert oasis and paradise.

SILK TRAINS 1929
by A.C. "Dutch" Walters, Santa Fe Conductor
(Reprint Needles Desert Star)
Edited by Germaine L. Moon

Silk trains, the fastest trains on the rails, ran from the West to the East Coast to beat the steamship's arrival carrying raw silk from Japan.

The trains consisted of three to five cars, usually with a double-header, in case one engine "went bad," the other providing the spare. Prairie type oil burning steam engines meant fast locomotives which came in different classes, such as 1200, 1300, 3500 or 3600.

From Barstow, California, one afternoon in 1929, two silk trains were called. The two engineers were Jack B. Potter and Billy Galbraith, "the little giant." Jack Potter had a prairie type engine which he backed out on the lead toward west, when he ran into a Johannesburg (Jo Burg) coach, knocking a hole in its tank (water and oil tank or tender). He took the engine back to the roundhouse where it was condemned. Billy Galbraith was oiling a "3600" all around when the roundhouse foreman ordered him to give Potter the engine. Billy smiled knowingly, the 3600 had the reputation of being top heavy and it was the only one there.

The road foreman of engines, "Grisley" Anderson and trainmaster, E.B. Hebert rode with Jack Potter.

"Do you want to work or deadhead, Jack, since this is your last trip?" asked Mr. Hebert. Jack was a small man and wore a jockey cap; he was also a good throttle man and known as a fast roller.

"I would like to work, this run pays $4.00 more. Are you gentlemen going with me?" he asked, and turning his cap around, he said: "If you are going, then tie yourself on, 'cause this is my last trip. I always wanted

73 *Traveling engineer, Earl Gilbert*

76 *October 31, 1932*

77 *August 3, 1932*

FLASH—While engineer Tom Cogley and his fireman stopped for lunch, a flash flood swept the engine from the track at Keene in 1937.

Wrecker Crew Goes To Work

74 *October 28, 1932*

78 *Barstow wrecking crew at Del Mar, Ca. 1936 - Abraham Lara, Coleman Payne, James Villares, Hugh Hamilton, Clifton Denney, Thomas Byrnes, John Goss, Louie Gliebe and Charles Davis, foreman*

75 *The "Wall" 1932*

to know how fast these engines would run, and now I am going to find out!"

They stopped at Bagdad 14 minutes to cool down a hot pin, and take on a tank of water. Hebert and Anderson got off, but Ralph Hogedon, the motor car maintainer, hopped on the rear coach to go to Needles. There he told me:

"It didn't sound like a locomotive, down through Amboy. It sounded like an explosion!"

It was two hours and 51 minutes from the time they left Barstow until they stopped under the water tower at Needles, a distance of 171 miles. I asked Jack how he made such a good time with a top heavy engine. He said:

"Dutch, I pinched her down on the curves and let her up on the straight-away."

If I remember right, the fireman was J.L. Ballard, who had said at departure:

"Ain't no use to change clothes, we'll be in Needles in a little while." When he got there, he looked like he had been firing soft coal, he was so dirty!

To my knowledge, the record has never been broken with a steam engine. This can be verified by retired engineers C.M. Richardson, Frank Barnum, Bush Bradford and retired conductor Bill Potter, Jack's brother.

I've never seen the 3600 engine any more. I think they scrapped her after that trip.

REMEMBRANCES OF FRANK E. McCONNELL

by A.F. Kitts

Mac is a retired Santa Fe station agent. He was at Cadiz from 1945 until his retirement in 1963.

He tells us that he first came to the desert in July, 1925, when he was ten years old. The family was on vacation, traveling through on what is now Highway 66. They came in a Model T roadster, with 30 x 3 tires on the front and 30 x 3½ on the back, and five spares of each size piled on the turtledeck.

As they were returning to Indiana, they stayed at Ludlow the first night. Mac believes the hotel was run by a Chinaman.

Model T Ford roads were mostly trails—one lane tracks. When two cars met, one pulled off the road, while the other went by and waited until they were both back on the road.

Mac's family intended to travel from Ludlow to Goffs, one day's trip. When they arrived at Goffs the hotel and tourist home were both full. Mac recalls seeing people asleep on the ground. There were mostly people from Needles up there to get a little relief from the heat. The family went on to Needles, staying at the old Gateway. Mac states it was too hot to sleep, but not as hot as the place got later. (It burned down about 1970.)

Mac stated that he told his dad he was going to walk across the bridge over the river, since he didn't trust his dad's driving. However, he rode across, due to a little persuasion from a razor strap.

Mac says:

Somehow, I decided I wanted to come back to the desert. Either I didn't see what I was looking for, or I did see it, I don't know. I came back in December, 1944, and went to work for the Santa Fe; worked one night at Ludlow. I was supposed to have stayed in the room in back of the Post Office, but never got to sleep there. I was told that I was to go to work the following evening at Goffs, so caught a train to Goffs.

He worked the second "trick" (shift) at Goffs until June 1945, when he was "bumped" and went to Blythe for the melon rush.

Goffs still had the two story depot, a signal maintainer lived on the second floor. There was a pump house and a house for the pumper. Across from the depot there was a two room "prefab" for one of the operators. The regular operator-agent lived in a house still at Goffs. The third operator lived in a little two or three room house just west of the depot. There were two or three houses north of Highway 66. The school building was unoccupied. There was no store in Goffs then. Mail came to Fenner. Not too much highway traffic (Highway 66 had been built over South Pass about 1938), but plenty of trains.

Power was about 50-50 steam and diesel—helper engines were steam. Passenger trains were almost all steam, as diesels were used mainly on freight. You could hear the diesels coming up the hill for a long ways.

Mac worked a couple of months in Blythe during the melon rush, but the Bagdad station job opened in July, 1945, and he bid on the job and got it. The Cadiz station job was opened up, and when he bid on that he got it before he could get to Bagdad. He worked at Cadiz from July, 1945 until he retired in 1963.

Helpers were used on passenger trains from Needles to Ash Hill, then to Pisgah.

Many engines came back to Cadiz "light" (a single engine), then helped east bound trains up to Goffs. Some engines double-headed to Needles, but most went from Goffs to Needles "light." Steam engines were still helping diesel power on the grades. Mac stated many passenger trains used light, high wheeled 1300's which were very fast.

A bunk car was at Cadiz for engine men, mainly for the helpers, but it offered a place for crews to stay when caught by the 14-hours-law.

Mac's house, the front part moved from Bagdad, and the back, a remodeled box car, burned on March 17, 1955. As he states, "On St. Patricks Day—The Luck of the Irish."

When Mac retired, he bought property north of Highway 66 at Cadiz, built a house of ties faced with native stone, and has lived there ever since. He has a beautiful garden, and raises chickens and rabbits. Mac says, "This old desert will grow anything in the world if you put water to it."

Mac comments about the desert weather, "I've seen it 135°, and 120° at midnight. I've also seen seven inches of snow."

He concludes, "I guess the reason I like the desert is I know where I'm going when I die. It ain't gonna hurt me like it does a lot of people."

RANSOM D. (BABE) STILES
Former Santa Fe Employee
by Louella Bishoff

Babe was born in 1902, in Needles, the son of a railroad family. He lived there until 1926 when he came to work in Barstow's rail yards as a clerk. When he came to Barstow the population was about 1,200. Between that year and the time of his retirement on December 21, 1963, he saw many changes take place.

Before the bridge was built over the tracks about 1930, Babe remembers spending about half his time just getting from his place on one side over to the other side of the railroad.

Babe's father was a railroad conductor on passenger trains running between Los Angeles and Needles. His mother lived in Inglewood. Later Babe's father worked a train between Los Angeles and Parker, Arizona, so Babe didn't get to see him very often. It was that move that prompted Babe to transfer to Barstow. In that way, he could visit with his father as the train made its regular stop here.

When Babe and his first wife, Myrtle Willows, (a Harvey girl), were going together in 1930, he remembers walking with her up to the Beacon Hotel and going through the rooms as they were under construction. He remembers the elegance of that hotel which was one of two built by Richfield, the other being in Santa Barbara. It was supposed to be the best hotel between San Bernardino and Albuquerque, New Mexico. The beacon tower which was in front of the hotel had a large light on top, but due to some complaints from local residents, the bright light was removed.

In Babe's file of early memories he recalls nothing on the hill where Dana Park is now, and only two streets, Main and Hutchinson. But, then, change did come quickly.

SANTA FE INVESTING HEAVILY
Reprint from: San Bernardino Valley Centennial
Edition of *The Evening Index*—October 18, 1910

The Santa Fe Railway Company seems to be all alive to the fact Barstow is located and clearly defined on the map of San Bernardino County. This gigantic corporation has made appropriations close to the million dollar mark for improvements in and around Barstow, a massive depot and hotel are beginning to rear their heads to a pretentious height above ground and a big gang of men are fast pushing the work along. Those structures are being built of reinforced concrete and when completed will be among the most imposing and commodious on the Santa Fe line. Comfort and ornamentation will be combined in making the edifices a luxury for travelers and employees of the Santa Fe Railroad alike, and included in the new structure will be a large reading room and a library in which free

concerts will be given from time to time by some of the leading talent and foremost artists. A recreation hall, bowling alley, pool and billiard hall is also a part of the arrangement provided for in the new building specifically. Extensive work is also going ahead at a rapid pace on the roadway, a cut through the hill at the east end of town, on which two steam shovels and a crew of men are making the dirt fly will obviate the inconveniences that the present sharp curve causes. The roadway is also being double tracked, and is underway between Los Angeles and Chicago. The contractor in charge of the work between Daggett and Cottonwood (Hodge) is working towards Barstow from both those towns and is daily shortening the gap and nearing completion of that stretch.

BUSY SPOT IS HARVEY HOUSE
by Virgie Timmons
(Reprint *Printer Review*, January 5, 1950)

One of the busiest and most interesting spots in Barstow is the railroad terminal station with its varied activities.

J.A. Klug is manager of the Harvey House, built in 1911.

The Santa Fe Eating House cafeteria counter seats 36 and the tables 16, an average of 600 patrons being

served daily. During the war as many as 2,400 were fed daily, in addition to as high as 2,200 troops in the old dining room. The equipment throughout is of stainless steel. Handsome hand-hammered copper light fixtures hang from the ceiling, with copper wall brackets scattered about the room.

Forty-six persons are employed at present. Mrs. Addie Bassett, head waitress and charming little lady,

79 Barstow Harvey House Employees 1934

82 Early 1900's

80

83 The new Harvey
House rises - 1910

Casa Del Desierto—Barstow

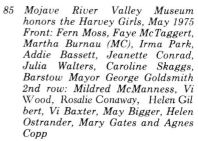

84

81 Frank Bassett and railroad dog 1935

85 Mojave River Valley Museum
honors the Harvey Girls, May 1975
Front: Fern Moss, Faye McTaggert,
Martha Burnau (MC), Irma Park,
Addie Bassett, Jeanette Conrad,
Julia Walters, Caroline Skaggs,
Barstow Mayor George Goldsmith
2nd row: Mildred McManness, Vi
Wood, Rosalie Conaway, Helen Gil
bert, Vi Baxter, May Bigger, Helen
Ostrander, Mary Gates and Agnes
Copp

has been there 22 years. Jack Turman, chef, while not in Barstow that long, has been with the company 21 years. The attractive waitresses wear white uniforms with small black ribbon bows at the throat.

In addition to their salaries, the company provides the employees with meals and maintains dormitories for both men and women, with showers and hot and cold running water in each room.

The newsstand, adjoining the cafeteria, is under the management of Mr. and Mrs. Bert South. The latest magazines, cigarettes, candy bars and curios are carried by the stand at all times.

A.J. Morgan, Santa Fe and Union Pacific joint agent, states that thousands of bags of first-class mail and sacks of parcel post, as well as outside packages of parcel post, pass through the Barstow transfer terminal daily. This year Christmas shipments were so heavy that it was necessary to handle them on freight trains, as many as 35 cars of mail per train. Special freight trains expedited shipments from Chicago to Los Angeles and from Los Angeles to Chicago over a two weeks' period, starting the second week in December and extending thru the third week.

Mr. Morgan also mentioned that the reading room with the latest periodicals and a dormitory are maintained for the use of railroad men on their stopovers. Here is a place for sleep and relaxation. An average of 100 men per day avail themselves of these privileges.

A.L. Imel, railway express agent estimates that at least 3,000 Christmas transfer shipments were handled daily by the company this year.

THE HARVEY HOUSE GIRL
by Frank Hutt, a Santa Fe Employee 1898

There's a girl that for me, is a pleasure to see
    She brings me my coffee and pie
I know every curl, on the head of this girl
    I watch her as she passes by
I sit on my seat, she glides on her feet
    She has gotten my brain in a whirl
I know not her name, it will be just the same
    If I call her my Harvey House girl
Her cheeks they are red, as pure as a rose
    She uses no powder, just a dab on her nose
She dresses so neat, from her head to her toes
    I love her, — my Harvey House girl.

FERN QUINT MOSS
Harvey Girl 1918-1938
by Louella Bishoff

Some time before 1918, Fern Quint's grandmother, living in Los Angeles, had died, and her father came out to settle the estate. He liked it so much that he persuaded his wife to move to California. Fern had been widowed by then; she let her mother take her young daughter with her while Fern remained at work in Missouri. However, Fern couldn't stay parted from her child very long, and finally she too, left Kansas City.

After Fern arrived in Los Angeles, her father was talking to Mr. Sullivan who was telling him about the problems of hiring girls and then losing them because of the flu epidemic that was running rampant through the nation. Fern's father told Mr. Sullivan he had two daughters that could help. Her sister had broken some ribs in an accident, so only Fern was able to be hired. She had never heard of the Fred Harvey system before that.

They paid for her transportation to Barstow, and her room and board while there, as well as her laundry fees. She also worked in Needles, Gallup, Winslow and for about 10 years in San Bernardino where she met George Moss and was married. George was a railroad man working out of San Bernardino, and that is where they lived.

As a Harvey Girl, Fern said she was no good as a waitress herself, but as head waitress, taught many girls to be one. The girls bought their own uniforms, but, after a while, the management didn't want the "heads" to wear the same uniform as the other girls and outfitted them in dresses. Fern said Miss Steel wasn't happy about that. In Needles, during the summers of 1931 and 1932, the girls wore the cooler white aprons and blouses. They liked it so much they eventually did away with the black dresses there.

Fern first went to work for one dollar a day. When she was head-waitress in San Bernardino, she got up to $75 a month.

She has been living in a retirement home since December 1974 and is very happy there. Her daughter, who lives in Los Angeles and her two granddaughters and five great grandchildren are nearby.

Fern said "I met Hazel Hallock (Needles). She just never lets up on me about making the best of being a Harvey Girl.—It seems as if I've been a Harvey Girl all my life."

86 Santa Fe Car Inspectors - 1917: Ted Wallen, John Wheeler, Fred Perchell, John Storey, Clarence Crooks, Sid Grady and Walter Dixon

Santa Fe
Yards, The
Hub of Activities

89 Roundhouse 1929 - A.T. & Santa Fe

87 Roundhouse remains after fire

90 Hand operated switches - east end of yards

88 Barstow Yards, Harry Kelly, Sr. on left

91 Santa Fe employees 1926

92 Barstow 1915 - astride engine's headlight, Donaciano Varela and Calixto Varela, white coated and leaning

95 Camilo and Guadalupe Duran 1918

93 Ragnon Robles and Donaciano Varela

They Came To Work For Santa Fe

96 Barstow 1918 - Pedro Duran in Santa Fe roundhouse's tool room

94 Senon Ramos, aged 96

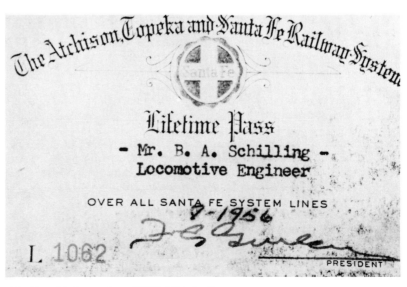

97 Can this be used on AMTRAK today?

DESERT MEMORIES

by Vernon Hallock and Hazel Poe Hallock 1971

On October 17, 1971, Santa Fe Park became an avenue of memories as Mr. Riley Witty, manager of the Fred Harvey House of Needles, California (1928 to 1938) returned to visit this once stately hotel and eating house. Accompanying him were Vernon and Hazel Hallock.

Built to accommodate Santa Fe passengers, the Harvey House became a mecca for weary travelers crossing the desert and a meeting place for townsfolk. The hotel boasted about 30 spic-and-span guest rooms, plus living quarters for the manager and 75 employees. The lunch room and dining room were geared to feed 300 guests; trains would unload their passengers to be fed in 30 minutes. Gourmet food and gracious service was a Fred Harvey tradition. Besides operating two separate kitchens, they baked all their own bread and pastries, made their ice cream and

sherbet, and operated their own laundry.

Mr. Witty, who passed his 89th birthday on July 31st, 1971, retired from the Santa Fe in 1948 after managing 22 Harvey Houses across the country for 50 years.

The Wittys and Hallocks met in Needles, California in 1930. Mr. Vernon Hallock worked in the hotel office and Mrs. Hallock, then Miss Hazel Poe, was hostess in the main dining room, which had all silver service. In the following years she became head waitress. And now, almost 42 years later, the old boss and two faithful employees were retracing steps and reliving events of an era past.

Besides Needles, they made other stops along the Santa Fe line to see old Harvey Houses, including Barstow, Seligman, Ashfork, Williams, Flagstaff and Winslow.

"Dad" Witty passed away in 1974.

ADDIE PARK BASSETT
Harvey Girl
4 July 1927 to 30 September 1967
by Louella Bishoff

After Addie Park's sister, Jessie Park Potter, completed a business course, she went to Kansas City to get a job. She couldn't get an office job that could pay enough to make ends meet, but she did see a newspaper ad about the hiring of Harvey Girls. When she applied, they asked her where and when she could go to work. She said, "anywhere, anytime." The next day she was on her way to Vaughn, New Mexico, where she worked for two years.

When Jessie came home for a vacation, two years later, Addie went back with her and became a Harvey Girl too, in Vaughn, then in 1927 her duty station began in Barstow. She worked as a waitress, head waitress, and eventually cafeteria manager. At first the girls

bought their own uniforms, but in the late 1930's they were furnished these as well as free food and transportation for a yearly vacation. They had to sign a contract for the first six months of their employment.

One special memory that Addie has about being a Harvey Girl is that she met her husband Frank while working in Barstow. She said they had 29 really good years together.

Addie thanks God every day because He sent her to Barstow. She says, "The town, the Fred Harvey system, have all been good to me. When we signed up, the folks in Missouri thought we were coming to the end of the world. We said we could stand it for six months." Addie has stayed for nearly 50 years.

JULIA SLOVICK WALTERS
Harvey Girl 1931-1935
by Louella Bishoff

Early in the years of the depression, Julia Slovick was employed as a comptometer operator in the audit department of Sears in Chicago. As economic conditions worsened, she was working only a week or so out of each month. When the banks closed, Julia lost her $30 deposit.

At this time a girl friend told her that the Fred Harvey system was hiring girls to act as waitresses at the railroad meal stops in the far west. They offered free transportation and food on the way to duty stations, free room and board, plus on the job training. To a young 19 year-old practically out of work, a job as a Harvey Girl sounded good. Until this time, Julia had never heard of Fred Harvey.

She was favorably impressed with the climate in

Needles when she arrived on May 9, 1931. While bitterly cold weather still prevailed in Chicago, Needles was a wonderful place; Julie thought that it was the most beautiful place she had ever seen.

The salary of a Harvey Girl at that time was $35 a month, but was lowered to $30 during the depression. They had to appear neat at all times, keeping their hair cut short and under a hair net while on duty. The girls bought their own uniforms, but the company paid for their laundry.

There was no air conditioning, as we know it today, in the girls' rooms, there were circulating fans on the ceiling. When the nights were particularly warm, they would pull their beds out onto the upstairs porch, apply citronella to their skin to combat the mosquitos, and cover their beds with netting. With some ice water and the alarm clock nearby, they would settle down for the night.

Julia worked at the lunch counter most of the time, but occasionally she would serve as head waitress. Although there were fewer of them, the dining room girls got more tips than the lunch counter girls. Mr. Riley Witty was their manager at Needles and Julia said he was very good to the girls.

She remembers how interesting it was to meet the public who traveled to and from so many different places. The trains were only in the station for 30-45 minutes, so the girls were sometimes hurried. There were several passenger trains a day and the girls usually worked split shifts, three hours in the morning and three in the afternoon. In between trains they had to set up the dining areas to be ready for the next train.

Julia's sister also became a Harvey Girl, working at Winslow, Grand Canyon and other places. Maybe they didn't earn a lot of money, but they used to get to go on free trips, and as recreation they swam in the river and Lankey's Pool and used the recreation hall nearby the depot where they stayed.

In 1933, when Julia's father died, Mr. Witty got her a pass so she could go to Illinois for the funeral.

There were all ages of Harvey Girls and many lasting friendships were made; it was like a sorority. As Julia said, "We were a bunch in those days."

CAROLINE SMITH SKAGGS
Harvey Girl 1928
by Louella Bishoff

During the latter part of 1928, Caroline Smith was living with a great aunt in Los Angeles and was happy there. However, she wanted a job of her own so she wouldn't be a burden on her relatives.

Caroline had a cousin who worked for the railroad eating facilities, and whose husband was a cook on a dining car. She often went along with her husband as he traveled. It was Caroline's cousin who suggested that she see the Harveys. She went to the Los Angeles headquarters, and the first thing she knew she was working in Barstow.

As a Harvey Girl, Caroline did a little bit of everything, but mostly worked the lunch counter. Addie and Jessie Park trained her and they roomed together. Her room and board was paid by the company. There were two girls in a room most of the time, except when she roomed with Addie and Jessie. Most of the time, their rooms were upstairs, except when in Seligman which had only one floor.

She worked nights for quite a while in Needles, Seligman, Gallup and liked that shift very much.

One of Caroline's fond memories was serving meals on an excursion train full of teachers who went to Yosemite.

After their return, the girls were asked if they wanted to go there on their own vacation. Two of the girls took the opportunity and had a nice little trip out of it.

Caroline said, "It would be nice if the Harvey Girls got together more often." She remembers the pay wasn't like today, but "then you don't get room and board and free laundry today either."

DESERT RAILROADS OF TODAY
by Pat Keeling

World War II placed great stress and strain on all railroads, and the desert railroads were able to meet the challenge. Steam engines pulled trainloads of men, machinery and supplies through the desert to points of distribution. At first manufacturers produced diesel locomotives only for use on the new passenger streamliners, but Santa Fe was a good customer and was finally able to obtain diesels to replace steam engines on freight trains.

The Union Pacific and Southern Pacific resisted dieselization, but by 1960 the steam locomotive had become a museum piece.

The new iron work horse "The Diesel" brought about many changes. The repair and maintenance facilities were not large enough at Barstow, the Needles property had no room for expansion, and San Bernardino was too far away from the hub of operations. The Santa Fe started plans for construction of a new type of maintenance house called a diesel shop in Barstow. The *Barstow Printer*

Review April 5, 1945, wrote:

> The Diesel maintenance house is the first of its kind and size built. The Diesel maintenance program is in a pioneer stage since freight Diesels have been in use only three years . . ., the entire Diesel locomotive history in this country is but little more than ten years.

The diesel shops brought a new era to Barstow. The shop cost $980,000. Machinery, equipment and yard facilities brought the total cost to several million dollars when operations began in 1945.

Following the war, Santa Fe built a new fleet of streamlined trains. This new fleet and their diesel locomotives caused the decline of the steam engine and service repairs from the Barstow round-house. In 1947 Santa Fe closed the roundhouse and Master Mechanic's office at Needles. The offices were moved to Barstow, thereby bringing a large influx of people to jobs at the shop. William Ellison was the first general foreman of the Barstow Diesel Shops in 1945. The shop later became the largest running diesel maintenance shop in the United States.

On September 11, 1947 Santa Fe launched an expensive expansion program to increase diesel shop facilities by 50 per cent. They added new building equipment and fixtures, and a large 60 ton crane. The enlarged main shop building measured 213 by 325 feet, on two levels, with ten working stalls, deep drop pits, depressed floors adjacent to the pits and steel platforms called ramps at engine room level.

Passenger train service in the United States, at its height in 1929 with 20,000 trains daily, by 1970 had dwindled to 400. This was due to the competition from airlines, buses and private automobiles. Passenger service losses totaled over $200 million dollars a year by the time the new quasi-governmental National Railroad Passenger Corporation took over all long haul passenger trains on May 1, 1971.

California stops on the Amtrak Santa Fe line include Pasadena, Pomona, San Bernardino, Barstow and Needles on one train a day schedule each way between Los Angeles and Chicago, the only railroad passenger service on the Mojave Desert. Amtrak eliminated all services on the inland route from Barstow through Bakersfield, once a beautiful route along the Garcés and Frémont trail through the Tehachapi Mountains. The colorful names that Santa Fe gave its passenger trains—The Super Chief, El Capitan, California Limited, The Chief, San Francisco Chief—are part of the past. The red and yellow diesels with their silver streamline cars are no more.

Along with the colorful names that the railroad gave to passenger trains have gone the many towns and water stations along the way, leaving only the trees and cemeteries with the crosses and flowers as mute symbols of the past.

Meanwhile, two of the few railroad extensions since the depression have been built in the Mojave Desert.

The Santa Fe built a 29-mile branch from Hesperia to Cushenberry in Lucerne Valley to serve a new limestone processing plant in 1956.

Southern Pacific, in 1967, built a 78-mile cutoff route linking Southern Pacific terminals at Palmdale and Colton. It enables the Southern Pacific to bypass Los Angeles in moving freight between the Pacific Northwest and Southeastern line. The line was the first totally new rail route to be constructed in the United States in nearly a quarter century. Built at a cost of some $22 million, it preceded the construction of a major rail car classification yard in Colton.

Jacob Nash Victor, builder of the California Southern, predicted:

No other railroad will have the nerve to build through the San Bernardino Mountains. All who follow will prefer to rent trackage from us.

He was right for 90 years.

Residents of Barstow, Daggett, Hinkley, Lenwood and Yermo, joined the Santa Fe to celebrate "Santa Fe Appreciation Day" in 1961. Chairman of the steering committee was Frank R. Hunt.

L.B. English, Superintendent of Shops in 1961, was coordinator of events in behalf of the Santa Fe Railway. The day long program included a Kiwanis Club open air breakfast, a parade featuring the famed Santa Fe Indian Band from Winslow, Arizona, a Chamber of Commerce luncheon honoring local railroad management, and a Barstow Women's Club flower show dedicated to Santa Fe Appreciation Day. The Barstow Optimist Club sponsored a Santa Fe Appreciation Hour before the dinner.

Mrs. Ida K. Pleasant was mayor of Barstow and hostess on behalf of the city. Ernest S. Marsh, then president of the Santa Fe, was guest of honor. Many Santa Fe officials were present at the Barstow Junior Women's Club dinner, held at Waterman School.

In May 1970, Santa Fe completed the new "High Bay" repair facility at Barstow, a diesel dismantling area built at a cost of $600,000; it roughly doubled the size of the teardown shops. The facility is 225 feet long, 90 feet wide and 49 feet high. It is equipped with two wheel truing machines and a 50-ton overhead crane.

Search, a super-sophisticated electronic computer device for preventing problems in the complex circuitry of modern, high powered diesel electric locomotives, is in use at the shops. "SEARCH," a trademarked acronym for "system evaluation and reliability checker," is used as a diagnostic device. The operations supervisor, W.A. Keeling, was promptly dubbed the "Iron Horse Veterinarian."

Open house, 1970, hosted by William M. White, Barstow Superintendent of Shops, and other supervisors and their wives, gave 2500 citizens a fine view of the new facilities. Visitors toured the apprentice school classroom, dispatching offices complete with a computer scanning plate on each engine, regular engines and radio-controlled power setups. They saw radio operated controls for extra engines under a master unit control. Honored guests at the gathering were Assistant to General Manager-Mechanical Department, L.B. English, who declared "Railroads are here to stay, no matter what anybody says to the contrary," and H.J. Briscoe, Superintendent of the Los Angeles Division. Adults and children of the community were allowed to toot diesel horns, wear paper trainmen hats, while enjoying refreshments.

The Mojave Desert today is crossed by three major railroads, the Santa Fe, the Southern Pacific, and the Union Pacific. One short line common carrier, The Trona Railway, connects Searles Valley to the Southern Pacific at Searles. One industrial road, the Mojave Northern, no longer a common carrier, carries limestone from quarries northeast of Interstate 15 to the cement plant at Leon, north of Victorville.

Among some of the newest projects initiated by the Santa Fe was the relocation project at Summitt. Presiding at the ground-breaking event were Larry Cena, Chicago, Santa Fe Vice-President and Operation and Construction Engineer Edmund T. Lucey of Los Angeles. The railway spent $4.3 million for three miles of double track relocation, completed

October 1, 1972. Coincidental with the track relocation was installation of a traffic control system enabling a dispatcher at San Bernardino to operate trains over either of the two tracks in either direction by simply moving a lever.

The latest project of the Santa Fe is the freight car classification yard at Barstow. The Santa Fe Railway has built the $50 million dollar yard to increase the efficiency of its western operation. Construction began in late January 1974, and was completed in February 1976. Situated just west of the company's original yards, the four mile long, 600 acre facility will be fully automated and computerized and have a maximum handling capacity of 2700 cars daily. The completed complex will embrace a 48-track classification yard, 10-track receiving yard, four track local yard, nine track departure yard and 36 tracks for diesel engine servicing, car repair and other services. A total of 113 miles of new trackage was installed, and a new bridge over the Mojave River was erected.

Cars are shoved over a hump at one end of the new yard by switch engines, and continue by gravity into the classification tracks. As cars roll down the hump they are weighed, measured for length, tested for rollability, automatically switched to the correct track and controlled for speed, all through use of computers.

Santa Fe's transcontinental main line from Chicago branches at Barstow, with one track extending to the San Joaquin Valley and San Francisco Bay area, and the other to San Bernardino and other Southern California points. The new yard sorts out both eastbound and westbound freight cars, assembling them into blocks destined to various stations along the line.

Before the yard construction started, Santa Fe employed over 1,000 persons with a payroll of $13.5 annually. The new yard operations increased that work force to 1,521 with an annual payroll expected to reach over $17 million annually.

Construction of the new facility further enhances Barstow's strategic position as a railroad operating and repair center. Santa Fe currently operates about 76 freight trains daily in all directions to, from and through Barstow. Additionally, there are 14 Union Pacific trains and two Amtrak trains in each direction through Barstow daily on Santa Fe tracks.

An open house and dedication of the new yard was held in the spring of 1976.

August 8, 1976 was the 100th Birthday of the desert railroads. Santa Fe, Union Pacific, and the Southern Pacific are today three of the nations major railroads.

Many railroads have served the desert; some have consolidated with the larger companies; others have passed from the scene. The great surge of western movement began with the railroads, and the results of that massive movement is still being served by these lines today.

Chapter VI

Traders and Merchants

Back packer's relief,
Over the counter discourse,
Outfit an empire.

DID YOU KNOW THAT . . .
by Clifford Walker

The Calico area had several types of lodging in 1885. Two of these lodging places, the Whitfield House and the "Rooms and Lodging" offered by James Applewhite, were located in Calico. The Railroad Hotel was in nearby Daggett.

The Whitfield House, located in the business part of town, boasted "clean, well ventilated, nicely furnished rooms. Good meals prepared from the best edibles. Anchor and rope fire escape."

James Applewhite had expanded his residence and furnished a number of rooms, "in a tasty and comfortable style." He offered rooms suitable for both families and travelers, located in "the quiet part of town."

The Railroad Hotel in Daggett was run by W. F. Cornett. He boasted "first class in every particular" and also a "liberal discount to people boarding by the month."

J.A. Kincaid and Company were merchandise dealers. They dealt in general merchandise and specialized in mining supplies.

D.W. Earl & Company was wholesale dealers of flour, grain, hay and lumber.

The Pioneer Meat Market, established in both Daggett and Calico, sold fresh pork, mutton and sausage. Daggett had a slaughter house.

The Calico Stage Line (owned by William Curry) operated between Calico and Daggett.

On March 19, 1885, the Daggett Glee Club scheduled a performance. Admission was $.50 (children half price) with proceeds going to the benefit of the Rev. D. McCunn of Calico. The program included quartettes, duets, solos, instrumental music, plantation character songs, dialogues, and recitations.

THE ALFS AND MEDLINS
by Walter Alf

Seymore Alf and his wife, Mathilda, with their three daughters, Rosa, Emma and Lena, came to California from Colorado in 1881. After spending several months in San Bernardino, they moved to a farm in Helendale, formerly called Point of Rocks. There a fourth daughter, Molly, was born.

Alf produced one successful crop, but found no market for it. He moved to the Fish Ponds Station, directly in back of and across the Mojave River from the present Marine Base. He bought the station from the Medlins who had come to the desert in 1852.

Fish Ponds Station had a large pond fed by a stream of water at the surface of the river bed. Cottonwood, willow and mesquite trees surrounded Fish Ponds and extended to within a mile of what is now the town of Barstow.

The Medlins moved to Daggett, where the Southern Pacific Railroad was under construction. Supplies and food were freighted to Daggett from San Bernardino until the railroad was finished, then they were sent from Los Angeles to Mojave by rail. A stage ran from San Bernardino through Stoddard's Wells bringing miners and settlers to the Calico mines which employed many men. No housing was available. Most miners carried their own beds and slept out on the hillsides in any caves or protected areas they could find. Food was available from stores and boarding houses in Calico. One of the first merchants, the Oliviers, had their store operating in 1884. John Lane had the general store there for years.

After settling at Fish Ponds, Seymore Alf freighted supplies to and from San Bernardino. He saw the need for fresh meat and began to buy and butcher cattle which he delivered every day to the miners. Often he killed and sold two beefs a day, lacking refrigeration, unsold stock was given away to widows or large families.

The Alfs moved to Daggett in the spring of 1885. The town boasted several adobe buildings erected by "Dolph" Navares' father. Seymore bought the old Stone Hotel built by District Attorney Kavanaugh's widowed mother.

In August, 1888, after their son Walter was born, the family squatted on the property at First and Santa Fe Streets until it was determined that the land was part of the railroad section. They leased it and finally bought it from the railroad. During this time, Alf started a small blacksmith shop across the street from the house. After it had burned, the present blacksmith shop next door to the residence, was built in 1890. It was not only a center in the desert mining area for horseshoeing, wagon repair, Fresno scrapers, mining machinery and construction equipment but tools were also made there.

The construction of huge borax wagons, pulled by 20 mule teams from Borate through Mule Canyon to the mill at Daggett, were built in Alf's shop. It was the headquarters for a large freight business; sixty head of mules were available for use or rent by Alf.

In 1903, Seymore graded the roadbed of the Salt Lake Railroad, (the San Pedro, Los Angeles and Salt Lake Railway), from Daggett to Yermo. He also built all the roads up the Johnson grade, and around Baldwin Lake and Big Bear Lake in the summers of 1915, 16, and 17. He maintained the county roads from Ludlow to Barstow.

The Alf children were all sent away to school. Mollie graduated from Pomona College and later taught school in Death Valley. Emma graduated from Woodbury College, Los Angeles, which Walter also attended. Rosa married Dr. McFarlane, Daggett's practitioner and druggist.

When he became old enough, Walter worked in the family business and continued after his father's death

1 *Mr. Williams, Santa Fe Telegrapher, Chris Weidman · Blacksmith's helper, Bill Borham - Smithy, Adams - express messenger, ————.*

2

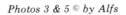

5

4 *Mathilda Alf, mother of Walter*

The Alfs -

Photos 3 & 5 © by Alfs

6

3

7 *Mr. and Mrs. Walter Alf in front of blacksmith shop 1965*

in 1922.

After the Armistice was signed in November, 1918, Walter and Gertrude Hadley, a local school teacher, were married. They moved into an old adobe house on the Alf property, which, over a period of years, was remodeled. Now it is used as a residence and houses a museum collection of memorabilia.

Gertrude and Walter had three sons, Walter S. of Banning, Hadley E. of Australia, and Lawrence living in Daggett at the family home with his mother since the death of his father in 1970.

DESERT MERCHANTS AND TRADERS
by Pat Keeling

Among the many early settlers of Needles were Francis Monaghan and Daniel Murphy. In 1883, they opened their first store, in an abandoned box car. A very profitable general merchandise business was established, expanding into almost every mining camp on the desert and along the Colorado River by 1917.

The Monaghan and Murphy stores were found in California and parts of Nevada and Arizona. The large two store building erected in Needles in 1898 burned to the ground in 1970. The buildings at Ludlow erected in 1908 (by John Denair), now abandoned, still stand on the street facing Santa Fe's main line.

A DAGGETT FAMILY SAGA
by Margaret A. Fouts

It was Canada's loss and Daggett's gain when Frank Ryerse and his family came to the high desert.

Born in Canada on February 18, 1866, Frank went to live with his uncle George Ryerse when he was ten years old. Later, in 1887, he worked as a telegrapher for the Atlantic and Pacific Railroad at Prescott Junction, Arizona Territory, now Seligman.

Frank met Hettie Swayze during a 1888 vacation in Canada. Her brothers didn't like him, they even threatened to shoot him. To thwart them, in 1889, Hettie slipped away by train to Albuquerque, New Mexico, where she and Frank were married on December First. They had four children. Their first, a son, was born and died in Canada. Myrtle, the first daughter, was born in the depot at Fenner, California. After Frank's telegraphy job was terminated, Hettie returned to Canada temporarily where daughter Hazel was born. Clarence was born in Daggett where the family settled in 1894. Their grandson Keith Kenney, Myrtle's son, lives in the same house today.

Early in 1894, Frank was employed by Fred Brooks in the Pioneer Meat Market. Some of Myrtle's and Hazel Ryerse's playmates in those days were Vera, Lionel and Marion Brooks. Myrtle remembered playing with them in an abandoned Calico Stage Coach parked in an alley behind their houses.

Frank's first wife, Hettie, and son Clarence died June 15, 1896. At 30, a widower and in debt, Frank never lost heart. After working and saving, he bought the Pioneer Meat Market. He had sent his two girls to Canada to board with John R. Butler. John's son, Ben quit his railroad job to become Frank's partner.

Cattle were shipped to Daggett in carload lots by rail or driven cross country by cowboys, corralled, fed and watered until slaughtered. Frank raised his own hogs which roamed the streets upsetting garbage and uprooting dooryards to the dismay of the townspeople. This surely would have lost customers had this not been the only market for miles around.

Besides local trade, meat was supplied to Calico and the Mule Canyon mining camps. Frank made deliveries before dawn by buckboard two or three times a week. In 1903, when the railway (now the Union Pacific) was extended to Salt Lake City, this market was the only source of meat supply to construction crews in the area.

While visiting in Canada, Frank Ryerse married Annie Fonger October 4, 1905 and brought her to his home in Daggett. Guests at Frank's and Annie's wedding included Frank's two daughters and his cousin Homer Ryerse and fiancee, Mabel Scott.

August 8, 1910, Frank's younger daughter Hazel, and Harry McInally married in Canada, and came to Daggett for several months. Returning to Canada, they lived in Toronto while Harry studied Dentistry. Graduating in 1916 from the Royal College of Dental Surgeons, he volunteered his services during World War I. Their son, Walter McInally was born October 3, 1918.

After schooling in Canada, and employment as a dressmaker, Frank's older daughter, Myrtle, married William Earl Kenney on September 4, 1912. Born in Canada on October 30, 1891, Earl worked farm seasons with his father and as a railroad extra in slack times. He attended business college in Canada in 1908-9. After marriage, he and Myrtle farmed for 11 years, then they too moved to Daggett on November 23, 1923. The day they arrived, their three children began to come down with the measles and one or another of them was sick until after Christmas.

Homer Ryerse was born October 29, 1878 in Canada, and was educated there. He was employed as a bookkeeper in Jersey City, New Jersey for three years. When his father George, died June 14, 1902, he returned to Canada to help his mother, Jane, with the farm. He married a local school teacher, Mabel Scott, on February 7, 1906. A year later, tired of farming, they moved to Daggett, April 21, 1907 to join cousin Frank and Ben Butler in the Pioneer Meat Market, which really was too small for a third partner.

About two weeks later, on May 9, 1907, Frank bought the General Store owned by George Mier and managed by George Toennies. Homer became Frank's partner in the General Store. Frank and Ben still operated the Pioneer Meat Market. After Ben Butler and family moved away January 11, 1908, Frank and Joe McCue became new partners in the Pioneer Meat Market. Homer and Mabel moved into the house where the Butlers had lived.

Though the General Store ran under the title "H.C. Ryerse and Co." Frank had little to do with its operation. Daggett was the outfitting point for early day miners and prospectors, and this store furnished almost anything from lamps, lanterns, matches, kerosene, yard goods, shoes, hats and coal to liniment, pills, and hair nets. Later, a lumber yard and chicken feed business were added. Many customers paid their bills in gold dust weighed on scales in the office.

On July 13, 1908, a fire left most of the north part of Daggett in smoldering ruins. The Ryerses were lucky, for some time before this, a large cellar had been dug at the rear of the store by Will and Frank La Mantain. Protected by a huge hand-made iron door from one of the old mines, the stock of merchandise stored there was saved. Afterward, Homer and Frank ordered a carload of cement and erected the fireproof cement building which today is called Scott's market and is Daggett's only store.

In 1908, Mabel's mother, Mrs. Roxa Scott, of Canada visited the Ryerses, later making Daggett her home. Other members of Mabel's family who moved to California were her sister, Maria "Molly" Scott and brother, George P. Scott. Molly met and married Lester A. Todd, June 23, 1909. George, who had visited them following College in Indiana, Class of 1909, settled in Daggett about 1918 and began working at Ryerson's store. After Homer and Mabel died, George bought and operated the store until his own death September 16, 1961. His widow, Helen Scott, ran the business for several years, later, renting the building to different proprietors. The current proprietress is Corrienne Sanders.

In 1914 Homer decided to modernize his name, changing it from Ryerse to Ryerson.

Before Highway 66 was completed, the main Highway was the old dirt road, now Santa Fe Street, which ran past the store. Countless horses and wagons used it, and in 1914, the drivers of the famous automobile race from Los Angeles to Phoenix came past the Daggett Store. According to Mabel Ryerson's diary, on May 4, 1914, Homer bought Frank out for $6,500. Her May 9, 1914 entry states, "Went to our own store for the first time."

In 1922, Frank was told his wife Annie had the then fatal pernicious anemia. She was never told. They returned to Canada where Frank was building a house when Annie died early in 1923. Frank and Nelson Watts had opened a market, but only a month after Annie's death, Frank returned to the desert and again operated the Pioneer Meat Market until it burned November 30, 1926.

Following the fire, Frank joined Joe McCue who had established a market in Yermo. In 1976, the same building is being used by Western Auto Supply. In 1929, Frank entered into a partnership with Arthur H. and Jennie M. Pendleton in a Barstow market which became known as Pendleton and Ryerse. Part of their slaughterhouse still remains two miles from Daggett on land which was Frank's.

Arthur started the original Pendleton's Market in 1902. It was located "between the tracks" in old Barstow. City Market, City Meat Market, and Pendleton & Lazenby City Meat Market are some of the names by which it was known. In 1925, the store was moved to West Main Street. In April, 1937, Arthur Pendleton died of pneumonia and on September 30, 1940 the partnership was dissolved; Frank sold out to Jennie Pendleton and retired.

To some retirement means "No more work!" Not so with Frank Ryerse. He and Donato Ramirez, Barstow grocery store owner, invested in grazing land and cattle, and supplied meat to several stores, including Kenney's Market (his son-in-law), Ryerson's General Store (Frank's cousin), Pendleton's Market (former partner) and to Ramirez Grocery Store. Besides the cattle, there were Frank's bees and honey to care for.

Although 60 years old, Frank learned to dance in the 1920s. He did them all, Spanish Two-Step, Fox Trot, Virginia Reel and Paul Jones. Dances were held in school houses in Daggett, Ludlow, Yermo or Newberry, and absolutely nothing interfered with Frank's attendance at these affairs. Not even chickenpox in 1934. He worked in the back room of the market during the day, but come night, he spruced up, placed his toupee a bit forward and to one side to cover the worst spots, and he was off to trip the light fantastic to the tunes of "Tippi Tin," the "Merry Widow Waltz," "Ukelele Lady" and others.

Nothing interfered with Frank's dancing until a heart attack in 1943, which kept him quiet for a few months. In 1952, he broke his hip, and after surgery, therapy and a year of recuperation, Frank walked again. However, he could only look on longingly when dance music struck up. Frank died in a San Bernardino nursing home on September 8, 1953, at the age of 87. Of his 66 years on the Mojave Desert, at least 60 of those were spent in Daggett.

Earl Kenney had originally sold his farm and come to the desert to help his asthma and sciatic rheumatism. It seemed to have agreed with him, for he led a very active life here. He ranched, worked for Western Borax Company in Boron, and for a number of years was employed by Homer Ryerson to deliver large orders of lumber and grain to customers in outlying areas. In 1942, he built and operated his own store, Kenney's Food Market, in Yermo. After an operation and serious illness in May 1958, he retired from his store in May of 1959.

Always interested in civic affairs, he was a member of the Daggett Chamber of Commerce, contributed to the Daggett Mutual Water Company and belonged to Daggett's Chapter of the American Association of

8 Store leased in 1887, Homer Ryerse, Frank Ryerse, Bernie La Montain, Ben Butler.

11 Frank's first business venture - Homer Ryerse, Bill and Bernie LaMantain

Ryerse Ventures

9 Pig pens with slaughter house at center

12 Frank and Hettie (first wife), daughters Hazel and Myrtle

10 Frank and Annie's wedding day 1905

13 Cattle pens with Calicos in background

14 Rowena Ryerson (Homer changed name), Charlie Nolan and Bill Parker early 1920's

Retired Persons.

Although retired, he was ever busy with one or more community improvement projects. Early or late, he could be seen with a rake, shovel, buckets and a gray 1941 Ford pick-up cleaning debris from vacant areas, filling in holes, leveling washed out desert roads, and trimming and watering abandoned trees. He was instrumental in starting the fencing of Daggett's Pioneer Cemetery, doing a tremendous amount of the work himself.

In the meantime, Earl's wife Myrtle was very active also. In 1934, she helped organize Daggett's Parent-Teacher Association, and served as its first president. She did office work at the Ryerson Store until 1938, when arthritis forced her to quit. At home, she kept books for the Daggett Mutual Water Company, from 1929 to 1938. In 1942, when Earl built and operated Kenney's Food Market in Yermo, she managed to do their bookkeeping until Earl retired in 1959.

In 1924-25, Viola Shea, the new school teacher from San Francisco gave dancing lessons in Myrtle's parlor. The phonograph issued forth with "Three O'clock in The Morning" or "Yes Sir, That's My Baby." It was "step, glide, close" or "one, two, three, four" until all hours. No neighbors complained; they were all there. In 1934-35, Myrtle's dancing days were cut short by the painful and crippling rheumatoid arthritis, with which she suffered until her death, April 4, 1967.

This story is not the complete saga of the Ryerse/Ryerson/Kenney family, for there are descendants of the clan still living in Daggett, carrying on the traditions begun there nearly a hundred years ago.

HENDERSON FAMILIES
by Alfred C. Henderson

When Al Henderson was contacted in Laguna Hills to write a history of the Henderson family for the Museum, he first wrote back a short note to indicate his interest. It read,

Those names you mentioned in your letter brought back some fond memories—Charlie Mitchell worked at my grandmother's store, took care of the horses, wagons, lumber, hay, grain, coal, etc., probably fourteen hours a day! Lavella Crooks, Bud Crooks' mother, worked for my grandmother. WOW!! Did we, as little kids, mind her? No monkey business or we'd get a clout across the side of the head; and we loved her . . . Dr. White delivered me as well as Bob White. Gene White was really my second father—Nowe Platt, if I remember correctly, worked at the Bagdad Mining Co. mill on the west side of "B" Hill,—May Murray, who lives on Bear Valley Road (Barstow Road) in Barstow, is the daughter of my Uncle Archibald Henderson and Mary Deuchriss Henderson.

A second letter was received, written in the first person, containing history of the Hendersons. It read as follows:

First you will have to remember that both sides of my family, paternal and maternal, were named Henderson, so don't become confused.

All my forebearers (including my brother George, and my two sisters, Madge and Flora) were born in Scotland. D.C. Henderson, on my mother's side, was an asthmatic. He left his family and three businesses in Glasgow, Scotland, to seek a climate that might offer him some relief from this condition. After seven years in Africa, Australia and South Africa, with little relief, he returned to Scotland, but his health worsened. He left again to try Southern California. He arrived in Los Angeles about 1888. He heard about a mining town called Calico. He came to Daggett, a shipping point for Calico and the Borax Company. He immediately felt better and was actually never able to leave the desert for more than a short time after that. D.C., as he was known, did return to Scotland to entice his wife, my grandmother, to return with him, but no luck. However, his youngest daughter, Jean, age 10, did come back with him. (This Jean, my aunt, was for whom the town of Jean, Nevada was named in 1906.) She attended grade school in Daggett.

Grandfather worked briefly for the railroad, and for a short time was stationed in Hinkley. During this period he wrote glowing descriptions of the desert to his wife back in Scotland and she joined him there, where their youngest child, called Hinckley, was born. Shortly thereafter, D.C. and his wife returned to Daggett where he opened a general merchandising store.

My maternal grandmother's brother, George Brown, came to Daggett to visit and liked the country so much (or disliked the climate of Scotland so much) that he decided to stay. He also opened a store in Daggett. This store was called the "Shamrock" and is still standing next door, to the west, of the old "Stone Hotel." (If one gets in the right light, the painting of a large thistle can still be seen.) At this same time, D.C. Henderson's son, Donald, arrived in Daggett from Scotland with his bride.

My father, Lubin J. Henderson, and my mother, Annie Henderson, brought their three children, Madge, Flora and George from Glasgow, Scotland to Barstow in the year 1902. Their daughter, Flora, who also suffered from asthma, found relief in the Mojave desert. My maternal grandparents, D.C. Henderson, built a home on 10 acres of land on the west end of Barstow, directly across from the puzzle switches. You can imagine the noise of the trains, both passenger and freight, as they were switched over the puzzles, the steam engines, sounding their signals with their whistles and "blowing off their cocks" (the water out of their cylinders). They also had to contend with the Mojave River rising each winter and covering the area with three or four feet of water, the mosquitoes and flies, the outdoor plumbing and the lack of fresh

15   *A Busy Corner*

From Calico Junction to Daggett

16   *Bahten Meat Market 1880's*

18   *Mr. and Mrs. D.C. Henderson*

17   *Mary Deuchress Henderson and children*

19   *Daggett*

vegetables and milk. Water was obtained by driving a "sandpoint" into the ground to a depth of four or five feet, attaching a hand pump and exerting a little "elbow grease." All heat and lighting was by coal, oil or wood. Cooling was done by home-made tents made with a frame covered with sacking over which water was allowed to drip—this, usually under a tree for shade and access to any breeze that might wander by. There was no viaduct at that time and, as the school was on the other side of the tracks, we crossed these tracks by climbing under or over the box cars, moving or still. (The only person I remember of being killed doing this, was a Mrs. Wells, wife of the Santa Fe Agent.)

Into this, I was born in 1903—delivered by Dr. J.O. White, Santa Fe doctor and father of Gene White.

My father, Lubin J. Henderson, brought his mother from Scotland to Barstow in 1910—his father had died shortly before in the "Old Country." This grandmother was accompanied by dad's two sisters, their husbands and children.

The original D.C. Henderson store, in old Barstow, was opened in 1897. In 1909 a large part of the town was burned down, including grandfather's store and warehouses. These were rebuilt, but this time of concrete. This store and the warehouses dealt in coal, lumber, hay, grain, feed, fuel, groceries, hardware and clothing. It also contained the Post Office and bakery, where most of the town's bread was baked.

Mrs. D.C. Henderson separated from the Congregational Church in Barstow in 1915. She built and donated a church (Free Methodist) which was more to her beliefs. This church is still standing in the 300 block on North Second Street. (The Free Methodist Church has since moved to a new location.) The original Free Methodist Church was used as a classroom after the Barstow High School burned down in 1917.

My maternal grandfather, D.C., died in Barstow in 1912 and was buried on the back approach to the School Hill. His remains were removed to Inglewood Cemetery in 1919.

My father, Lubin J. Henderson, opened his own store, in old Barstow, in 1903. In 1920 he bought 55 acres of land from a man named Otis Lowell (there is a short street named for him in Barstow) for $710. This property was subdivided and known as the Henderson subdivision. He also bought the stores and property formerly owned by Mr. and Mrs. D.C. Henderson (Mrs. D.C. Henderson died in Los Angeles in 1921). This property was on Elm Street (the name of Main Street in old Barstow) between Santa Fe passenger tracks on the north and the freight tracks on the south.

In 1918, Lubin J. renovated the store buildings in old Barstow and turned them into a temporary hospital during the 1918 "flu" epidemic. Following this, the buildings were used as an office and classroom for the Barstow Union High School. (For instance: I would arrive at this building at 9:00 a.m., attend a math class, then go over the footbridge to the Free Methodist Church for English, then to the Congregational Church for Latin and Study Period, then to the house adjacent to the old church on the corner of Third & Hutchison Streets for Science.) After the new high school was built, in the new town, in 1918, the main store, in old Barstow, was leased to Mrs. Lillian Jones, a long time businesswoman.

The Henderson store, and other stores, moved from old town to what is now First and Main Streets in 1925. Lubin J. Henderson conducted his clothing business there with his two sons, George and Alfred, until his death in 1954—at age 83. He, indeed, participated in the development of Barstow. He became a naturalized citizen in 1907. Also, in this year he organized the first Chamber of Commerce. He was elected Justice of the Peace in 1922 and served for 20 years. He was President of the Barstow Kiwanis Club and head of the War Bond Drive in World War II; a trustee of the Congregational Church for many years and an active member of the Masonic Order; a member of the Barstow Elementary School Board and instrumental in the forming of a High School District. His wife, Annie, was a charter member of the Barstow Women's Club, the Eastern Star and White Shrine.

George was active in the Chamber of Commerce, a charter member and Lt. Governor of Kiwanis International and a Life member of the B.P.O.E. His wife, Eda, was active in the Barstow Women's Club and the Mojave River Valley Museum. The Eda Henderson Pool at Fogelsong Park was named after her in recognition of her work for the Park District.

I was active in the Kiwanis Club, Congregational Church and served 24 years as an Elementary School Board member. I also organized and was first President of the Barstow Shrine Club. One of the proudest moments in my life was when the Alfred C. Henderson School was named in my honor, in 1953.

WHITE AND PLATT FAMILY
by Celestia Gilliam
(From an interview with Elma June Payne)

The names of White and Platt are synonymous with the history of Barstow. They ran the only drug store serving the area for many years, also providing ambulance and mortician services.

Dr. John Ogden White and his wife, Eugenia, came to Barstow from Nashville, Tennessee in 1900. Dr. White was employed as a Santa Fe doctor in association with Dr. Rhea. The Whites were the parents of three children, Marietta, Gene and Arthur, and the family lived in old Barstow on Cottage Street as most people did at that time. The house they lived in had been moved from Calico and was later moved to 227 North First Street where it still remains.

Dr. Rhea was operating a drug store along with his practice, and in 1903 Dr. White bought this business.

Meanwhile, Nowe Platt arrived in Barstow to work as

a cyanide man at the Bagdad Chase Mill on "B" Hill. He met and fell in love with Marietta White and they were married in 1909. They also made their home on Cottage Street and their three children, Ogden, Elma June and Lois, were born there. Their children, and many other babies, were delivered in Barstow by Dr. Anderson and Nurse Dalman.

Gene White became a druggist and operated his father's business. He married Stella Reynolds and they became the parents of Robert and Bernice.

In 1921, Gene White and Nowe Platt became partners in the drug store and also in the ambulance and undertaking business in old Barstow. They became staunch members of the community and medicinal counselors in many cases. Gene made his own "desert skin lotion" which would make a fortune if we still had the formula. He was also a jeweler and did a fine job of cutting glass.

Both men were active in local affairs for the betterment of the community. Gene organized the first volunteer fire department. Nowe was a member of the Elks and the Masonic Lodge and performed many fine services including the organization of the first March of Dimes here. On occasion he would find the time to take a fishing trip with Al Mudgett or Forst Dillingham.

Their ambulance and undertaking business served the entire desert. The hearse was a large Lincoln automobile which was also often used to haul ice cream to the drug store from the Santa Fe Railroad. Johnny Thursby was a right-hand-man and close associate of White and Platt.

Life was interesting in "old Barstow." Those who conducted business's along with White and Platt included: Henderson's Clothing and Tailoring, Dillinghams Market, Pendleton's Butcher Shop, Gilhams Dry Goods, Hillis' Garage, Sloan & Hart Saloon, and the Melrose Hotel.

The Harvey House was the center of entertainment and out of town performers, including "Chatauquas," were brought in by the Santa Fe for the townspeople to enjoy. School graduation parties were held at the Harvey House reading room. The first movie house was "Fletcher's Opera House."

Old town included the telephone and water company buildings; also the Catholic, Christian Science and Community Churches. The school was located at Second & Hutchison, a small building with a steeple and bungalows. It was built by Robert Waterman, a mining engineer who owned the Waterman Mine and realized the need of an education for the miners' children. The school was named for him. It served many purposes over the years—Sunday School and Church was held there before the Congregational Church was built.

The children swam in the river, enjoyed Buzzard Rock and played a lot of baseball. After the games it was great fun to go to White & Platts Soda Fountain for a soda or a special drink called "Green River." They also spent much of their time jumping the freight and passenger tracks or dawdling on the foot bridge, much to the consternation of their parents. Many of them took music lessons from Marietta Cook and can remember her riding in her buggy, drawn by "Teddy," her horse. Christmas was a wonderful time with the first organized service club, Kiwanis, giving a party. Leon Whitney played Santa Claus. These "children" could have been one of the Deskins, Conaways, Leaks, Eddys, Schmidts, Crooks, Thursbys or Copps, many of whom still live in Barstow.

Old Barstow was not without its disasters; floods and fires shaped much of its history. In 1906, a $100,000 fire on Elm Street burned the Sloan-Hart building and Henderson Dry Goods. In 1908 a $150,000 fire started in the saloon and destroyed the Harvey House. In 1921, a blaze which started in the grocery burned toward the west and took the hotel, Post Office and butcher shop. Then in 1923, a fire started at the lunch counter and burned Gilham's general store. It was after this last fire that most businesses moved to their present locations on Main Street. The move was caused not only by the fires but, coincidentally the Santa Fe Railroad was enlarging its operation and needed the "old town" space. In 1930, the viaduct was constructed connecting old and new town. White & Platt, along with others, built their new building on Main Street where they continued to conduct their business until their deaths.

DILLINGHAM FAMILY

by Celestia Gilliam

The Dillinghams—Reese M. Dillingham, his wife, Lucy, and their children, who moved from Ohio to California in the 1890's—were one of the earliest families to settle in Barstow. Dillingham's first contact with Barstow was in 1896. His job as conductor on the Santa Fe took him through the area.

By 1900, he became fascinated with the prospects of a business in the desert and bought Bodine's mercantile business. He moved his wife and three of their four children, Wilda, Jean, and Reece Jr., to Barstow where they all soon became involved in helping in the family enterprises. Forst, their oldest boy who worked as a sports reporter in Los Angeles, soon

joined the family in Barstow. When Reece Jr. graduated from high school in Los Angeles, he and his brother, Forst, became the mainsprings in their father's business in old Barstow. By 1924, they not only sold groceries, hardware and lumber, but had also built rental housing, the best known was the Dillingham Apartments still standing at the west end of Cottage Street.

When business interests were moving to Main Street in 1925, Forst continued to operate the mercantile business on Cottage Street, and Reece opened a cash and carry grocery in a new building on Main Street. Later, the business on Cottage was discontinued, and

20 Visiting Mr. Lane (left) at Calico. Forst and Reece Dillingham

23 Dillingham family and friends on their way to Calico in a Stanley Steamer

The Dillingham Clan

24 Dillingham store on Cottage Street 1914

21 Dillingham apartments

25 Reece in front of his home, Cottage Street, Barstow 1917

22 Reece hauled his boat to Big Bear 1915-1917

26 Outing to the Ord Mountains April 29, 1924

the building was moved to what is now the 200 block of Main Street where it became a rental. It is now Victor's Music Store.

At the same time, the San Bernardino Valley Branch Bank occupied the corner of Second and Main. It closed in the crash of 1929, and Forst and Reece used the building for a general mercantile business until their deaths. In converting the bank building to a grocery store, they ingeniously turned the bank vault into a cold box. Bob Hartwick ran the produce stand and Ed Lisenby ran the butcher shop. The Dillingham lumber yard was located on the east side of Second Street behind what is now the Sears store.

The Dillinghams were active in the community serving as volunteer firemen, and Reece became Fire Commissioner. Both were members of the Masonic Lodge and the Elks.

Forst married Ethel Reynolds and they became the parents of Forst Jr. and twins, Mike and Margaret. Reece married Hila Orner and they had two sons, Leon and Reginald.

The families had a cabin at Big Bear to escape the desert heat. They were often joined by the Nowe Platt family, Al Mudgett or Johnny Sloan. It took days by horse and buggy to reach the mountains. Later the family bought a White steamer car, only to discover that trips took as long as with the horse and buggy because of flat tires and unkept roads.

The Dillinghams had one of the first businesses on Main Street in Barstow, along with Hendersons and White & Platt. Slaton and Bauer, who had operated stables in old Barstow, opened a garage at First and Main. Soon came Cunningham's Drug, Old Trails Diner (O'Hara), Kinleyside Hardware, Eva Tabor's "Tony's Cafe," and Pendleton's Market on West Main. The colorful Beacon Hotel was built on East Main and became a landmark in the city for many years.

Dillingham's Market was a household word for two decades, not only in Barstow but for all those people who were served in the outlying areas. The two brothers, Reece and Forst, proved themselves industrious and many of their buildings in Barstow still stand as a testimony to their farsightedness.

OLD BARSTOW ROAD
by Mrs. Aileen McCue Powell
as told to Pat Keeling

When we came to Barstow, we would always take the livery stable road, in our wagon, and travel up the river road, over the hill across the railroad tracks; the railroad track went around the hill. Then we would come down the hill and over the railroad tracks, through town down to the west tower and up and over the hill by the Dillingham (Foley) apartments, and over another hill on to San Bernardino. It was a winding road. Old Barstow was built in the center of what is now the railroad tracks. Its main street had Pendleton's Meat Market, Gene White's Drug Store, a bakery, the Chinese restaurant, a saloon, and the dance hall, with a picture show above, owned by Johnny Sloan.

Near the railroad tracks, the forerunner of the Elks, the Antlers Lodge members, held their meeting in a building which was later moved to Third Street and Hutchinson where it was again used as a church.

ELLA B. PITCHER 1877-1969
by Nell Woolford

Ella B. (Connors) Pitcher was born July 15, 1877, in Vurita, (Indian Territory) Oklahoma. In 1896, at the age of 19, Ella Connors came to Barstow to visit her brother who was a road-master for the railroad. She met Ed Pitcher who drove a 20-mule borax team, and they were married. After the railroad replaced the mule teams, Ed Pitcher went to work for the railroad, but resigned when he was elected constable of Barstow. He appointed Ella as his deputy. He later resigned as constable because he didn't like to lock up the prisoners.

The Pitchers then acquired the Inez Hotel, the swankiest place in Barstow. As hostess, Ella met many notables, among them the Prince of Belgium, Theodore (Teddy) Roosevelt, General Pershing, Champ Clark, President Taft, and Governor Stephens.

Always civic minded, Ella Pitcher worked for women's suffrage, acted as United States census marshall in 1900, 1910 and 1920. She was the first lady to perform jury duty in Barstow. She and two other women circulated a petition to obtain names needed to form a high school district. She served on the Waterman School board for many years.

During the First World War, she was president of the local Red Cross, and at the end of the war she won the highest award from the organization, a four-stripe badge. As Chairman of the Council for Defense, she sold the largest amount of Liberty Bonds and Stamps in San Bernardino County, winning a bronze medal from the Federal Government.

In 1922 Ella Pitcher organized the first women's service organization, the Barstow Women's Club, and served as its first president. She was later made an Honorary Life Member and Mother Emeritus of the Club.

Ella Pitcher was the first woman member of the Barstow Chamber of Commerce; she opened the first real estate office in Barstow. In 1942 an NBC radio program honored her as the "Good Neighbor for the Day." She had no children of her own, but she raised 21

27 Elm Street 1910

30 Ella and Ed Pitcher owners of Inez Hotel. Ed drove Borax wagons

28 Lisita Pico Williamson, Castilian descendant

32 Death Valley Scotty (arrow) visits Barstow 1906

Old Town Barstow

29 Newspaper - "The Printer" Nov. 23, 1912

33 Inez Hotel and Fletcher Opera House

children of relatives.

In 1958, when the Barstow Freeway was to be opened, a slogan contest was conducted. Ella Pitcher submitted the slogan "Trails of Pioneers—Mules to Missiles," and as winner of the contest was presented a trophy when the freeway opened.

Ella Pitcher was a charter member of the Barstow Chapter No. 546, Order of the Eastern Star, a charter member of the Odessa Rebekah Lodge No. 388,

Independent Order of Odd Fellows. In 1962, the Altrusa Club of Barstow voted her the first, and only, honorary member of the Barstow Altrusa Club.

Ella B. Pitcher devoted most of her life to working for the growth and advancement of Barstow. Our country and the community have grown and prospered because of the strength and determination of citizens like Ella B. Pitcher.

CONAWAY FAMILY

by Ray Conaway as told to Pat Keeling

Grandad Oscar Bigelow Conaway and his children Fred, Clarence, Oscar "Louie", Laverne and Agnes arrived in Randsburg about 1905. They had formerly lived on a land claim in the Oklahoma Territory.

Grandad was a freighter, with headquarters in Johannesburg and Mojave. He drove an eight and ten horse wagon team for the H.D. and L.D. Freighting Company of Johannesburg. His family then lived at Old Wells, east of Red Mountain. Grandad and Fred Conaway had claims near the Yellow Aster Mines at Randsburg.

Part of the Conaway family moved to Westminister, where Grandad went into the real estate business. Another daughter, Mina, was born in Westminister. Every year they would return to do assessment work on the claims in the Randsburg area. Fred and Louie stayed in Johannesburg with Aunt Minnie Boling.

Fred helped his brother Louie operate the pumps for Charles Chase, owner of the water system. Fred went to work when he was 14, driving the stage and mail coach between Johannesburg and Ballarat. On one occasion he had a load of gold to deliver valued at over $10,000. To avert suspicion, he put the gold under his feet, threw mail sacks over it, and drove it and his passengers out of "Skidoo" to Ballarat. He was considered one of the best teamsters around, and never had a holdup.

Dad (Louie) as a teamster and freighter in 1906, used the road to Goldstone via Black Canyon which had water holes for the mules. There were rock corrals to pen the mules overnight. The date of 1906 was branded by him at Granite Wells. They followed the road from Barstow via the Copper City to Johannesburg. The same route started at Daggett, through the hills across Red Mountain, over the Copper City road and on to "Joberg." At that time, Crutts had water and a Post Office. In the 1920's, there was lots of water, people had orchards, fields and cattle. Dad, "Louie" Conaway, died in 1956.

I was born in Westminister in 1906, and have a younger brother Harold and sister Edna. Our dad, Louie Conaway, was later a stationary engineer at the Barstow Power Plant. One day, in 1915, he needed a substitute boy to call crews. Although I was under age, I was flattered to be asked. He sent me to the Japanese compound where those workers were housed, on Hutchinson Street, between Sixth and Seventh Streets.

One did not yell out for crews but talked to the "Number-One-Man;" then I was allowed to enter the house. Much to my astonishment I found a number of people, stark-naked, having a steaming-warm bath in a tub as big as a small swimming pool in the middle of the room. I found their customs strange and quickly ran out of the house.

During World War I, the Santa Fe Railroad employed many Japanese at the roundhouse, most were loyal American citizens. A few were suspected of tampering with the water tanks of the steam engines when it was found that carbonaceous dust had been added to the water.

After the sabotage to the water tanks, the Master Mechanic sent to the main office for a new boilermaker. Alex Kiss was to arrive from San Francisco in the near future. A telegram arrived stating "Sending you A. Kiss." A return wire was quickly dispatched, "I do not want a kiss, I want a boilermaker!"

Little has been recorded about an engine that made electricity in the communities of Barstow, Daggett, Ludlow and Goffs, before World War I. It was unique in the fact that it did not have an electric starter. It started with a blow torch and ran for two or three years at a time, occasionally having to be lubricated with oil.

When Grandad and his family moved to Barstow, in 1916, they arrived by train. They moved to the desert for the health of Walter Upton, son of daughter Agnes. Her husband James Upton, brought his family by wagon and team over Cajon Pass. The doctor in Westminister told them that the fresh air and getting out of the dampness would help Walter get well. The family lived on Crooks and Pierce streets until 1922, when they moved uptown to the Coddinger's duplex on Hutchinson Street. Later, they lived at a ranch on Irwin Road and Rodeo Road Drive.

Barstow sustained a very serious influenza epidemic in 1918 which was also world-wide. A building set aside for use of contagious cases was situated on the edge of town and known as the pest house. It had a windmill that pumped water.

Barstow's other water supply was pumped from Charlie Williams' well, situated on the southwest corner of First and Fredricks streets. His well was 300-400 feet deep and pumped the water into a large reservoir for the use of the citizens of Barstow. Occasionally Williams would imbibe too freely and let the reservoir run dry. My grandfather, father, and I would have to start up the motor for the water to refill all the water pipes in the city. Everyone was well aware of why there was a sudden lack of water.

I worked for the Santa Fe night shift in Barstow for the American Railway Express. The train to "Joberg" ran on Monday, Wednesday and Friday. The agent always, asked for volunteers to work up the line because it was overtime. I would go to pick up the gold shipment the Yellow Aster Mine brought into the depot at Johannesburg. The baggage cars used kerosine lamps, but kept a spring loaded candle holder for emergencies when the fuel ran out. These candles were always at the top of the holder ready to burn due to their unique design. I saved one when they hauled all of the materials to the dump after the line was abandoned.

My family have been long time residents of the Barstow area and have seen many changes. I married a Harvey Girl named Rosalie R. Frankovich in 1937, and we have five children, Ruby Ann, Charles F., Mary Ellen, John R. and Christina M. Remembering how Barstow used to be brings back many hours of happy memories.

HELEN MORRISETTE
by Louella Bishoff

Helen Morrissette, owner of the Budget Shop at 224 East Main Street, came to Barstow as a young high school student along with her mother, Lillian Jones, and a younger brother.

They had first come to San Bernardino at the suggestion of a cousin who was a judge in San Diego. In 1918, doctors advised Mrs. Jones to move to a higher and drier climate for the sake of her son's health.

The opportunities for employment here at that time were few for a young woman who had two children to support. She could have become a waitress at the Harvey House or a domestic for the Melrose Hotel. There was little else to choose from. Not having ever worked as a waitress, Lillian Jones served as a hotel maid, for a few weeks.

Meanwhile, a friend who was working for Harris' Department Store in San Bernardino, told Mrs. Jones that Harris' would extend her credit for the merchandise if she would like to start a store of her own in Barstow.

It seemed as though the time was right, for a store building by the railroad tracks had recently been vacated by Lubin J. Henderson and was for rent, including the much needed display cases and shelves. That was to be the first of several locations for the Jones Department Store.

The store was moved to Crooks Avenue in 1922 when Santa Fe began expanding their facilities. It stayed in the "River-bottom" until 1926, when Mrs. Jones moved to the Griffith house at 224 East Main Street. The Ryerson Lumber Company of Daggett remodeled the front of the house for use as a store in 1928. In 1931 it became the first location of Barstow's Sprouse-Reitz Variety Store.

The Hayward Lumber Company did extensive remodeling for Mrs. Jones at about the same time they were also building their own facilities farther down on East Main Street. They told her that the town was moving east as evidenced by the recent construction of the beautiful Beacon Hotel, which was west of where the Beacon Bowl is now. There was talk even then of a super-highway that was to come through soon.

While the remodeling was going on at 222 and 224 East Main Street, Mrs. Jones moved her store to a building in the 300 block of East Main, next door and just east of where Albert's Levi's is now. When the remodeling was finally completed, she moved her store to 222 and in 1942 moved into 224. That's the location where this writer first remembered going as a child in the early 1940's when an addition to the wardrobe was needed.

During a slow business day Mrs. Jones would sit in the front of the store and watch the transcontinental traffic passing by. She had predicted such traffic more than 20 years before. One of her favorite pastimes was to recite poetry in her North Carolina accent which she never lost.

In 1950 the Jones Building, at 305 East Main was built and housed the store until 1954 when it was sold to Rude's Department Store.

Mrs. Jones passed away on July 4, 1954. Helen Morrisette continued doing business in connection with LaMarr's Men's Wear and Carmel's Clothing Store until 1966.

After hearing of the success of several other consignment stores over the state, Mrs. Morrisette decided to start one of her own. The Budget Shop opened its doors at 222 East Main in 1970, and moved to 224 in 1973.

Mrs. Morrissette and the author had a lot of fun recalling their early childhood in Barstow. The one memory Helen holds most dear was the atmosphere of "one big happy family," which prevailed at the time.

She recalled that individuals and businesses each donated their share and the whole town would have a picnic or barbecue. They sometimes held dances in the old Waterman School, a wooden building on Hutchinson Street. She remembers the school was heated with an old fashioned pot-bellied wood burning stove. Sometimes the entertainment included a free picture show or a trip to Yermo for a Saturday night dance.

Needles Nuggett 5-15-42

Office of Price Administration warned all sugar users to guard their ration books jealously. When a book is lost or destroyed it will be impossible to obtain a replacement until at least two months.

LOVE STORIES DEWOLF & KUHN

by Celestia Gilliam

Carl DeWolf and Mabel Bowman arrived in the west from Kansas and Indiana respectively, meeting and marrying in Pasadena, California in 1914. Carl was a general contractor in the city but soon became interested in moving to the desert, having heard of the wonders of a farming community called Hinkley. He and Mabel negotiated to homestead 160 acres in Hinkley Valley. They packed their belongings and two children, Marion and Irene, and set out to new adventure on their newly acquired property.

It was their dream to raise turkeys and to farm enough ground to make a profitable living. However, Carl found it necessary to supplement their farming enterprise by returning to contracting and building. Also, their family had increased by two sons, Jimmy and Earl (Buster), and Mabel found it difficult to watch over her four children and help her husband with the chores.

Bad luck struck the DeWolfs in 1922, a load of tainted feed killing their entire flock of turkeys just before Thanksgiving. Carl and Mabel decided to move to Barstow where Carl would go into his own construction business.

At this time, the desirable area in Barstow was in the district of Pierce, Crooks and Willow Streets. There was always a flow of water in the Mojave River and the streets were lined with shrubbery and trees. Carl acquired property on Willow Street where he built a residence for his family and also four other houses which he rented.

Their family grew, by one, with the birth of a daughter, Patsy, in 1931. All the older children attended Waterman Elementary School and later Barstow High School on Main Street.

Carl did well in general contracting and built many structures in Barstow, including the original Standard Oil Station which stood at the corner of First and Main Streets (now the location of Winchell's Donut House). He also did the cement work on the sidewalks on First Street and much of Main Street. From time to time he took contracts out of town, and one of the most interesting jobs he completed, in 1926, was the sidewalks at the Amargosa Hotel in Death Valley Junction for the Pacific Coast Borax Co. It is remembered that these sidewalks were a major addition to the area, being the only ones within a radius of 100 miles. For the first time parents there were able to include rollerskates in their order to Sears Roebuck at Christmas time!

The DeWolf also bought property on East Buena Vista which they leased to the government for housing called "Victory Homes" during World War II.

The DeWolf sons, Jimmy and Earl, entered the service upon graduation from High School. Jimmy married Kathryn Kuhn, whose family history in Barstow dated further back than the DeWolfs.

Kathryn's mother, Kathryn Borowski, arrived in Barstow as a Harvey girl in 1909. As a teenager, she had been sent from Poland to America to seek her fortune, and went to work for Fred Harvey in New York in 1908. As customs were, she was moved around from city to city in the Harvey system and finally at her request, was sent to the country and found herself in Barstow. Here she fell in love and married a handsome Austrian named Paul Kuhn who worked in the baggage area of the Santa Fe trains. They bought acreage in the Highway 58 area from Charlie Mitchell, built a home there and eventually became the parents of three children, Kathryn, Bill and Paul Jr. As a child, Katie remembers walking to Compton's Dairy where she washed milk bottles for a nickel.

The DeWolfs and the Kuhn children attended Waterman Elementary School and Barstow High School, where Katie and Jimmy were destined to meet. They married in 1941.

It will be remembered that Katie and Jimmie owned and operated DeWolf's Market on Second Street from 1950-1960. Jimmy was also a member of the City Council from 1952-1960. They still reside in Barstow.

The marriage of Kathryn Kuhn and Jimmy DeWolf united two pioneer families who had, in their own times, contributed to the history and growth of our area. A similar story could be told about many other long standing desert families, namely: Hoskins-Kuhn, Gibson-Leak, Thrasher-Bye, Fairbanks-Haimut, Dolph-Dillingham, Belsher-Butler, and White-Crooks. After all, that's what it's all about!

THE HOUCK TWINS
by Evelyn Askren Stafford Bruce

Nell and Stell, the twin daughters of Mr. and Mrs. Joseph Houck, can remember moving to Barstow with their parents in 1911. Their father had come to California to work on the railroad as a section foreman for the Atchison, Topeka and Santa Fe. They later moved to Minneola, a little railroad "whistle stop" east of Daggett. They also resided in Ludlow before returning to Barstow as brides, living for a while in the Dillingham apartments on the north side of "B" hill.

They vividly recall their earlier school years in Barstow. Their teacher was Clarence Brown, the classroom one large room shared by sixth, seventh and eighth grades. They left school after the eighth grade, because Barstow had no high school at that time. Their father thought no self-respecting young lady of that age should be finished with schooling and have nothing to do, so he made them repeat the eighth grade two times.

Some of their classmates were Ike Warwick, Reece Dillingham, Bertha (Griffith) Schmitt, Harold Wilson and Walter Mudgett.

With laughter and happiness in their hearts, they remember how they looked forward to fun filled social events, the Saturday night dances held at the club named "Our Nite Out," owned and operated by Santa Fe road engineer Casey Lee and his wife Edna. It was located above the saloon. Once a person entered the dance hall, absolutely no one, boy or girl, could go out that door and expect to re-enter. This was a staunch rule and Mrs. Lee was always there to enforce. it.

Stell and Nell have often laughed until the tears rolled down their faces, remembering how they made the trip from Minneola to Barstow. They would spend much time dressing beautifully in their finest dresses and ribbons, then, putting on their oldest, most scruffed, every-day shoes, they would start walking down the railroad track towards Barstow. Each carried her best dress shoes in hand, to slip on when they arrived. If they were in luck, a freight train might come rumbling by and they would flag it to a stop, climb aboard the caboose, and sit in the cupola with the conductor and brakemen the rest of the way to Daggett.

Arriving at the home of their friend Aileen (McCue) Powell, they put on their good dress shoes and be on their way to the dance with Aileen, her brothers, and friend Walter Alf. Sometimes they would all stop by the home of Mr. and Mrs. George Deskins (in Barstow) who would also join them.

They spent happy times dancing with their friends to the current popular tunes played by a small orchestra. The piano was sometimes played by "Scotty" Thursby. When the evening came to an end, they would exchange new shoes for the old and start walking back home to Minneola.

After a few years, their family moved to Ludlow. Both girls later married former boy friends from Kansas and returned to Barstow to raise their families. Stell married Bernie Stafford who became Yardmaster General for the Santa Fe Railroad. They had four children, Gene, Bill, Grace and Sue. Nell married Roy Canady another Yardmaster. Their son, Mack, was born when they lived in the Dillingham Apartments.

The twin "girls" now reside in San Bernardino, where they still reminisce about their many happy experiences. They recently shared a party celebrating their 80th birthday and are now looking forward to sharing their 81st in this bicentennial year.

"HELLO, CENTRAL"
by Martha Burnau

Years ago having a telephone was considered a luxury. In these "modern times," however, the telephone is such a necessary part of our lives that we take it for granted (unless we decide to move out to a remote part of the desert where the cost of acquiring telephone service is still prohibitive).

Service came to settled portions of the Mojave Desert in 1913. In 1911 the Interstate Telegraph Company which was providing service to Inyo and Mono Counties and several Nevada counties was purchased by a power company. This company extended telephone lines along its own power transmission facilities to the south, reaching Victorville in 1912 and Oro Grande and Barstow in 1913.

An agent of the power company handled original telephone communications in Barstow. The first switchboard was located in the lobby of the Hotel Melrose on Main Street in "old town." It was later moved to the library building between the tracks.

Bertha Schmitt, one of the first switchboard operators in Barstow, recalls that in 1913 the few calls coming through gave her plenty of time to do her knitting. On February 21, 1913, the *Barstow Printer-Review* reported "32 phones in service and more being applied for."

After WW I the Santa Fe Railway needed to enlarge its Barstow yard facilities. The citizens who owned homes and businesses were urged to sell their holdings, which were located in the center of the railroad yards. Agreement was reached between the railroad and concerned citizens and an exodus began in 1925.

The telephone company constructed a reinforced concrete building in the 100 block of North First Street in the center of town. All equipment and employees were moved into the new facility on November 5, 1926. This date also marked the beginning of an automatic dialing service. The newly constructed Melrose Hotel

8-12   Picnic at Newberry 1910

Daggett At Play

9   Picking wild grapes at Newberry 1910

13   Touring Calico on the AB & C

10   Sporting event, Marion Mill stacks in background

14   Exploring Odessa Canyon

11   Helen Muir Funk target shooting at Van Dyke Ranch

15   Serenading a cholla

16 Independence Day celebration Old Town 1911

Barstow At Play

20 Hunting season

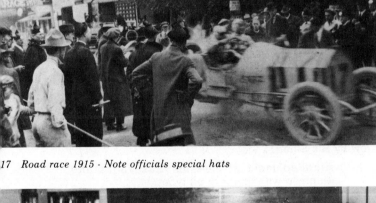

17 Road race 1915 - Note officials special hats

21 Daggett Light House 1936, one of several desert beacons used to guide travelers

18 Celebrating 44th wedding anniversary of Mr. and Mrs. R.L. Teague Oct. 25, 1933

22 Addie Bassett

24 Odessa Canyon picnic spring 1934

23 10¢ a dip at Harlan's ranch. Jamie and Harry Kelly, Sr.

193

19 Margaret Fink, Ollie Fink, Ina Marvin

on Main Street housed the first day and night long distance telephone booth.

Records left by Jimmy Mullen, trouble shooter for the Interstate Telegraph Company, reveal the following from February 8, 1923: Number 22-M issued to People's Home Laundry; Number 8-R issued to Electrical Plumbing Shop, formerly known as the Dresie and Hoxie Plumbing and Electrical Shop; Dr. Pratt had two phones installed, one at his office and another at his residence; Jones Department store, "Washie" Laundry, and Billie the Tailor's residence also received new phones.

January 1954 marked the end of the telephone service as a power company subsidiary. California Interstate Telephone Company was incorporated and began independent operations on March 24, 1954.

In 1964, another change came when with the acquisition of all properties Continental Interstate Telephone Company (CITelCo) was born. The company added the Television Cable System to its holdings in 1967, but was required by the federal government to sell these facilities in the early 1970s. Today the local office supplies telephone service to Newberry Springs, Yermo, Daggett, Hinkley, Lenwood, Goldstone, Fort Irwin and the Marine Base as well as Barstow.

We are now able to maintain contact with just about anyone nearly anywhere in the world by just pushing a few buttons. Have you ever imagined what communications must have been like before the telephone became a reality on the desert?

DAGGETT FUN TIMES
by Mrs. Aileen McCue Powell as told to Pat Keeling

Many times on the Fourth of July, we would go on a picnic on the old canal down inside the Van Dyke ranch. Other recreation was music from my piano, which was sold to us by a Santa Fe agent, who sold instruments as a side line. The piano was the center of attention in our home. People came over, including Mr. Ryerson, to sing and get together for an evening of fun.

I also remember as a child standing outside the dance hall and looking in, watching the old time waltzers.

Later, after the mines were closing, Al and Fanny Mudgett played the fiddle and piano for the small dances in town. The dance hall stood out in the street, down from the Stone Hotel.

REMEMBER PROHIBITION
by Pat Keeling
(as told in interview by Bill Smart)

Bill Smart moved to Needles as a young man in the 1920's. He had fun telling about the "stills" that were in operation near the town of Searchlight:

A man had quite an operation going up there in the mountains. Many armed guards patrolled all the time. The only reason we weren't shot at and killed was because we were with the boss. He

supplied most of Needles, Las Vegas and Kingman with liquor of all types.

For entertainment, during the prohibition, people came to the wide open city of Needles. Like most of San Bernardino County, slot machines, gambling, ladies of the night and illegal booze were the order of the day. Several houses of ill-repute flourished in communities on the desert.

THE TEAGUES
by Celestia Gilliam
(as told in interview by Gladys Thursby McGinnis)

Dick and Rachel Teague who lived on Main Street in 1928 moved to Barstow from the South. It was a matter of great curiosity that Teague reportedly kept a KKK flag in his garage. Mrs. Teague sold home-made vegetable soup; each Saturday one could go to her house and buy a lard can full for 25 cents. When Mrs.

Teague's birthday came, her husband held a surprise birthday party at Waterman School and invited the whole town. He had given her all new furniture for their home, which was out of line with life in the depression. One can imagine the comments.

DID YOU KNOW THAT
by Clifford Walker

The Mojave Desert was a hotbed of prohibition activity. Bootlegging was a favorite occupation for clandestine entrepreneurs of the "Roaring Twenties." One local Hinkley resident remembers seeing at night

the fires from the stills near Black Canyon. One ranch owner in Helendale was sentenced to seven years in prison for his excellence in beer production.

At an abandoned ranch in Hodge, one may see the

hidden basement where illegal alcohol was made.

Within 20 miles of Yermo, especially around the Coyote Lake area, there were three large stills and several smaller ones. In a single raid, police confiscated 180 gallons of whiskey hidden in a cave.

Four men were killed at Sheep Springs in the early 1920's as a result of internal strife between the bootleggers.

On several occasions, guilty parties were not convicted—law officials and others drank all the evidence.

THE DEVELOPMENT OF THE DESERT COOLER

by Pat Keeling

In the 1930's, William Smart was responsible for an invention most people of the desert now take for granted. Without the cooler fewer people would be living in the desert. There would be fewer jobs, shopping centers and certainly a great discomfort during the summer months when the temperatures go over the 90 degree mark.

William Smart came to Needles in 1920 to visit his cousin Lula Perkins and her family. He got a job with Santa Fe and made Needles his home. He moved to Barstow in 1945 and retired in 1969. Bill notes that:

Needles had about 3,000 people in 1920. There was no pavement on any street except Front Street. The Santa Fe Railroad had large engine shops, a round house with 30 stalls, a car department, a large ice house for icing refrigerator cars, a store department, water service, carpenter department, and in the rush season the railroad sometimes brought in coal burning steam engines. The Santa Fe had over 600 employees in the mechanical department, as well as section crews, telegraphers and others in little towns between Needles and Barstow.

I think back to 1920 when Needles was very hot in the summer time and people kept cool by sleeping outside on the grass, or on their screened-in porches. There was no other way to stay cool. My cousins' used to spray water on sheets hung from the trees and let the little breeze blow through to keep cool. Sometimes in Needles in July at midnight it would be 115 degrees and without a breeze; it was hard to sleep.

Bill built the first desert cooler in Needles from an idea of a desert cooler to keep vegetables and butter in good condition in areas without ice. It was a square box open on both sides, covered with burlap on the outside. Water ran over the burlap and kept it constantly wet. This was in the days before refrigerators and ice boxes were a daily expense. A fellow had built one box over an outside door of his home and with a breeze of cool air the box cooled the front room. Bill wondered if he couldn't put a fan in the box to cool the room or the house. The only fans in Needles in the 1930's were desk fans, or the large ceiling fans at the County library, the Santa Fe Harvey House, or Recreation Room. Bill remembers how he started:

I went to the fire hall (as Santa Fe Fire Chief) and built one of wood that I had gathered up. I tore up some gunny sacks and covered it and put a fan in, with no results. I was disappointed, but I sat down to study it. I thought if I covered the opening, it would have a chance to pull cool air into the room, and it worked. There was a Japanese carpenter at the Santa Fe shop and when I went over to show him what I had done with the frame, the carpenter built me a real nice one. I used tar paper on the outside of the first cooler, then I measured a board and put it in the frame to set it upright. I then experimented from this cooler. I put tar paper on the inside, but it got a lot of moss on it and it was not practical. I tried a burlap grain sack because I thought the burlap would not moss up. I had an idea of building a drain through for the water, filling it with charcoal to hold moisture, but it just didn't work. I took excelsior from the Santa Fe store department (it was used for packing items) and built a frame, covering the inside with burlap, then with the excelsior on the outside, and covered it with chicken wire.

Bill was very lucky in working on the first cooler because the Master Mechanic, Roston Tuck, was very interested and did not bother him while he was working on it. Mr. Tuck did not know for sure what he was doing, but he left him alone to work on the invention. He wanted one of those THINGS on his office, and when it worked Mr. Tuck had Bill put a lot of the coolers on all the Santa Fe offices in Needles. When this happened, Bill said:

I had graduated to better materials such as flooring from the Bridge gang, which didn't leak like the old scrap lumber. Everyone got interested in the coolers because they really worked. The word got around real fast about my invention and people flocked over to see it.—It was anything to keep COOL IN NEEDLES!! Everyone went home to build one of his own to keep his family cool. Claypool and Sons store ordered burlap by the roll to help us get away from the burlap grain sacks and cement sacks, which were very dirty.

I remember Dad (D.E.) Jernigan building his very first one at our home at 615 Cibola Street, Needles. It was just a big box at the front window with burlap on the outside and just a trace of water running over the top. Dad put a board into the middle of it, with a huge fan mounted on that board. Bill and Dad worked and worked on various ways to get water to stay in the back of the cooler, to pull in cooler air. It was wonderful and did help. At least we could sleep in the house at night; and if we were lucky, even to take a nap in the middle of the afternoon without waking up in a pool of perspiration. We did not have to use the screen porch on the back of the house anymore. The cooler changed our way of life, and my folks remodeled the porch into three more rooms before 1940. Dad took the new cooler invention to Barstow to be added to his Cottage Street apartments. Many other railroad men who had to sleep during the daytime soon added the coolers to their dwellings.

Bill had this to say about his invention:

After people started building their cooler frames, the stores, such as Claypools and the Lumber

Yard, took the responsibility of ordering bigger fans for people to use in their home-made coolers. I did not take out a patent on my idea because the people in Needles were my friends and it was a needed item by all of us. I was just glad to see people get cool. If my cooler had not worked a lot of people that would have left Needles and the desert remained for many years.

The cooler changed the way of life for people of the desert. Everytime we have summertime storms that turn off our electricity, think about how it was before!

CABLE TELEVISION IN BARSTOW
by Dean M. DeVoe as told to LaRue Slette

Cable television in Barstow was a great boon to home entertainment, removing many obstacles to satisfactory television reception in this area. Previously to get any kind of reception at all required very high antennas, and then only few broadcasting stations could be reached.

In August 1952, two San Bernardino men, Charlie Ball and his friend Jerry, who were in the television set sales and services business, proposed a television cable system to Roy Brown, owner of Barstow Furniture Co., Inc., and later to Dean M. DeVoe, a local businessman. They explained that Barstow could not receive good television reception without a cable because television signals, unlike radio signals, do not follow the contour of the earth's surface, but are transmitted in a straight line. Because of this, mountainous terrain or even the curvature of the earth would block out a television signal, causing either poor reception or none at all. By placing an antenna on top of a mountain, a strong signal could be received and, by way of coaxial cable, that signal could be brought into the town to serve the people.

The first cable system was promoted in Astoria, Oregon, and a second in Palm Springs; Barstow would be the third. Work on the cable system began in June 1952, and was completed in time for Barstow to view that year's election returns. By 1954, there were 1,200 subscribers.

At first, the company was able to pick up only three signals strong enough to put on the system, channels 2, 4, and 5. The company had many problems with cable and electronic equipment which was just about as new as the business itself. Because of the high cost of construction, the company charged $59.50 for a hook-up fee, and $4.00 per month for the service, plus 50 cents for each additional outlet. With the help of Bank of America and Security Pacific Bank, the company was able to expand.

DeVoe tells an amusing anecdote from the company's early days of growth and expansion:

We were constructing our line out to the Marine Base and we had two sets of telephone poles on which we could string our line, one on each side of the highway. We chose the one route because there were half a dozen people on that side of the highway who were anxious to get the service.

Suddenly the office got a call from the construction foreman saying that some woman had driven a pickup truck over the cable which was still on the ground, and had tied a rather vicious dog to the truck so that no one could approach it. She said she would not move the truck until she had talked to me. I rushed out there to find out what the problem was, and she informed me we had no right on her property even though we were on the utility right-of-way, and she was going to leave the truck there until I agreed to give her free television reception for the rest of her life. I told her we had no other choice then but to cross the highway and string the cable down the other side, but in so doing it would eliminate the possibility of giving TV reception to the six neighbors on down the street from her. Her answer to that was she could care less about her neighbors. We had no choice but to move our cable and it was several years before we were able to finally provide all those people on that side of the road with cable reception.

DeVoe also commented:

In the early period of development, we were hard put to find qualified, experienced men to string cable, which had to be done on telephone poles. As a result, a great deal of our early construction was done on weekends when we could hire electric company and telephone company men to do the work. We had the same type of problem with electronic technicians. For a while we used a chap who maintained all the radio equipment for the Santa Fe Railroad. Joe Dugan, whom I had known for sometime, came to me and wanted a job. He had just closed out a highway garage and cafe he had out toward Baker. I was not quite sure of his ability so I hired him on a part time basis. His abilities were such that within a month he became an expert in the field of electronics. He already knew the pole construction business. As the company grew, Joe became the chief engineer of all the construction and maintenance of the system.

The signal picked up at the original antenna site on Block B Hill was so weak that the picture quality was poor. Company technicians were constantly testing for a site with stronger reception. One was finally found just off Ft. Irwin Road, west of the cemetery. At this location, the system was able to expand to five

CALICO  PRINT.

VOL. IX.   CALICO, CALICO MINING DISTRICT, SAN BERNARDINO COUNTY, CAL., OCTOBER 10, 1886.   NO. 14.

197

THE BARSTOW PRINTER

Mojave River Valley and Desert Interests

The Barstow Printer first edition rolled off the press July 1, 191_
Results of a contest renamed the newspaper *The Desert Dispatch*
October 28, 1958

VOLUME 1   BARSTOW, CALIFORNIA, FRIDAY, FEBRUARY 27, 1914.   NUMBER 35

...ALIFORNIA, FRIDAY, JANUARY 30, 1914. No 3_

INTERIOR VIEW OF THE HOME OF THE BARSTOW PRINTER—MECHANICAL DEPARTMENT

FRIDAY, JANUARY 23, 1914. No. 30

Barstow Brevities

The north side is on a boom as a residence section. Two new houses are being erected by Clarence H. Crooks and Lynn Crooks on lots purchased in the new addition along the north road.

Episcopal services will be held in Fletcher's Opera house Sunday morning at 10 o'clock. A cordial invitation is extended to all to come and hear a good sermon by Rev. J. J. Perry.

Dr. H. W. Linhart paid a professional visit to Ryan, Inyo Co., this week.

Mr. and Mrs. W. B. Sullivan are now settled in their new home, the Bedell place in West Barstow, Mrs. Sullivan having returned to Barstow last week.

Mrs. D. C. Henderson has fitted up the old telephone exchange, next to the toy store, for a mission hall, where gospel meetings will be held.

Mr. and Mrs. T. A. Kuhn and little daughter, and Mr. and Mrs. Morris Paul of Kansas City, are on a lake to San Francisco. They arrived in Barstow Sunday and stopped over until Tuesday evening, when they resumed their visit. They are all in excellent health.

MINERS AND MINING

Copper ore is being hauled out from the Greenwater mine in Death Valley by auto truck to the L. A. P. road at the rate of a carload a week for shipment to the Salt Lake smelter.

Rails are being shipped in for the proposed railroad from Death Valley Junction to the borax deposits by the Pacific Coast Borax Co.

Ben Hemus' camp was robbed recently while he was away. Several tools and machinery parts were taken. He has no clue to the robber. His grub supplies were short at the time, or his loss might have been greater.

George Parks will return to his gold property near Killeck soon to continue operations.

C. E. Goodrich will leave for Amboy next week to put in some more machinery for the Gold Belt Mining Co., whose property lies south of Amboy.

Buell Funk, Walter Olivier and J. B. Osborne will shortly put new life into an old silver property at Calico by resuming operations in mine and mill. C. E. Goodrich will put their five-stamp mill in shape for working on his return from the Gold Belt in a couple of weeks.

A. Ferguson, of Pasadena, manager of the American Opal Co., expects to resume work very shortly at the mines north of Barstow.

NEW MANAGEMENT

With this issue of the Barstow Printer the old management steps down and out and Mr. Oswald Wilson and his son Mr. J. Harold Wilson, successful newspaper men of wide experience, assume editorial and business management of the Barstow Printer. These gentlemen fully appreciate the opportunities for development in the Mojave Valley, and we feel sure that they will make the Barstow Printer a success and a credit to the community. We ask the people of Barstow and the Mojave Valley to give these gentlemen their hearty support and help to make the Barstow Printer the best paper in Southern California.

Thanking our friends for support given and wishing each and every one a Merry Christmas and a Happy New Year, we are, yours truly,
G. E. CAPPS.

BARSTOW, CALIFORNIA, FRIDAY, DECEMBER 4, 1914. No. 29

UNDER NEW MANAGMENT

National Highway Notes

H. P. Hosken of the Desert Auto Co., Kingman, Ariz., came in from Los Angeles, Wednesday, in a new Studebaker 6. He brought a team of horses thru the pass with him to make sure of getting thru with the machine. He left here Thursday morning for Kingman.

The first move in Congress toward the construction of a bridge over the Colorado river at Needles has been made by Congressman Hayden, of Arizona, supported by Congressman Kettner, in the introduction of a bill for that purpose. It calls for an appropriation of $1000 to investigate conditions and make plans.

Railroad Affairs

Since the recent floods caused some bad washouts on the S. P. from Mojave south, trains from that road have come over the Santa Fe and turned here for the north and south. The Santa Fe has furnished oil and water for their engines.

PERSONAL

W. R. White, of Winslow, Ariz., arrived in Barstow today to take up his duties as local agent for the Santa Fe. Mrs. White and daughter are here also, and the Printer extends a hearty welcome to them in behalf of the people of Barstow and vicinity. Here other branch...

Barstow Brevities

Daggett and Barstow schoolboys baseball clubs will play here tomorrow (Saturday) afternoon. Get out and root.

Mrs. Lubin J. Henderson, who is with her children in San Bernardino, visited Barstow a few days ago on the occasion of her wedding anniversary. She returned to the city Tuesday.

E. L. Stanfield visited Los Angeles on business this week.

Dr. H. W. Linhart spent a few days in San Francisco on business.

E. T. Hillis, G. D. Hutchison, W. C. Deschler and Lon Reedy were in the Kings River country for a few days looking over a land proposition. Lon Reedy picked up 20 acres of it. Before returning, Mr. Hillis paid a visit to relatives in Fresno.

The man arrested here last Friday by Officer Wells by request of Officer Cahill of Salt Lake City, proved to be Carlson, and not Applequist who was wanted for murder at Salt Lake. He was turned loose.

C. E. Williams is again in the hospital at Los Angeles, with stomach trouble. Thursday morning he came through an operation successfully and was reported as doing well. Mrs. Albright is at the hospital today, to learn his exact condition.

Down on the Farm

B. A. Harland recently had an I. H. engine of 12 h.p. installed on his place east of Barstow. He is preparing to make final proof on his homestead, and has been having some trouble with his old engine. With his new outfit he feels that his success is assured.

F. G. Mitchell has three acres in alfalfa and 17 more leveled for that crop and will have a larger garden patch this year than last. Eight acres have been prepared for fruit trees, and Mr. Mitchell will put in several acres of kafir corn and other forage crops. His application has been made for final proof. He is sinking his big well deeper for greater supply of water.

Zanini Brothers are connecting the residences on the ranch by private telephone. About a mile of wire will be used. Four or five acres will be added to their alfalfa fields, making over acres all told. A large variety of garden truck will be raised on the ranch this summer, as usual.

W. D. Riche is deepening his well in North Barstow and will prepare for planting 850 fruit trees and grapevines. He will put in 10 acres to apples, and one acre each to cherries and grapes, also one acre to a variety of other fruits. He intends to test out a variety of vegetables this summer.

BARSTOW, CALIFORNIA, FRIDAY, FEBRUARY 13, 1914. No. 3_

Barstow Brevities

Phone your news items to 92.

E. L. Stanfield is posting 75 signs on the roads indicating distances and direction to the Central Garage, Barstow

Donald Henderson, at Ramona hospital, San Bernardino, is able to be about and will shortly return to Barstow.

T. G. Nicklin is in Los Angeles for a couple of weeks.

W. W. Jones is spending a few days in Colton and Los Angeles on a mining deal.

The ladies of the Catholic church of Barstow will give an oyster supper for the benefit of the church building fund at Fletcher's Theatre, Monday, Feb. 16, from 4:30 p.m. to 7 p.m. All are invited.—Advertisement.

Something new in the "For Sale" column, on fourth page.

Robert Bentley, a barber recently employed in Barstow, died of tuberculosis Wednesday morning at the hospital in San Bernardino, and was buried Friday. He came here from Bakersfield about four months ago. He was 30 years old and married. Bakersfield papers please copy.

The Orange Show edition of the Kingdom of the Sun, Mrs. Gregory's souvenir publication is off the press and is a splendid piece of work in the artistic sense as well as a good adjunct to the show.

Spend your money with Printer advertisers.

We hear on good authority that Charlie Williams is making good pro-...

Bond Election Tuesday

An election will be held next Tuesday to vote on the proposition to bond San Bernardino county for $1,750,000 to build good roads in this county.

The sum of $1,625,000 is proposed to be spent in building cement roads south of the mountains—146 miles at about an average cost of $10,000 per mile.

The desert's share, according to the assessed valuation, is $104,000, but we have been apportioned the round sum of $125,000 to build 225 miles of desert road and bear one-third the cost of building a bridge across the Colorado river as a link in the Santa Fe-Grand Canyon-Needles National Highway.

This question of bonds or no bonds has been thrashed out all over the county. The conditions in the citrus fruit districts of the county are entirely different to the conditions on the desert. The great amount of assessable property in those districts demands that good roads be built. The people there can afford to bond themselves to build the finest cement roads. That section is what is known in the east as a metropolitan district. The distances between cities are short, some of the cities adjoin each other. The roads in many cases are short connections between the streets of different small cities. The demand is to make the country roads there as good as the city streets.

What kind of roads can the desert expect for $550 per mile, while the cement roads in the citrus section are to cost $10,000 per mile? An estimate given by a practical road man states...

National Highway Note_

Several applicants have made propositions to the city council of Needles for the operation of a ferry across the river to the Arizona side, until such time as a bridge is built. This will be an additional help in boosting the Santa Fe-Grand Canyon-Needles National Highway, in fact, one of its most important links.

The Victor Valley people are boosting for a road to Palmdale to connect with the road now under construction from that town to Los Angeles. This would save the desert traveler a distance of 28 miles in the trip from Victorville to Los Angeles.

The Needles' Eye says that a proposition was submitted to the Chamber of Commerce of that city by the "Chamber of Commerce of Barstow" for an automobile trip to the Grand Canyon on April 17. The matter was given to a committee for consideration but was turned down, as weather conditions at the Grand Canyon at this time of the year are not conducive to the happiness of pleasure seekers. But the strange part of this is that Barstow has no Chamber of Commerce, but ought to have one. Anyone representing himself as an officer of the "Barstow Chamber of Commerce" should be given no consideration.

FROM THE TOURISTS' REGISTE_

W. A. Bohland, J. S. Sophy and S. _. Braggs, of Lindsay, passed through Barstow last Saturday returning from a business trip to Parker and Blyth_ channels.

The industry was so new and knowledge so limited all of us building these systems were hard put to know proper procedures. We were being harassed by legislators on both the federal and state levels who wanted to place tight controls over us so we had to combat them in some way. We formed a national television cable association with less than one hundred members throughout the nation at the time. In January of 1953, the association met in San Francisco, with manufacturers showing their wares, and so on. You never saw such a bunch of scared people as those attending. None of us knew how to approach the legislators on the state level, much less in Washington. One of the manufacturers of equipment, who exhibited at the meeting and later came to Barstow selling some of his equipment, was a man named Milton Shapp. He is now Governor of Pennsylvania and a candidate for the Presidency.

Early in the cable company's history, some unscrupulous people discovered that if they punched a hole in the cable and moved their antenna close by they could pick up a pretty good signal. This, of course, was easy to detect. Others were more clever; they put a small hole in the cable, inserted a thin wire, taped it to the telephone drop, and ran it into the house for free TV. This practice was finally stopped by taking a few people to court, as there were laws against such misuse. In every case the judge found in favor of the company and ordered violators to pay the company for the whole time involved.

By this time, the company consisted of five individuals: Dean DeVoe, president, Dorothy Jones, vice-president, Gladys McMullen, credit manager, Harry Ford, auditor, and Irene DeVoe, a member of the board.

During this period, the technical advances in the industry made it possible to locate an antenna site closer to the transmitter on Mt. Wilson and beam, via microwave, to the receiver in Barstow. This microwave made possible a total of seven channels, and reception of superior quality.

Prior to the installation of the microwave, the stock holders sold their interests in the company. Western Video bought the cable company with its 4,000 subscribers, and owned it for approximately one year. It was then sold to the Jack Kent Cook interests. Two years later the Continental Telephone Company bought the cable system. Eventually the Federal Communications Commission handed down a ruling which forced the telephone company to sell all their television cable interests. Warner Cable, a subsidiary of Warner Pictures, was the successful bidder, and is the present owner of the Barstow system, with over 6,000 subscribers.

Dean DeVoe was active in the National Television Cable Association and served on the Board for several years. He was one of the organizers and twice president of the California Cable Association. In the beginning, there were only eight members. It presently has a membership of over 500. Because of his activities in both associations, Dean DeVoe was one of the first of ten men to be recognized as pioneers in the industry.

Chapter VIII

Progress and Promises

*The beauty of God
In lonely desert landscapes . . .
Tomorrow's bright hope.*

EARLY MAP NAMES FOR BARSTOW

by Mrs. Ralph (Alice) Salisbury
Barstow Womens Club 1963-1964

The earliest known reference to the site of the present town of Barstow was a verbal one. Though for a long time the site listed no permanent white homemakers, it was widely known as the meeting place of four old pioneer trails that continued as one trail along the course of the Mojave River and over Cajon Pass to the coastal basins of California.

The "upside down" Mojave River flowed extensively enough above ground to enable this trail junction to offer shade from old cottonwood trees, fresh drinking water and animal forage, features gratefully enjoyed by desert-wracked early explorers, and later by mule caravaners and covered wagon travelers.

Inevitably a trading post appeared on this site where an enterprising businessman, Ellis Miller, supplied trail travelers and prospectors with groceries, meat brought by local hunters, hardware, hay and mining equipment. A few families settled near Miller's trading post. From the abundance of wild grape vines growing on the nearby river banks, Miller called his post Grapevine. Lafayette Mecham established Fish Ponds, a second trading post a few miles down the river to the east.

It was at Grapevine that Robert Whitney Waterman heard rumors of a heavy silver vein some three miles north of the station. The richly yielding silver deposit that Waterman located and developed resulted in the birth, in 1880, of a lively little community surrounding his mill. Waterman boasted a well-stocked store, a Post Office, a small school (the first one to appear in the Barstow region) and a number of dwellings.

Various railroad enterprises began to shape desert community development. From 1882 Southern Pacific freight and passenger trains ran between the towns of Mojave and Needles. The California Southern laid tracks between San Diego and San Bernardino. Santa Fe engineered a merger of these lines to add to its transcontinental system. The union point for this merger was a rail locale so close to Waterman's little settlement that the name Waterman's Station or Junction appeared on 1885 maps of the region displacing the map name Grapevine.

With Waterman Mine closing and the historic down plunge of the price of silver, the little Waterman community declined rapidly and was finally absorbed into the fast growing Santa Fe headquarters developing in the Mojave River bottom area. This site promptly took the middle name of William Barstow Strong, to honor this noted pioneer president of the Santa Fe organization. The name Waterman's Station disappeared from the maps and the name Barstow was established permanently and officially as the name of this rapidly growing community in 1886.

This river bottom "town site" featured a two story brick station with a Harvey House eating place annex, several stores and saloons, private dwellings and boarding houses, all in close contact with a big roundhouse, repair shops and a constantly growing number of freight and passenger rails. Inevitably its history was bound to be dramatic and hazardous.

On five occasions "jinx" fires violently assailed the crowded civilian quarters as well as Santa Fe railroad facilities until finally river bottom dwellers, generously backed by the Santa Fe organization, formally decided to initiate a wholesale "exodus" from the crowded river bottom to "the heights" now known as Main Street.

Although this general exodus occurred in the 1920's, some of the households had already moved up the south side of the river bottom to an area now referred to as Hutchison Street.

Also, this exodus in the 1920's had been anticipated by a farsighted individual. Charlie Williams, who had put through a homestead deal in 1911, and from that date had been busily selling lots in the Main Street area to a number of early Barstow residents.

In 1915, on one of Charlie Williams' lots, appeared the first building to house Barstow High School.

A half century later Barstow claimed a population of over 17,000.

BARSTOW FIRE DISTRICT

by Willis Pinkerton, Jr., Fire Chief

Barstow was known in its earliest days as Waterman and received its first fire protection from the steam locomotive switch engines in the yards of the Atchison, Topeka and Santa Fe Railroad. The only buildings protected were those within several hundred feet of the railroad tracks and the only water available to fight a fire was the water in the tanks (tenders) of the steam locomotives. Water pressure for fire-fighting was generated by a steam-driven pump.

There were several serious fires in 1906, 1908, 1921 and 1923 which led to the formation of the Barstow Fire Protection District. Throughout all those years, there was no fire insurance to help recover fire losses because no insurance company would take a chance of providing such coverage where no organized fire protection was available.

On May 24, 1926 the Barstow Fire District formed under Act 1174 of the General Laws of the State of California as it appeared in the State Statutes of 1881, amended in 1899, and 1909, and then becoming Act 2593 in the year 1919.

The County Board of Supervisors appointed Dr. A.C. Pratt, Reese Dillingham, and E.L. White as Commissioners. The first fire engine, a 1922 Model T Ford combination hose and chemical, was purchased in September 1926. The original list of volunteer firemen

1 *Barstow Old Town June 11, 1921*

included: F.E. Slaton, E.C. Saunders, George Cunningham, N.F. Platt, J.J. Taylor, Fred Bauer, Ed Burke, Ed Harris, R.R. Burke, A.R. Meek, Harvey Mosier, A.H. Pendleton, Homer Martin and James Leggett.

On October 16, 1929 Fire Commissioner Chairman, George Cunningham, called a meeting with Fire Commissioners R.M. Dillingham, J.A. Morgan and Fire Chief E.L. White. They purchased a Chevrolet-Yeager pumper with a 300 gallon per minute capacity prospect pump for $1,117.00. Throughout the town the pumper was called "the little red fire engine."

The volunteer firemen depended on the Santa Fe Power House steam whistle to call them to duty. It was also the only place where someone was always present who could receive a fire call and notify the firemen by a coded signal. There were very few telephones, but there was a single party line to the powerhouse for the purpose of reporting fires.

Fire insurance protection became available in 1926 with the forming of the fire district and the acquisition of the Model T Ford chemical fire engine, but in the fall of 1930 the Board of Fire Underwriters of the Pacific made their first actual survey of Barstow's fire protection that provided the basis for a class eight grading.

On May 5, 1931 Fire Commissioners George Cunningham, George Henderson and C. Edwin Hill resolved to purchase property on First Street from Harry Kelly for a fire station. A contract to W.W. Clark to build a house for the fire engine at a cost of $1,035.00 was awarded in 1932.

A contract had been previously awarded to the Gamewell Fire Alarm Company to install seven street fire alarm boxes on September 23, 1931.

The water system providing the few fire hydrants had been installed by the Atchison, Topeka and Santa Fe Railway in 1919, and, aside from supplying the rail yards, only extended south from the yards one street. The American States Water Service Company of California acquired the water system in 1923, and in later years changed their name to the Southern California Water Company.

On June 13, 1934 a meeting was called at the White and Platt Drugstore to organize a more effective fire brigade with E.L. White continuing as Fire Chief; Ed Harris, George Henderson, and George Cunningham, Assistant Chiefs; Engineers Ed Hill, Russell Riley, Evert Williams and A.S. Schmitt; Firemen Ogden Platt, Harvey Rowe, Herb Brandon, Clarence Crooks, Ollie Finke, Kenneth Marvin, Fred Steward and a Mr. Cole and Duncan.

After several years of planning a Town Hall-Fire Station, ground was broken on January 13, 1936 for the building at 209 North First Street. Funds for the construction were made available through the Federal Public Works Administration, and work began on the two-and-one-half story building.

The need for a more dependable fire engine was met when, in August 1938, a 600 gallon per minute Seagrave fire engine was purchased. The new engine was painted white instead of the traditional red, so it could be seen better.

On August 4, 1938 Fire Commissioners George Henderson, Ed Hill and George Cunningham ordered Board Clerk E.L. White to file an application with the Federal Public Works Administration for additional financing to complete the construction of the Town Hall. On September 23, 1939 the building was appropriately dedicated by the Native Sons of the Golden West with the laying of a plaque in the entry to the building. Quoted the *San Bernardino Daily Sun* of September 25, 1939:

> The dedicatory ritual of the Native Sons of the Golden West was performed by Grand Officers of the lodge Saturday afternoon, September 23, 1939, at the dedication of Barstow's new Town Hall. The rites were identical with those at the dedication of the Golden Gate Bridge, the California building on Treasure Island, and at the new San Bernardino City Hall.

> Following the dedicatory address by Eldred L. Meyer, Acting Grand President, the bronze plaque was set into the threshold of the building, pledging to the preservation of Truth, Liberty and Toleration. E.L. White, Clerk of the Board of Fire Commissioners, accepted the building in the name of the Board and also accepted the Bear Flag presented by Leon Gregory, President of the Arrowhead Parlor of the Native Sons.

> Especially gratifying to the large audience of townspeople was the introduction by Judge L.J. Henderson of E.L. White as the one man whose untiring efforts and unswerving faith have made the erection and completion of the new building a reality . . . .
> Following Chief White's address, Mrs. C.C. McClellan, President of the Women's Club, introduced Mrs. Ralph Salisbury who presented the "Father of the Town Hall" with a token of appreciation from the women of the community.

> Distinguished guests present for the ceremonies included Judge Donald E. Van Luven, Supervisor A.L. Doran, Supervisor John Andreson, Eldred L. Meyer, Herman Lichenberger, Walter C. Richards, John Olivas, Dr. Herman Katz, Douglas Mecham, Elmer Hoien, Leon Gregory, and William Allen. Dr. R.L. White of San Bernardino, Past President of the Arrowhead Parlor of the Native Sons of the Golden West and son of Chief E.L. White received special mention.

During 1938, a new fire station under construction and an improved record of fire protection, the Board of Fire Underwriters of the Pacific regarded the fire protection a one-grade improvement to a Class seven.

In 1939 the firemen organized the Barstow Firemen's Service Club, a social and civic organization. Their first effort was a Firemen's Ball, using the profits from this dance in 1940 to purchase the first resuscitator. Profit from their Second Annual Ball, in 1941, was used to purchase the first protective coats and pants for the firemen.

In the early months of 1940 E.L. "Gene" White resigned as Fire Chief, but he had become a fire

2   Barstow fire 1921 - Note double roof on the right

3   1938 Seagraves engine "Bud" Crooks driver
old engine on right

5   Fire engine with crews 1940-41

4   1952 Seagraves engine

Barstow
Fire
Department

6   oops

department legend in his 14 years of service. Russell Riley was appointed Interim Fire Chief in January 1940.

O.C. Gilson became Fire Chief in July 1940 by the appointment of the Board of Fire Commissioners who, at that time, were Russell Riley, Earl Barton and Leonard Zagortz.

In 1941 a new Ford-Seagrave 500 gallon per minute fire engine was purchased to replace the 1929 Chevrolet engine.

O.C. Gilson resigned as Fire Chief in 1942. A. Howard Pendleton was appointed by the Board of Commissioners to the Fire Chief's position; he had been Assistant Chief. Pendleton with his Mother, Mrs. Jennie Pendleton, and his brother, Glenn, who in past years had also been a volunteer fireman, operated Pendleton's Market at 114 West Main Street. With the war expanding in 1942 and 1943, men were being drafted or volunteering for military duty, and the ranks of the volunteer firemen were dwindling. Pendleton trained firemen's wives to fight fire and to perform first aid: he met with school officials and received cooperation in allowing him to recruit 10 high-school boys for a fire auxiliary that would respond from school to assist his firemen. Under the training of Captain E.R. "Ed" Amende, the 10 young men learned quickly and several went on to become professional firefighters. That auxiliary force included: Alfred B. Willis, Bill Robbins, Louis Winningham, Maurice Howland, James Howland, Willis R. Pinkerton Jr., William "Sonny" Wright, Robert Miller, Robert Rowe and Robert Newbrough. Regulars on the rolls in January 1943, besides Pendleton as Chief, included: Assistant Chiefs Homer Wynn and Reece Dillingham; Captains Ardell Schmitt, Leonard Zagortz, Thomas Earls and E.R. Amende; Drivers Frank Good, Omer Johnson, Chester Byrnes and Percy Mitchell; Firemen Thad Covington, Ray Dutcher, Bert Bruning, George Beardon, Louis Hopkins, Bill Horsman, Nick Keating, Larry Lovelady, Earl LaFont, N.K. "Bud" Millett, Dale T. Mossburger, Walter Lauterback, E.S. Thrasher, James DeWolf, Alfred Campbell and Edward King.

In 1947 the town of Barstow became the City of Barstow, by election of the people. But as city functions were being established the City Council determined that the fire protection responsibility should remain with the Barstow Fire District.

In 1952, a new 1,000 gallon per minute Seagrave fire engine was purchased and a second fire station built at the corner of Nancy and G Streets to provide protection for the growing west side of town. Land was purchased from R.W. Fogelson and the building constructed by George Warner from Victorville. In January of 1955 the district received a Class six grading.

Also in 1955 the first two-way radio communications equipment was installed in the fire engines, and the Fire Chief's pickup truck. The San Bernardino County Sheriff's radio frequency was used and their dispatcher became the base station. At this time the fire apparatus consisted of the 1938 and 1952 Seagrave Pumpers and the 1941 Ford Seagrave Pumper. Those men serving on the Board of Fire Commissioners in 1955 were: Leonard Zagortz, Dr. Bruce Wilkes, and L. Paul O'Donnell. Earl Stanton, City Clerk for the City of Barstow, served as Secretary to the Fire Board also.

A.H. "Howard" Pendleton, who had served 14 years as Fire Chief, and a total of 30 years on the fire department, resigned the position in January 1957.

Arthur Mitchell, who had been serving as a part-time Fire Inspector along with his duties as a Building Inspector for the City of Barstow, assumed the added responsibility of Interim Fire Chief until a permanent appointment could be made.

1956 was also an election year for two seats on the Board of Fire Commissioners. The two new members were Alfred B. Willis, a volunteer with nine years service, and E.R. Amende, also a former volunteer fireman who had retired from ten years active service in 1948. Leonard Zagortz remained on the Board as its third member. Willis was chosen Chairman and Amende as Clerk.

Willis R. Pinkerton, Jr., a 14 year veteran of the volunteer fire service with the rank of Assistant Chief and a full time Crew Captain with the U.S.M.C. Supply Center Fire Department, was selected Fire Chief effective July 1, 1957. Since its inception in 1926 the fire department had been a total volunteer operation. The Fire Chief's salary was set at $500 per month, and a full-time Fire Inspector was employed in February 1958 at a salary of $450 per month. R.R. "Rex" Dillingham, a 10 year volunteer fireman, was employed as the Fire Inspector.

Property was purchased at 441 Adele Street in August 1958 for a third fire station to serve the east end of Barstow which was developing at a rapid pace. This was to be but a temporary location and a small, single stall building was constructed by Stanley & Rognlie Contracting firm.

On July 1, 1959 three additional full time men were employed; two drivers, Stanley Murphy and Eugene Reed, and one fireman, Donald C. Burgett. Murphy and Burgett were promoted to Captains in 1962. Volunteer firemen began a night sleeper duty schedule for faster response to alarms.

The district boundaries were expanded in October 1959 to include the community of Lenwood when the people of that area petitioned for annexation. A used fire engine was purchased, and the Lenwood Town Hall, in its unfinished stage of construction, was given to the district for a fire station. An additional 10 men were trained, the building completed, and a small park developed by the firemen. The fire station was dedicated to public fire protection in 1961. The original 10 men at this station included: Wesley Jaska, Assistant Chief; Gordon Stricler and Richard Thomas as Captains; Drivers Joseph Hawkins, Walter Van De Walker and Tommy J. Craig; and Firemen Ernest McMichael, Ladell Proctor, Robert Avery and Jim Whitaker.

The State Civil Defense Office Fire and Rescue Division, recognizing the ideal location of Barstow for the placing of backup equipment, offered a heavy-duty rescue truck and a fire pumper to the district to be used locally or to dispatch in the surrounding area or Southern California in disaster situations. The district accepted this equipment which meant added protection for the people of the high desert area at no cost to the local taxpayer.

During 1961 and 1962 the District and the City of Barstow worked closely in developing a Civil Defense Plan that received state-wide recognition. Alfred Willis, Chairman of the Board of Commissioners, was named Citizen of the Year in 1962 for his leadership. Three underground, radioactive fall-out proof shelters were constructed at fire stations and eight other shelters were built at firemen's homes during this period. All labor was donated by the local firemen with the district paying for material only on its premises and the respective firemen paying for the material in their personal shelters. John Patton, a long-time volunteer fireman, was recognized for his leadership in this program also by being named "Fireman of the Year" in 1961.

In 1962 the Board of Commissioners, comprised of Alfred Willis, Homer Wynn, and E. S. Thrasher, awarded a bid to the Seagrave Corporation for three new 1,000 gallon per minute pumpers, and a contract to the Gamewell Fire Alarm Company for the installation of 30 additional street fire alarm boxes and new receiving equipment at the headquarters station.

The big sirens that had summoned the volunteer firemen for over 20 years were replaced by radio receivers for each fireman in 1963 when the firemen, in a money-make project, raised the funds for the receivers and the District installed their own radio base station. Ray Eddy, President of the Firemen's Service Club, was awarded the Fire Chief's "Fireman of the Year" honors for his leadership in the radio fund-raising program in 1963.

With the new fire engines in service, the 1938 Seagrave Pumper was sold to the Barstow Lion's Club, who, in turn, gave it to Tecate, Mexico, in a "Hands Across the Border Program." The 1941 Ford Seagrave was sold to the Hinkley Volunteer Fire Company for one dollar in a "Help-Thy-Neighbor" activity, and the 1952 Seagrave was moved to Station four in Lenwood.

The improvements made with the new pumpers, new radio system, full-time personnel, added fire alarm equipment and updated records system, was sufficient evidence to the Fire Underwriters of the Pacific to award a better fire insurance class following their grading in 1963.

The personnel roster in January 1963 read: L. Rowe, Leon Dillingham, and Wesley Jaska, Assistant Chiefs; Rex Dillingham, Battalion Chief; Engine No. One Captain S. Murphy, D. Burgett and Bob Rowe; Engineers Gene Reed and Tommy Craig; Firemen John Patton, Lloyd Munson, Bob Washa and Dick Jacobsen. Engine No. Two Captains Clinton Proctor and Bob Mitchell; Engineers Bill Zualet, Ray Eddy and Bob Luse; Firemen James Bellomy, James Van Brunt, Q. Arend, and Bob Welker. Engine No. Three Captains Don Rowland and Ed Trowbridge; Engineers Bob

Stapp, H. Cockrell and Clyde Hessom; Firemen J. Myers, Don Braucher, Jerry Strong and Larry Hodges. Engine No. Four Captains Walt Van De Walker and Jim Whitaker; Engineers Joe Hawkins, Ernest McMichael and Ladell Proctor; and Firemen Bob Avery, Ken Curd, Bob Brunner and Carl Dickerson.

By 1965 the building, that had served the community well as its Town Hall, at 209 North First Street was fully utilized by the fire department. Through the years the building had been the meeting place for the local civic and fraternal organizations, the Office of Price Administration during the World War II years, California Highway Patrol, Barstow Justice Court, Barstow Police Department, City of Barstow, Council Chambers and County Assessor.

In 1961 the State Legislature passed a new statute that replaced all previous fire district laws including the original act under which Barstow Fire District had been formed in 1926. The Board of Fire Commissioners acted in December of 1965 to bring the Barstow Fire District under the "Fire Protection Act of 1961," in order to preserve local autonomy.

In August 1966 Barstow experienced its greatest fire loss when an 80,000 square foot warehouse totally burned out and an estimated $1,000,000 loss was recorded. In that fire it became evident that the capability to project high volumes of water from an elevated source was sorely needed. In 1968 the District acquired a 65-foot elevating platform, commonly referred to as a snorkel truck. An additional crew was trained in its operation and placed in service.

In the mid-1960's it had become evident that the fire headquarters building at 209 North First Street was outgrown for the amount of fire equipment and the job that had to be done from that location. A site was chosen at the corner of Virginia Way and Barstow Road as the best site for serving the greatest part of the district and the best location from which to serve the future population growth.

The site was acquired from the Barstow Park and Recreation District in 1969 at no cost, but with an agreement that the Fire District would level and grade the remaining park property along with the Fire District property for an expansion of their recreation programs.

The Board of Fire commissioners, whose title had become Board of Directors by the Fire Protection Act of 1961, was expanded from its original three-member status to a five-member board by a vote of the people on November 6, 1973. Edward Duitsman and Peter Duran were appointed to serve with Alfred Willis, Cleveland Harris and Joseph McMullin. McMullin had replaced Homer Wynn upon his retirement in 1970 after 32 total years of service as a fireman and board member. Alfred Willis resigned from the Board in July 1973 when he moved from the area and Guy Sawyer was appointed to fill his unexpired term. Willis' service had covered some 28 years as a fireman and board member.

At a special meeting, July 16, 1975, the Board of Directors made a decision to enter into a paramedic program and to send personnel for training at Riverside General Hospital. With this decision and the training and equipping of fire paramedics, a new dimension of service was provided for the people of Barstow Fire District.

At the District Board of Directors election on November 4, 1975 Joseph F. McMullin retained his seat on the Board, and Cleveland C. Harris was replaced by James H. Van Brunt, a former volunteer fireman and later a full time employee who had earlier retired.

The personnel roster at the close of 1975 included Fire Chief Willis R. Pinkerton; Assistant Chiefs Larry Rowe and Wesley Jaska; Battalion Chief Rex Dillingham; Inspector David Mathews; and Office Manager Jane Eddy. Engine No. One Captains S. Murphy and D. Burgett; Drivers Gene Reed and Lee Divine; and Firemen Jerry Trowbridge, D. Martinez, R. Ramos, P. Beltz, and J. Carpenter. Snorkel No. One, Captains Bob Mitchell and Bob Stapp; Drivers V. Wright, F. Sicks, K. Mack; Firemen M. Rowland, A. Carruthers, R. Ober and J. Harris. Engine No. Two, Captains C. Proctor and T. Craig; Drivers B. Luse, K. Amari and D. Milligan; with Firemen J. Bellomy, L. Hodges, J. Stapp

and M. Franey. Engine No. Three, Captains D. Rowland and E. Trowbridge; Drivers B. Zualet, J. Strong and M. Isaacson; and Firemen B. Wallace, R. Sanchez, A. Schroeder and C. Ward. Engine No. Four, Captains E. McMichael and W. Raley; Drivers R. Avery, S. Arges, and G. Edwards; and Firemen C. Dickerson R. Menie, M. Denbo, G. Milligan, B. Hogan, T. Welsh, B. Kinder and E. Johnson.

As Barstow Fire District prepared to celebrate its Golden Anniversary on May 26, 1976 it was interesting to note the meager beginning with one fire engine, a chemical and hose wagon, and a handfull of dedicated volunteer firemen and commissioners, which provided fire protection to a 1,000 population, and an assessed valuation tax base of less than $1,000,000 had grown to four fire pumpers, one 65-foot snorkel truck, four fire stations, 56 fire personnel—of which 15 are full time professionals, an office manager, and a five-member Board of Directors, providing modern fire suppression, fire prevention, and rescue service to a 25,000 population in an area of 31 square miles, on an assessed valuation tax base of $47,076,173.

INTERVIEW WITH JAMES KELLY LIFE-LONG RESIDENT OF BARSTOW
by Jack Westfall

Mr. Kelly was interviewed as a representative of that sizeable group of Barstow citizens who have lived here all their lives and seen many changes in the city and in our way of living, and yet is young enough not to be considered an "old timer."

Jim, as he likes to be called, was born in Barstow January 20, 1922. His parents, Harry and Jamie Kelly, came to Barstow three years earlier from Beaumont, California. Harry Kelly was the first male white child born in Beaumont (in 1887). He became a railroad engineer for the Southern Pacific while in Beaumont and was an engineer for the Santa Fe after moving to Barstow, continuing in that position until he retired in 1952.

Jim was born in a house not far from the former west tower of the Santa Fe railroad. The "old town" of Barstow was located on land which is now part of the Santa Fe yards, passenger train tracks on one side, and freight tracks on the other. An old photo, taken about 1918, shows the yard office, a ramp for foot traffic over the freight yards and up to Second Street, the Melrose Hotel, a blacksmith shop, a saloon and some other buildings. He said that Barstow "moved" from that site in the early 1920's.

Jim attended school through the 8th grade in an old school called simply "the grammar school," now Central High School. He recalls that it was built after the Long Beach earthquake "in 1930, I think." With memories of the damage done by the Long Beach quake, the builders of the Hutchison School constructed it very substantially.

As a boy, Jim and his friends hunted rabbits in the river bottom area and went swimming in pools scooped out of the river to provide storage water for the railroad

locomotive. He recalls that the town was friendly and neighborly, almost like a big family. The Hill family, who owned a dairy, gave a town picnic once a year for the entire community. Such treats as watermelon, peaches, and roast corn were served, and, of course, milk and ice cream. He remembers that, in the late '20's and early '30's, Jeramiah McCartney and George Boyd owned a mine about where the present drive-in theatre is located. Jim says the miners didn't get much valuable ore, just enough to keep them working at it.

In the 1920's and 1930's the railroad was the chief means of transportation. Six or seven passenger trains a day passed through Barstow. Automobiles were expensive and unreliable and service stations and garages were few and far between; it was risky to venture very far from home by car. An automobile trip to San Bernardino was a real adventure. The road through Cajon Pass was narrow, steep, and twisting; a tough test of a car's ability. The most popular car of that day, the Ford Model T, had more power in reverse gear than in forward gear, so drivers would sometimes back their cars all the way up that steep, twisting road on the return trip.

During prohibition there was some bootlegging, and a fair amount of "home-brew" manufacturing. Jim tells that his dad made one unsuccessful attempt to brew some homemade beer. Jim himself, and some of his friends, made and bottled a large batch of root beer one summer, putting it under the house to age. The root beer fermented and blew up, scaring the Kelly family nearly out of their wits, smelling up the place for weeks.

Entertainment was simple. There was a weekly dance in town, church "socials," but mostly at-home types of entertainment, hearts, flinch, pinochle, and

Uptown Barstow

7 Classroom bungalows Waterman School

10 Beacon Hotel—700 block East Main

11 Barstow grows late 30's

8 Forum Theatre—200 block East Main 1940's

11a Barstow grows late 50's

9 100 Block East Main 1930's

12 Snow on West Main 1949

later contract bridge. In the early 30's some of the more well-to-do families owned a marvelous new device, a radio. Some had speaker horns, others had to be heard by earphones.

In 1939 Jim graduated from the new Barstow High School. Previous to that the high school had been located where the El Rancho is now. With the outbreak of World War II in the autumn of 1939 Jim's older brother Harry enlisted in the British Royal Air Force, became a pilot, and was killed. Kelly Drive is named after him. Several other streets are named for Barstow men who were killed in World War II, including Bigger Street, Lance Street, Collins Court and Dolph Court.

Jim was attending Junior College in San Bernardino when America entered World War II in December 1941. He left college and was employed as a civilian at Camp Marr, the site of the present Fort Irwin. His job was helping to test missiles in the desert near the Goldstone area. In July 1942 Jim entered the Navy for the duration of the war and was discharged in December 1945 with the rating of chief radio technician.

He later worked for a couple of years with the Santa Fe Railroad and Shell Oil Company, then two years with the Marine Corps at Barstow as an electronics technician. Meanwhile, the Korean war had broken out, and Jim, who was in the Naval Reserve, was called to active duty. He served in the Navy from 1951 thru 1967 at Treasure Island, San Bernardino, Flagstaff and on the east coast, on cruisers in the Caribbean, and on a destroyer out of Japan.

Following discharge from the Navy in January 1967, Jim worked at the Marine Corps in Barstow as an electronics technician for two years, retiring in 1969.

Jim says that although he has seen a good deal of the world, Barstow is the place for him. In 1949 he married Barbara VonBrecton and they have three children. They have seen a lot of changes in Barstow over the years and are glad that the changes in the main have been gradual rather than abrupt.

While looking back fondly at the "old days," Jim feels that Barstow's future will be great and worthy of the heritage of the pioneers who struggled to establish the town.

MRS. ANTONIA V. ESPINOZA
by Richard V. Espinoza

Antonia V. Espinoza was born in Barstow February 11, 1917, where the present Santa Fe Railway shops are located. The houses there were later moved to Williams and Fredrick Streets to make room for the diesel shops.

Her father came to Barstow from Arizona in January 1913 as a track layer and worked for the Santa Fe until he retired in 1967. He and his father made cement blocks for the old Forum Theatre (now the Sears store) at Second and Main. Mrs. Espinoza still has the block-making machine they used at her home.

Antonia completed the eighth grade at Waterman school; in 1938 she graduated from Barstow High School, which was then located at First and Main.

Dillingham's grocery store was at Third and Cottage, across from Waterman School playground; a duplex is there now. A loaf of bread cost 10 cents and a pound of steak cost 25 cents. Coal for heating and cooling was delivered from Daggett.

When the flood of 1938 hit Barstow, only one house in the riverbottom area was not seriously damaged or washed away. It was a cement block house located behind the Chili Bowl on Irwin Road.

ONE BLOCK ON MAIN STREET
by Pat McCall Jackson

When we came to Barstow in 1945, the face of Main Street was much different than it is now. A good example is the block from the northwest corner of First and Main Streets (going west).

On the corner stood a Standard Service Station. The station was unique for two reasons: first its size, and second the fact that the entire area was covered with a roof. With twelve gas pumps, it was one of the largest in the state of California.

Next, looking west, was the Gold Star Cafe, run by "Pop" O'Hara and his family. Then came Lee Poole's A & C Cafe, which served American and Chinese food.

The Bank of America had a small branch next to Cunninghams Pharmacy. The pharmacy is still in the same place, although the building front was remodeled and the store has changed owners several times.

In these days the "one stop center" for Barstow residents was next to Cunninghams where the gas, electric and telephone companies had their business offices.

The Katz bar is another place of business that has retained the same name and address over the years. Next door was a Western Auto store operated by Chet Byrns.

The blacktop area where buses now park was the site of the Old Trails Inn, operated by the Papayianis family, Greek-Americans.

The Barstow Hardware Company at 139 West Main dealt in over ten thousand items. Next door west a small building shared by a Texaco Service Station and a shoe repair shop is now a parking lot.

Times change, businesses change, and buildings change. What does this block on Main Street look like today?

THIRTY YEARS WITH
BARSTOW WOMEN'S CLUB 1922-1952
excerpt: Friendly Relations with
Early Chamber of Commerce
by Alice Richards Salisbury

The effectiveness of Mrs. Pitcher's club stimulated the Barstow Chamber of Commerce. Leading members of the Chamber often addressed the Women's Club on various civic projects—to the mutual strengthening of both groups. Legend says the Chamber members never failed to find Women's Club refreshments most enticing, and bountiful too!

Old timers hereabouts still chuckle over the story of the first official community act of the club. Governor Stephens was due to make a speech in Barstow and a welcoming committee from the Chamber was to meet him on a train arriving in Barstow at a very early hour.

However, the night before Chamber members had attended a banquet and every one of the appointed welcoming committee overslept. Someone "in the know," realizing a crises was at hand, telephoned frantically to the President of the Women's Club to do something fast about meeting that approaching train!

Mrs. Pitcher certainly *DID* work fast, and Governor Stephens was delighted at the effusive welcome given him by a group of charming, wide-awake Club women bearing armfuls of exquisite desert lillies (a glamour feature hastily filched from Harvey House dining room decorations intended for the gala day ahead!)

BARSTOW LAGUNA COLONY
HISTORY OF THE MODERN INDIAN
by Winona Kenyon, 1963-64 Barstow Womens Club

The local Laguna colony is patterned after and is a branch of the parent body on the Laguna reservation in New Mexico.

Three Laguna Indians were sent to Barstow in 1942 to work for the Santa Fe Railroad according to the treaty between the railroad and the tribe. If their reception was favorable, they would remain; if not, they were to move on to San Bernardino. Mr. Henry Pachecho was their leader.

In 1942 the Lagunas lived in a camp built by Santa Fe. Here approximately 18 families lived in a communal manner. The homes were built of abandoned "reefers" (refrigerator cars). There was a courtyard surrounded by apartments. This colony kept alive their dances, weaving and silver jewelry making, selling whenever they could. Their dance groups entertained at P.T.A. affairs and in parades. Two champion hoop dancers were members of the dance group.

Other Laguna colonies were established in Richmond, Winslow, Los Angeles and San Bernardino. The Laguna men worked as laborers on the railroads, at Fort Irwin and Barstow Marine bases; many women worked also. Each colony keeps the other informed and local colonies take part in the politics of the parent group.

In the fall of 1964 the camp was torn down. The Barstow Women's Club gave the leader the form sent by the California Commission on Indian Affairs which investigates problems involving Indians, hoping some solution could be found to their plight. The majority bought new homes in a low cost subdivision.

The Laguna Tribe provided many evening entertainments at P.T.A. meetings. They presented tribal dances, after which native food and crafts were exhibited and sold. The dance group also performed at the Orange Show, Halloween Mardi Gras Parade and Daggett Pioneer Days.

(At the January 1976 Meet, LeRoy Pellman was elected to serve as Governor for the 18th time.)

BARSTOW NAVAJO TRIBAL COUNCIL HISTORY OF THE MODERN INDIAN

by Winona Kenyon — 1963-64, Barstow Womens Club

The Barstow Area Tribal Council was organized by Steve Gorman of Daggett, California approximately five years ago. Its main purpose is helping Navajo Indians find their place in society. There are approximately 80 members with dues of four dollars per year. This organization is a branch of the parent group in Window Rock, Arizona, which started after World War II.

Funds for the parent group are derived from natural resources: oil, uranium, gas, coal and timber. With these funds the tribe has set up its own government, museum, newpaper, arts and craft guild, motels, restaurants, furniture company, training schools, housing project and heavy equipment pool. These funds provide clothing for the school children and eye-glasses for the needy. The reservation is divided into 18 districts with funds being allocated to each, and to Area Councils.

There are many families in Barstow who board relatives to enable them to receive an elementary education. Many of these children need clothing. In 1964 more than 100 pupils were outfitted. Children who need eye-glasses are examined and fitted by an optician in Riverside, transportation is paid for by the

Council.

The local Council raises money through raffles and membership dues. Needy families are furnished loans without interest. The Council has the services of a qualified attorney; Mr. Gorman serves as liaison to assist the Indians in their trials and tribulations.

A Navajo Tribal dance group has been created and has performed at several functions. Some of the dances performed are: The Hoop Dance—of recent origin, representing all tribes and is a most competitive dance; Yei-be-chai—a nine day healing dance and a sacred ceremonial dance, held after the first frost and during the winter months; Corn Grinding Ceremony—a chant is sung while the women grind corn; and the traditional Riding Song—a song expressing their feelings to the Great Spirit and fellow man. This group keeps the Navajo culture alive, acquaints others with their customs and is excellent public relations.

NEW MEXICO TO BARSTOW

From family histories by Annie Barajas, Filomena Moya, Lugarda Silva Wallis, and Helen Torrez

Introduction by Thelma M. Carder

In the years following World War II Barstow unexpectedly became a Mecca for Hispanic residents of New Mexico, especially the community of Belen, just South of Albuquerque. Workers laid off by the Santa Fe Ice Plant or from other jobs in Belen found employment at the Marine Corps Supply Depot and Santa Fe Railroad in Barstow and sent for their families. Today these former New Mexicans—or Manitos—are an important part of the Barstow community.

Involved in this emigration to Barstow were several courageous women who decided a few years ago to enroll in a program to train bilingual aides for the local schools. Some became so enthusiastic about going to school after years spent rearing families that they went on to obtain Barstow College AA degrees.

Filomena Moya and Lugarda Silva Wallis graduated from the college with high grade-point averages—3.5 and 3.4. Mrs. Moya represented the New Mexican women in her class in receiving the John F. Kennedy award for courage.

One instructor asked the bilingual aide students to write the family histories which are the sources for this article. The idea originated with Dr. Carlos Cortez of the University of California, Riverside, Cortez asserts that most of the printed materials historians use for sources ignored the presence in the Southwest of residents of Spanish or Mexican descent. One way to recover this otherwise lost history is the writing of family histories.

Former New Mexicans do not regard themselves as Mexicans. They look back to a Spanish rather than a Mexican past. New Mexico had been governed by Spain for 200 years before becoming part of independent Mexico in 1821 and of the United States in 1848. Some typical Barstow surnames appear on the Belen census for 1790—Baca, Chavez, Peralta, Padilla, Luna, Lucero, Silva, Montoya.

Although they came from older communities, New Mexicans found Barstow to be more modern—"like moving to the city"—in comparison with the living conditions they had left at home. Some of their experiences and reactions to early days in Barstow follow:

FILOMENA MOYA:

After Pearl Harbor the Belen community was worried because many of the Belen boys were in the New Mexico National Guard, one of the first to go to war. Many never came back. Next came practice in air raids, blackouts, the drafting of our young men and fathers. Others went to defense jobs at home or came to the Naval shipyards in San Diego. Dad worked for the Santa Fe Pullman Company in Belen, servicing the troop trains that went by. He also formed a band, mostly family members, his four half brothers and myself. A guitar player, the only outsider, later became my husband. We played for wedding dances and receptions. This helped me pay my high school expenses.

In May 1947 dad was laid off by the Santa Fe in Belen, but he had heard of plentiful jobs at the Marine Base in Barstow, California.

He came to Barstow and was immediately hired as a cement mixer operator. He and other friends roomed together and we stayed home with mom. I began my high school as a senior in September 1947. My dad wrote about all the clerical jobs available at the Marine Base for after I graduated. Dad came for my graduation and I returned with him to a job waiting for me in Barstow. The rest of the family came two months later. I went to work at the Nebo Marine Base as a clerk-typist, GS-2.

My first home in Barstow was in a very small house on Main Street where Rosita's now stands. The Post Office was where Barstow Academy of Beauty is, the Bank of America where David's shop for men is and the rest of Main Street only went as far as the old Beacon Bowl Hotel.

I was afraid to walk down town by myself as my dad had warned me about Pachucos, Zootsuiters, and the rivalry between Barstow and New Mexican youth. I had no trouble and soon many Barstow girls became my friends as well as my co-workers.

I worked at the Marine Base until November 1949, when I was laid off in a reduction in force and by then my family had decided to go back to Belen, which made me happy because I was still going steady with my husband of today. My father went to work for Kirtland Air Force Base in Albuquerque and I remained at home with my parents until my marriage on April 26, 1950. My husband and I lived in his community,

Adelino, for two years.

Good-paying jobs weren't available and my husband worked on his father's farm, played in my dad's band, and took cabinet making under the G.I. bill.

He also worked part time in the summer for the Santa Fe Ice Company servicing refrigeration cars. After my husband had held several other temporary jobs, we again heard that the Barstow Marine Base was hiring. When we got to Barstow in January 1954 jobs were frozen, but I was hired at Ft. Irwin in April and about the same time my husband was called to the Marine Base where he still works.

ANNIE BARAJAS

My father came to Barstow in 1952 to find a better job. He was born in Santa Rita, New Mexico, where he helped his father deliver mail. My grandfather was a farmer and ran a Post Office. My father met and married my mother in Belen..

My father wanted his children to better themselves. He remembered Barstow from vacation trips and thought Barstow would open up new opportunities and better education for his children. He and mom made plans and we all moved to Barstow.

At first he worked for Santa Fe, but saw no way to get ahead. He quit and worked for almost a year at the Brubaker-Mann mill. Then he got an opportunity to work for Industrial Milling and Mining on Irwin Road. He managed this mill until he was murdered in 1960 by unknown persons.

Our way of life changed when we moved to Barstow. In Belen we had cold running water in our home. We also had electricity, which meant that we could have a radio, iron, and electric refrigerator. We also had a telephone. We bathed in a big tin tub. We had a garden in which we raised our own vegetables, our own chickens for eggs, and chopped our own wood for fuel. Our life was simple.

Sometimes on Sundays we would go to the theater and see the double feature. But, most of all I remember my mom and dad playing games with us in the evening.

When we came to Barstow all this changed. Here we had cold and hot running water, a big white shiny bath tub, and an inside toilet. No running outside in the middle of the night! Also electricity, radio, refrigerator, iron, and a black and white television. This we thought was really living. No chickens to take care of and no garden. Here we went shopping for our groceries and all our other needs. We didn't have to chop or cut wood. All we had to do was turn on the gas and right away you had heat or could start cooking. After a couple of burned fingers we learned how to regulate the flame. We missed our games with our parents. Father worked harder and he was tired most of the time. Or we had places to go—school games, parties and dates.

LUGARDA SILVA WALLIS

When my ex-husband Querino Silva was discharged from the service he couldn't find a job. Many other men were also getting out of the services and looking for jobs. He worked at the Ice Plant in Belen for a while and then was laid off. Since he couldn't find another job around home he decided to go west looking for one in Arizona. He wrote and said he was going on to California. He arrived in Barstow in February 1947, worked for Santa Fe, and later went to the Marine Base as a painter and later a painter foreman. He lived in Barstow about ten months before I could afford to come out with the children.

When I got here housing was so scarce that I had to live with one of my cousins. Eight of us shared one bedroom. At this time the sanitation board controlled the number of people who lived in one building. This board found out that we and our children were living with my cousin and I was called to appear before them. They told me that either I find a place of my own or I would have to go back to New Mexico. After a week or so of looking, this same sanitation board called me and we were able to rent a trailer from them. It was very small and I had three of the four children with me, but that was home for us.

As time went by we moved to a one bedroom apartment and as the family grew we moved to a two-bedroom apartment where there were ten children and the two of us. As time went on three of the girls were married, and in 1960 we moved to Montara to a three bedroom house.

In 1972 I married Harold Wallis. I have 23 grand-children and one great-grandchild, and one child still at home. Since earning my teachers' aide certificate and AA degree I have worked in several schools.

We would still like to go back to New Mexico, especially because my mother and sister live there. We may return if Santa Fe in Belen has their big opening.

HELEN TORREZ

Our lives changed totally when we came here. We came from the country to live in the city. When we came to California we moved right into a furnished house with refrigerator, washer, bathroom. We even had a telephone and television, which was a luxury for us.

Our religious ways changed. We would go to church every Sunday back home even if we had to walk about five miles, but we didn't mind or forget. Here it was too easy.

My children don't know what it is to go hungry or cold. Doctors are handy. They go to school by bus. We had to walk. Sometimes we couldn't go because the snow was too high and we didn't have warm clothing. In Adelino, New Mexico, our school rooms were heated with pot-bellied stoves. The janitor brought in the wood and coal. All the teachers were Spanish. And so were all the children. We were not allowed to speak Spanish. I didn't know any other way to speak so I didn't want to go to school.

Today my children are learning Spanish in school. They speak English all the time at home. Most of my brothers and sisters graduated from high school and some are attending or have attended college.

They have good jobs, and good homes. We were able to better ourselves when we came to Barstow.

CITY OF BARSTOW

by Celestia Gilliam

The comparative peaceful life of the community of Barstow was preceded by a long drawnout fight that prompted the editor of the *Printer-Review* to call the effort for incorporation the "Battle of the Century."

The contention between the citizens and civic groups of Barstow and the San Bernardino County Board of Supervisors began March 18, 1946 when Eugene White, pioneer resident of Barstow and "Father of every worthwhile project," presented petitions containing 586 signatures to the Board asking that a hearing be held on the matter of incorporation.

The signatures represented approximately 60 per cent of the 700 property owners within the proposed City boundaries, while only 25 percent was required by state law.

"While it will take time," said the *Printer-Review*, "most of the balance of the procedure toward making Barstow a city is merely routine."

But the procedure turned out to be anything but "merely routine." It was nearly a year and a half before the matter reached the voters in an election held September 16, 1947.

Barstow was one of the largest, isolated, unincorporated towns in the United States. But the Board of Supervisors was not ready to allow Barstow to incorporate.

Merchants and homeowners were asked to contribute to a Chamber of Commerce fund to take the matter to the Supreme Court. A total of $1500 was turned over to the incorporation committee, headed by Caryl Krouser.

In October, 1946 the state Supreme Court issued a writ of mandamus compelling County Clerk, Harry Allison, to accept and file the petition. It also ordered the Supervisors to proceed with the hearing on incorporation or show cause why they should not.

In July, 1947 the Supervisors set final boundaries and called for an election to be held. Barstow citizens voted 620 to 450 to incorporate and Barstow became a city.

At this same election the first councilmen were voted into office: Robert Hartwick, Joe Gintz, E.L. White, Leonard Zagortz and Clyde Boucher. Hartwick was named Mayor by his fellow-councilmen, as he was the top vote-getter. Skipper Winfield was named the first judge; Virgil Beavers—Police Chief; Earl Stanton—City Clerk; and William Newbrough—City Treasurer.

Meetings were held at the Fire Hall on First Street and it was here that our various departments of city services were organized. There was no City Hall, as such, and the Fire Hall was used by many civic organizations. The Police Department was located on Cozy Lane, an alley running parallel to Main Street on the North and West of First Street.

In the early 50's, the City built a Post Office and small City offices on Buena Vista. They also built a new Police facility on Mt. View. Eventually the Police facility

was sold to the County Sheriff's Department and a new City Hall and Police Department completed in 1962 on Mt. View Ave.

All of these changes were a part of a master plan for a civic center to be completed combining City and County services in one area. This 11 acres, located west of Barstow Road, bounded by Mt. View on the south and Buena Vista on the north, had been occupied by "Victory Homes" during World War II, and city officials fought hard to hold on to it. Today one can see this master plan coming to fruition with buildings all about.

Not least among the accomplishments of the City was the building of a Community Hospital in 1957. This was done through Hill-Burton funds which included extensive donations of time and money from citizens of the Mojave Desert.

There have been three City Clerks elected since incorporation in 1947: Earl Stanton, LaRue Shaffer Slette and Betty Rowe; Mrs. Rowe has served since 1963. The City Treasurers elected have included William Newbrough, Evelyn Lee, Annette Roloff and Thomas Meade. Five Police Chiefs have headed the Police Department: Virgil Beavers, Floyd Howard, Max Pierce, Bill Grissom and H.O. "Sonny" Davis (Sonny has more seniority than any other city employee). Gale Kenyon was the first City engineer to be hired and he served from 1949 to 1959. Following him have been Robert Russell, Bernard Schattner, Craig Leland, Wayne Harris, Robert Beach and Juan Majares.

Other elected Councilmen through the years will be remembered as George Oakes, Leonard Zagortz, James DeWolf, James Gilliam, Bill Casey, Ida Pleasant (the only woman), Paul Christianson, Blendon Beardsley, Burt Johnson, Barney Keller, Richard Padilla, Margo Saenz, Al Vigil and George Goldsmith. They have been cussed and discussed, as with all elected officials, but continued to serve, many of them for several years without salary. They, and all those working in the City departments, have managed to guide the growth of Barstow in an orderly manner. We hope it continues to grow and to be worthy of its adopted slogan "Intersection of Opportunity."

Needles Nugget 2-7-1941

Diesel Freight Engine Arrives here tomorrow. Tomorrow morning at 3 o'clock, the Santa Fe freight locomotive will pull into Needles yards . . . The engine —193 feet in length—is pulling a 70 car freight train and is en route from Fort Madison, Iowa to Los Angeles on its regular run from east to west.

A "2" wide vermillion strip separates the yellow bands from the dark blue body color. The use of the wide yellow bands, running the full length of the locomotive is in keeping with the Santa Fe's policy of providing maximum safety at crossings.

INCORPORATED CITIES OF THE GREATER MOJAVE DESERT 1976

CITY OF ADELANTO
Government 1976

Mayor .... Joan Robinson
Vice-Mayor .... Dr. Hastell S. Hollis
Councilmen .... Ed Dunagan
Rex Bean
Councilwoman .... Karen Kamp McClure
Treasurer & Clerk .... Peggy Smith
Administrator .... Gilicerio Ramirez
City Attorney .... Ivan Hopkins

CITY OF BARSTOW
Government 1976

Elected

Mayor .... George Goldsmith
Mayor-Pro-tem .... H. James Gilliam
Councilmen .... Bernard Keller
Richard Padilla
Al Vigil
City Clerk .... Betty Rowe
Treasurer .... Thomas Meade

Appointed

City Manager .... Robert Beach
City Attorney .... Conrad Mahlum
Police Chief .... Homer O. "Sonny" Davis
City Engineer .... Juan Mijares
Chief Building Inspector .... J. Art Mitchell
Hospital Administrator .... James Harrell

COUNTY OFFICIALS

Municipal Court Judge .... Ted L. DeBord
Librarian .... William Christiansen
Park & Recreation Director .... Terrance Johnston
Sheriff's Department .... Captain Joseph Karr

CITY OF NEEDLES
Government 1976

Elected

Mayor .... Huey O'Dell
Mayor Pro-tem .... Louise Corey
Councilwoman .... Shirley Lackey
Councilmen .... Richard Telles
David Daniel
Darwin Richardson
A.J. "Pete" Jewell

Appointed

City Clerk and Treasurer .... Vern Bailey
City Attorney .... Ed Heap
Chief Building Inspector .... Harrison Dohrman

COUNTY OFFICIALS

Municipal Court Judge .... James Barnes
Librarian .... Dick Goto
Park & Recreation Director .... Robert Posey
Sheriff's Department .... Captain Walter Acuna

CITY OF VICTORVILLE
Government 1976

Elected

Mayor .... Humberto Lugo
Mayor Pro-tem .... Peggy Sartor
Councilman .... Terry Caldwell
Councilwomen .... Jean DeBlasis
Gladys Butts

Appointed

City Clerk .... James Cox
Treasurer .... James Cox
City Attorney .... Anthony Piazza
Chief Building Inspector .... Jerry Brummett
City Engineer .... Kent Davis

COUNTY OFFICIALS

Municipal Court Judge .... William Johnstone
Librarian .... Mary Crenshaw
Park & Recreation Director .... Tom McCourt
Sheriffs Department .... Captain Earl Campbell

SAN BERNARDINO COUNTY OFFICIALS 1976

Board of Supervisors:

Chairman .... Dennis L. Hansberger
Members .... James L. Mayfield
Daniel D. Mikesell
Robert O. Townsend
Nancy E. Smith

STATE OFFICIALS

Assemblyman .... Larry Chimbole
State Capitol
Sacramento, CA 95814
Senator .... Walter W. Stiern
State Capitol
Sacramento, CA 95814
Governor .... Edmund G. Brown, Jr.
Governor's Office
Sacramento, CA 95801

FEDERAL OFFICIALS

Representative .... Shirley Pettis
House Office Building
Washington, D.C. 20515
United States Senators .... Alan Cranston
452 Russell Ave.
Senate Office Building
Washington, D.C. 20510
John V. Tunney
1415 New Senate Office
Building, Washington,
D.C. 20510

BARSTOW ECONOMIC CONDITIONS
by BHIDC

SANTA FE FREIGHT CLASSIFICATION YARD

Completion of the facility was February 1, 1976. Updated cost figures indicate a $50 million price. An additional 240 new personnel are employed in connection with this operation. A grand opening ceremony was held May 15, 1976, at which time the Senior Executives of this company visited the Barstow facility.

NEW SHOPPING CENTER

Barstow Station, a unique railroad car shopping center was completed and opened in July 1975. This first of a kind facility was designed and built entirely utilizing old railroad cars for shops and dining facilities in conjunction with McDonald's Restaurants. The primary purpose of this project was to offer visitor services to the 6 million cars which pass through Barstow annually.

INDUSTRIAL SITES

There are 3100 acres in the city limits zoned for light and heavy industry; about 76 per cent is vacant and available in parcels ranging in size from 2 to 200 acres. Included in this acreage total is one industrial district. Typical sales price during 1974 ranged from $6,000 to $12,000 per acre.

BARSTOW MALL

The Barstow Mall which will be anchored by Sears, Roebuck & Co., and K-Mart was a long time becoming a reality but many of the buildings for the mall are now under construction. A completion date of October 20, 1976 has been announced.

CITY CORPORATION YARD

New city yard facilities were constructed and opened in September 1975 at a cost of $353,000. This complex consolidates and provides a modern maintenance shop for all city owned vehicles and equipment. Additional space is available for expansion in future years.

SOUTHERN CALIFORNIA EDISON

A complete new structure to house all of Edison's facilities was completed in May 1976. Their location in downtown Barstow was no longer considered adequate. Cost of this project was $734,000.

NEW LAW AND JUSTICE CENTER

Currently under construction in Barstow Civic Center is a new Law and Justice facility. This project is under the auspices of San Bernardino County and will house a branch of the Superior Court of San Bernardino County as well as new jail facilities, district attorney's offices and other related services. A cornerstone laying ceremony was held in late March 1976 with completion scheduled for this year. Cost of this project is estimated at $2,093,812.

CITIZENS SAVINGS & LOAN BUILDING

Completed and opened a $36,000 facility in June, 1975, this compay adds to the many already existing financial institutions located in Barstow. Other savings and loan corporations located here are First Federal of San Bernardino and Home Savings and Loan. Home Savings has completed a new facility which opened in March 1976 at a cost of approximately $100,000.

BARSTOW COLLEGE

A new administration building was completed and opened in December 1975 at a cost of $305,000. With the addition of this facility the college will be able to expand many of its present facilities thus providing better service for its ever increasing student population.

CITY REDEVELOPMENT

The City of Barstow's Redevelopment Agency is well underway with a project which will add considerable off-street parking to the downtown shopping area. This project will also provide a mini-mall for smaller shops and update and enhance the ever deteriorating condition of many of the older buildings. Completion is anticipated to take about two years.

Major Employers	# of Employees	Payroll
U.S. Marine Base, Civ.	2,200	$35,042,736
U.S. Marine Base, Mil.	650	
Santa Fe Railway	1521	$17,000,000
School District	642	$ 8,970,225
Goldstone	470	$ 8,048,200
Fort Irwin	187	$ 2,597,908
Yellow Freight	442	$ 6,000,000
Others	2368	$13,916,736

FISH POND SCHOOL
by Eunice Bush Leak

There are several families farming along the river, east of Barstow. Asher Harris tells me that his family came in 1910. The lead mine north of Highway 91 had just closed down. The manager was anxious to dispose of lumber, etc., he had there, so Asher's father bought it for $24.00. Mr. Harland, a neighbor, helped him haul it. With this lumber the Harrises built a house and barn. Mr. Harland, for his work and a silver watch, was given enough lumber to build a barn.

The people around were anxious to have their children in school. About 1912, Mr. Harris gave some of the lumber to build a small room near the Harland's house. Beulah Harris, who had some high school education, taught the children. They were able to get books from the County. Those participating paid her in produce, cattle, etc. She was able to go to Los Angeles to high school the next year.

In 1913 the County took over and furnished funds to build the Fish Pond School. Miss Clark was the first teacher. The following year another teacher was em-

A Day At Fish Pond School

ployed, but I don't remember her name. When I came in September 1915 to teach at Fish Pond School, I had a room in the Harris home, which was about four miles from Barstow, out Highway 66 and across the river bed to the north side. I had a small wood stove where I did my cooking.

The Harris family were Mr. and Mrs. Enoch Harris, Farris, Beulah, Ephraim, Charles, Asher, Electa, Huldah, Clara, Mattie, Oscar, and Joseph. We had many interesting times. Harris worked at the Waterman Ranch, when needed. Ephraim had bees and sold honey. Buelah and Charles were in Los Angeles attending high school. Mr. Harris grew alfalfa and vegetables, and had some fruit trees.

It was a nice walk through the woods to the school house next to the hills. It was on Soapmine Road about one-half mile east of the present George McGinnis home, which was owned at that time by Gladys McGinnis' grandfather, D.T. Chilson, who had worked in the Calico Mines.

One Sunday afternoon we walked down to the fish ponds, about two miles east of the school house, where the old stage coach stop had been. Asher says that when they came here in 1910 some of the corrals were still there and fireplace chimneys on a little higher level. The fish ponds were owned by Matthew Kurtzan, a sort of hermit, who guarded the place carefully. The ponds were fenced. He had signs around saying, "No Trespassing." There were fish in the ponds, and ducks swimming on them. Matt was friendly when he saw it was the Harris boys. But, he had had trouble with people coming out from town to help themselves to his fish and shooting his ducks. I have been told that he lived there until the 1938 flood when the river came down so full that it filled the ponds with sand and washed out trees and everything.

On Saturday Mrs. Harris fixed a picnic lunch and we all went to Calico in the wagon to spend the day. We went east on Soapmine Road to the fish ponds and over the hill north on the old stage coach road. It was a good road at that time.

The mines were still being worked by the Mulcahy brothers, from Daggett, so the tunnels and ladders were kept in repair. They allowed the older boys and me to go through. We went in a tunnel above the town of Calico, explored awhile, then went down several ladders and came out a tunnel down on Wall Street. My white middy blouse, skirt and shoes were red from the dust in the mines. What an adventure!

During Christmas vacation and the first of January in 1916 a great deal of snow had fallen in the mountains. Then it rained there and also here in Barstow. One day one of the Harris boys heard in town that the river was rising, so that evening we went to the river and watched it flow downstream, in the moonlight. In the middle of the night a messenger knocked on the door and told us that a 12 foot wall of water was coming down the river and we had better get out. The boys hurried to hitch the team to the wagon. I put on my suit and high laced shoes I had just bought, packed a few clothes in my suitcase and we all went to the school house, which was on higher ground. The Harland family came, too. When it was time to open school, we had a crowd. Gradually the men drifted out. They found that there was a stream going down the north side of the valley, but the farms and homes were not damaged. The stream soon abated, so we were able to walk to school as usual. The river flowed for about three months that year.

One Saturday, in the spring, Mrs. Harris fixed a picnic lunch and most of the family drove to Ord Mountain in the wagon for the day. We saw

13 School on Waterman Ranch about 1882 note Mill in background

16 First Elementary School built in 1905

Local Schools —

14 Hutchinson school prior to new construction 1935

15 Fishpond School

17 Hutchinson St. School, 3rd and 4th grades late 1920's Mrs. Blevins, teacher

18 Fishpond School 1916: back row—Wilber and Guy Harland, Electa Harris; front row—Martha, Huldah and Clara Harris, Daisy Stone, Harriet Lazenby

wildflowers, apricot mallow and blue bells, also a diamondback rattlesnake. There were cabins where the miners lived.

In the spring the children often saw sidewinder rattlesnakes, on the way to school. One day, one came onto the school yard. The older boys killed it.

At recess and noon time the children played baseball, hopscotch, pompom pullaway, dare base, and ran relay races.

We heated the school house with a pot-bellied wood stove. The water supply was a hand pump, south of the school building. The boys kept the water bucket filled. The teacher did the janitor work, the children helped sometimes.

Mrs. Grace Stanley was the County Superintendent. She came to visit the school once a year.

The Board of Trustees consisted of Farris Harris, Mr. Harland, and D.T. Chilson. There were eight months of school each year. My salary was $60.00 per month for the 1915-16 school year and $65 per month for the 1916-17 school year.

During the 1916-17 school year I had board and room with Mr. and Mrs. Chilson. Alice and Adele, their daughters, were living in town. I enjoyed hearing stories of early days and Calico.

During the year the Harris family moved to a ranch in Hinkley. The Stone family moved away to find work elsewhere. The Lazenbys moved into town; he was a butcher. At the end of the term the Fish Pond School was discontinued. Later, the building was bought by

Newton Henderson and made into a dwelling at 232 E. Williams Street, Barstow.

FISH POND SCHOOL
Fall 1915 - May 1917

Teacher: Eunice Bush
Families that lived in the area:
 Mr. and Mrs. D. T. Chilson, Alice and Adele
 Mr. and Mrs. Richard Harland, Guy and Wilbur
 Mr. Howard
 Mr. and Mrs. Enoch Harris, Farris, Ephraim, Charles, Asher, Electa, Huldah, Clara, Mattie, Oscar, and Joseph
 Matt Kurtzan lived at the fish ponds
 Mr. and Mrs. Stone, Sylvia, Amy, Daisy lived at the soap mine, two miles east of school
 Mr. and Mrs. Ed Lazenby, Harriet
Across the river were:
 Mr. and Mrs. Charles Leak, Burton, George, Donald, Elmer
 Mr. and Mrs. John Sturnacle, George, John
Children in school:
 Fall 1915—Amy Stone, Daisy Stone, Guy Harland, Electa Harris, George Leak, George Sturnacle, Huldah Harris, Wilbur Harland, Clara Harris, Mattie Harris and Donald Leak.
 Fall 1916—Daisy Stone, Guy Harland, Electa Harris, George Leak, Huldah Harris, Wilbur Harland, Clara Harris, Mattie Harris and Harriet Lazenby.

DAGGETT SCHOOL BUILT 1884
by Margaret Fouts

The first Daggett School District report to the county was for the year 1885-86:

 Daily attendance - 23
 Teacher's yearly pay - $480
 Year's operation cost - $494.07
 District fund balance - $5.95
 School property value - $500

Financed by Daggett residents, the school house was built in 1884 on Mill Street and used until 1951 when Daggett's new elementary school was dedicated.

During World War II, Government employee's children had increased the student population until the second addition built near the old school house wasn't adequate. The Daggett Firehall and several military

buildings near the Daggett Airport were used until completion of the new school.

Larry and Lucille Coke of Yermo bought the old school property and converted the second addition into two apartments (at present, owned by Charles and Cathie Wilson).

The original 1885 school house made one apartment. William and Beverly Venner, Daggett teachers, rented it. Later, Mr. Chambless, the school custodian, and his family occupied it. He was the school custodian.

After being vacant for several years, the first school building burned to the ground.

A TEACHER'S LIFE
Edited by Margaret Fouts
Barstow Printer Review January 11, 1951

On a September evening in 1924, a teacher sent out by the county school superintendent got off a Union Pacific train at Cima, California. She stayed in the home of the agent's family until an abandoned cabin was prepared for her living quarters.

School began next morning in a very good building that had been closed a few years due to lack of pupils in

the district. One eighth grade girl swept the classroom and the others helped dust; soon all were doing some writing on the blackboards.

In those days all children learned to write a flowing script and enjoyed the lessons. The usual books for the three R's were on hand and the county library mailed supplementary material. Due to the distances and

22 *Hinkley School—Hinkley 1912*

19 *Class of 1937-38, Hinkley*

Grammar Schools

23 *Daggett School class of 1897-98*

20 *Daggett School 1898-99*

24 *Daggett School after renovation 1923*

21 *Snow fun Daggett School 1906*

conditions of desert roads, visits of a school supervisor were infrequent, but were a source of inspiration to teacher and pupils when made.

Before Christmas, the county superintendent was receiving requests from Afton to have an emergency school opened at that point also. The Cima teacher stopped there on her return trip following the holidays to investigate the necessities and possibilities. She found several eager little Mexican children at the section quarters and on reporting this to the county office, was asked to spend a part of every alternate week there. So for several months she made the train trips between Cima and Afton, finding the warm sheltered climate in the canyon a welcome change from the chilly, windswept summit of Cima in the winter months. Because school time was so short for these children, she taught them Saturday mornings on her own time. She devoted Saturday afternoons to exploring the scenic region around Afton, climbing hills and taking snapshots of the curious formations in the narrow canyons and the age-old eroded river banks. She enjoyed watching wild sheep that came to the river to drink while the lookout ram stood on a high point above.

The conditions for school work at Afton were unusual but did not prevent learning on the part of the pupils, nor did they make instruction a hardship for the teacher. The section foreman, a bachelor away from his house all day, assigned the use of the large center room of the section-house for classwork. Flexible blackboard material was stretched across the wall at one end of the room and a table and simple benches served as desks. Mothers urged the teacher to use corporal punishment if their youngsters were inattentive, even bringing a strap for the purpose, but these eager and affectionate children required no flogging. Some wept when the teacher left in the spring.

The teacher became increasingly interested in the desert, her life enriched by the experiences at Cima and Afton and she continued to be concerned about the education of desert children when, as the wife of Jim Lucas, constable and Santa Fe special officer, she came to live in Daggett in 1927.

The teacher, Jean Lucas, served for 12 years on the local school board and assisted children in choosing books at the Daggett branch of the county library.

HISTORY OF BARSTOW HIGH SCHOOL
by Tom Percy

A high school? On the Mojave Desert? in 1915?

A law requiring children to attend high school had not been enacted and the grade school principal was regularly threatening prosecution of Barstow parents whose children did not attend classes.

Barstow was the largest of a couple of dozen Mojave Desert towns. The *Barstow Printer* wanted to see construction of desert highways that would bring "thousands of cars" to the desert, development of high school and a junior college. Four decades passed before the latter became a reality.

As early as 1912 petitions circulated for the opening of a high school. Miss Abby L. Waterman, whose father, Robert Waterman, owned the earliest silver mine here and later served as Governor of California, did much of the petition-circulating, traveling the desert in her buckboard. Miss Waterman was named the first board president.

Formation of a high school district was approved by a "majority of 192" on June 23, 1915. In July of that year, a five man Board of Trustees was elected. In addition to Miss Waterman, these were W.B. Allen of Hinkley, G. Clyde Compton, A.H. Pendleton, Oswald Wilson, the Printer publisher and editor, and Thomas Williams of Yermo. Compton, a Barstow resident, served as the district board's first clerk.

Polling places were located at Todd (where Grace Hill was the inspector), Fish Pond (near present Nebo Marine Base), Waterman (Barstow), Daggett, Yermo, Kramer, Rasor, Newberry, Ludlow, Mojave and Hinkley.

School opened on September 20, 1915, with 14 boys and 12 girls, none of whom were required by law to continue their formal education. There were 20 freshmen, three sophomore transfers and three special students.

The school house stood one-half mile out on the desert, east of today's First & Williams Street. It was a two-story residence where two classrooms were created out of four small rooms by removing two partitions. The principal set up his office, a desk, filing cabinet, and several chairs in the kitchen. An inside toilet was used by the faculty, while the students used a divided outside facility.

Opening day found them without books, desks or equipment, but students and faculty made do with tables and folding chairs for a month or so until the desks came.

Students were enthusiastic about extra-curricular activities and red and white were chosen as the school colors.

James Mudgett was the first president of the student body; Laura Goodrich, Vice President; Mabel Hill, secretary; Fred Owen, Treasurer; and Walter Mudgett, athletic manager and also manager of the school's annual, *The El Desierto*. Cleon Hill was the first editor.

Numbers and isolation handicapped the sports program, but competition was found in contests with Santa Fe teams, town teams and elementary school teams. Boys and girls played together, the boys changing in a chicken shed and girls in a storage room of the school. Without showers, the students returned to classes hot and sweaty.

The second year with enrollment up to 46, theater

came to Barstow High School. The first production was "Fanny's Funny Furniture" directed by Mrs. Hoagland. Muriel Hindle, Barstow High School's first graduate, played a popular young lady with too many gentlemen callers.

Barstow churches united to conduct the first baccaulaureate service, with a Rev. Price of Pomona officiating.

In its second year, the Barstow Union High School acquired three board members, E.A. Erikson, C.J. Lingenfelder, and Mrs. Robert H. Greer. Erikson served a year, succeeded by Claude O. Gillett of Daggett, while Lingenfelder, also of Daggett, would serve two years and Mrs. Greer seven years.

The United States entered World War I in the spring of that second year and Barstow High School was the country's first school to organize a Junior Red Cross chapter. They raised money for war relief by a musical, the sale of Liberty Cook Books, and handmade infant clothes. The whole school—led by a Jr. Class Cake sale, raised $150 for aid for the Armenians.

The bitterest sacrifice was to mimeograph, instead of printing, *the El Desierto*. Money raised for printing was combined with school play receipts to purchase a $50 War Bond. Barstow's only mimeographed edition of *the El Desierto* was dedicated to the high school's iron-willed founder, Miss Abby L. Waterman.

The Trustees proposed a $30,000 bond issue to be repaid over 20 years at $2,475.00 per year for the construction of a school building. The bond issue failed to get the required two-thirds vote of approval. One problem, the 1916 *El Desierto* reported, too many people were not convinced that the high school was here to stay.

In the spring of 1918, an explosion in the kitchen started a fire and everything was gone, main building and bungalows, in 26 minutes. This disaster was followed by an outbreak of flu that forced the school to close down. In the midst of its afflictions, two students graduated, in June of 1918; Ora Luther Johnson and Myrum James Mudgett.

A $30,000 bond issue was finally approved. The delay had proved costly. Inflation hiked construction costs to the point where, even with an auditorium dropped from the plans, the building alone cost $36,397.46. New furniture added $2,300.00 and other equipment $3,500.00. The costs above $30,000 were handled out of operating expenses and property owners saw their one-time 15¢ tax rate soar to $1.06.

The site chosen for the new school building was the present site of the El Rancho Motel. On September 28, 1918, Judge Wm. Rhodes Hervy, Grand Master of the Masons of California, conducted a cornerstone laying ceremony. Addresses were delivered by Judge J.W. Curtis and Prof. R.B. Stover. A banquet on January 24, 1919, celebrated the opening of the new school.

"Flu Vacation" ended December 30, 1918 when students began attending classes in the new building six days a week to make up for lost time.

Those graduating on July 16 were: Madge Henderson, Merton Dexter Harlow, Verda May Haws, Byron

Arthur Hill, Cleon Leslie Hill, Mabel Eva Hill, Marry Hillis, Bertha Adelaid Kennedy, Agnes Price, Mellie Lee Riha, Marguerite Valerie Wells and Eva Elizabeth Wilhelm.

The enrollment the fourth year was 45. The *Barstow Printer* reported on June 12, 1919, that the high school had been accredited after an examination by Dr. Thomas. This meant that Barstow's graduates could enter university without taking an examination.

The Barstow trustees requested approval of $35,000. for construction of a 40 by 80 foot auditorium to be built on the south side of the school, with manual training and gym rooms below. This proposal failed approval in the March 26, 1920 election. Nine months later the Barstow Chamber of Commerce called for a new vote. The Trustees asked for $10,000.00 for high school beautification. This issue failed as did the previous one.

In the 20's, enrollment almost tripled—climbing from 60 in 1921 to 93 in 1925, 111 in 1929 and 153 in 1930.

Barstow was rapidly growing and by the middle of the decade, the paving had reached Hicks, ten miles west of Barstow. With National Old Trails slated to pass through, Lenwood to the west was reported to be a fast-growing suburb in 1923. By 1927, Yermo business had moved away from the railroad to the new busy highway. In that year, 189,717 cars passed through the Daggett check station. The following year the check station counted 213,717. Barstow grew as the traffic swelled. In 1923 the Printer reported that many new businesses were going up. The next year it declared that "new Barstow" was well established.

Charles Williams, a miner was selling land and Barstow High School District bought five city lots for $250 each.

However crowded, Barstow High continued its business of education through the 20's serving both adults and students. People came from distant areas as far as Helendale, Red Mountain, and Ludlow. A dormitory was set up to house these students. A teacher served as matron while another woman was employed to cook and keep house. The boys had quarters in the basement and the girls slept upstairs. The dorm was set up in a residence that the district leased near Third & White Streets.

The dorm was closed in 1922 when the board stated transportation was adequate. The students were transported in a touring car that rattled over unpaved roads. In early years bussing was by private contract, but, in the late 20's, the district began acquiring its own buses and hiring drivers. At one time, Ray Langworthy, then a young Barstow High School teacher, agreed to live in Ludlow and make the bus run. Barstow High School's small fleet of buses grew into a huge one, bussing not only hundreds of high school students thousands of miles a week, but, also, by contract, moving hundreds of Barstow elementary students to and from school.

Faculty members did not increase with student enrollment; the number ranging between six and seven all through the 20's. One problem, of course, was that there would have been no classrooms for them. Two members of the faculty remained in the community. These were Ray Langworthy, who served part of the time as Vice-Principal—until his retirement in the 50's. The affection and esteem that he earned during those years was reflected in naming the upper level athletic field for him in 1957. The other was Ethel Prather who married Al Henderson, a Barstow High School alumnus and Barstow merchant.

The decade of the 30's opened with over 150 students crammed into a building that was too small when one-third that number first occupied it a decade before.

The board had to decide whether to remodel at the present site or rebuild at a new location. The board decided to remodel and went to the voters three times in 13 months for the money, and each time the voters were more decisive in registering a veto. Sherman S. Hill, whose credentials in support of education could not be challenged, was among those arguing that no more money should be spent at the Main Street site. On one hand, the present site was too small and was poorly located on a busy highway. But, on the other hand, the building was relatively new.

The first bond election, held March 30, 1930, narrowly failed to achieve the two-thirds majority required for passage. The board asked for $60,000. It again asked the next month for $70,000 to add on an assembly room and three classrooms and to purchase 15 acres to the south from Williams for an athletic field. This was defeated 320-357. One year later the board asked for $60,000 to remodel, it was also defeated 266-304, in April of 1931.

The board nursed its wounds for two years and then called a bond election that was not held. In February 1933, the board said it would ask for $25,000 to remodel. Many opposed and, after an informal poll of citizens by board members, Board President, Charles Garver announced that the board had decided against a bond election. He pointed to 16 percent tax delinquency and detailed cost-cutting by the board. These included a salary reduction for teachers two years before and the use of the manual training class to build a school garage.

Grace Hill returned to the board in 1933 to serve for 15 more years. Mrs. Hill's election, and events, tipped the board to building at a new site. One of these events was a vigorous recommendation by state authorities to move from the Main Street site. Points made by the state were:

1. Students (now almost 200) were "working under a tremendous physical handicap in the present building";
2. Under the new "earthquake law," alterations to the Main Street building would cost more than a new building;
3. The Main Street site was too small; and
4. A busy highway was a poor location for a school.

A second important event was the advent of the federal Public Works Administration program of assistance to school building. Trustees proposed an

$87,500 bond issue, with PWA to buy the bonds and contribute 30 percent of the cost. This would have provided the money to purchase acreage at the Williams Aviation Field to the south and to erect a school to accommodate 350 students. The issue failed to get the required two-thirds vote, being defeated 446-366.

At this point, Barstow Union High School District had lost seven out of eight of its bond issues. It had lost the last six in a row, four of them within five years. This was in stark contrast to the elementary district which had never lost a bond election.

The board waited nearly two years before going to the voters again with a bond proposal. In the meantime, the district acquired 15 acres of Williams Addition land, and the federal government was developing a football field there. This was named Gordon W. Park Field in honor of the man who had succeeded Hurst as principal in 1931 and who had introduced football to Barstow High School. The federal government had also agreed to construct a swimming pool at the new site.

A new event was that the state returned the utilities to the district's tax rolls, swelling the district's assessed valuation from $1,688,400 to $8,132,955 and slicing the operation tax rate from 75 cents to 34 cents.

In December of 1935, the district trustees proposed an $85,000 bond issue. The federal government would contribute $62,500. The voters agreed overwhelmingly, giving the bond issue their approval, 591-130, in January 30, 1936 election. The bonds were sold in April, plans for the new school were approved by the state in June.

And then nothing happened! Five months later, the newspaper reported that the federal government was withholding funds because of a shortage of skilled labor in the Barstow area. Six months after that, the newspaper reported that new federal ruling would require that the project be resubmitted for a new division of cost between the district and the federal government.

Meanwhile, the need had become even more critical. Enrollment had soared to 240 and the board had voted to partition the school's undersized auditorium into three classrooms. The trustees appealed to Congressman Harry R. Sheppard for help. He immediately proposed a Congressional resolution allowing school districts to go ahead with building plans where bonds had been voted. Franklin D. Roosevelt announced his approval the following month.

On August 26, 1937, the *Printer* announced a federal WPA grant of $198,544 for projects in Barstow. Barstow High School District was to receive $66,272 as their share.

The high school district went back to the federal government for help on its gymnasium and cafeteria. The district originally proposed that the federal government would put up 55 percent of the cost, with the district paying the balance out of receipts from the sale of the Main Street school site and direct taxes. A $115,000 contract was let in September of 1938.

However, a great flooding of the Mojave River in 1938 not only closed the high school for two days but also wiped 10 percent of the tax valuation from the books. In addition, school trustees were not finding any buyers for their Main Street property at the price they were asking.

The trustees announced a new bond issue for $90,000 gym and cafeteria, and also to build a classroom-assembly building. The reaction must been explosive; as the board scheduled a $35,000 bond issue for the gym and cafeteria, the next week.

The bond issue carried, seven to one. The great wartime growth would soon make educators regret that the school did not have the classrooms proposed in the $90,000 bond issue.

At the time the board purchased 37 acres for $3,500, it could have brought 37 more acres to the south with $1,500 additional funds. Within a few years, lots in that area were selling for that price. However, the board could not visualize the need for that much land. The classroom-administration building, gymnasium, cafeteria and swimming pool must have looked like a vast lot of high school to the few thousand people residing in Barstow in 1939.

Far from being faulted for what was not done, the leadership that produced that plant must surely be honored for its remarkable achievement.

On December 14, 1937, the elementary and high school students of Barstow assembled at the spot where the single-story, Spanish style school building was to be erected. Lawrence Lewis, the high school student body president, and Vincent Claypool, who had succeeded Gordon Park as high school principal in 1936, spoke, and then Board President Garver turned the first spadeful of dirt, followed by Mrs. Hill and L.C. Powell. The following March, the California Masonic Grand Lodge conducted the cornerstone laying for the $137,000 building erected by Willard Lutz of Los Angeles. In September 1939, nearly 300 students began classes in the building that had been a long time coming.

The school board had added two new members, both were former Barstow High School students. Mrs. Gertrude Northrup of Daggett ended nine years of board service in 1938 and was succeeded by Robert H. Greer, Jr., a member of the school's first freshmen class. The second new board member was Charles C. Burden, Class of 1922 and operator of a general store in Helendale.

The changes were gradual but steady. A cafeteria, managed by Mrs. Abner Cunningham, was opened in the fall of 1941. During the five years that Gordon W. Park served as principal, courses in printing, salesmanship and advertising were added. Howard Irwin, instructor in music, Spanish and journalism, wrote the Alma Mater in 1935. The Class of 1937 set the tradition of white-washing the giant "B" atop what is now known as "B" Hill.

The biggest change was the introduction of football to the sports scene. Coach John Brose had only two weeks to form a team out of a group of boys who had never played football before matched against Tehachapi. Barstow lost its first two home games and the Riffians scored their first touchdown in the last game of the season against Needles. By the fifth season of competition, the Barstow team had the knowledge of the game and lost only one game all season.

Vincent P. Claypool, who served seven years as high school principal and five years as high school principal and district superintendent, was the first administrator to bear the title of "superintendent."

During the decade of the 30's, the enrollment grew from 153 in September, 1930 to 281 in September, 1940, while the graduating classes grew to 53 in May 1940 and the faculty had increased to 13 by the 1939-40 school year.

Bill Collins, honorary captain of the 1939 basketball team, killed at Pearl Harbor, was the first of 15 Barstow High School boys to die in the war. The 1942 *El Desierto* was dedicated "to the boys from BHS who are now men in the armed forces all over the world and on whom we are basing our hopes of ultimate victory."

The board lost its longtime president, Charles L. Garver, who died from cancer in 1941.

The war brought growth to Barstow and crowding to the schools; three major developments, Camp Irwin, Marine Corps Supply Center and Douglas Aircraft plant located in the area.

A Victory Corps was formed and the students purchased $3,200 in war bonds. They earmarked $1,200 for scholarships, $500 for a bronze plaque in memory of WWII servicemen and $500 to be used by the 1957 student body.

One wartime sacrifice was imposed by the federal government, when it took over six typewriters under a wartime order requiring high schools to give up 20 percent of their typewriters.

Before the war ended, the business of disposing of the Main Street school site would be taken care of, but not to the satisfaction of many citizens. Its disposition had been an issue since before the new school was built. The school Board wanted building money but couldn't get the price that other Main Street land sales indicated as the property value. The high school district maintained offices there until September 1942.

The district went to bid on the Main Street site in July 1943 and accepted a $2,500 bid by Arthur L. Doran. The El Rancho Motel, a desert landmark for many years, arose there.

Barstow kept growing. A park and recreation district was formed and two decades later, they developed an Olympic-sized swimming pool, four parks and a community center building. A cemetery district was formed in 1947 and a cemetery was developed on the hills north of Barstow.

Barstow was incorporated. Caryl Krouser, city-builder, had to appeal to the California Supreme Court for the right to hold an election. After a unanimous favorable decision by the court, north and west Barstow were excluded from the annexation proposal. Incorporation carried 620-450. In an election, September 16, 1947, Robert R. Hartwick was elected Mayor.

A sanitary district, uniformed police force, street paving, city planning, Post Office, county services, jail and library were developed. The Marine Base was announced a permanent base in 1949 and the tracking station, Goldstone, located in the area. Calico was restored by Walter Knott.

Barstow's population grew from 2,500 in 1940 to 5,000 in 1950 to over 11,000 in 1960 and an estimated 17,000 in 1966. Housing went up in all directions and motels, service stations and restaurants boomed. KWTC began broadcasting in 1947 and KIOT came a decade later. The weekly *Printer-Review* became the *Daily Desert Dispatch*.

In 1966 the number of elementary schools had increased from one to nine. There were two high schools, which now had more teachers than the students in the beginning. In addition, the town had a growing junior college on its own campus and two parochial schools.

Classrooms were being squeezed again, especially fo seventh and eighth graders.

In August 1945, the high school board proposed a $450,000 bond issue to finance construction of administration facilities, 12 classrooms, library, mechanics shop, music hall, and girl's gym. These were to serve a combination junior-senior high school on one campus.

Some 453 junior high school students (grades seven, eight and nine) began classes along with 305 senior high school students, on the campus in 1947.

In February of 1949 with 810 students enrolled in grades seven through twelve, the school was again overcrowded. At an election on April 21, 1949, a $495,000 bond issue drew approval 423-81. This financed construction of a music building, a girl's gym and four classrooms.

In February 1953, voters approved a $634,000 bond issue 938-95 to finance construction of 23 classrooms and a library. Two federal grants totaling $252,893 provided money for constructing two shop buildings on the hill next to Langworthy Field.

This completed the building on this campus during the fifties. Some remodeling, the girl's gym addition, cafeteria, varsity locker room and landscaping would follow in the sixties.

In 1955, a $750,000 bond issue was approved for the construction of a separate Junior High School campus.

The achievements of those first years following the end of World War II were almost miraculous. Somehow these dedicated men and women maintained quality education as the student body enrollment leaped from 350 in 1945 to 1,500 in 1960.

A faculty of 20 launched post-war education at BHS in the fall of 1945. Vincent B. Claypool was principal, Ray Longworthy was vice-principal, and Mrs. Betty Ruth Crane was the Dean of Girls.

Walter Andrews, who later succeeded Dr. Grossbach as Barstow High School principal, was the founding principal of the summer school, in 1957.

As the post-war years went along, names of more and more faculty members whom students of 1966 would recognize appeared in the pages of *El Desierto*. These included Robert M. Stapp, Ray Langworthy, Leona Evans, Majorie Havens, Juanita Thompson and Grace Laudon. In the fall of 1951, Jean Hutchinson (Christensen) began teaching music and Oliver Osborne was teaching English and history. By 1954, Wilfred McKendry, Maxine Smith, Lawrence Cady and Leon Hunter had joined the faculty. Winnetta Clark joined the next year, with Mary M. Flanagan, Donald C. Lipking, Leona M. Matson, Donald E. Phelps and Cliff Walker arriving the fall of 1955. Don Bilsborough, John Hansard, Lorenzo Osborne, George and Gloria Pelkey, and Vincent Zivelonghi arrived the next year and Roy Gray, Gerald Harvey, Thomas Hare, Dorsey Lightner, Kenneth Mack, Kenneth Schleusner, Fred Sharp, Samuel Sochis and Robert Thompson followed in 1957.

The Muriel Street site was purchased as the site for the new high school at $3,000 per acre. Schoolmen knew the trick was to move students to the new campus without squabbles about who must, and must not, attend the new school. It was decided to let the 1966 seniors graduate as a single class from the Barstow School campus, opening the new campus with but three classes in the fall of 1965. The new school was to be named after the late President John F. Kennedy, proposed by Bill Jackson and overwhelmingly approved by the students.

The 1965 *El Desierto* celebrated two historic events, the 50th anniversary of the founding of the Barstow Union High School District and the founding that year of John F. Kennedy High School. Black and gold were chosen as the school colors and the Spartan warrior as their mascot. Approximately 900 students began their first year on the Kennedy Campus in the fall of 1965.

The campus left behind got some of the bond issue money to expand the girls' gym, build a cafeteria and varsity locker room, construct a new track around Langworthy Field, turf the football field and landscape the grounds. The student body was visibly proud and happy to remain behind on a campus steeped in tradition, while the Kennedy students revelled in a new school.

Needles Nugget 9-25-42

Yucca Harvest Approved for Public Lands

The public lands of California, Nevada, Arizona and New Mexico have been made available for harvest of Yucca, to over come the shortage of fibers from which most rope is made . . . The Federal government is making the yucca on its lands available, Secretary Harold L. Iches said, because such preferred raw materials such as manila, hemp, jute and vegetable fibers are scarce or soon will be, because of curtailed war-time shipping . . . The yucca fiber was used to some extent for rope substitute during the First World War.

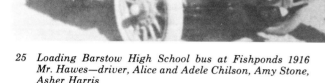

25 Loading Barstow High School bus at Fishponds 1916
Mr. Hawes—driver, Alice and Adele Chilson, Amy Stone,
Asher Harris

28 English class at the old Free Methodist Church 1918

29 First school bus for new Barstow High School

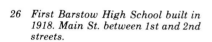

26 First Barstow High School built in
1918. Main St. between 1st and 2nd
streets.

27 Mollie Alf Harris teacher of Philander
Lee's children at Resting Springs 1912

30 Barstow Union High School bus at Yermo after snow storm of 1945.
Mr. Shaffer, driver

BARSTOW UNIFIED SCHOOL DISTRICT

9,500 square miles

1966-1976 by Lewis Allbee, Superintendent

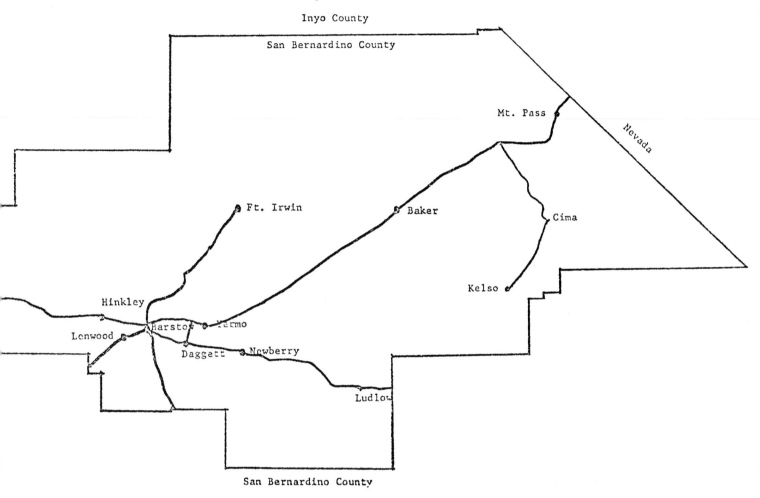

DEVELOPMENT OF THE SCHOOLS

The Barstow Unified School District is composed of 9 school districts, encompassing an area of some 9,500 square miles, which became unified on July 1, 1966. Their student enrollments in October 1964 were as follows:

Barstow Elementary	5,033 students	Kelso	17 students
Barstow Union High	2,305 students	Ludlow	20 students
Cima	43 students	Newberry	112 students
Daggett	771 students	Yermo	404 students
Hinkley	750 students	Total	9,455 students

227

UNIFICATION OF THE SCHOOL DISTRICT - July 1, 1966

School	Established	Present Building	Additions
Adult Evening School	1964		
Baker		1952	1965
Baker High School	1973	1973	
Barstow High School	1915	1939	
Barstow Junior High School		1957	1958 & 1962
Cameron		1955	
Continuation High School		1969	
Crestline		1966	
Daggett	1884-85	1954	1959 & 1963
Ft. Irwin (deactivated in 1970)		1953	1962 & 1963
Henderson		1953	
Hinkley	1909-10	1937	
Ingels		1958	1960
Kelso (closed in 1975)	1911		
Kennedy High School	1964	1965	
Lenwood		1956	1958 & 1965
McKinney		1958	
Montara		1961	1964 & 1965
Mt. Pass	1909-10	1954	
Newberry	1912-13	1947	1964
Pitcher Junior High School		1971	
Skyline North		1964	1967
Thomson		1947	1954
Waterman (converted to Central High in 1973)	1885-87	1936	
Yermo	1906-07	1950	1955, 1958, 1964 & 1967

NUMBER OF STUDENTS -- BY SCHOOL

(As of September of each year)

SCHOOLS	1966-67	1967-68	1968-69	1969-70	1970-71	1971-72	1972-73	1973-74	1974-75	1975-76
Baker	50	47	103	74	82	102	114	106	105	112
Barstow Junior High	1069	1173	1281	1289	1283	883	872	807	827	825
Cameron	768	755	704	761	631	557	595	540	510	352
Crestline	400	468	538	432	604	556	577	581	522	483
Daggett	213	339	331	327	303	299	186	126	125	138
Ft. Irwin	456	404	397	373	162	10	--	--	--	--
Henderson	655	597	589	622	556	534	541	453	394	410
Hinkley	466	416	451	414	419	396	340	345	325	325
Ingels	339	325	270	275	252	247	230	212	212	190
Kelso	20	28	40	28	33	38	35	21	15	--
Lenwood	482	485	456	452	438	397	355	331	323	307
McKinney	423	429	407	355	308	251	315	282	254	217
Montara	621	655	654	724	615	543	507	529	507	490
Mt. Pass	83	82	84	76	79	64	56	89	81	92
Newberry	135	146	125	120	141	144	136	151	138	171
Pitcher Junior High	--	--	--	--	--	417	400	399	390	343
Skyline North	388	396	396	375	416	425	383	377	363	330
Thomson	481	497	454	410	385	357	359	353	364	353
Waterman	275	265	230	251	214	218	--	--	--	--
Yermo	376	468	501	507	365	344	323	299	282	305
Individual Instruction	--	3	5	5	5	4	4	6	3	--
Total K-8	7700	7978	8016	7870	7291	6806	6328	6007	5740	5651
Headstart	30	30	45	77	60	60	--	--	--	--
TOTAL K-8 + HEADSTART	7730	8008	8061	7947	7351	6866	6328	6007	5740	5651
Baker High School	--	--	--	--	--	--	--	39	51	58
Barstow High School	1361	1417	1485	1542	1562	1529	1495	1467	1479	1476
Central High School	9	8	25	27	41	37	46	84	104	124
Kennedy High School	1212	1210	1204	1321	1264	1294	1300	1219	1217	1188
Individual Instruction	--	6	2	3	6	3	1	6	1	5
Total 9-12	2582	2641	2716	2893	2873	2863	2842	2815	2852	2851
Total K-12	10,312	10,649	10,777	10,840	10,224	9,729	9,170	8,822	8,592	8,502*
Adult Education	688	785	800	997	882	932	1,062	1,119	1,200	1,273
DISTRICT TOTAL	11,000	11,434	11,577	11,837	11,106	10,661	10,232	9,941	9,792	9,775

*This represents a loss of over 2,338 students since 1969-70.

BARSTOW UNIFIED SCHOOL DISTRICT
GOVERNING BOARD

NAME	1966-67	1967-68	1968-69	1969-70	1970-71	1971-72	1972-73	1973-74	1974-75	1975-76
Forrest Bruton	☆									
Herschel Clemmer	☆									
Dr. T. R. Fredricks	☆	☆	☆	☆	☆					
Dr. C. Dean Hammans	☆	☆	☆							
Antonio Leon	☆	☆	☆							
Genevieve Lewis	☆	☆	☆							
Norman Smith	☆	☆	☆	☆	☆	☆	☆			
Harold Bailey		☆	☆	☆	☆					
Richard Flores		☆	☆	☆						
Donald Burgett				☆	☆	☆	☆	☆	☆	☆
Anthony J. Piazza				☆	☆	☆				
S. Vincent Sisneros				☆	☆	☆				
Lavergne A. Gallagher					☆	☆	☆	☆	☆	
Gary Mitton						☆	☆	☆		
E. A. Trowbridge						☆	☆	☆	☆	
Tom Hicks						☆				
Ann Walton							☆	☆	☆	☆
Tom Hunt								☆		
Jim Rapponotti								☆	☆	☆
Nancy Martin									☆	☆
Ralph Conner										☆
Deloris Garrett										☆
William Bryan									☆	☆

230

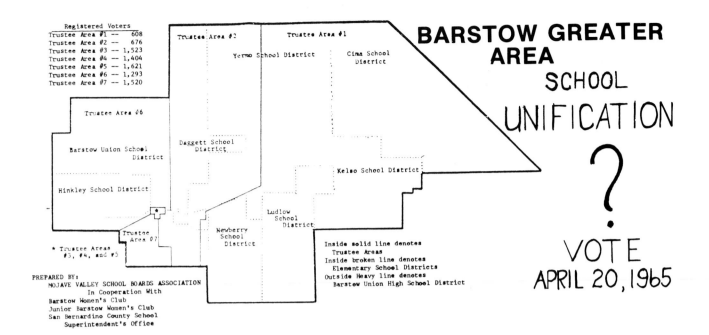

Registered Voters
Trustee Area #1 -- 608
Trustee Area #2 -- 676
Trustee Area #3 -- 1,523
Trustee Area #4 -- 1,404
Trustee Area #5 -- 1,621
Trustee Area #6 -- 1,293
Trustee Area #7 -- 1,520

Trustee Area #2
Trustee Area #1
Yermo School District
Cima School District

Trustee Area #6

Daggett School District

Barstow Union School District

Kelso School District

Hinkley School District

Ludlow School District

Trustee Area #7
Newberry School District

* Trustee Areas #3, #4, and #5

Inside solid line denotes
Trustee Areas
Inside broken line denotes
Elementary School Districts
Outside Heavy line denotes
Barstow Union High School District

PREPARED BY:
MOJAVE VALLEY SCHOOL BOARDS ASSOCIATION
In Cooperation With
Barstow Women's Club
Junior Barstow Women's Club
San Bernardino County School
Superintendent's Office

BARSTOW GREATER AREA
SCHOOL
UNIFICATION
?
VOTE
APRIL 20, 1965

A COMMUNITY COLLEGE FOR THE HIGH DESERT

by Ruth Paget and Thelma Carder

Barstow College can trace its beginnings to March 11, 1957, when the Barstow High School Board, with Melvin Hill as president, asked Superintendent Robert Hilburn to investigate the possibility of establishing a junior college in this area. All high desert high school districts except Victorville responded favorably.

To satisfy the state's requirement of demonstrated need, Dr. Hilburn got special state legislation to permit San Bernardino Valley College to offer fifteen extension classes beginning September 29, 1958. The classes were very successful.

By a majority of eight to one in 1959, the voters approved the formation of a junior college district within the high school district.

On April 1, 1960—the college's birthday—the first director, Dr. Charles Chapman, was ready to select a staff and establish a program for the following September. He had one secretary in a small office on the Barstow High School campus. Of the eleven certified instructors and administrators who formed the original full-time college faculty, three are still on the staff today. They include Thomas Kimball, Librarian; Ruth Paget, Chairman of the Business Division; and Robert Vencill, Chairman of the Science Division.

A half hour before the first scheduled registration in September, the waiting line extended a block down First Street. College officials processed 750 students that evening. More than 1800 different persons enrolled at the college during its first year. Classes met on the high school campus from 3:30 to 10:00 p.m. every day.

At the end of that year, in June 1961, Barstow College graduated its first class, thirteen persons who had enough work from other colleges to obtain the AA degree in two semesters. When the academic procession came through the audience, it included as many staff members, wearing the graduate robes indicating

their degrees and universities, as it did candidates for the AA degree.

During the next year the college offered some day classes in rented facilities at a nearby church. But, a full day program was not possible until after the move to the new campus in 1964.

The citizens of the community voted on October 18, 1960, by more than a five to one majority to authorize a three-million dollar bond issue to purchase a site and build campus facilities.

In November 1961, again by ballot, the community selected the present 200 acre site on Barstow Road. Ground was broken March 14, 1963.

The first classes on the new campus were held in February 1964, but the administrative wing, library, and gymnasium were not ready until later in the semester.

The technical-vocational building was completed for use in September 1968; and the most recent campus addition, the administration building, in December 1975. The college celebrated its sixteenth anniversary in April 1976 by inviting the public to view the new administration building and its work-saving computer, automatic typewriters, and copy machines.

When the college moved to the new campus it had eighteen full-time instructors. That number had more than doubled by 1976. Through the years the college has added new courses needed by students or requested by the community. And, in addition to instructors, it added support staff. The college has become one of Barstow's major employers.

Today students can complete the equivalent of the first two years of university academic work, earn an AA degree, complete occupational certificate programs, or simply enroll in courses to improve their skills or enrich their lives.

Like all junior colleges in California, Barstow College several years ago became a community college.

231

And like all California community colleges, it has simple admissions requirements. Students must either be high school graduates or eighteen years of age.

In addition to the expected crop of high school graduates, full-time students at the college include older adults—veterans, retired military men and married women whose children are in school or grown. Night classes attract a much higher percentage of veterans and other mature adults, many of whom complete the requirements for graduation. In 1975 the average age of Barstow College graduates was 28.

While day classes can still be accommodated on the campus, night classes overflow into classrooms at Kennedy High School, the fire station, and other locations.

The college also offers courses for enlisted Marines at the Marine Supply Depot. And in the spring of 1976 President R. William Graham launched the college into a new program of providing high school and junior college courses for servicemen overseas. This program should add to the income of the college and enable it to provide better services for local residents.

BARSTOW COMMUNITY COLLEGE BOARDS OF TRUSTEES MEMBERS
1960-1976

THE POST OFFICES OF SAN BERNARDINO COUNTY
by Martha Burnau

NAME	FORMERLY	ESTABLISHED	DISCONTINUED	RESCINDED	MAIL TO	NAME CHANGED TO	
Adahi		11/01/1934	9/30/1935		Twin Peaks		
Adelanto		10/26/1916					
Alessandro		1/18/1888				Into Riverside Co.	5/3/1893
Alta Loma	Iomosa	4/18/1913					
Amboy		12/21/1903		6/14/1904			
		10/14/1904					
Apple Valley		4/16/1949					
Arlington		6/15/1881	11/23/1882		Riverside		
Arlington Place		10/15/1891				Into Riverside Co.	5/3/1893
Arrow Bear		12/31/1927	7/14/1928			Arrowbear Lake	
Arrowbear Lake	Arrow Bear	7/14/1928	5/31/1929		Running Springs		
		6/19/1931					
Arrowhead		10/17/1895	10/30/1906		San Bernardino		
Arrowhead Sprs.		5/13/1887	7/13/1895		San Bernardino		
		2/17/1906	1/14/1924		San Bernardino		
		1/03/1925	6/30/1942		San Bernardino		
Atolia		5/10/1906	8/15/1922		Osdick		
		11/10/1927	7/31/1944		Randsburg		
Avawatz	Crackerjack	8/13/1908	12/15/1910		Silver Lake		
Bagdad		5/31/1889	12/15/1921				
		10/28/1922	4/30/1923		Amboy		
Bairdstown		2/1/1875	9/28/1875				
Baker	Silver Lake	2/ /1933					
Baldwin Lake		8/17/1916	7/31/1917		Pine Knot		
		6/10/1924	9/19/1931		Big Bear City		
Banning		10/11/1877				Into Riverside Co.	5/3/1893
Barnwell	Manvel	2/21/1907	4/15/1915		Goffs		
Barstow		5/15/1886					
Baxter		6/06/1914	3/31/1919		Yermo		
		6/21/1923	6/15/1926		Crucero		
Bear Lake		8/30/1924	11/30/1931		Pine Knot		
Beaumont	San Gorgonia	9/09/1886				Into Riverside Co.	5/3/1893
Bell Mountain		6/01/1953					
Big Bear City	Van Duesen	10/01/1927					
Big Bear Lake	Pine Knot	10/01/1938					

NAME	FORMERLY	ESTABLISHED	DISCONTINUED	RESCINDED	MAILTO	NAME CHANGED TO	
Big Bear Park		7/30/1934	8/31/1945		Big Bear City		
Blake	Goffs	6/13/1893		7/07/1893			
		8/24/1896				Goffs	11/8/1911
Bloomington		7/14/1892					
Blue Jay		6/17/1924					
Blythe Junction		11/5/1910	9/30/1916		Blythe		
Borate		7/07/1896	12/14/1907		Daggett		
Borosolvay		8/13/1917	3/31/1921		Trona		
Brynmawr		1/22/1895				Bryn Mawr	9/2/1924
Bryn Mawr		9/02/1924					
Burcham		1/13/1893				Summitt	9/15/1898
Burris		12/08/1908	7/30/1910		Mentone		
Cadiz		7/31/1939					
Cajon		2/20/1889	12/31/1818		Summitt		
		12/06/1919	12/31/1944		San Bernardino		
Calico		5/18/1882	11/30/1898		Daggett		
Calzona		10/29/1909	9/15/1914		Vidal		
Camp Angelus		3/21/1924	7/31/1943		Mentone		
Camp Baldy		4/23/1913	7/1/1951		Mt. Baldy		
Cedar Glen		3/18/1939					
Cedarpines Park		4/29/1927	4/15/1943				
		8/16/1946					
Chino		7/28/1873	3/16/1887				
		11/09/1887					
Chubbuck		5/06/1938	8/31/1950		Cadiz		
Cima		12/26/1905					
Colton		5/22/1876					
Columbia Mines		9/03/1901	11/15/1902		Manvel		
Coyote		10/24/1879	10/05/1880				
Cracker Jack		2/26/1907	8/13/1908		Avawatz		
Crackerjack							
Crafton Retreat		6/03/1886	4/16/1887		Lugonia		
Craftonville		8/04/1892	6/23/1899	7/26/1899	Mentone		
		7/29/1899	10/15/1920		Mentone		
Crestline	Skyline Hts.	9/05/1919					
Crest Park		9/16/1949					
Cross Roads		7/30/1935					
Crucero		4/18/1911	6/30/1917		Stagg		
		2/09/1926	5/25/1943		Kelso		
Crutts		4/21/1916	8/31/1922		Barstow		
Cucamonga		3/23/1864					
Daggett		4/12/1883					
Dale		11/19/1896	10/30/1915		Amboy		
Danaher		4/23/1892	6/07/1893		San Bernardino		
Danby		9/10/1898	5/31/1900		Blake		
		5/24/1901	12/31/1913		Goffs		
Declez		12/22/1900	9/15/1913		Bloomington		
Declezville		12/18/1888	11/04/1898		Colton		
Delrosa		6/16/1893				Del Rosa	6/9/1895
Del Rosa		6/09/1895	6/29/1901		Highlands		
		2/09/1903					
Desert		3/28/1881	12/17/1883				
		6/30/1908	11/15/1912		Nipton		
Desert Springs		2/16/1949					
Devore		3/07/1908	6/30/1930		San Bernardino		
Doble		7/27/1900	8/31/1906		Victorville		
Dunbar		10/17/1912	5/31/1914		Lanfair		
Earp		1/04/1930					
E. Highlands		11/11/1892	6/29/1901		Highlands		
		1/02/1902					
E. Riverside		6/26/1888				Into Riverside Co.	5/3/1893
El Casco		5/23/1888				Into Riverside Co.	5/3/1893
El Mirage	Gray Mt.	4/17/1917	2/28/1923		Victorville		
		5/02/1927	5/15/1934				
Essex		5/21/1932					

NAME	FORMERLY	ESTABLISHED	DISCONTINUED	RESCINDED	MAILTO	NAME CHANGED TO	
Eswena		7/29/1892	4/27/1898		Cucamonga		
Fallsvale		11/25/1929					
Fawnskin	Oso Grande	5/18/1918					
Fenner		2/24/1892	7/11/1893		Goffs		
		1/17/1902		11/25/1902			
		10/05/1905		3/31/1912	Goffs		
		8/09/1928	7/9/1972				
Fontana		8/05/1914					
Forest Home		5/01/1906					
Fredalba		2/08/1896	6/15/1915		San Bernardino		
		7/28/1920	2/29/1924		San Bernardino		
Geiger		3/25/1908		Rescinded			
Glenn Ranch		8/08/1921	12/01/1953		Lytle Creek		
Goffs		3/25/1893	11/03/1894		Needles	Blake	6/13/1893
						Change rescinded	6/13/1893
		8/24/1896				Changed to Blake	
		11/08/1911				Changed to Goffs	
Goldbridge		5/15/1917	8/15/1918		Barstow		
Gold Park		1/11/1908		7/29/1908			
Grapeland	Hesperides	2/08/1889	12/31/1905		Etiwanda		
Gray Mountain		10/27/1913	4/17/1917			El Mirage	
Green Valley Lake		5/17/1939					
Guasti		7/16/1910					
Halleck		1/03/1881				Oro Grande	5/1/1925
Hart		4/30/1908	12/31/1915		Goffs		
Hawley		6/25/1883	12/10/1883		Daggett		
		4/09/1884	10/13/1888		Daggett		
Helendale	Judson	9/30/1918					
Hesperia		5/25/1889					
Hesperides		10/02/1888				Grapeland	2/8/1889
Highland	Messina	8/29/1898					
Hinkley		3/16/1908					
Hodge	Palliser	10/30/1925	5/31/1941		Barstow		
Ibis		12/21/1904	7/15/1908		Needles		
Idlewild		8/21/1890	7/12/1895				
		10/07/1896	6/30/1897		San Bernardino		
Incline		6/18/1907				Skyland Heights	4/04/1910
Ioamosa		4/23/1895				Alta Loma	4/18/1913
Ivanpah	Leastalk	6/17/1878	4/24/1899			Rosalie	4/24/1899
		8/12/1903	5/31/1906		Manvel		
		10/10/1914	1/31/1927		Goffs		
Joshua Tree		7/16/1946					
Judson		12/08/1909				Helendale	9/3/1918
Keenbrook		2/07/1894	8/16/1894		San Bernardino		
		9/27/1910	5/31/1921		Cajon		
Kelso		5/20/1905					
Kingston		5/27/1924	5/14/1938		Goodsprings		
Klinefelter		5/08/1894	5/10/1895		Needles		
Kramer		12/20/1896	8/31/1911		Hinkley		
		3/02/1912	11/30/1918		Hinkley		
Lacey		12/07/1897		2/11/1898			
Lake Arrowhead	Sagital	2/24/1922					
Lanfair		9/21/1912	1/31/1927		Goffs		
Lavic		9/02/1902		5/23/1903			
		6/04/1904	8/31/1909		Stagg		
Leastalk		6/01/1906	12/31/1911		Nipton		
		4/11/1912				Ivanpah	10/10/1914
Little Bear Lake		2/16/1917				Sagital	2/24/1922
Lockhart		1/01/1953	7/—/1957				
Lomalinda		1/14/1901	6/07/1905		Redlands	Changed Spelling	Loma Linda
Loma Linda		7/01/1908					
Lucerne Valley		9/09/1912					
Ludlow	Stagg	9/15/1926	7/—/1974				
Lugo		4/02/1917	4/30/1924		Hesperia		
Lugonia		9/05/1882	9/22/1888		Redlands		

NAME	FORMERLY	ESTABLISHED	DISCONTINUED	RESCINDED	MAIL TO	NAME CHANGED TO	
Lytle Creek	Glen Ranch	12/01/1953					
Manvel		3/30/1893	8/24/1893		Goffs		
		10/03/1893				Barnwell	2/21/1907
Marida		10/04/1893				Verdemont	3/25/1895
Maruba		8/27/1915	3/15/1926		Lanfair		
Mentone		5/15/1891					
Messina		5/26/1887				Highland	8/29/1898
Minnelusa		5/31/1928	6/30/1940		Fawnskin		
Minneola		4/17/1896	5/05/1897		Daggett		
Moonlake		10/24/1929	5/01/1939		Switzerland		
Moreno		2/19/1891				Into Riverside Co.	5/3/1893
Morongo Valley		7/01/1947					
Mound Station		5/15/1876	5/11/1877				
Mt. Pass		6/15/1929	3/31/1932		Nipton		
Mt. Baldy	Camp Baldy	7/01/1951					
Nantan		3/10/1887	12/31/1890		Ivanpah		
Needles		8/28/1883					
Newberry		3/11/1899		6/15/1899		Wagner	10/12/1911
		5/15/1924					
Newberry Springs		1/-/1967				Newberry Springs	1/-/1967
Nipton		10/05/1905	10/30/1909		Desert		
		9/16/1911	6/30/1919		Desert		
		3/31/1932					
North Cucamonga		9/28/1888	8/31/1923		Cucamonga		
North Ontario		9/10/1887				Upland	3/21/1902
Ontario		2/19/1883					
Oro Grande	Halleck	5/01/1925					
Osdick		2/14/1922				Red Mountain	9/14/1929
Oso Grande		3/22/1918				Fawnskin	5/18/1918
Palliser		8/05/1914				Hodge	10/30/1925
Parker Dam		12/05/1935	1/31/1939		Cross Roads		
		1/24/1940					
Patton		8/06/1897					
Phelan		11/25/1916					
Pine Knot		7/01/1912	5/31/1913		Redlands		
		10/03/1916				Big Bear Lake	10/01/1938
Pinelake		12/15/1891	12/15/1905		Redlands		
Pioneertown		3/16/1950					
Providence		6/05/1882	5/03/1892		Needles		
Reche		5/03/1883	9/13/1888		Colton		
Redlands		11/05/1887					
Red Mountain	Osdick	6/15/1928					
Reservoir		2/08/1892	8/24/1892		Pinelake		
Rialto		1/10/1888					
Rice		3/01/1933	5/01/1943		Earp		
		7/01/1946					
Richie		4/03/1883	4/27/1883				
Rimforest		1/01/1949					
Rincon		12/12/1870	8/24/1874				
		11/19/1887				To Riverside Co.	5/3/1893
Riverside		6/12/1871				Into Riverside Co.	5/3/1893
Rochester		9/22/1890	1/31/1911		Cucamonga		
Rock Springs		1/08/1866	12/06/1866				
Rosalie	Ivanpah	4/24/1899	7/31/1900		Manvel		
Rosemine		4/04/1899	2/15/1900		Victor		
Rosena		7/28/1893	9/20/1901		Rialto		
Running Springs		4/25/1927					
Sagital	Little Bear Lk.	9/24/1922				Lake Arrowhead	4/22/1922
San Antonio		3/09/1891	10/14/1905		Upland		
San Bernardino		2/19/1855					
San Gargonia		8/21/1879	5/23/1881				
San Gorgonia		4/14/1884	9/09/1886			Beaumont	9/9/1886
San Gorgonio		6/29/1868	4/25/1870				
San Salvadore		11/17/1873	2/21/1896				
Sevenoaks		4/23/1894					
Seam		4/07/1906	2/28/1907		Danby		

NAME	FORMERLY	ESTABLISHED	DISCONTINUED	RESCINDED	MAIL TO	NAME CHANGED TO	
Silver Lake		3/27/1907	2/ /1933		Baker		
Skinner		8/18/1894		11/05/1894			
Skyforest		9/27/1928					
Skyland Heights	Incline	4/04/1910				Crestline	9/5/1919
Slaterange		4/27/1900	12/14/1901		Johannesburg		
South Riverside		8/11/1887				Into Riverside Co.	5/3/1893
Stagg		2/15/1902				Ludlow	9/15/1926
Stedman		3/28/1904	11/30/1907		Stagg		
Stonewall		5/28/1873	8/01/1876				
Sugarloaf		1/01/1947					
Summitt	Burcham	1/22/1898	3/05/1898				
		9/15/1898	4/30/1901				
		8/13/1901	6/31/1910		Cajon		
		2/05/1915					
Switzerland		5/01/1939	9/30/1941		Crestlne		
Tecopa		5/24/1877				Into Inyo Co.	1880
Temescal		2/12/1861	11/12/1861				
		9/27/1890				Into Riverside Co. 5/3/1893	
Terra Alto		3/03/1893		5/10/1893			
Trona		3/27/1914					
Twentynine Palms		10/28/1927					
Twin Peaks		7/29/1916					
Ulmer		11/14/1888	2/16/1890		Barstow		
Upland	N. Ontario	3/21/1902					
Vanderbilt		2/01/1893	3/31/1900		Manvel		
Van Duesen		10/01/1927				Big Bear City	3/16/1928
Verdemont	Marida	3/25/1895	6/18/1895		San Bernardino		
		9/10/1922	4/30/1924		Devore		
Victor		4/10/1886				Victorville	9/24/1903
Victorvile	Victor	9/24/1903					
Vidal		3/19/1910					
Viento		5/22/1903	4/15/1910		Bloomington		
Vontrigger		5/07/1907	10/15/1913		Dunbar		
Wagner	Newberry	10/12/1911				Water	7/9/1919
Water	Wagner	7/09/1919				Newberry	5/15/1924
Waterman		10/25/1881	4/19/1887		Barstow		
Watson		2/19/1883	7/25/1883		Calico		
Westend		10/11/1919					
Whipple		4/24/1935	7/15/1935		Earp		
Wild		3/12/1928	10/15/1931		Helendale		
Wild Rose		5/23/1907					
Wrightwood		9/27/1928					
Yermo		10/21/1905					
Yucaipa		6/08/1895	1/25/1896		Redlands		
		2/25/1908					
Yucca Valley		11/15/1945					
Zanja		5/16/1917	11/15/1920		Mentone		
Zucher		3/22/1887	8/31/1900		Ontario		

BARSTOW POSTAL SERVICE

Postal service for Barstow began on May 15, 1886, when an office was established in this then small desert rail center. Myron E. Beach was the first Postmaster to serve.

Although the Barstow Post Office now looks back over almost a century of service to desert residents, at the time of its inception it joined an already established and expansive postal system in the San Bernardino area. The Barstow office was preceded by those at San Bernardino, Calico, Daggett, Halleck, Hawley, Ivanpah, Needles, Providence and Waterman, near Barstow.

Postmasters: From September 1887 to November 1906, a family named Gooding had a corner on the postmaster's job. Three of them held that post in succession—Leonard, Joseph and Annie.

In November 1906, Reece M. Dillingham was appointed postmaster.

Mrs. Alpharetta Gilham, mother of Mrs. Joseph H. Gray, served from June 1916 until November 1921.

Arthur Doran, served from November 1921 to May 1922.

Alfred A. True held office from June 1922 until June 30, 1940.

31 Late 1896 Barney the horse, Frank Ryerse, A. LaMantain, Ben Butler, Mulcahy and McCue, Daggett

34 Post office and general store—Hinkley 1916

Telegraph and Postal Service

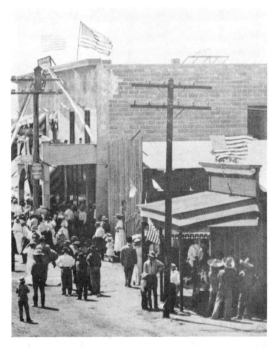

32 Postal telegraph services in the Melrose Hotel, Old Town July 4, 1911

35 & 36 1924-1948 on South Second

33 Another loser—post office and store at Crackerjack

37 1948-1956, now the Barstow Beauty Academy 423 E. Main

Carl McClellan held the post from July 1, 1940 until June 30, 1949, at which time Walter Upton was promoted to Postmaster.

Three other men held the position, but only for very short periods of time—Charles H. Cook, 1886; Thomas Twaddle, 1887, and Clarence E. Kendrick, 1908.

Gordon Clancy has been the Postmaster since 1965 until the present time. Jack Upton is Superintendent of Postal Operations and Dale DeWitte is Superintendent of Mails and Delivery.

The Barstow Post Office presently serves the area within Community Boulevard, Fort Irwin, the United States Marine Corps Supply Centers at Nebo and Yermo, and Rimrock Road.

After occupying many locations in Barstow, the new U.S. Post Office Building, at 425 South Second Street, was occupied and dedicated on November 2, 1968. The staff has grown from one person in 1886 to 44 in July of 1975.

MORE ABOUT DORSEY
by Helen Graves

What ever happened to Dorsey, the famous canine Calico United States mail carrier? He was employed at a time when the booming mining town found that most anything could happen.

A lost chapter in Dorsey's life came into view recently at the San Bernardino County Library, California Room. A roll of microfilm containing copies of the *San Bernardino Index* revealed the following item:

> February 27, 1886: Last Tuesday a mail sack, Dorsey, and Major Gillis departed for San Francisco, the dog's future home. He had been given to W.W. Stow of that city.

Today, Calico visitors hear stories about Dorsey who carried the United States mail for over a year between that bustling community and Bismark or East Calico as some called it. Brothers E. E. Stacy and O.T. Stacy owned the mail contract for Star Route delivery, a distance of seven miles on foot over a tedious trail, with delivery promised three times a week.

Wells Fargo had the contract to bring mail from Los Angeles at ten cents a letter, with service taking eight to ten days before arriving at Calico. Mail laid over in San Bernardino until a stagecoach brought it. The Stacy brother, known locally as Bill, opened the first Post Office in Calico May 18, 1882, and his brother, who lived in Bismark, received the mail at the other end of the line, although no official Post Office was recorded at that point.

Dorsey first appeared as a stray, desperate for food and water, footsore as though he had traveled a long way. He would whine and crawl on all fours, pleading with Bill Stacy who tried to run the collie off. Bill weakened and adopted the collie.

Showing unusual intelligence, the animal began to accompany Bill on the Star Route. If a piece of mail dropped, especially in the desert winds, Dorsey would pick it up, delighting in retrieving it for his master.

One day Stacy was quite ill on delivery day. Someone suggested letting Dorsey deliver the mail bag alone. A crude harness was constructed, not unlike a saddlebag, with pouches on each side. For a trial run the daily newspapers were inserted and a note tied on his collar suggesting that mail from the other end be sent back with the dog. A newspaper was rubbed across Dorsey's nose and he was told of the emergency. Record time was made on the mail run this day. It seemed as though the animal preened and strutted as never before, proud of the faith and trust his master had in him.

More tests were made to make sure Dorsey could not be distracted on his important mission. A safer harness was made to insure no chance of loss. Even the newspaper, the Calico Print, was precious in those days, read and re-read by all within reach. When it seemed unreadable it was used to patch chinks in crude buildings.

Miners who were hard pressed for amusement were skeptical about Dorsey and would try to meet him on the trail to waylay him. The dog would either see or smell them, leave the trail with a wide detour, then circle onto the trail again.

The Collie became famous throughout the country and he has been painted by many artists. Walt Disney Productions made a movie about him. His employment was terminated after more than a year of service because the Star Route was abolished and the contract cancelled.

Dorsey was restless in his retirement, which led to his placement with the Stow family in San Francisco. Thus he was provided a special army escort for the long journey to his new abode.

EARLY NEWBERRY POSTAL HISTORY
by Beth Pinnell

In Miss Morris Wagner's letter to the museum, in June 1971, she writes of some of her experiences while a homesteader and postmistress in Newberry:

In applying for the Post Office in 1911, I offered three names as was required: (1) Newberry, (2) Wagner, (3) Water. Newberry was refused because of fear of confusion with Newberry Park in Southern California. Wagner was chosen as second choice. We often received packets of mail intended for Wagner, Arizona, and our mail would sometimes go there. Finally jt was changed to Water. I believe there was a Water also in some other desert area. I understand that it is now Newberry Springs.

Lew Page, another homesteader, was appointed deputy postmaster and when I left the desert, he became postmaster. The Station Master of the railroad was a man named Fordhan.

The mail train took the outgoing mail off a crane as it slowed slightly, and the incoming mail was thrown off—I think at top speed! When I sent a watch to be repaird, I had it returned to Daggett, and I had to ride the 12 miles on horseback to pick it up.

I had purchased a small building on the railroad land across the track from the station, and beside the Station Master's home, near that of the other two agents. The post office was housed in this building, and I opened a small grocery store. About the only customers were myself and Lew Page, and an occasional tramp or prospector seeking a grubstake.

The crews on the freight trains were friendly and often would slip me a chunk of ice from the caboose. I would ride my horse to the end of the train and a man (the conductor I think) would drop off a big chunk of ice onto the horn of my saddle. I would balance it there and ride off across the desert. The saddle horn would sometimes melt a hole in the block so that it was easier to balance by the time I got back to my homestead on a hot August day.

Miss Wagner presently lives in Redwood City in Northern California, but still owns property in our area to retain ties with the desert.

THE GENERAL DELIVERY LINE
by Pat Keeling

Home delivery mail service began in the Barstow community when the City of Barstow was incorporated on September 30, 1947. Until the city incorporation the Post Office was ineligible for home delivery.

The old Post Office on South Second Street in early 1947 was the hub of a busy community with growing pains. Old family residents with post office boxes were fortunate to have their mail "put up." The other newcomers to Barstow received their mail in the "General Delivery" line. There were two service windows: one for stamps, money orders, Postal Savings at 2%, parcel post and the various other services; and, one for "General Delivery" which always had a very long line.

The Post Office was a friendly place where the women and children would visit to renew acquaintances. They would find out the latest news and happenings in the area. If you wanted your mail, a trip to the Post Office became a daily necessity!

MEDICAL CARE IN THE MOJAVE RIVER VALLEY
by Juanita Atkinson & Caryl Krouser

In 1882 the discovery of silver created the town of Calico with approximately 3500 area residents. Records are sketchy . . . who were the doctors administering to the physical needs of miners, tradesmen and their families? In 1886, Calico physicians were Drs. R.A. Goodenough, G.R. Johnson and A.R. Rhea. A Dr. Holmes had already left when physician-surgeon Rhea moved into the same office. Medical services were plentiful then. Calico had at least a pharmacist, H.J. Jordan and a drugstore, —L. Patterson. At Daggett, J.F. Davis, druggist, would later either sell or compete with Dr. Rhea who settled in town. He owned a drugstore, promoted unprofitable mining ventures and held an interest in the Van Dyke ranch. In those days medicines were freely sold and prescriptions were seldom necessary. Sears in its 1890 catalog advertised various patent medicines like Dr. Barker's Blood Builder; "Nature's Most Wonderful remedy for destroying poisons in the blood;" Brown's Vegetable Cure for female Weakness; Pasteur's Microbe Killer, and most were guaranteed to cure all the diseases known to man.

The Atlantic and Pacific Railroad had been taken over by the Atchison, Topeka & Santa Fe Railroad. Business was good on the Santa Fe and the blowing of steam from the locomotives was a welcome sound to the residents of fast growing Barstow. The town was then located "between the tracks." In 1900 Drs. Riley Shrum and John Ogden White came to work for the Santa Fe.

Dr. Rhea moved from Daggett and practiced in Barstow until 1906. Filling the medical vacancy created in Daggett, were Drs. Lindhart and MacFarlane; the latter staying until 1905. Calico resident physician in 1907 was Dr. Albert Ray.

In population growth, Daggett was losing out to Barstow, and in 1903 Dr. White purchased Dr. Rhea's drugstore which in later years became White and Platt's Drug Store.

To care for their employees, Santa Fe induced Dr. C. B. Anderson to come to Barstow. In June 1906 he arrived from Rockford, Illinois. His nurse being Miss Thecla Dolman, now Mrs. Peter Boutakes of San Bernardino. Dr. Anderson was the first doctor hired on a monthly basis, previously physicians had been paid for each consultation of railroad employees. He not only cared for the railroad men and their families but also for any sick or injured.

The Santa Fe doctors had little more than an office in the old Harvey House. They peered over their glasses at their patients and took the little black bag when making house calls. In 1911, the new Harvey House was completed. This was a great improvement, giving the medics a reception room, office, space for laboratory and room for several cots for the seriously ill.

Getting off the train at Barstow in 1916 were the next two Santa Fe physicians, Drs. Benson and Hall, who remained in town for several years. They worked extra long hours in September, 1918, when the flu epidemic hit nationwide. In ten months half a million people died in the United States, and Barstow suffered proportionately. After reaching its peak in the winter months, the epidemic tapered off by July, 1919. Dr. Lyle Graham, who settled in the community of Newberry, 20 miles to the east, assisted in the epidemic.

Woodrow Wilson was President; the nation voted dry, causing numerous stills to spring up on the desert; and the Model T Ford, or Tin Lizzy made its appearance in Barstow; Jazz was born.

Dr. McKenzie came to Yermo in 1920 and remained for ten years, while in Ludlow, D.S. McCall, a Santa Fe physician, started practice. In 1930, Dr. Miller opened an office in Barstow.

In the 1930's doctors attended to inpatients in private homes such as "Ma" Denney's.

During the depression years of 1933, the Santa Fe brought in R. J. McDonald, to Barstow. He left the railroad in 1945 to open up his own practice with offices in the newly completed El Rancho Motel on Main Street. His practice grew and he enlarged to a suite of rooms and brought in his brother Dr. C.A. McDonald. Their practice expanded and in 1951 they built their own clinic at 200 South First Street, now occupied by William Channel, Optometrist.

The first physician to come to Barstow not employed by the Santa Fe was Dr. Milford Nelson, in 1932. Six years later he moved into medical and dental facilities at 209 North Second Street. His adobe building was designed for the practice of two doctors and one dentist. His associate was Dr. Joel Gibbons.

From 1937 to 1940, Mrs. Robina McLaren provided practical nursing, home care, to many Barstow residents. She fondly recalls Drs. Nelson and Gibbons as well as their patients.

Both physicians held reserve officer commissions in the United States Army Medical Corps. After Pearl Harbor, they were ordered to active duty and served for the war duration. Upon discharge, both doctors took specialized training and opened offices near Los Angeles. Taking over their practice in 1941 was Dr. Georgie Rue, who apparently did not like the rigors of the desert as he did not finish out the year.

In 1938, Dr. Bruce W. Wilkes, came to Barstow and opened an office at 210 North First Street. On February 7, 1938, while getting the building cleaned, furnished and equipment moved in, he received his first patient but was unable to care for the lady who wanted an abortion. One February 9th he saw his first paying patient; his first employee was Betty Amende, a secretary, followed by his first nurse Margaret Rahn, R.N.

In 1940, Dr. Wilkes realized he must provide for his growing crop of prospective mothers closer to his office. He had been using the home of Mrs. Ova Eddy at 417 Hutchison Street for delivery and maternity care. This proved inadequate so Dr. Wilkes opened the first "licensed" hospital between Needles and San Bernardino. It was located at 112 E. Williams and consisted of two patient beds and an office. The first patient was a maternity case from Baker and the second was Mrs. Floyd Henderson, who gave birth to her son David.

The patient load grew and Mrs. Helen George, now Mrs. Payne, joined the nursing staff. Meals brought in from a nearby restaurant were kept warm on a hot plate.

Dr. Wilkes' maternity facility soon became an emergency stop for ambulance drivers with accident victims on their way to San Bernardino hospitals. An addition was necessary. Accordingly, the hospital was enlarged to include one four-bed ward; two two-bed wards, an operating room, a delivery room, a nursery and a drug room. The addition opened in 1943.

In May 1941, Dr. Glen A. Graybill came to Barstow locating in the Second Street medical facility, taking over the practices of Drs. Nelson and Gibbons. At that time the maternity patients of Dr. Graybill's were cared in his home or the medical-dental building, with the dental suite being pressed into use as the patients ward. Dr. Graybill's wife Esther, an R.N., assisted him with his maternity patients, as well as his office patients. In 1945, nurses were hired to care for the patients during their convalescence.

Robert Combs, D.O. became associated with Dr. Wilkes. In 1946, Robert Nafzgar, D.O. joined the staff. In 1948, Sheridian Griffith, D.O. became a member of the group. Dr. Griffith was born and raised in Barstow and is the only native son in the roster of local doctors. Drs. Carl Taylor and T.R. Fredericks arrived later. By an act of the legislature, the D.O.'s became M.D.'s in 1964.

In 1952 the overcrowded facility was increased by another four-bed ward, a two-bed ward, a kitchen and laundry. Even enlarged many times, patients still lined the halls on stretchers, awaiting transportation to San Bernardino hospitals. In emergencies, surgeons and specialists were brought to Barstow from Los Angeles.

In 1957, the facility was converted from a hospital to a convalescent home and later to the Hi Desert Mental Health Center.

In 1957, the new Barstow Community Hospital was completed and Dr. Wilkes became the first medical chief of staff. The hospital attained national publicity when Life Magazine ran a full page picture of the hospital with the caption, "Hospital completed but too broke to open." The city attorney had ruled that the use of city funds to either build or operate a municipal hospital was illegal. The hospital remained closed until the people of Barstow, by special election, authorized the city council to use city funds for its operation. The hospital opened in 1958.

In 1945, Dr. David Parker, came to Barstow as Santa Fe physician. In addition to railroad employees and their families, he cared for outside patients. He remained for five years, leaving to accept a position as dermatologist with the Veterans Hospital at Sawtelle.

In 1951, Dr. Thadeus Jones, became the Santa Fe doctor. He did not take outside patients. He was followed by another doctor named Jones, who shortly left Santa Fe to go into private practice. In 1955, Santa Fe transfered Dr. Marion Fink, to Barstow from the Santa Fe hospital in Los Angeles, where he had served his internship. He was also in private practice for Barstow and desert residents. Joining Dr. Fink in 1957, was Alejandro P. Vincente, a Navy Doctor stationed at the Marine Corps Supply Center dispensary at Barstow. In 1963, the two physicians began a private partnership practice specializing in obstetrics and gynecology.

Other physicians came to Barstow via the Santa Fe route. They were Drs. W. M. Clover, Anthony Samorajski, and J. F. Narkevitz. Dr. Clover left Barstow to practice in the Los Angeles area, and Dr. Narkevitz entered private practice in Barstow.

With the opening of the new and larger hospital, in 1958, more physicians began establishing private practices in the area and it was not long before Barstow had the much needed physicians to care for the population increase.

One of the first to come in 1960 and establish a surgical practice was Dr. Sanford W. French III, the first general, thoracic and cardiovascular surgeon at the Barstow Community Hospital. Dr. French, a retired Colonel, United States Army Medical Corps who, after arriving in Barstow, was appointed expert surgical consultant to the Surgeon General, U.S. Army in 1961. He was available to the Fort Irwin Hospital medical staff for their difficult surgical cases, in many of which Dr. French participated.

Dr. Graydon C. Sanders, came to Barstow in 1966 and associated with Dr. French. Dr. Sanders was a general and plastic surgeon; he remained in Barstow until 1972.

Joining Dr. French in 1970 was Dr. Rogelio A. Arosemena, a general surgeon.

Serving the medical needs of Barstow today are Drs. Rogelioa Arosemena, Marion F. Fink, T. R. Fredericks, S. Griffith, Paul J. Musgrave, Robert L. Nafzgar, J. F. Narkevitz, D. J. Owens, Anthony Samorajski, C. J. Taylor, A. P. Vincente, R. L. Woodyard.

Santa Fe's policy of bringing doctors to the area has now been supplemented by the City of Barstow. A new Medical Clinic complex was completed in 1974. Several suites are leased to the County, one being a Medical Health Clinic. The city provides office space for incoming doctors to set up practice in Barstow. Thus far, three doctors, Drs. Gebre C. Gobezie; Tak Chow, W. H. Luke Huang have been induced to settle in our town.

Medical care for the Santa Fe employees and the general public was supplemented by the San Bernardino County Health Department. This, in itself, is a fascinating story. These public programs began in 1940 and were geared to immunizations for all and referrals to doctors. They provided Well Baby Clinics for pre-school children. Originally, one nurse covered Barstow, Victorville, Needles, Ludlow and all points between, including the section houses. The program was under the direction of Dr. Wynetta Simpson, Public Health Doctor, and Miss Clara Annabelle, Director of Public Health nurses. In 1953, the office was increased to two nurses stationed in Barstow. By 1956, this had increased to three nurses with headquarters on Seventh Street. In 1958 the present San Bernardino County building was completed on East Mountain View and two rooms were assigned for the Health Department. In 1964 three nurses and a secretary staffed a newly built addition in the rear of the county building. With the unification of the Barstow School District, the school hired its own staff of nurses and the Health Department began the present community programs.

Barstow's health needs have been well cared for during its nearly one century of existence.

Needles Nuggett 2-7-41: Ad

Looking for Something To Do? Next Sunday motor to Mitchell's Caverns north of Essex to view the underground caves. Then have a fame bird dinner with us, We raise our own birds including: Gambels Quail, Chucker Partridge, Pheasant; All cooked by Mrs. Mitchell and served with hot delicious biscuits and other trimmings which you will enjoy.

38 John Sloan, Stanley Cutler with Dr. W. MacFarlane in front of his store at Daggett

41 Daggett, Rosa Alf MacFarlane 1906 Mrs. Hallery was a seamstress for the Alfs

Doctors and Druggists

39 Doctor's fee for delivery 1921

42 Soda Fountain in White and Platt drug store 1930, Barstow

40 Corner of First and Main St. 1930's, Barstow

LIFE ON THE MOJAVE RIVER VALLEY
Excerpt—Doctors of the Area (1904-06)
by Dix Van Dyke

Dr. A.R. Rhea had been a pioneer doctor (listed in the 1886 Directory) in Calico and Daggett. Like others, he had dabbled in mines and three years before had been lucky enough to sell some mining claims for $35,000 cash. In 1904, tired of bachelorhood, he brought from the east an old maid he had known in his youth. She was a thrifty wife and a shrewd trader. He gave her a small amount of money which, with careful manipulating, she increased. In her old age she possessed $80,000 which she lost to two slick oil stock swindlers. But, that is another story.

Dr. Rhea had been one of the original incorporators of the Silver Valley Water Company, the first water company, and had provided money to begin the Van Dyke Ranch. He and Kerckhoff had agreed to furnish the funds to pay for the pipe. Rhea's intentions were good, but like many who have been lucky enough to gain sudden wealth, he was an incurable optimist. He also had an unfortunate habit of consulting spirtualist mediums about investments and was a firm believer. His wife was a devout church member, but each respected the other's belief and they refrained from quarrels.

Rhea had invested all of his funds in a mine in the Panamint Mountains far out in the desert. He was so sure of it that he induced various of his friends to invest. He had trusted the optimistic report of another sent to investigate the mine and had now learned too late the mine was worthless and the whole investment was a total loss.

In 1906, Dr. Rhea was killed by a street car while riding a bicycle in the city of Long Beach. He was quite deaf and, not hearing the car, had ridden in front of it. His widow inherited his property and sold his interest in the ranch to Funk. Rhea was a fine honorable man and well liked and respected by all who knew him. He had grieved very much over his folly in persuading many friends to invest in his unprofitable mining venture and had been anxious to, in some way, make enough to repay their losses.

In 1906, replacing Dr. McFarlane who moved elsewhere, came Dr. Lindhart, a middle aged adventurer who had roamed about the world. Driven from Manchuria by the Russo-Japanese, he had been attracted to Daggett by the prospective mining boom. He was lucky enough to locate and sell a claim for $2500, which was bad luck for him! It caused him to spend several years locating more claims and making futile endeavors to sell another. Lindhart cared nothing about anyones ill will and feared no one.

THE ERADICATION OF POLIO

by Pat Keeling

Until 1958 when the control of polio began, mankind was held in the grip of a deep, unending fear—Polio: the disease that could cause a lifetime of tortured twisted limbs, death, or a living death in an iron lung. In conjunction with a State project, the Barstow Junior Women's Club began making arrangements to hold Polio immunization clinics.

New polio cases in the State of California had reached epidemic proportions when Dr. Jonas Salk announced the release of his serum for immunization. Every parent lived with the fear of polio. Cases abounded everywhere. The ability of the disease to cross boundaries of age, race and social status was apparent. The new serum was a necessity.

The Barstow Juniors, under the direction of local doctors, held clinics from 1958 to 1962 at the new County building, 301 E. Mt. View, Barstow. The shots were administered by local doctors with a minimum donation of one dollar toward community service projects. An isolette for the hospital, and a resuscitation unit for the Fire Department were purchased with these funds.

In 1962, the announcement of Sabin (Live Virus) vaccine was made. The Junior Womens Club again undertook an area innoculation project, this time under the direction of the County Health Department. The last Salk Vaccine was administered April 3, 1962 at the County building on Mt. View with two doctors present.

The new Sabin Polio Clinics were held at East Barstow and Intermediate Schools on May 18, 1962, and 13,289 people received their first sugar cube of serum. There was another clinic held on Wednesday, May 16, and 1,682 received their first serum. At the second clinic, June 9-10, 1962, Sabine Type III was given, and the third clinic, August 1962, Type II was administered.

The disease is almost eliminated, and there is a law requiring pre-school children to be immunized before entering public school. The Public Health Department of San Bernardino County now gives a trivalent Sabin immunization with just two drops on the tongue, these are given one month apart. A booster at intervals of one year, three years and every ten years for lifetime protection. The last known polio case in Barstow was in 1955.

Sept., 1966—Barstow City Police always operating with a close eye on the boys who like to drag their cars on the city streets, were summoned to Ann Street yesterday by an irate homeowner, but on arrival the drag artist had disappeared. According to the report telephoned to police headquarters, the kids were really "cutting up the street."

MENTAL HEALTH SERVICES

by Helen Bond

The official opening of the "Hi-Desert Mental Health Center," September 29, 1972, coincided with the Barstow's Silver Anniversary. Its first permanent location was at 112 E. Williams Street—long known as Dr. Bruce Wilkes' "Barstow Hospital."

On May 22, 1957, "The Mojave Valley Coordinating Council," was incorporated as a non-profit organization. The Articles of Incorporation were signed by Robert F. Ballanger, Irwin F. Long and L.A. Cochran.

A group of local citizens, under the leadership of Chairperson, Mrs. Edith Gold, proved the need for a "Family Counseling Service" in the community and sponsored several fund raising projects to support the first service, before being accepted as a committee of the "Mojave Valley Coordinating Council," subsequently sponsored by the Mojave Valley United Fund.

The first service to the community was one professional counselor who saw clients at the DeVoe-Stewart Real Estate Office. Sometime in the early '60's the Pendleton Building was utilized, when the staff was increased to two counselors. Mrs. Maggie Carson was the first receptionist and continued in this capacity until November, 1963 when Mrs. Helen E. Bond became associated with the Service and remained until August, 1973.

With increase of staff to three and four, Mrs. Gold procured the Guidance offices of the Barstow High School. During the greater part of the tenure in this location, Dr. William W. Clover donated consultant-service time to the staff of Social Workers.

Through the effort of Mrs. Celestia Gilliam, who became Chairman of the Board in 1965, office space was made available to the agency at the County Health Department in 1968, until mid-July, 1972. Again, through the effort of Mrs. Gilliam, the "Barstow Hospital" building was leased from Dr. Bruce Wilkes, to the newly incorporated Hi-Desert Mental Health Center, which continued under sponsorship of the United Fund.

After 15 years as a committee under the Mojave Valley Coordinating Council, who no longer felt they could be responsible for so great and expanding service, a Board of Directors was formed. They were: Mrs. Clara McKinney, President-Chairman; Eldon Schmidt, Vice-President; Dave McCartney, Treasurer and Mrs. Frances Weygandt, Secretary; with 15 dedicated enthusiastic citizens comprising the first Board of Directors of the Hi-Desert Mental Health Center.

In February 1970, it was learned that grant monies were available through the Medical Assistance Program—Short Doyle Act—Lanterman-Petris-Short Act, to be administered through the San Bernardino County Mental Health Program. With the funding were guidelines for service and staffing. The first hurdle was surmounted when the services of Dr. R. Warburton Miller, Psychologist of San Bernardino, was named Director, and Mrs. Carol Moser, Clinical Psychologist, who after one year became the Director. The search for a Psychiatrist was more difficult, but a former local youth, Dr. Robert Wyckoff, joined the staff, which also included three psychiatric social workers.

A "WE CARE" crisis line was instituted soon after the opening of the new facility. A Drug Abuse Program has been in existence since the opening of the Center in various degrees of operation due to funding and staffing. In 1975 an Alcoholic Program, with Mrs. Helen Wilson as coordinator, was effected.

In July 1973 Mike Mathis was named the first full-time Director. The following year Richard McCoombs was named Executive-Director, and Dr. Richard Steele, Psychologist and staff supervisor. A children's service was added in 1975.

With the resignation of Mrs. Clara McKinney in 1973, Mrs. Jane Chamberlin was named President-Chairman of the Board.

CHURCHES OF THE BARSTOW AREA
1976

Seventh Day Adventist Church
Desert View Seventh Day Adventist Church
Bethal Temple Spanish Assembly
First Assembly of God Church
Trinity Assembly of God Church (Daggett)
Arrowhead Baptist Church
Calvary Baptist Church (Yermo)
E. Barstow Southern Baptist Church
First Baptist Church of Barstow
Oasis Missionary Baptist Church
Union Missionary Baptist Church
Trinity Conservative Baptist Church
Community Bible Church of Daggett
Hinkley Bible Church
Lenwood Community Church
Newberry Community Church
Yermo Bible Church
Mt. Saint Joseph's Catholic Church
Our Lady of the Desert Catholic Church (Baker)
First Baptist Church of Hinkley
Grandview Baptist Church
Landmark Missionary Baptist Church
Church of Christ
Church of God
Church of God in Christ
The Church of God of Prophecy
First Congregational Church

Community Congregational Church (Yermo)
Mexican Congregational Church
Pentecostal Church of God
First Christian Church
Jehovah's Witnesses Kingdom Hall
Congregation of Beth Israel
Church of Jesus Christ of Latter Day Saints
Reorganized Church of Jesus Christ of Latter Day Saints
Concordia Luthern Church
Shepherd of the Desert Lutheran Church
First Church of Christ Science
St. Paul's Episcopal Church
Bethany Foursquare Gospel Church
First Church of the Nazarene
First Church of Religious Science
Bethel A.M.E. Church
First United Methodist Church
Free Methodist Church
Minor Chapel C.M.E. Church
United Pentecostal Church
Baker Bible Church (Baker)
Bible Way Mission
U.S. Marine Corps Center
Northside Church of Christ
Church of the Holy Spirit
Christian Science Reading Room

CHURCHES OF THE NEEDLES AREA

Seventh Day Adventist Church
Needles Assembly of God Church
First Southern Baptist Church
Mojave Valley First Baptist Church
St. Ann's Catholic Church
Needles Christian Church
Church of God
Church of Jesus Christ of Latter Day Saints

St. John the Evangelist Episcopal Church
Jehovah's Witnesses Kingdom Hall
Grace Lutheran Church
Community United Methodist Church
Indian Church of the Nazarene
Church of Christ
Apostolic Church

CHURCHES OF VICTORVILLE

First Assembly of God
Latin American Assembly of God
Bethany Baptist Church
Bible Baptist Church
First Baptist Church
High Desert Baptist Church
First Missionary Baptist Church
St. Joan of Arc Catholic Church
Church of Christ
Church of God in Christ
Church of Jesus Christ of Latter Day Saints
Reorganized Church of Jesus Christ of Latter Day Saints

Foursquare Gospel Church
Free Methodist Church
Zion Lutheran Church
Seventh Day Adventist Church
Mt. Carmel Community Church
First Christian Church
First Church of Christ Scientist
Jehovah's Witnesses Victorville Congregation
Trinity Luthern Church
United Pentacostal
Victorville Chuch of the Nazarene
United Methodist Church
Church of Religious Science

43 Barstow First Congregational Church 2nd and Cottage Sts. 1904

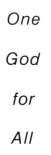

One

God

for

All

46 Fray Francisco Garcés 1738-81 portrait executed after his death

44 Above church moved to 3rd and Hutchinson in 1923 (1976)

47 Looking east 2nd and Hutchinson center left: Free Methodist Church right: Catholic Church Barstow

45 Bible class Yermo Union Church 1936

48 Barstow, Lucille Thursby, Betty Ryan, Frances Gibson, Ruby Jones, Marion DeWolf—seated

"Vanished Indian of the Mojave Valley"

INDEX TO AUTHORS AND STORIES

PHOTOGRAPHS, MEMORABILIA AND ART CREDITS

Alf, Gertrude (Alf Collection)
Atchison, Topeka and Santa Fe Railway Company
Barstow Fire District
Berry, Lee
Bruce, Evelyn (Askren-Stafford-Bruce Collection)
Burnau, Martha
Carson, LaVera (Failing Collection)
Clancy, G. W.
Cochran, Lee
Conaway, Ray
Crooks, Clarence (Crooks-White Collection)
Department of Interior
    Bureau of Land Management
Dillingham, Reginald (Dillingham Collection)
Drenk, R.M.
Duran, Frank
Eddy, Jane
Elliott, K. Dean (Art)
Fouts, Margaret (Ryerse-Ryerson-Kenney-Butler
    Collection)
Gibson, Fred (Leak-Gibson Collection)
Gilliam, Celestia (Fairbanks-Brown-Gilliam
    Collection)
Goldstone Photo Laboratory
Gould, Bobby
Graves, Helen
Gray, Nancy (Gilham-Gray Collection)
Harmel, Ed
Henderson, Alfred (Henderson Collection)

Hinkley Women's Club Collection
Keeling, Pat (Jernigan-Keeling Collection)
Kelly, James (Kelly Collection)
Krouser, Caryl
Lemus, Richard
Leroux, Dolores
Lyles, Donald
McCormick, Jessie
McGinnis, Gladys (Thursby-McGinnis Collection)
Miller, Elmer (Rivas-Miller Collection)
Moon, Germaine
Murray, May (Henderson-Murray Collection)
Olsen, Laura and E. J. (Honey-Olsen Collection)
Payne, Elma June (White-Platt-Payne Collection)
Powell, Aileen McCue (McCue-Powell Collection)
Prescott, Kathy Art
Schilling, B. A.
Shaffer, Roy C.
Union Pacific Railroad Company
U.S. Marine Corps.
Varela, Donaciano
Walker, Clifford
Wilkins, Bill
Williamson, Mary (Pico-Williamson Collection)
Wilson, James
Zeitelhack, June
Needles Museum Chapter of the San Bernardino
    County Museum Association (McNeil-Vary
    Collection)

MOJAVE RIVER VALLEY MUSEUM ASSOCIATION
Collections'

Barstow Women's Club (Henderson-Woolford Photo
    Story Book)
Bassett, Addie (Park-Bassett Collection)
Copp, Agnes (Copp Collection)
D.W. Earl Collection
Greer, Robert (Greer Collection)
Hallock, Hazel (Poe-Hallock Collection)
McCoy, Raymond (Burns-McCoy Collection)
Mitchell, Charles (Mitchell Collection)
Pinnell, Clara Beth (DePue-Pinnell Collection)
Ramirez, Felix (Ramirez Collection)
Whilhelm, Walter (Wilhelm Collection)

INDEX TO PHOTOGRAPHS

BIBLIOGRAPHY

BOOKS:

Abdill, George B. *Pacific Railroads From 1854-1900.* Seattle: Superior Publishing, 1959.

Adler, Pat & Walter Wheelock. *Walker's R. R. Routes 1853.* Glendale: La Siesta Press, 1965.

Armstrong, Mary Francis. *Desert Gem Trails.* Mentone: Gem Books, 1966.

Bancroft, Hubert Howe. *The Works of Hubert Howe Bancroft.* 24 vols. San Francisco: History Co., 1890.

Beattie, George William and Helen Pruitt Beattie. *Heritage of the Valley: San Bernardino's First Century.* Oakland: Biobooks, 1951.

Beck, Warren A. *New Mexico: A History of Four Centuries.* 2nd printing. Norman: University of Oklahoma press, 1963.

Beebe, Lucius. *Trains in Transition.* New York: Bonanza Books, 1951.

Biberson, Ralph P., ed. *Exploring Southwest Trails 1846-1854.* Southwestern Historical Series. Glendale: Arthur H. Clark, 1938.

Bolton, Herbert Eugene. *Anza's California Expeditions.* 5 vols. Berkeley: 1930 (Reissued: New York, 1966.)

————, "Early Explorations of Father Garcés on the Pacific Slope." *Pacific Ocean in History.* Macmillan, 1917.

Borax Consolidated, Limited. *The Story of the Pacific Coast Borax Co.* Los Angeles: Ward Ritchie Press, 1951.

Broadhead, Michael J. *Soldier-Scientist in the American Southwest.* Historical Monograph No. 1. Arizona Historical Society, 1973.

Brown, John Jr. and James Boyd, eds. *History of San Bernardino and Riverside Counties.* Western Historical Association, 1922.

Bryant, Keith L., Jr. *History of the Atchison Topeka & Santa Fe R. R.,* 1974.

Burmeister, Eugene. *Early Days in Kern.* Bakersfield: Cardon House, 1963.

California Interstate Telephone Co. *Romantic Heritage of Mojave River Valley, A Saga of Transportation and Desert Frontiers.* 1961.

Casebier, Dennis G. *The Battle at Camp Cady.* Tales of the Mojave Road Series. Norco: by author, Sep 1972.

————, *Carleton's Pa-Ute Campaign.* Tales of the Mojave Road Series. Norco: Tales of the Mojave Road Publishing, Sep 1974.

————, *Rock Springs.* Tales of the Mojave Road Series. Norco: Tales of the Mojave Road Publishing, Jan 1973.

Chalfant, W. A. *The Story of Inyo County.* Bishop, Calif. 1933.

————, *Death Valley—The Facts.* Bishop, Calif. 1933.

Chapman, Charles E. *A History of California. The Spanish Period.* New York: 1921. (Eighth printing, 1958.)

Coke, Lucille & Larry. *Mining on the Trails of Destiny.* New York: Vantage Press, 1969.

Coues, Elliot. *On the Trail of a Spanish Pioneer: The Diary and Itinerary of Francisco Garcés in His Travels Through Sonora, Arizona, and California 1775-1776.* New York: 1900.

Dale, Harrison C., ed. *The Ashley-Smith Exploration and the Discovery of a Central Route to the Pacific 1822-1829.* Cleveland: Arthur H. Clark, 1918.

Death Valley—A Guide. Bret Harte Associates, 1938-1939.

Drago, Harry S. *Notorious Ladies of the Frontier 1850-1929.* New York: Ballatine Books, 1969.

Elliott, Wallace W. *History of San Bernardino and San Diego Counties with Illustrations 1883.* Reproduction Sponsored by Riverside Museum Asso., Riverside: Riverside Museum Press, 1965.

Foreman, Grant, ed. *Pathfinder in the Southwest. The Itinerary of Lt. A. W. Whipple During His Exploration for a Railroad Route from Fort Smith to Los Angeles in Years 1853-1854.* Norman: University of Oklahoma Press, 1941.

Fox, Theron, *Arizona Treasure Hunters Ghost Town Guide.* San Jose: Harlow Press, n.d.

Frémont, John C. *Memoirs of My Life.* New York: Belford, 1877.

Frickstad, Walter N., ed. *A Century of California Post Offices, 1848-1954.* Oakland: 1955.

Glasscock, C. B. *Here's Death Valley.* North York: Grosset and Dunlap, 1940.

Garcés, Francisco. *A Record of Travels in Arizona and California. 1775-1776.* A new translation, ed. by John Galvin. San Francisco: John Howell, 1972.

Gilmore, N. Ray & Gladys Gilmore. *Readings in California History.* New York: Thomas Y. Crowell, 1966.

Goodykoontz, Colin Brummitt. *Home Missions on the American Frontier.* 1939. (Reissued: New York, 1971.)

Hafen, LeRoy & Ann W. *Journals of Forty-Niners, Salt Lake to Los Angeles with Diaries and Company Records.* Glendale: Arthur H. Clark Co., 1954.

————, *Old Spanish Trail Santa Fe to Los Angeles with Extracts from Contemporary Records and Including Diaries of Antonio Armijo and Orville Pratt.* Glendale, Calif: Arthur H. Clark 1954.

Harvey, Lois F., Dir. of Education. *Toyanuki's Rabbit—A Story of the Paiutes.* Office of the County Superintendent of Schools, Independence, Calif., 1956.

History of San Bernardino County, California with Illustrations, Descriptive of its Scenery, Farms . . . Including Biographic Sketches. San Francisco: Wallace W. Elliott, 1883.

Hunt, Rockwell, ed. *California Californians.* Los Angeles: Lewis Publishing, 1932.

Ingersoll, L. A. *Ingersoll's Century Annals of San Bernardino County.* Los Angeles: 1904.

Keenan, George. *E. H. Harriman, A Biography.* New York: 1922.

Keyes, Charles R. *Borax Deposits of the United States.* (Spokane Meeting) Des Moines: 1909.

Korn, Bertram Wallace. *Incidents of Travel and Adventure in the Far West by Solomon Carvalho.* Centenary Edition. Philadelphia: Jewish Publication Society of America, 1954.

Leaderbrand, Russ. *Guidebook to the Mojave Desert of California in the Death Valley, Joshua Tree National Monument and the Antelope Valley.* Los Angeles: Ward Richie Press, 2nd printing, 1967.

Lee, W. Storrs. *The Great California Deserts.* New York: G. P. Putnam's Sons, 1953.

Marshall, James. *Santa Fe, The Railroad That Built an Empire.* New York: Random House, 1945.

Morgan, Dale L. *Jedediah Smith and the Opening of the West.* New York: Bobbs-Merrill, 1953.

Myrick David F. *Railroads of Nevada and Eastern California,* vol. II. Berkeley: Howell-North Books, 1963.

Nadeau, Remi. *Ghost Towns and Mining Camps of California.* Los Angeles: Ward Richie Press, 2nd printing, 1965.

Newmark, Maurice H. & Marco R., eds. *Sixty Years in Southern California, 1853-1913, Containing the Reminiscences of Harris Newmark.* New York: Knickerbocker Press, 1938.

Norman, Arthur A. & A. Graebuer. *A Study in American Continental Expansion-Empire on the Pacific.* New York: Ronald Press, 1955.

O'Conley, Mary Ann. *Upper Mojave Desert, A Living Legacy.* Detroit: Harlo Press, 1969.

Pierson, Erma. *Kern's Desert.* Bakersfield: 2nd printing, 1965.

Richards, Elizabeth. *Guideposts to History Concerning Origin to Place and Street Names.* San Bernardino: Santa Fe Federal Savings & Loan Asso., 1966.

Riegel, Robert E. *The Story of the Western Railroads.* Lincoln: 1964.

Rusling, James F., Brevet Brigadier General. *The Great West and the Pacific Coast.* New York: Sheldon, 1877.

Schurler, Montgomery. *Westward The Course of Empire.* New York: 1906.

Spears, John R. *Illustrated Sketches of Death Valley and Other Borax Deserts of the Pacific Coast.* Chicago: Rand McNally, 1892.

Story of San Bernardino County. San Bernardino: Title Insurance & Trust, 1966.

Sullivan, Maurice S. The Travels of Jedediah Smith: A Documentary Outline, Including the Journal of the Great Pathfinder. Santa Ana: Fine Arts Press, 1934.

Thwaits, Ruben Gold. The Personal Narratives of James Ohio Pattie of Kentucky. Cleveland: Arthur H. Clark, 1905.

Trottman, Nelson. History of the Union Pacific. New York, 1923.

Walker, Ardis M. Francisco Garcés Pioneer Padre of the Tulares. Limited Editions of Visalia, 1974.

Wedertz, Frank S. Bodie: 1859-1900 Chalfant Press, n.d.

Weight, Harold C. 20 Mule Team Days in Death Valley. Twenty-nine Palms: Calico Press, 1955.

White, Douglas, The Story of a Trail. Los Angeles: 1905.

Wilson, Neil C. Silver Stampede. Mac Millian, 1937.

Winn, Marcia. Desert Bonanza. Glendale: Arthur H. Clark, 1963.

PERIODICALS

"Along the Route of the Super Chief, El Capitan, The Chief, San Francisco Chief, and Texas Chief." Santa Fe Magazine, July 1967.

"Bicentennial Series." Westways Magazine, March 1969 thru June 1969.

"Brief History of Santa Fe." Santa Fe Magazine May 1968, Jul 1975, Oct 1975.

Camp, Charles L. "The Chronicles of George C. Yount, California Pioneer of 1826." California Historical Quarterly, Apr 1923.

Cullimore, Clarence. "The Martyrdom and Interment of Padre Francisco Garcés." California Historical Society Quarterly, Mar 1954.

Foy, Mary E. By Ox Team From Salt Lake to Los Angeles, 1850: A Memoir by David W. Cheesman. Annual publication, Historical Society of Southern California, 1930.

Hill, Joseph H. "Ewing Young in the Fur Trade of the Far Southwest, 1822-1834." Reprint from Oregon Historical Quarterly, Vol. XXIV, No. 1, 1923.

Knight, Emily M., Andrew M. Knight, & Gerald A. Smith. "Historic Chronology of San Bernardino County." San Bernardino County Museum Quarterly, Summer 1962.

"Manifest Destiny." Westways, May 1969.

Mecham, G. Frank. "The Discovery and Locating of the Silver King Mine in Calico Mountains." The Pioneer Cabin News. Society of California Pioneers, 1968.

"Milepost 100." Santa Fe Magazine, May 1968.

"Mrs. Laura King." Desert Magazine. May 1948.

Penick, James Jr. "I will stand on the ground with my foot and shake down every house." American Heritage, Dec 1975.

Pleasants, J.E. "Ranching on the Mojave River in 1864." Touring Topics, Mar 1930.

Reynolds, Robert E. "Exploring the Calico Mining District." (The Mineral Information Service of California Division of Mines and Geology.) San Bernardino County Museum Quarterly, Winter, 1967.

Robinson, John W. "San Gorgonio Mountain: The Early Years." San Bernardino County Museum Association Quarterly, Winter & Spring 1976.

Rousseau, Mrs. J. A., "Rousseau Diary, Across the Desert to California From Salt Lake City to San Bernardino In 1864." San Bernardino County Museum Quarterly, Vol. VI, No. 2, 1958.

"Saga of the 20 Mule Team." Westways, Dec 1939.

Staples, Douglas W. "The Calico Print, Pioneer Newspaper of the Mojave Desert." Historical Society of Southern California Quarterly, Sept. 1960.

Van Dyke Dix. "A Modern Interpretation of the Garcés Route." Annual of the Historical Society of Southern California, 1927.

Waitman, Leonard. "The History of Camp Cady." The Historical Society of Southern California Quarterly, Mar 1954.

_____ , "Horse Soldier Forts of the Mojave Desert." San Bernardino County Museum Association Quarterly, Spring 1968.

_____ , "The Watch Dogs of San Bernardino County." San Bernardino County Museum Association Quarterly, Winter 1973.

Walker, Clifford, "Opening the Mojave River Trail," San Bernardino County Museum Quarterly, Summer, 1971.

Wood, Raymund F. "Francisco Garcés, Explorer of Southern California." Southern California Quarterly, Sep 1969.

NEWSPAPER ARTICLES:

"Amtrak," San Bernardino Sun-Telegram.

Barstow Printer-Review, 5 Jan 1950, 21 Feb 1913, 23 Jan. 1913, 30 Jan 1913, 13 Feb 1913, 27 Feb 1913, 4 Dec 1914.

Battye, Charles, "The Changing Desert," Barstow Printer-Review, 12 Apr 1951.

_____ , "here and there on the Desert," Barstow Printer-Review, 10 Jun 1943.

_____ , "A Desert Journey of Battye," Barstow Printer-Review, 10 Dec 1943.

_____ , "Railroads Thrilling Battle for Water on the Desert, Recounted by Oldtimer," Barstow Printer-Review, 18 Mar 1943.

Belden, L. Burr. "History in the Making Series: Clarence Rasor Discovers New Borax Ore Type," San Bernardino Sun-Telegram, 22 Mar 1953.

_____ , "History in the Making Series: Daggett, Long Metropolis of Mojave Valley," San Bernardino Sun-Telegram, 30 July 1961.

_____ , "History in the Making Series: Death Valley Has New Resort Era, T & T Abandoned," San Bernardino Sun-Telegram, 8 Feb 1953.

_____ , "History in the Making Series: Double Cross by Senator Delays Borax R. R.," San Bernardino Sun-Telegram, 25 Jan 1953.

_____ , "History in the Making Series: Early Edition Depicts Courts In By-gone Era." San Bernardino Sun-Telegram, 15 Jul 1962.

_____ , "History in the Making Series: Forgotten Towns Found Listed in Postal History." San Bernardino Sun-Telegram, 29 Jan 1961.

_____ , "History in the Making Series: Long Teams of Mules Capture Public's Fancy," San Bernardino Sun-Telegram, 7 Apr 1957.

_____ , "History in the Making Series: Obscure Borax Chapter Found in Traction Road." San Bernardino Sun-Telegram, 18 Jan 1953.

Bishoff, Louella M. "Citizen of the Week: Lisita Pico Williamson." Mojave Valley Times, 6 Mar 1975.

_____ , "Citizen of the Week: Lee Berry." Mojave Valley Times, 27 Feb 1975.

_____ , "Do You Remember?" Desert Dispatch, 17 Jun 1974.

"Cajon Pass: A Way to Get There By Car or Train." San Bernardino Sun-Telegram, 1 Jun 1975.

"Calico Edition." Desert Dispatch, Oct. 1974.

Calico Print, 15 Feb 1885; 29 Feb 1885; 7 Mar 1885; 21 Oct 1882; 20 Apr 1885; 14 May 1885; 1 Oct 1886; 10 Oct 1886.

Coke, Lucille & Larry. "Calico." Barstow Printer-Review, 1951.

Daily Missouri Republican, 17 Feb 1853.

Daily Morning Argus, Vol. VI, No. 104, 23 May 1877.

_____ , Vol. VI, No. 106, 25 May 1877.

Desert Dispatch, 28 Sep 1972, 5 May 1971, 7 Oct 1974, 20 Apr 1976.

"Diesel Shops Near Completion in Barstow," Barstow Printer-Review, 5 Apr 1945.

"Expansion Program," Barstow Printer-Review, 11 Sep 1947.

Graves, Helen. "Once Upon a Desert—Historian Explores Willis Wells." Lucerne Valley Leader, 3 Dec 1970.

"History of Barstow School District." Desert Dispatch, 11 Dec 1958.

Los Angeles Examiner, 12 Nov 1905.

Los Angeles Star. 27 May 1851; 12 Jul 1851; 8 Nov 1851; 31 Jul

1852; 28 May 1853; 29 Sep 1860.

Minton, Meredith. "John Brown: His Life and His Toll Road." *Victor Press*, 26 Jul 1974.

Needles Eye, 3 Jul 1907; 3 Jul 1909.

Needles Nuggett, 27 May 1942; 29 May 1942; 26 Jun 1942; 17 Jul 1942.

"Old Government Road," *Los Angeles Star*, 25 Jun 1853.

"Railroads to End All Passenger Service." *San Bernardino Sun-Telegram*, 1 Apr 1971.

Salisbury, Alice, Dix Van Dyke, "A Bedtime Story," *Printer Review*, 5 January 1950.

San Bernardino Evening Index, "San Bernardino Valley Centennial," 18 Oct 1910.

San Bernardino Guardian. 24 March 1868; 25 Apr 1868; 2 May 1868; 30 May 1868; 26 Oct 1867, p. 2, Col. 1; 16 Aug 1868; 31 Aug 1867; 24 Aug 1867; 28 Sept 1867; 12 Oct 1867; 13 June 1868.

San Bernardino Sun-Telegram. 30 Jul 1961; 10 May 1968; 1 Jan 1906; 29 Jan 1961.

San Bernardino Weekly Argus, 1 Nov 1875; 29 Nov 1875.

San Bernardino Index, 27 Feb 1886.

"San Bernardino Will Be Stop On Chicago-LA Rail Route." *San Bernardino Sun-Telegram*, 23 Mar 1971.

San Francisco Chronicle, 2 Nov 1889; 13 Feb 1889.

_____, (Year of 1890, microfilm at State Library.)

San Francisco Daily Herald, 25 Feb 1853.

Santa Fe Gazette, 24 September 1853.

Santa Fe Republican, 1848: 12, Feb, 3 May; 18 May; 9 June; 9 Aug; 12 Sep.

Spackman, Ellis L. "Why San Bernardino Is Not L. A. Hooray!" *San Bernardino Sun-Telegram*, 19 May 1972.

Timmons, Virgie, "Busy Spot Is Harvey House Built in 1911," *Printer Review*, 5 Jan 1950.

Van Dyke, Judge Dix. *Barstow Printer-Review*, 28 Dec 1939.

_____, "Life On the Mojave Valley." *Barstow Printer-Review*, 1958.

Waterman, R. W., ed. "San Bernardino County Silver Boom Recalled." *Los Angeles Times*, 1 Jan 1956.

"Waterman Recalls History of Mining and Pioneer Days." *San Bernardino Sun-Telegram*, 21 Apr 1950.

Wilmington Journal, 28 Sep 1866.

GOVERNMENT PUBLICATIONS:

California Division of Mines & Geology. *Basic Placer Mining.* (Special Supplement to Mineral Information Service.) San Francisco, Dec. 1963.

California Gazetter & Business Directory, San Francisco: R.L. Polk, 1888.

California State Mineralogists Report, 1888-1889, VII-IX, San Bernardino County Library.

California State Mining Bureau, *California Journal of Mines and Geology*, Vol. 29, No. 1 and 2, Jan to Apr 1953, Sacramento.

Darton, N.Y. *Guidebook of Western U.S. Part C., The Santa Fe Route, with a Side Trip to the Grand Canyon of The Colorado.* Dept. of Interior, U.S.G.S. Bulletin 613, Washington, D.C., 1915.

DeGroot, Dr. Henry. *San Bernardino County, Its Mountains, Plains and Valleys.* California Mining Bureau, Report 10, Sacramento, 1890.

Fremont, John C., Brevet Capt. *Report of the Exploring Expedition to the Rocky Mountains in the year 1842 and to Oregon and North California in years 1843-1844.* Sen. Doc. 166, Washington, D.C., 1845.

Irelan, William. *Eighth Annual Report of the State Mineralogist.* California State Mining Bureau, Sacramento, 1888.

Ives, Lieutenant Joseph C. *Report Upon the Colorado River of the West.* Washington D.C., Government Printing Office, 1861.

Mendenhall, Walter C. *Some Desert Watering Places in Southeastern California and Southwestern Nevada.* U.S. Dept. of Interior Geological Survey, Water Supply Paper No. 224, Washington, D.C.: U.S. Govt. Printing Office, 1909.

San Bernardino City & County Directory & Business Directory of San Bernardino City & County, 1889. San Bernardino: McIntosh, Flagg & Walkens, 1889.

San Bernardino City & County Directory, 1886. Los Angeles: F.L. Morrell, 1887.

San Bernardino County Books of Assessment. Tax Assessor's Archives, 1870, 1883, 1885, 1887, 1889, 1903 through 1910.

San Bernardino County Post Offices. Records from General Services Administration, National Archives & Records Service, Washington, D.C., n.d.

San Bernardino County Tax Rolls, 1862-1864. Hall of Records, San Bernardino, Calif.

San Bernardino County Index to Mines, 1880-1883, Vol. II, Hall of Records, San Bernardino, Calif.

San Bernardino County Delinquent Assessment Book of Property for the year 1880-1881. Hall of Records, San Bernardino, Calif.

San Bernardino, Riverside & Colton Classified Business Directory, San Bernardino: Flagg & Walkens, 1889.

Sitgreaves, Lorenzo, Capt. *Report of an Expedition Down the Zuni and Colorado River.* (33rd Congress, 1st Session.) Washington, D.C.: Public Doc., 1854.

Storms, W.H. *Old Mines of Southern California.* (Reprinted from the Report of the State Mineralogist, 1893.) Toyahvale: Frontier Book Co., 1965.

U.S. Congress, 37th, Sess. II. *Railroad Land Grant Act, 1862.* Ch. 110, 120, pn/489-499.

Thompson, David G. *The Mojave Desert Region, California.* (A Geographic, Geologic, Hydrographic Reconnaissance.) U.S. Dept. of Interior, Water Supply Paper #576, Washington, D.C.: Govt. Printing Office, 1929.

U.S. Dept. of Interior Geological Survey. *Water Supply Paper #578.* Washington, D.C.: U.S. Govt. Printing Office, 1928.

U.S. National Archive & Record Service. *Fort Mojave Record of Events*, (Fort Mojave, Ariz., Abandoned Military Reservation File, microfilm.) Washington, D.C., 1 Apr 1861.

U.S. Surveyor General's Office. *Township 10 North, Range 2 East of San Bernardino Meridian.* San Francisco, 1882.

U.S. Treasury Dept. *Report of the Director of the Mint Upon Production of the Precious Metals in the United States During the Calendar Year 1888, 1893.* Washington, D.C., 1889, 1894.

Utilizing of Mojave River for Irrigation in Victorville, California. Calif. State Water Supply Paper, Dept. of Engineers Bulletin #5, Sacramento, 1918.

W.P.A. Writers Program. *Old West Pioneer Tales of San Bernardino County.* San Bernardino: The Sun Co., 1940.

Walker, Joseph, Capt. *Report on Committee and Statements of Captain Joseph Walker before them on the practicability of a Railroad from San Francisco to the United States.* California State Legislature, Senate Session of 1853.

Weber, F.H. *Silver Mining In Old Calico.* Calif. State Mining Bureau, Sacramento, Calif., n.d.

Williamson, Robert S., Lt. *Report of Exploration in California for Railroad Routes to Connect with routes near the 35th and 32nd Parallels of North Latitude.* Pub. Doc. #72, Vol. V, p. 354. Washington, D.C.: 1855.

Yale, Charles. *Old California Mines, 1899.* (Phamphlet from California Mines & Minerals, 1899.) Fort Davis: Frontier Book Co., 1967.

PERSONAL INTERVIEWS & DOCUMENTS:

Alf, Mrs. Gertrude. Personal interview w/Pat Keeling, 25 Oct 1968, 17 Dec 1975 & 17 Jan 1976

_____, Personal interview w/June Zeitelhack, 18 Apr 1970.

Alf, Walter. Personal interview w/Gregg Morris, 11 May 1968.

_____, Personal interview w/Ronnie Moore, 15 May 1968.

_____, Personal interview w/Pat Keeling, 25 Oct 1968.

Bassett, Addie Park. Personal interview w/Louella Bishoff, 3 May 1975.

Berry, Lee. Personal interview w/Louella Bishoff 27 Feb 1975.

Brimmer, Chloe. Personal interview w/June Zeitelhack, n.d.

Bureau of Land Management Representative. Personal interview w/Germaine Moon, Oct & Nov 1975.

Clancy, Gordon. Personal interview w/Pat Keeling, 6 Jan 1976.

Conaway, Ray. Personal interview w/Pat Keeling 10 Nov 1975.

Coleman, William T. Letters: 12 & 14 May 1883.

Cook, Mr. & Mrs. Personal interview w/T. L. Merchant, 23 Dec. 1969.

Crooks, Clarence. Personal Interview w/Celestia Gilliam, June 6, 1975.

DeVoe, Dean. Personal interview w/LaRue Slette, n.d.

De Wolf, James. Personal interview w/Celestia Gilliam, Oct 10, 1975.

Dorrance, Dutch. Personal interview w/Charles McCoy, 1 May 1968.

Dillingham, Margie Dolph. Personal interview w/Celestia Gilliam, Sept 30, 1975.

Duffey, Loleta Clark. Personal interview w/Pat Keeling, 10 Jun 1970.

Earl, D. W. & Co., Forwarding & Commission Merchant, List of Accounts, 1883.

Elliott, Clarence Roy. Personal interview w/Louella Bishoff, 7 Aug 1974.

English, Mrs. Lyle. Personal interview w/Pat Keeling, 17 Feb 1976.

Fink, Marion F., M.D. Letter to Juanita Atkinson, 2 Feb 1976.

Fouts, Mrs. Margaret Kenney. Personal interview w/Pat Keeling, 17 Jan 1976.

Frazer, Clinton. Personal interview w/Pat Keeling, 12 Oct 1970.

French, S. W., III, M.D., F.A.C.S. Letter to Juanita Atkinson, 30 Jan 1976.

Graves, Helen, Personal interview w/June Zeitelhack, 2 May 1970.

Haenszel, Arda, Information on Garcés Trek, 1976.

Henderson, Alfred C. Letter to Celestia Gilliam, Feb. 17, 1976.

Hill, Mrs. Okarita Henderson. Personal interview w/T.L. Merchant, 10 Nov 1969.

Hill, Melvin. Personal interview w/Thelma Carder, n.d.

Madden, Frank. Personal interview w/Martha Burnau, 8 Oct 1970.

Mitchell, Charlie. Personal interview w/Celestia Gilliam, July 18, 1975.

Moss, Fern Quint. Personal interview w/Louella Bishoff, 3 May 1975.

Morrisette, Mrs. Helen. Personal interview w/Pat Keeling, 20 Nov 1975.

————, Personal interview w/Louella Bishoff, 17 Feb 1975.

McConnell, Frank. Personal interview w/A.F. Kitts, n.d.

McConnell, Oliva. Personal interview w/Sachiko Kitts, n.d.

McCoy, C. B. Tape-recorded interview w/Charles McCoy, 28 Apr 1968.

McCoy, Marvin. Personal interview w/Charles McCoy, 5 May 1968.

McCoy, Raymond. Personal interview w/Charles McCoy, 6 May 1968.

McGinnis, Gladys. Personal interview w/Celestia Gilliam, June 9, 1975.

McLaren, Robina. Personal interview w/Germaine Moon, Dec 1975, Apr & May 1976.

McShane, Mr. Personal interview w/Ronnie Moore, 15 May 1968.

Newschuconda, R. Letter, 22 Feb 1883.

Parks, George B. Personal documents & interview w/Mrs. J.M. Duarte, n.d.

Payne, Elma June Platt. Personal interview w/Celestia Gilliam, 11 Oct 1975.

Powell, Mrs. Aileen McCue. Personal interview w/Pat Keeling, 30 Sep 1970.

Pyeatt, Mrs. H. P. "Nell" McNeil. Personal interview w/Pat Keeling, 29 Jul 1970.

Russell, O. A. Personal interview w/June Zeitelhack, 8 May 1970.

Skaggs, Caroline Smith. Personal interview w/Louella M. Bishoff, 3 May 1975.

Smart, William. Personal interview w/Pat Keeling, 19 Sep 1970.

Stickney, Jud. County Agriculture Advisor, Personal interview w/June Zeitelhack, 3 Feb 1970.

Staudinger, Percy. Personal interview w/Dave Oxley, n.d.

Stiles, Ransome D. "Babe." Personal interview w/Louella Bishoff, 3 May 1975.

Sutcliff, Mina. Personal interview w/Pat Keeling, Oct 1, 1975.

Terry, Walt. Personal interview w/Martha Burnau, n.d.

Torbett, H.G. "Jerry." Assessor Office, Barstow. Personal interview w/Germaine Moon, Oct & Nov 1975.

Vincente, Alejandro P., M.D. Letter to Juanita Atkinson, 2 Feb 1976.

Wagner, Morris. Letter to Beth Pinnell, June 1971.

Waterman, Robert Wood. Handwritten notes to Ron Brubaker, 29 Apr 1963.

Walters, Julia Slovick. Personal interview w/Louella Bishoff 3 May 1975.

White, Winifred. Letter to LeRoy L. Bishoff, 25 Aug 1965.

Wilhelm, Walter. Personal interview w/Clifford Walker, 1967.

Wilkes, Bruce, M.D. Letter to Juanita Atkinson, 30 Jan 1976.

Williamson, Mary Fran. Personal interview w/Louella Bishoff, 27 Apr 1975.

————, Personal interview w/Germaine Moon, 28 May 1976.

MAPS:

Bancroft, *Map of California, 1868.* (Photocopy at the University of Southern California Library.)

Biberson, Ralph P., ed. *Exploring Southwest Trails, 1846 - 1854.* Glendale: Arthur H. Clark, 1938. (Index Map, Mojave Desert Region, Calif.)

California State Water Supply Paper #578, "Plate 2," circa. 1928.

Carter, Harvey L., ed. *Dear Old Kit, The Historical Christopher Carson, with a New Edition of the Carson Memoirs.* Norman: University of Oklahoma Press, 1968. (Map p. 51.)

Dunnett Bros. *Map of San Bernardino County California,* 1908.

Font, Pedro. "Map, 1775-1776" from *A Record of Travels in Arizona and California, 1775-1776, Fr. Francisco Garcés.* ed. by John Galvin. San Francisco John Howell Books, 1972.

Fox, Theron. "Arizona Territory, 1868-1881." from *Arizona Treasure Hunters Ghost Town Guide.* San Jose: Harlow Press, n.d.

Galvin, John, ed. *A Record of Travels in Arizona and California 1775-1776,* Fr. Francisco Garcés. San Francisco: John Howell Books, 1972. (Endpiece map.)

Hicks, Sharon L. *The Greater Mojave Desert.* City of Barstow, 1976. (Map)

Holmes, Kenneth L. *Ewing Young: Master Trapper.* Portland: Binfords & Mort, 1967. (Frontspiece map.)

Ives, Lieutenant Joseph C. *"Report Upon the Colorado River of the West"* Washington, D. C. Government Printing Office, 1861 (Map.)

Nadeau, Remi. *Ghost Towns and Mining Camps of California.* Los Angeles: Ward Richie Press, 2nd printing, 1965. (Map.)

Preston, R. N. *Early California, Southern Edition.* Corvallis: Western Guide Publishers, 1974: maps dated 1873, 1891, 1903, 1910.

Reynolds, Robert E. "Mines of the Calico District." (Map.) from *San Bernardino County Museum Quarterly,* Winter, 1967.

San Bernardino County, California. (Map.) Punnett Bros., 1908.

"Santa Fe Lines & Trails." *Santa Fe Magazine,* July 1967, (2 maps.)

Waitman, Leonard. "Old Government Road, 1867." (Map) from *San Bernardino County Museum Association Quarterly,* Spring, 1968.

U.S. Dept. of Interior Geological Survey. Topographical Maps, San Bernardino County: 15 Minute Series, *Barstow Quadrangle,* 1953.

————, *Daggett Quadrangle,* 1956.

_____, Newberry Quadrangle,_ 1955.

_____, _Opal Mt. Quadrangle,_ 1955.

_____, 7.5 minute series, _Yermo Quadrangle,_ 1953.

_____, U.S. Army Map Service. _Langford Well, California._ Series V895, Sheet 2654 II NW. Corps of Engineers, U.S. Army, Washington, D.C., 1952.

MISCELLANEOUS PUBLICATIONS:

Atchison, Topeka & Santa Fe Railway Co., _Statement on Needles,_ on file Mojave River Valley Museum, n.d.

_____, _Statement on Barstow,_ n.d.

_____, _Statement on Mojave,_ n.d.

Atchison, Topeka & Santa Fe Railway Co. _Dedication of New Facilities, Diesel Shop._ (Brochure.) 20 Jan 1976.

_____, _Barstow Hump Yard Main-Line Realignment._ Letter dated 28 Oct 1975.

_____, _Time Tables:_ 9 May 1920; 20 May 1943, #85; 1888; 1911; 1920; & 1934.

Barstow Women's Club. Colorful History of Barstow and Vicinity. Barstow, 1938.

_____, Unpublished notes for _Colorful History of Barstow and Vicinity._ Barstow, 1938.

_____, History and Landmarks Reports 1963, 1964, 1965.

_____, _Thirty Years With Barstow Women's Club, 1922-1952._ Alice Salisbury, ed.

Campbell, N.R. _Borax Deposits of Eastern California._ Bull. 213-03-26. (Contributions to Economic Geology.) 1902.

Davenport, Lawrence C., dir. _Halleck-Oro Grande-Mojave._ (Local historic research.) Victorville: Victor Valley College, 1963.

Dictionary of American Biography—II Vol. 1964-1974. Scribners publisher.

Encyclopedia Britannica, Vol. 1, Chicago, 1954.

"Fremont," _Compton's Pictured Encyclopedia,_ 1956.

"Homestead Law." _Encyclopedia Americana,_ Vol. 14, 1955.

The McGraw-Hill Encyclopeadia of World Biography, published McGraw-Hill, 1973.

Perez, Don Dometrio. "Tragica Muerta de Francis Aubry." _Benjamin M. Reed Papers._ Mss. No. 30, Historical Society of New Mexico. Santa Fe: State Records Center & Archives. n.d.

"Railroad and other Land Grants" _Encyclopedia Americana,_ Vol. 23, 1955.

Riegel, R.E. "Story of the Western Railroads." _Dictionary of American History,_ Vol. 2.

Salisbury, Alice. _Collection of Papers._ San Bernardino County Branch Library, Barstow, Calif.

Santa Fe Appreciation Day. (Program.) City of Barstow, 15 Apr 1961.

Sears, Roebuck & Co., Catalogue, 1890.

Simpson, Ruth DeEtte. _Coyote Gulch._ Archeological Survey Association of So. Calif., Paper No. 5, 1961.

Southern Pacific R. R. _Time Table,_ 1884.

Tonopah & Tidewater R. R., Bullfrog Goldfield R. R., _Time Table_ 1927.

Towne, A. N. _R. R. Transportation & Construction._ Manuscript, Bancroft Library.

U.S. Borax & Chemical Corp. _The Story of Borax._ Calif. Public Relations Dept., Los Angeles, 1961.

_____, 3rd ed., VI, 1969.

Van Dyke, Dix. _Notes on Daggett._ Barstow College Library.

_____, _Van Dyke Ledger._ (Unpublished)

Walker, Clifford. _History of the Mojave River Trail._ University of Southern California, Master Thesis, Unpublished, 1967.

Wentworth, J. P. H., ed. & Proprietor. _Resources of California, 1886._

Who's Who. Black & McMillan, London an New York, 1929-1970

Who's Who In America. Black & McMillan, London and New York, 1960-1975

Who Was Who. Marquis Co., Chicago, 1929-1970

Who Was Who In America. Marquis Co., Chicago, 1951-1974,

GENERAL INDEX

INDEX Editor & Preparer: G. L. Moon
Assisted by Patricia Keeling & C. J. Walker
Typeset by Theron J. Egg

This annotated index corrects errors in the First and Second Printings and clarifies variation in spellings. It also clarifies changes in place names over the years.

ABBREVIATIONS TO THE INDEX

A

ABC   - American Borax Company
Agt   - Agent
Aka   - Also known as
A & P   - Atlantic & Pacific Railroad
Assn   - Association
A, T &
  SF   - Atchinson, Topeka & Sante Fe Rwy Co.
AZ   - Arizona

B

B   - Base
BHS   - Barstow High School
Bk   - Book
Bldg   - Building
Bros   - Brothers
Btw   - Barstow
BUSD   - Barstow Unified School District
Bvt   - Brevet

C

CA, Ca
  or Cal. - California
Ca So.
  or CS - Californa Southern Railway
Capt   - Captain
Co   - Company or County
Col   - Colonel *or* Colorado
Comdr   - Commander
Cons   - Consolidate
Corp   - Corporation
C S   - Californa Southern Railway

D

DA   - District Attorney
Dag   - Daggett
Dble   - Double
Dept   - Department
Dist   - District
Div   - Division
Dr(s)   - Doctor (s)
D.V   - Death Valley

E

E   - East
Eng   - Engineer

(E cont.)

Etc   - Et cetera
Et ux   - And others

F

FAA   - Federal Aviation Agency
FHA   - Federal Housing Authority
Frt   - Freight
Ft   - Fort

G

Gen   - General
Gov   - Governor
Govt   - Government

H

HADEC - Hour Angle Declination
Hd   - Homestead
Hqts   - Headquarters
Hse   - House
Hts   - Heights
Hwy   - Highway

I

I   - Interstate
Id   - Identification
IFC   - Inside Front Cover
Improv - Improvement
Inc   - Incorporate
Ind   - Indian(s), Individual
Int   - Internment

J

Jap   - Japanese
Jct   - Junction
JFK   - John Fitzgerald Kennedy
JPL   - Jet Propulsion Laboratory
Jr.   - Junior

K

KKK   - Ku Klux Klan

L

LA   - Los Angeles
Lt   - Lieutenant
Ltd   - Limited

M

MAAR - Mojave Anti Aircraft Range
Maj   - Major

Mdse	- Merchandise		**S Fe´**	- Santa Fe´ Railway
Mex	- Mexico & Mexican		**SFP**	- Santa Fe´ Pacific Railway Rwy/RR
Mg	- Mining		**Sh'g**	- Shipping
Mil	- Military		**So**	- Southern
Mkt	- Market		**SP, LA**	
Moj	- Mojave		**& SL**	- San Pedro, Los Angeles & Salt Lake Railroad
Mr	- Mister		**Spr(s)**	- Spring(s)
Mrs	- Mistress		**SP**	- Southern Pacific Railroad
MRVM			**Sr**	- Senior
Assn	- Mojave River Valley Museum Association		**St**	- Street
Mt(s)	- Mountain(s)		**Sta**	- Station
			Supt	- Superintendent

N

N	- North
NASA	- National Aeronautics Space Administration
Nat	- National
NL	- National Lead
NM	- New Mexico
NV	- Nevada

T

Tch	- Teacher
T & T	- Tonopah & Tidewater Railroad
TX	- Texas

O

O G	- Oro Grande

U

UC	- University of California
UP	- Union Pacific Railroad/Rwy Corp
US	- United States
USA	- United States Army
USAAC	- United States Army Air Corps
USMC	- United States Marine Corps
USN	- United States Navy
UT	- Utah

P

PCB	- Pacific Coast Borax
Ph	- Telephone
Pk	- Peak
PO	- Post Office
POW	- Prisoner of War
Pres	- President
Pt	- Point
Pvt	- Private

V

Vet	- Veteran
VFW	- Veteran of Foreign Wars
VOR	- Vector (Automatic) Omni Range

W - X - Y - Z

Q

Q	- Quartz
Qtrs	- Quarters

w	- water
W	- West
WADC	- Women's Ambulance and Defense Corps
Wks	- Works
WWI	- World War I
WWII	- World War II
Yd	- Yard
Yr	- Year

R

Rch	- Ranch
Rd	- Road
Red	- Reduction
Ref	- Reference
Rest.	- Restaurant
Resv.	- Reserve, Reservation
Riv	- River
RR	- Railroad
Rte	- Route
Rwy	- Railway

S

S	- South
S & L	- Savings & Loans
SB	- San Bernardino
SBCM	- San Bernardino County Museum
SBM	- San Bernardino Meridian
Sch	- School
SD	- San Diego
Sec	- Section
Serv	- Service

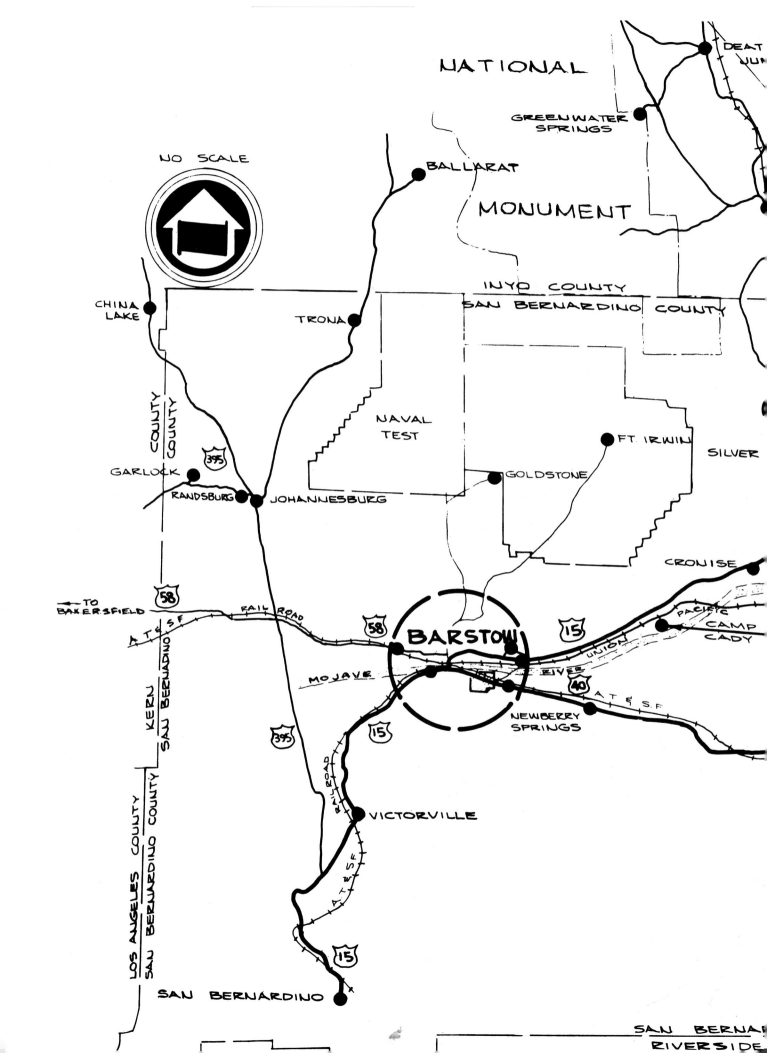